MW00477697

LETTERS OF PETER ABELARD,
BEYOND THE PERSONAL

MEDIEVAL TEXTS IN TRANSLATION

EDITORIAL DIRECTOR

Thomas F. X. Noble
University of Notre Dame

EDITORIAL BOARD

Paul Dutton
Simon Fraser University

Geoffrey Koziol
University of California at Berkeley

Carol Lansing
University of California at Santa Barbara

Barbara H. Rosenwein
Loyola University of Chicago

LETTERS OF PETER ABELARD, BEYOND THE PERSONAL

Translated by Jan M. Ziolkowski

The Catholic University of America Press
Washington, D.C.

Copyright © 2008

The Catholic University of America Press

All rights reserved

The paper used in this publication meets the minimum requirements of
American National Standards for Information Science—Permanence of
Paper for Printed Library Materials, ANSI Z39.48-1984.

∞

Library of Congress Cataloging-in-Publication Data

Abelard, Peter, 1079–1142.

    [Letters. English. 2008]

    Letters of Peter Abelard, Beyond the Personal / translated by Jan M.
Ziolkowski.

      p. cm.

    Includes bibliographical references and index.

    ISBN 978-0-8132-1505-1 (pbk. : alk. paper)   1. Abelard, Peter, 1079–
1142—Correspondence—Translations into English.   I. Ziolkowski, Jan
M., 1956–   II. Title.   III. Title: Beyond the personal.

    B765.A24A4 2007

    189'.4—dc22   2007012248

    [B]

To Liz,

with love,

these letters in lieu of my own

CONTENTS

Acknowledgments ix

Abbreviations xi

Map of Abelard's France xii

General Introduction: Life and Works xiii

PART I. HELOISE AND THE NUNS
OF THE PARACLETE

1. LETTER NINE. To the Nuns of the Paraclete 3

Letter Nine 10

2. PREFACES to the Three Books of
The Paraclete Hymnal 34

Preface to the First Book 40

Preface to the Second Book 47

Preface to the Third Book 50

3. DEDICATION LETTER to *The Commentary
on the Six Days of Creation* 52

Dedication Letter 60

4. LETTER SIXTEEN. Prologue to *The Sermons* 64

Letter Sixteen 70

PART II. BERNARD OF CLAIRVAUX

5. LETTER TEN. To Bernard of Clairvaux 75

Letter Ten 85

6. LETTER FIFTEEN. To His Comrades, against
Abbot Bernard   99

Letter Fifteen   108

7. APOLOGIA against Bernard of Clairvaux   111

Apologia   116

PART III.   OTHER CONTROVERSIES

8. LETTER ELEVEN. To Abbot Adam and
the Monks of St. Denis   133

Letter Eleven   138

9. LETTER TWELVE. To a Regular Canon   147

Letter Twelve   158

10. LETTER THIRTEEN. To an Ignoramus in the
Field of Dialectic   175

Letter Thirteen   179

11. LETTER FOURTEEN. To Bishop G[ilbert]
and the Clergy of Paris   188

Letter Fourteen   194

Bibliography   197

General Index   219

Index of Scriptural References   231

ACKNOWLEDGMENTS

Although I alone hold blame for the present book, Peter Dronke has responsibility for having proposed it to me fifteen years ago, and I thank him for both that initial incitement and for his meticulous reading of a recent draft. For their thoughtful attention to the same version, I am also grateful to the other reader for the Catholic University of America Press, Paul Dutton, as well as to the series editor. While the book was in production, I was fortunate to have the painstaking editing of Philip Gerard Holthaus.

Together with anyone else who works with most of the materials translated here, I owe a debt to the late Edmé Smits for his impeccable edition of the Latin. Originally, when my plan was a dual-language edition, he graciously extended to me the right to reprint his text. After Edmé's sadly sudden death, his literary executor, L. C. Engels, reaffirmed the permission with equal generosity.

At that stage, since scanning was not yet a possibility, Lenore Parker keyboarded for me the Latin of Edmé Smits's text and textual notes. (About the same time she also inputted on the basis of my longhand the rough drafts of the English translations: my warm thanks go to her for everything.) Years later Philip Kim proofread the Latin material (just as he later did the page proofs of this book), for which I am grateful even if it is not appearing alongside the English as I had once envisaged. It is splendid that the Latin will appear shortly in the Corpus Christianorum Continuatio Mediaevalis, where far more than a mere *corpusculum* of Peter Abelard's works has now come together.

Completion of the present project would have been inconceivable without the simultaneous sedation and stimulation that the Netherlands Institute for Advanced Study provided me for ten months in 2005–2006. For the privilege of being ensconced in the soothing environs of Wassenaar, I am deeply beholden. The librarians of the institute worked wonders in supplying me rapidly and copiously with books and articles, and my fellow medievalists in the attic bore with my occasional unsolicited monologues about Abelard's writings. In addition, Emily Vasiliauskas helped me ably again and again from afar as my research assistant in Cambridge to secure items and verify references more readily handled through Widener and other collections in the Harvard College Library. Finally, I thank Sarah Watson for generating the map. As the project was rounding the final bend, Chrysogonus Waddell did me the kindness of identifying two snippets from hymns that had been eluding my grasp, and I am glad to offer him my appreciation.

My greatest debt is owed to the dedicatee. A topos of acknowledgments would have me express appreciation to her for having borne with me as I talked over the years about the details of the project. Instead, I appreciate that she has allowed me to be absent. To her I send these letters.

ABBREVIATIONS

AH	*Analecta hymnica medii aevi.* Edited by Guido Maria Dreves, Clemens Blume, and Henry Marriott Bannister. 55 vols. Leipzig, Germany: Fues's Verlag (R. Reisland), 1886–1922.
CCSL	Corpus Christianorum, Series Latina. Turnhout, Belgium: Brepols, 1953–.
CCCM	Corpus Christianorum, Continuatio Mediaevalis. Turnhout, Belgium: Brepols, 1966–.
CSEL	Corpus Scriptorum Ecclesiasticorum Latinorum. Vienna: apud C. Geroldi filium etc., 1866–.
PL	*Patrologiae cursus completus. Series Latina.* Edited by Jacques-Paul Migne. 221 vols. Paris: apud Garnier Fratres, 1844–1855 and 1862–1864.
Schaller/ Könsgen	Schaller, Dieter, and Ewald Könsgen. *Initia carminum Latinorum saeculo undecimo antiquiorum.* Göttingen, Germany: Vandenhoeck & Ruprecht, 1977.

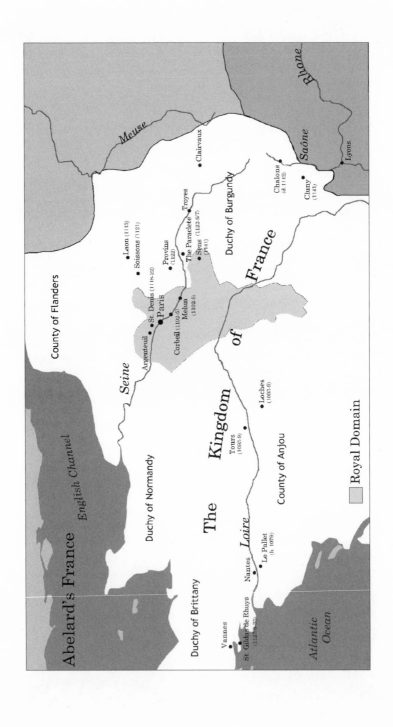

Abelard's France

County of Flanders

English Channel

Duchy of Normandy

Duchy of Brittany

Vannes

St Gildas de Rhuys (1126-32)

Nantes

Le Pallet (b 1079)

Atlantic Ocean

Loire

The Kingdom of France

Tours (1093-9)

County of Anjou

Loches (1093-9)

Seine

Argenteuil

St Denis (1118-22)

Paris

Corbeil (1102-6)

Melun (1102-6)

Laon (1113)

Soissons (1121)

Provins (1122)

The Paraclete

Troyes

Sens (1123-5?)

(?141)

Clairvaux

Duchy of Burgundy

Meuse

Chalons (d.1142)

Cluny (1141)

Saône

Lyons

Rhone

Royal Domain

LIFE AND WORKS

Life

The twelfth century has benefited from a disproportionate share of the curiosity, romantic attraction, and even daydreams and fantasies that have been elicited by the extraordinarily vibrant and variegated millennium to which the label the "Middle Ages" has been affixed. Attempts have been made to validate earlier spans of time within this thousand years as having undergone equivalently consequential and productive renewals, so that the terms "Carolingian Renaissance" and "Ottonian Renaissance" have sometimes been bandied about, but the first such formulation, and the most abiding one, remains the "Twelfth-Century Renaissance."

This period, often tacitly protracted to a hundred fifty years by appending at either end an additional quarter century (1075–1225), has been and continues to be scrutinized for such disparate phenomena as the creation of new religious institutions; the rise of universities; the salience of love (or at least of talk about love) in both secular and religious culture; changes in relations between women and men; the flowering of vernacular literature, especially but by no means solely lyric poetry; and even the discovery or alleged discovery of the individual.[1] The century calls to mind

---

1. The expression "Twelfth-Century Renaissance" owes its existence and dissemination to Charles Homer Haskins (1870–1937), *The Renaissance of the Twelfth Century* (Cambridge, Mass.: Harvard University Press, 1927). To bring Haskins's findings closer to the present day, an invaluable collection (linked explicitly with the earlier

contrasts and clashes in thought, such as nominalism and realism, reason and faith, and dialectic and Platonism. In all of these developments and debates the title character of this book played a role, sometimes on center stage.

Peter Abelard (1079–1142) ranks among the best-known thinkers, teachers, and personages of the entire medieval period. Although he is often designated *tout court* as Abelard (also spelled in English as "Abaelard" and "Abailard") and will be called so here, that name appears to be a cognomen he acquired only during or after his student years.[2] A person wishing to refer to him formally in his own day would have addressed him by the Latin *Petrus* or *magister Petrus.* Beyond being a logician, philosopher, and theologian of the first order, Abelard earned fame as a poet and songwriter.[3]

His reputation has only been enhanced by the controversy he provoked, both through the shocking outcome of the affair he had with a young woman who had been entrusted to him for private in-

book) is Robert L. Benson and Giles Constable, eds., *Renaissance and Renewal in the Twelfth Century* (Cambridge, Mass.: Harvard University Press, 1982).

2. For a list of thirty-seven medieval spellings of the name, see David E. Luscombe, *The School of Peter Abelard: The Influence of Abelard's Thought in the Early Scholastic Period,* Cambridge Studies in Medieval Life and Thought: New Series 14 (Cambridge, U.K.: Cambridge University Press, 1969), 315. On the nickname, see Constant J. Mews, "In Search of a Name and Its Significance: A Twelfth-Century Anecdote about Thierry and Peter Abaelard," *Traditio* 44 (1988): 175–200; repr. in Mews, *Reason and Belief in the Age of Roscelin and Abelard,* Variorium Collected Studies CS730 (Aldershot, U.K.: Ashgate, 2002).

3. On his logic and philosophy, the best starting place is John Marenbon, *The Philosophy of Peter Abelard* (Cambridge, U.K.: Cambridge University Press, 1997). On his achievements as a theologian, a compact introduction is furnished by Jean Jolivet, *La théologie d'Abélard* (Paris: Editions du Cerf, 1997). On Heloise's and Abelard's accomplishments and reputations in literature, some fundamental works by Peter Dronke have been gathered in his *Intellectuals and Poets in Medieval Europe,* Storia e letteratura: Raccolta di studi e testi 183 (Rome: Edizioni de Storia e Letteratura, 1992), 247–342. On what can be discerned of his skills in music, see Lorenz Weinrich, "Peter Abaelard as Musician I" and "Peter Abaelard as Musician II," *Musical Quarterly* 55 (1969): 295–312 and 464–86, and Gerard Le Vot, "Que savons-nous sur la musique des *Planctus* d'Abelard?," in Paul Zumthor, trans., *Abélard. Lamentations. Histoire de mes malheurs. Correspondance avec Héloïse,* Babel 52 (Arles, France: Actes Sud, 1992), 107–22.

struction, Heloise (often rendered as "Eloise" or "Héloïse"), and through his having been tried twice thereafter for heresy in his theological teachings and writings.[4] Although his encounters with the Church could call to mind the earlier trial of Socrates in 399 B.C.E. or the later one of Galileo in 1633, and although he has been coopted as a kind of precursor to the Reformation and the Enlightenment, it must not be overlooked when drawing such anachronistic analogies that Abelard not only became a monk and served as abbot of a monastery, but also helped to shape—if "founded" is too strong a word—a female religious order. There is no sense in tagging him so as to imply that he is exclusively conservative or innovative, orthodox or heterodox, monk or *magister*, or at the one or the other end of any other such polarities. His life and works have too many intricacies and idiosyncrasies to permit such reductionism.

Knowledge of his life has increased thanks to the continued mining and sifting of a rich and possibly growing but ultimately frustrating lode of twelfth-century materials about him, including an autobiographical letter as well as a subsequent correspondence between him and Heloise (around 1100–1164), which have secured them places among the most famous men and women of the twelfth century.[5] A few of the key dates in Abelard's biography remain hotly contested, and Heloise's age at the time of their love story has been estimated variously. For want of evidence, such details may never be fixed definitively.[6] Still more unsettling, spe-

---

4. The relationship between Heloise and Abelard has elicited vast amounts of attention, not all of it reliable as scholarship. For a recent specimen, see James Burge, *Heloise and Abelard: A Twelfth-Century Love Story* (London: Profile Books, 2003).

5. For an insightfully synthetic but not chronologically linear biography of Abelard, see Michael T. Clanchy, *Abelard: A Medieval Life* (Oxford, U.K.: Blackwell, 1997). The most recent appreciation of Abelard (with close scrutiny of Heloise as well) is Constant J. Mews, *Abelard and Heloise* (Oxford, U.K.: Oxford University Press, 2005).

6. For the common opinion on many major dates in Abelard's life as they are now generally accepted, see Michael T. Clanchy, "Chronology," in *The Letters of Abelard and Heloise*, trans. Betty Radice, rev. Clanchy (London: Penguin Books, 2003), ix–xi.

cialists have been sharply divided at times in their opinions on the authenticity of these letters. Yet despite all the uncertainties, the long-past affair that hangs over them and their lives long afterward has taken on an existence of its own in translations, adaptations of varying degrees of freedom, and even plays, operas, and films.[7] If it is an exaggeration, it is only a slight one to contend that Abelard and Heloise have gained the cultural status of Lancelot and Guinevere, Dante and Beatrice, Petrarch and Laura, or even Romeo and Juliet. The first four letters in this book pertain to the relations between Abelard and Heloise, but stem from a period somewhat after the better known correspondence.

Many basic facts of Peter Abelard's life can be pieced together from an autobiographical letter, or apologia, the *Historia calamitatum* (The Story of My Disasters; written around 1132), as well as from mentions in other texts.[8] He was born in 1079 at Le Pallet, a village about a dozen miles east of Nantes in Brittany. Although an eldest son of noble background, he was drawn to the world of learning or, to be more precise, to the domain of reasoning and debating.[9] Eventually he forsook his birthright as a knight to become a philosopher. Initially he devoted himself especially to logic or dialectic. Letter Thirteen in this volume does not date from this earliest stage in his career, but it gives an eloquent testimonial to the lifelong conviction Abelard cherished in the powers of dialectic, as well as to the impatience he evidenced for those who were not like-minded and who failed to grasp the utilities of formal

7. On the final three categories, see Raffaella Asni, "Abélard et Héloïse sur l'écran et la scène de 1900 à nos jours," in *Pierre Abélard. Colloque international de Nantes*, ed. Jean Jolivet and Henri Habrias (Rennes, France: Presses Universitaires de Rennes, 2003), 185–203.

8. The generally cited edition of the Latin is Jacques Monfrin, ed., *Abélard, Historia calamitatum* (Paris: J. Vrin, 1959). The standard translation is in *Letters of Abelard and Heloise*, trans. Radice, 3–43.

9. His father and mother belonged to the minor nobility. On Abelard's parentage and genealogy, see Brenda M. Cook, "Abelard and Heloise," *Genealogists' Magazine* 26 (1999): 205–11.

logic as a tool for problem solving and intellectual discovery and advancement.

Although the schools of Paris became paramount in his professional life, Abelard first journeyed to other places to obtain and offer an education in philosophy, especially in logic.[10] Letter Fourteen gives a picture of his combative relations, a quarter century later, with one of his principal instructors during this early phase of his education. His itinerancy in learning and teaching was at least a contributing factor in one of his nicknames, *Peripateticus Palatinus*. He qualified as "the Peripatetic" by virtue of both his traveling ways and of course his close acquaintance with (and resemblance to) Aristotle, the Greek philosopher of the fourth century B.C.E. whose followers were so called after the arcade in the ancient Athenian Lyceum where they walked about (*peripatos* in Greek) while debating. The epithet of "the Palatine" Abelard merited by way of his birthplace, Le Pallet, and perhaps by his own nobility as well as by his connections with the higher nobility (since the adjective associated him with the palace and would have carried undertones similar to "courtier").[11]

Abelard's earliest education in logic took place sometime in the

10. On his relations with the schools (particularly of Paris), see Jean Châtillon, "Abélard et les écoles," in *Abélard en son temps. Actes du colloque international organisé à l'occasion du 9e centenaire de la naissance de Pierre Abélard (14–19 mai 1979),* ed. Jean Jolivet (Paris: Les Belles Lettres, 1981), 133–60, and Stephen C. Ferruolo, *The Origins of the University: The Schools of Paris and Their Critics, 1100–1215* (Stanford, Calif.: Stanford University Press, 1985), 18–22.

11. Early in the *Historia calamitatum* (ed. Monfrin, p. 64, line 30; trans. Radice, p. 3), Abelard terms himself "Peripateticorum emulator" (emulator of the Peripatetics). The full nickname appears in John of Salisbury (about 1110–1180), *Metalogicon* 1.5, 2.10, 2.17, 3.1, 3.4, and 3.6, ed. J. B. Hall, with K. S. B. Keats-Rohan, *Ioannis Saresberiensis Metalogicon,* CCCM 98 (1991): 20, line 13; 70, line 5; 81, line 22; 103, line 6; 116, line 35; and 122, line 21; and John of Salisbury, *Policraticus* 2.22, ed. K. S. B. Keats-Rohan, *Ioannis Saresberiensis Policraticus,* CCCM 118 (1993): 129, lines 99–100. For a good introduction to John, see Southern, *Scholastic Humanism,* 1: 214–21. On the relationship between the two men as well as on the name, see François Lejeune, "Pierre Abélard et Jean de Salisbury," in *Pierre Abélard. Colloque international de Nantes,* 63–75.

final decade of the eleventh century (1093–1099) in Loches (Indre-et-Loire), which lies south of Blois and Tours, and in Tours itself under Roscelin of Compiègne (about 1050–about 1120), a logician and theologian who had formulated controversial thoughts on Trinitarian theology and who had been induced to recant them at Soissons in 1092. Beyond his notions on the Trinity, Roscelin also maintained that words and names are only a means of describing realities, both physical and conceptual, from which they remain discrete. His beliefs in this regard, which belong to an important school of medieval thought known as nominalism (or more precisely as vocalism), left an enduring mark on Abelard; but this is not to suggest that Roscelin had a true disciple in the younger man for long, if ever. On the contrary, Abelard later went out of his way to dissociate himself from Roscelin. Letter Fourteen, the one that caps this collection, relates to their final sparring, apparently just before Roscelin's death or retirement.[12]

In about 1100 Abelard studied in the cathedral school of Paris under William of Champeaux (about 1070–1122), archdeacon of Paris and master of the school of Notre Dame.[13] Abelard reacted just as strongly, and hostilely, against the realism of William and other twelfth-century Platonists as he had chafed against the nominalism of Roscelin, and he undertook to devise his own solu-

12. For details on Roscelin's thought and on the intellectual relationship between Abelard and Roscelin, see Constant J. Mews, "Nominalism and Theology before Abaelard: New Light on Roscelin of Compiègne," *Vivarium* 30 (1992): 4–33, and "The Trinitarian Doctrine of Roscelin of Compiègne and Its Influence: Twelfth-Century Nominalism and Theology Reconsidered," in *Langages et philosophie. Hommage à Jean Jolivet,* ed. Alain de Libera, Abedelali Elamrani-Jamal, and Alain Galonnier, Etudes de philosophie médiévale 74 (Paris: J. Vrin, 1997), 347–64, both repr. in Mews, *Reason and Belief.* Many of Jean Jolivet's numerous publications on Abelard's philosophy grapple with the task of situating the master's thought vis-à-vis the nominalists.

13. On William, see Jean Jolivet, "Données sur Guillaume de Champeaux, dialecticien et théologien," in *L'abbaye parisienne de Saint-Victor au Moyen Age: Communications présentées au XIIIe Colloque d'humanisme médiéval de Paris (1986–1988),* ed. Jean Longère, Bibliotheca Victorina 1 (Turnhout, Belgium: Brepols, 1991), 235–51.

tion to the old problem of universals.[14] More important in practical terms, he soon set up shop as master of his own school (about 1102–about 1105). He began to lecture in the royal towns of Melun and Corbeil.

Abelard's disagreements with William of Champeaux had consequences that extended far beyond the strictly intellectual, since Abelard's hounding of his onetime teacher contributed to William's decision in 1108 to resign his position at Notre Dame and to take refuge with some companions in the hermitage of St. Victor, not far outside the city walls, on the left bank of the Seine, where they became Augustinian canons and he headed the school.[15] Later, as bishop of Châlons, William installed Bernard (1090–1153) as abbot of Clairvaux (1115–1153), and the two grew to become friends. St. Victor became a breeding ground for canons distinguished in theology, foremost among whom was Hugh of St. Victor (died 1141), who taught there from 1115 until his death. Because Hugh

14. On Abelard and William, see Yukio Iwakuma, "Pierre Abélard et Guillaume de Champeaux dans les premières années du XIIe siècle: Une étude préliminaire," in Joël Biard, ed., *Langage, sciences, philosophie au XIIe siècle: Actes de la Table ronde internationale organisée les 25 et 26 mars 1998 par le Centre d'histoire des sciences et des philosophies arabes et médiévales (UPRESA 7062, CNRS/Paris VII/EPHE) et le Programme international de coopération scientifique (France-Japon) "Transmission des sciences et des techniques dans une perspective interculturelle"* (Paris: J. Vrin, 1999), 93–123.

On Abelard's responses to Plato and Platonism, see Tullio Gregory, "Abélard et Platon," in *Peter Abelard. Proceedings of the International Conference, Louvain, May 10–12, 1971,* ed. Eligius M. Buytaert, Mediaevalia Lovaniensia Series 1, Studia 2 (Leuven, Belgium: University Press, 1974), 38–64, repr. in Tullio Gregory, *Mundana sapientia: Forme di conoscenza nella cultura medievale,* Storia e letteratura 181 (Rome: Edizioni di storia e letteratura, 1992), 175–99; John Marenbon, "The Platonisms of Peter Abelard," in *Néoplatonisme et philosophie médiévale: Actes du Colloque international de Corfou 6–8 octobre 1995, organisé par la Société internationale pour l'étude de la philosophie médiévale,* ed. Linos G. Benakis, Rencontres de philosophie médiévale 6 (Turnhout, Belgium: Brepols, 1997), 109–29; and Lawrence Moonan, "Abelard's Use of the *Timaeus,*" *Archives d'histoire doctrinale et littéraire du moyen âge* 56 (1989): 7–90.

15. On the establishment of the abbey, see Robert-Henri Bautier, "Les origines et les premiers développements de l'abbaye Saint-Victor de Paris," in *L'abbaye parisienne de Saint-Victor au Moyen Age,* ed. Jean Longère, 23–52.

and Abelard flourished in Paris during the same decades, it is often illuminating to juxtapose their writings.[16] At the same time, it must not be overlooked that there seems to have been scant love lost between Abelard and any of the Victorines.[17] Consequently, comparison between them often brings out contrasts.

Eventually the pressures of teaching, probably exacerbated by tensions with William, Roscelin, and others, led to a failure of health that may have constituted what would be termed today a nervous breakdown (about 1105–about 1108), and Peter Abelard retreated to his native region for a few years to recover. It is likely that the concerns oppressing him exceeded the medieval equivalent of mere academic wrangles, since beyond the intellectual differences and teaching rivalries he and his antagonists had patrons in the highest reaches of contemporary politics who were themselves in conflict. William of Champeaux, associated first with the episcopally supported schools of Notre Dame and St. Victor, stood opposite to Stephen of Garlande, an archdeacon of Paris and chancellor (1106/7–1127/8) and seneschal to King Philip I (1052–1108, king of France 1059–1108), and Louis VI the Fat (1081–1137, king of France 1108–1137), who backed Abelard. Both Melun and Corbeil, the towns where Abelard taught, were affiliated with the king, and the public school of Mont Ste. Geneviève, out of which the University of Paris arose, was located in the cloister of secular canons where Stephen of Garlande was dean.[18] Thus it lay outside episcopal jurisdiction. It was on Mont Ste. Geneviève that Abelard became master of his own school (about 1110–about 1112) after his return from convalescence.

16. For a panoptic approach to Hugh's worldview through his *Didascalicon*, see Ivan Illich, *In the Vineyard of the Text: A Commentary to Hugh's "Didascalicon"* (Chicago: University of Chicago Press, 1993).

17. On Hugh of St. Victor in general, see Southern, *Scholastic Humanism*, 2: 56–65. On his criticism of Abelard's teachings, see Luscombe, *School of Peter Abelard*, 183–97.

18. On the importance of Stephen in Abelard's career, see Robert-Henri Bautier, "Paris au temps d'Abélard," in *Abélard en son temps*, 21–77.

Around 1113, Abelard determined that he needed to progress from what could be caricatured as a single-minded pursuit of logic, particularly the logic of Aristotle as mediated through Boethius (about 480–524). His interests had already ranged deeply into ethics and metaphysics, but his reputation rested on his teachings and writings on dialectic.[19] Now he began also to amplify his scope to accommodate the investigation of theology. To this end, he traveled in 1113 to the cathedral school of Laon to learn from Anselm of Laon (about 1055–1117), an exegete and theologian who was renowned among his many followers and who had initiated an undertaking to outfit the whole Bible with a continuous commentary (the so-called ordinary gloss, or *Glossa ordinaria*) that would supersede the partial ones that already existed.[20] Anselm had a reputation as a very successful pedagogue, but Abelard found his methods boringly dissatisfying and his erudition painfully pedantic. With the benefit of hindsight, the incompatibility of the two men seems to have been preordained. Anselm was text-driven, in that the information he imparted and the questions he posed emerged from within individual texts and the commentaries upon them; and he could be described as being allegorically inclined. In contrast, Abelard was question-driven, with a proclivity to favor logical analysis over all other forms of interpretation.

As Abelard had already done with both Roscelin and William of Champeaux, he made no bones about his quarrels with both the style and the content of the lectures his new teacher gave. At his most temperate, Abelard regarded Anselm as having acquired his authority mostly thanks to his advanced age.[21] Going further, the young upstart probably made known his opinion that Anselm was a fool.[22] Abelard managed, at least according to his own as-

---

19. On his ethics and metaphysics, see Marenbon, *Philosophy of Abelard.*

20. See Beryl Smalley, *The Study of the Bible in the Middle Ages,* 3rd ed. (Oxford, U.K.: Blackwell, 1983), and Southern, *Scholastic Humanism,* 2: 25–48.

21. *Historia calamitatum,* ed. Monfrin, p. 67, lines 161–63; trans. Radice, pp. 6–7.

22. Otto of Freising, *Gesta Frederici seu rectius Chronica,* 1.50, ed. Franz-Josef Schmale,

sessment, to outshine the revered old sage through his own teaching and thus instigated enduring hostility between his adherents and those of Anselm, particularly Alberic of Rheims (died 1141), who later led the cathedral school of Rheims and ultimately held office as archbishop of Bourges (from 1136/7 until his death), and Lotulf of Novara (also known as Lotulph of Lombardy).[23] Alberic and Lotulf pressed Anselm to ban Abelard from teaching in Laon, which as head of the school the older man was able to do in short order.

After the rift with Anselm, Abelard returned to Paris in late 1113 or 1114 and resumed lecturing. Students were enthralled by the novelty of his pedagogy, which challenged them not just to absorb the definitive statements (*auctoritates*) in revered authors (*auctores*), but also to interrogate the texts and passages with the strength of their own logic. His magnetism as a master at the cathedral school of Notre Dame contributed to the eventual ascendancy of Paris as a major university town, preeminent in the teaching of dialectic. By about 1116 he had completed a textbook, the *Dialectica*, that gave room to his own creativity qua logician as his earlier teaching had not done, which had hewed more closely to the set texts by Aristotle; Porphyry, the Neoplatonic philosopher (about 232–304); and Boethius. At the same time, his popularity also made him a lightning rod for monastic criticism, since many brethren would have regarded Abelard himself as well as the schooling and thinking he embodied as being irredeemably worldly.

Under these active and tense circumstances unfolded the cause célèbre of Abelard and Heloise. Fulbert, a canon of the chapter

---

2d ed., *Ausgewählte Quellen zur deutschen Geschichte des Mittelalters: Freiherr vom Stein-Gedächtnisausgabe* 17 (Darmstadt, Germany: Wissenschaftliche Buchgesellschaft, 1974), pp. 224, line 31–226, lines 1–3; *The Deeds of Frederick Barbarossa, by Otto of Freising and His Continuator, Rahewin,* 1.49 (47), trans. Charles Christopher Mierow, Records of Civilization: Sources and Studies 49 (New York: Columbia University Press, 1953), 83. For a sense of Otto, see Southern, *Scholastic Humanism,* 1: 208–12.

23. John R. Williams, "The Cathedral School of Rheims in the Time of Master Alberic, 1118–1136," *Traditio* 20 (1964): 93–114, at 108–9.

of Notre Dame cathedral, arranged for the rising star of logic to be lodged in his quarters and to tutor his niece, Heloise, privately. Sometime between 1115 and 1117 the renowned master and the considerably younger Heloise began a love affair under the good canon's very nose.[24] At first Fulbert failed or refused to recognize the romance, even when it evolved from being merely budding to being in full bloom, but eventually he learned or admitted the truth. Despite the obstacles that Fulbert raised, the two lovers persevered in their lovemaking and as a natural consequence conceived a child. Their son paid the price for having two unconventional parents by receiving from his mother the name of Astralabe, which refers at least in part to the astronomical device still designated now as the astrolabe.[25]

Abelard had sent Heloise to his sister in Le Pallet, where Astralabe was born (around 1118). When Heloise came back to Paris, Abelard and she were wedded secretly; the matrimony was a gesture to placate Fulbert, while the secrecy was a play to keep intact Abelard's reputation and career. Among other things, to be openly married would have ruled out most possible promotions within the Church. But Heloise seems to have been concerned with mar-

---

24. Her age has been estimated between the teens and late twenties.

25. The full import of the name remains murky. The astrolabe could have had symbolic meaning to Heloise (and Abelard?) since it used the positions of the stars to determine dates, to navigate, and to enable other calculations. Etymologically the two Greek elements of which the word is formed could have been construed together as meaning roughly "reach for the stars." Additionally, its letters (since it was probably written with an "a" instead of an "o" in the second syllable) could be rearranged to form an approximation to Abelard's name in the spoken language, such as *Abalarts*. Another, more elaborate anagram has been proposed, that resolves *Astralabius. puer.Dei* into *Petrus.Abaelardus.II*; see William G. East, "Abelard's Anagram," *Notes and Queries* 240 (1995): 269, and Brenda M. Cook, "The Shadow on the Sun: The Name of Abelard's Son," in *The Poetic and Musical Legacy of Heloise and Abelard: An Anthology of Essays by Various Authors*, ed. Marc Stewart and David Wulstan, Wissenschaftliche Abhandlungen/ Musicological Studies 78 (Ottawa, Canada: Institute of Mediaeval Music, 2003), 152–55. The last-mentioned hypothesis would carry more conviction if either of the Latin phrases in question had ever been attested.

riage as an impediment to a philosophical ideal that Abelard and she shared, rather than to any particular ecclesiastic advancement that either of them coveted for him. Before finally yielding, she pleaded forcefully against marriage, with supporting quotations from Jerome's (about 340–420) *Book against Jovinian* (393).

Whatever the motivations behind it had been, the wedding led to an even worse disaster than Heloise had feared. Fulbert tried to break the confidentiality about the marriage, which his niece, to protect Abelard's interests, then denied even existed. When Fulbert grew abusive toward Heloise, Abelard removed her from Fulbert's dwelling to the nunnery of Argenteuil, where she had been raised. Fulbert, convinced (and perhaps not incorrectly) that Abelard meant to repudiate the marriage, directed hoodlums to emasculate Abelard. Once his thugs had executed their mission successfully, Abelard insisted that Heloise become a nun, which she did at Argenteuil in about 1118.

After the castration and scandal rendered impossible the continuation of his secular career in Paris, Abelard retired to the Benedictine monastery of St. Denis. In personal terms, becoming a monk afforded a means to attain spiritual peace. Politically, it may have offered him a way to free himself from episcopal jurisdiction, since at St. Denis he would have been answerable to the abbot but not to the bishop. Even after taking his vows, he continued to teach—a not altogether monastic pursuit that only worsened his troubled relations with his fellow monks, with whom he seems to have had friction from his very arrival or soon thereafter.

While at St. Denis Abelard put together a first version of the *Sic et non* (Yes and No), a sourcebook of 158 chapters that placed extracts from the Bible and Church Fathers alongside others that were contradictory or at least inconsistent on many points, particularly with regard to Christian belief.[26] Although the main body

---

26. For a detailed analysis of the underlying interpretative principles set forth in the prologue, see Cornelia Rizek-Pfister, "Die hermeneutischen Prinzipien in Abae-

of the book contains nothing but quotations from earlier authors, the Prologue sets forth his motives, methods, and conclusions in presenting the excerpts, the authoritative texts. Since the excerpts, texts, and prestige vested in them all passed under the name of *auctoritas,* Abelard's undertaking involved wrestling with concepts and practices at the very heart of medieval culture.[27] A similar effort to collect systematically had been made by the canonist Ivo of Chartres (about 1040–1115/6), with whose modus operandi in the *Panormia* (also called the *Pannomia*) Abelard was familiar,[28] but no one before the Peripatetic Palatine had employed in the study of theology a deliberate confrontation of quotations that arrive or at least hint at opposite conclusions.

Abelard next applied his energies to problems pertaining to the natures of God and of the Trinity. He presented his findings in a treatise now known, in reference to its opening words, as the *Theologia "Summi boni"* and alternatively, following a description of it that Abelard himself gives, as the *Tractatus de unitate ac Trinitate divina* (Treatise on the Unity and Trinity of God).[29] By choosing the

---

lards *Sic et non," Freiburger Zeitschrift für Philosophie und Theologie* 47 (2000): 484–501. Abelard probably revised and expanded the work in subsequent years, perhaps during his teaching at the Paraclete.

27. On the semantic range of *auctor* and its derivatives, see Mariken Teeuwen, *The Vocabulary of Intellectual Life in the Middle Ages,* CIVICIMA Etudes sur le vocabulaire intellectuel du moyen âge 10 (Turnhout, Belgium: Brepols, 2003), 222–23.

28. The first form of the title plays on the Greek for "All" and the Latin for "Rules" or "Norms," while the second Latinizes the Greek for "All the Laws." For a sketch of Ivo's activities and writings, see Southern, *Scholastic Humanism,* 1: 252–61. On Ivo and other possible sources for Abelard, see Marenbon, *Philosophy of Peter Abelard,* 61–62. For a tabulation of correspondences among the *Sic et non, Decretum,* and *Panormia,* see Paul Fournier, "Les collections canoniques attribuées à Yves de Chartres," *Bibliothèque de l'École des Chartes* 58 (1897): 624–76, at 661–64. A thorough investigation of instances throughout Abelard's writings in which he relied on Ivo would be well worthwhile.

On earlier exegetes who had occasionally organized evidence according to a *Sic et non* dichotomy (or, in their terminology, "*Quod . . . et contra*"), see Ermenegildo Bertola, "I precedenti storici del metodo del *Sic et non* di Abelardo," *Rivista di filosofia neo-scolastica* 53 (1961): 495–522.

29. *Historia calamitatum,* ed. Monfrin, pp. 82–83, lines 692–93; trans. Radice, p. 20.

Trinity as his central topic, Abelard was almost inevitably doomed to incite the wrath of his many foes. Recall that his first teacher, Roscelin, had been condemned in 1092 at Soissons for work on the Trinity. Roscelin himself was bitterly critical of Abelard's treatise, and he and Abelard struggled in at least a small volley of letters to besmirch each other's reputation and reasoning and thereby to win the upper hand with the ecclesiastic authorities. As mentioned above, Letter Fourteen in this collection relates to their disputes.

But being entangled in a contention with a heretic did not suffice to immunize Abelard against the taint of unorthodoxy. He still incurred suspicion and, like Roscelin nearly two decades earlier, was found guilty (and was compelled to consign his book to the flames) in Soissons in March or April of 1121 after being put on trial before Bishop Cono of Palestrina (ancient Praeneste), the papal legate in France from 1111 until his death in 1122. Both Alberic and Lotulf, the two protégés of Anselm's of whom Abelard had fallen afoul in Laon, played contributing parts, by prevailing upon Raoul le Vert (died 1124), archbishop of Rheims, to have the council convoked. Despite its condemnation and burning, The Theologia "Summi boni" survived. In addition, Abelard incorporated approximately nine-tenths of it into a much-expanded revision that is entitled the Theologia Christiana, which he revised in turn into the Theologia "Scholarium."[30] What Abelard could not undo was the humiliation of having been forced to recite the Athanasian Creed, which affirmed all the divine persons to be omnipotent: the great magister was constrained to avow his faith before one and all, like a schoolboy being catechized.

After his public abasement, Abelard was sentenced to a short confinement in the monastery of St. Médard in Soissons. There, to add insult to injury, he was placed under the supervision of Prior Goswin (about 1086–1166), a former student at Mont Ste. Geneviève who had been antagonistic toward him. Before too long

---

30. Marenbon, The Philosophy of Peter Abelard, 58–61.

Abelard returned to St. Denis, but the stay lasted only one or two years. If he had not already merited the hostility of his fellow monks, he now earned it by not merely chastising them for indiscipline but also arguing, in vintage Abelardian fashion, that the patron of the abbey, St. Denis, bishop of Paris, the protomartyr and apostle of France (died about 250), was an altogether different person from the Dionysius the Areopagite, bishop of Athens in the first century, touched upon in the Acts of the Apostles (17.34). Long after the fact he cursorily described the imbroglio in the *Historia calamitatum*.[31] He dealt with the challenge much more fully in a letter (Letter Eleven in this book) he addressed to the abbot, Adam (1099–1122), and to his fellow monks. By teasing apart the various Dionysiuses, he simultaneously diminished the prestige of the monastery and rendered himself persona non grata among the brethren.

After fleeing to Provins (and probably in particular to the priory of St. Ayoul there) in the realm of Count Thibaud of Champagne (1107–1152), and after the death of Abbot Adam on 19 January 1122, Abelard negotiated permission from Suger (1081–1151), Adam's successor as abbot of St. Denis (1122–1151), to withdraw permanently from the abbey so long as he did not enter obedience to another abbot.[32] Thus he became a kind of monastic free agent, answerable fully neither to a bishop nor an abbot, able to establish himself where he wanted and to act as he wished. He was exempt from the sorts of obedience and stability that hemmed in most monks.

Thereafter he settled in a wilderness in Champagne on the bank of the river Ardusson, near Quincey (northwest of Troyes) and not far from the Seine, where he established a hermitage; but

---

31. See *Historia calamitatum*, ed. Monfrin, pp. 89–91, lines 941–81; trans. Radice, pp. 26–27.

32. Thibaud, or Theobald, was also count palatine, count of Blois and Chartres (1107–1152), and count of Troyes (1125–1152).

the hermitic life did not last long, since soon students sought him out in droves. They constituted a community devoted to learning, modeled upon the way of life that Jerome had ascribed to Greek philosophers of antiquity, but the utopia of an apostolicity based on the alleged modus vivendi of ancient sages lasted only a few years (1122–1125/7) before its dissolution. In the meantime the young men built a small chapter or oratory that Abelard dedicated first to the Holy Trinity but that he settled eventually on designating the Paraclete or "Comforter," an appellation of the Holy Spirit (John 14.16 and 14.26). This choice of name was itself unprecedented and controversial, probably because it plainly reflected Abelard's convictions about the Trinity, which galvanized excitement in some of his followers and decidedly more mixed reactions among many other contemporaries.

By sometime between 1125 and 1127 Abelard felt isolated and vulnerable, as a result of what he suspected to be a smear campaign against him by two "new apostles," perhaps by Bernard of Clairvaux and Norbert of Xanten (about 1085–1134), founder of the Premonstratensian Order, who (according to Abelard) had been whetted on by old rivals of his.[33] To make matters worse, in 1127–1128 Stephen of Garlande, who had sometimes backed Abelard, fell from grace with King Louis VI. To escape the deteriorating situation, Abelard departed to become abbot of St. Gildas on the Rhuys peninsula, near Vannes on the west coast of Brittany. An undated broadside in the present collection, Letter Twelve, gives vent to Abelard's vehement but coolly argued belief in the superiority of the monastic over the canonical way of life. His advocacy of rigor in monastic conduct had led to grief at least once before, at St. Denis, but throughout his life Abelard consistently refused to allow the foreseeably unappreciative reactions of others to dissuade him from any given course of action or self-expression. His efforts to strengthen discipline in the monastery met resentment and resistance to the

---

33. *Historia calamitatum*, ed. Monfrin, p. 97, lines 1196–1212; trans. Radice, pp. 32–33.

point where (if we credit Abelard) the mutinous monks schemed to assassinate him.

Around this time, in 1129, Heloise's community was displaced from the convent of Argenteuil, which had been expropriated by Abbot Suger.[34] Whether the expulsion by Suger had anything to do with Heloise's ties to Abelard is an intriguing question, but the most obvious motivation would have been greed rather than animosity. The paths of the two men seem to have intersected seldom, and their interests and ambitions differed greatly, to put it mildly.[35] Suger is now best known for the conception and construction of St. Denis chapel, which have earned him a reputation as the founder of Gothic architecture.[36] But in his own day his reputation (or disrepute) may well have owed most to the fundraising necessitated by such building enterprises. Argenteuil was located very close to the abbey of St. Denis, just down the Seine, and possessed valuable property. Discipline in the convent was sufficiently lax to have allowed Heloise and Abelard at least once to have sex in the refectory, during Holy Week no less, and Suger assailed the nuns on moral grounds; but he required and found (or fabricated) a more telling claim to arrogate its properties. In early spring of 1129 he attended a synod on monastic reform at St. Germain des Prés. There he achieved a coup by flourishing a forged docu-

34. See Thomas G. Waldman, "Abbot Suger and the Nuns of Argenteuil," *Traditio* 41 (1985): 239–72.

35. See Louis Grodecki, "Abélard et Suger," in *Pierre Abélard et Pierre le Vénérable. Les courants philosophiques, littéraires et artistiques en occident au milieu du XIIe siècle—Abbaye de Cluny, 2 au 9 juillet 1972*, ed. René Louis, Jean Jolivet, and Jean Châtillon, Actes et mémoires des colloques internationaux du Centre National de la Recherche Scientifique 546 (Paris: Centre National de la Recherche Scientifique, 1975), 279–86.

36. See Charles M. Radding and William W. Clark Jr., "Abélard et le bâtisseur de Saint-Denis. Études parallèles d'histoire des disciplines," *Annales ESC: Economies, sociétés* 43 (1988): 1263–90. For the same material in an expanded form in English (with better plates), see Radding and Clark, *Medieval Architecture, Medieval Learning: Builders and Masters in the Age of Romanesque and Gothic* (New Haven, Conn.: Yale University Press, 1992), 57–76.

ment to establish the original title of St. Denis to Argenteuil.[37] Soon thereafter, the papal legate, Matthew of Albano (1085–1135, cardinal-legate 1127–1135), issued a decree to authorize the transfer of Argenteuil to St. Denis, and Pope Honorius II (1124–1129) confirmed this decree in a document dated 23 April 1129. At least some of the nuns lodged at Ste. Marie de Footel, in Malnoüe in Brie, but others seemed to have been scattered.

When the convent found itself homeless, Abelard volunteered the Paraclete as a haven to Heloise and some of the nuns. After two or three years there, Heloise embarked upon a correspondence with Abelard, at the outset mainly for personal reasons but later partly on the basis of (or on the pretext of) her duties administering the convent and her questions about theological and liturgical concerns. These letters have been widely disseminated in translation for decades, usually in tandem with the *Historia calamitatum*, and they have accounted for most of the notoriety the two lovers continue to have.

Building upon the epistolary exchange, Abelard composed for the Paraclete, in response to repeated requests from Heloise, a cluster of writings that had the potential to make the convent a paragon of a new female monasticism, one designed on distinctively Abelardian lines. This volume presents a translation of a long text (Letter Nine) Abelard directed to the nuns of the Paraclete on his ideals for their education, with special praise for Heloise's linguistic and interpretative qualifications for delivering such instruction. Alongside Letter Nine is presented the English of prefaces and dedicatory letters to Heloise and sometimes to her fellow nuns that accompanied a hymnal, a commentary on the opening of Genesis, and a collection of sermons, all composed by Abelard at Heloise's instigation for the sisters in her convent. Later in this volume appears Letter Ten, half of which, though addressed to Bernard of

---

37. For the story, see Lindy Grant, *Abbot Suger of St-Denis: Church and State in Early Twelfth-Century France* (London: Longman, 1998), 191–93.

Clairvaux rather than the nuns, is taken up with the wording of the Lord's Prayer that Abelard had established for the Paraclete.

For nearly two hundred years debate, like a volcano that refuses to slip into dormancy, has raged intermittently over the authenticity of the letters between Abelard and Heloise. One of the three principal theories maintains that the correspondence was concocted by a later author in the thirteenth century to make an example of the two. Another holds that Abelard wrote all the letters, both the ones that bear his name and those that are ascribed to Heloise. A third advocates that the correspondence is genuine. The manuscript tradition, references to the letters in texts by other authors, and verbal and stylometric analysis are among the tools of analysis that have been brought to bear on this much-vexed question, with the result that a consensus (though far from unanimous) now holds Abelard and Heloise indeed to be the authors of the letters that begin with the *Historia calamitatum*. But let us return from the byways of philology to the vicissitudes of Abelard's existence, which from this stage on are no longer chronicled in the *Historia calamitatum* or letters.

After not a decade as abbot of the forsaken (and seemingly God-forsaken) cloister of St. Gildas, Abelard gravitated back to the environs of Paris to resume teaching on Mont Ste. Geneviève. This move would have occurred about 1133.[38] During this phase he addressed himself to two audiences, one being his students and colleagues in Paris and the other being Heloise and the nuns of the Paraclete. In sending forth texts he seems to have been feverishly productive. Once again, he aroused acrimony through his personality, his writings, and, perhaps especially, his teachings. This time the opposition against him rallied around a most formidable opponent, Bernard of Clairvaux, who took his anxieties and grievances to the highest reaches of the Church.

38. It is disputed how long he remained in Paris. Marenbon, *Philosophy of Peter Abelard*, 25–26, puts the case for 1139, while most others argue for 1136 or 1137.

In the end, Abelard sought to defend himself at the Council of Sens against charges based on the alleged content of his theological doctrines and treatises. The council took place in 1141, after Abbot William of St. Thierry (about 1085–1148, abbot 1119/21–1148) brought to the attention of his fellow Cistercian Bernard of Clairvaux as well as of the papal legate, Geoffrey of Lèves, bishop of Chartres (1116–1149), purportedly heterodox passages in what William believed (or maintained) were writings of Abelard.[39] Nearly twenty years earlier Geoffrey had been a supporter of Abelard's at the Council of Soissons, but in the two intervening decades much had changed.[40] Among other things, Geoffrey had been acquainted with Norbert of Xanten since 1114 or even earlier and had become at the latest by 1126 a close intimate of his, and Abelard and Norbert seem, to judge by remarks in the writings of the former, to have attacked each other. Count Thibaud of Champagne, who had thrown his weight behind Abelard in the past, had been an active antagonist of Geoffrey's and had driven him from Chartres after his appointment to the episcopacy in 1116, although there is no evidence that attests to subsequent battles between them. Geoffrey had been among the bishops who had favored the arrogation of Argenteuil by Suger.

But it would be wrong to overemphasize the role of Geoffrey of Lèves, since the council was filled with men who had ample cause to dislike or resent Abelard. Abelard would have been a fool not to take countermeasures against the likelihood that many ecclesiastics hostile to him would participate. In the present collec-

---

39. On the relations between William of St. Thierry and Abelard, see Ambrogio M. Piazzoni, *Guglielmo di Saint-Thierry: Il declino dell'ideale monastico nel secolo XII*, Studi storici 181–83 (Rome: Istituto storico italiano per il Medio Evo, 1988), 157–79.

40. The definitive source for the facts of Geoffrey's life are set forth in Wilfried M. Grauwen, "Gaufried, bisschop van Chartres (1116–1149), vriend van Norbert en van de 'Wanderprediger,'" *Analecta Praemonstratensia* 58 (1982): 161–209. On the length of Geoffrey's acquaintance and close friendship with Norbert, see 161–62 and 165; on Thibaud, 166–67 and 173.

tion, Letter Fifteen records Abelard's ultimately futile endeavors
to ensure, by rallying students and supporters, a favorable forum
for the presentation and defense of his doctrines. The *socii* upon
whom he called in this letter may have trooped to Sens, but the
council failed to live up to any of Abelard's hopes or schemes. Responsibility for its outcome must be accorded above all others to
one potentate of the Church, Bernard of Clairvaux.

Bernard's participation made Sens a collision between two no-
tabilities of the first order, as well as between two value systems.
The abbot of Clairvaux was not just among the most charismat-
ic men of his times but also a redoubtable broker of political and
ecclesiastic power. Both he and Abelard professed to revere the essential dogmas of Christianity and not to wish to subvert them.
Both were magnetic speakers who attracted and motivated devoted
retinues.[41] Both wrote extensively about love, gave and received it
in good measure, and yet were capable simultaneously of fiery and
even nasty intolerance toward others, perhaps most particularly toward each other. Both were monks who served as abbots.

Yet the manifold differences between the two outweigh the like-
nesses. From Bernard and most monastic brethren Abelard diverged
not only because he held views perceived to be unorthodox and in-
flammatory on theological topics such as the nature of the Trinity,
but also because he had been married, had been unmanned, persevered in teaching, and, perhaps most important, valued above all
the application of reason to the solution of problems and answer-
ing of questions. He and Bernard had locked horns even before
Sens, as Letter Ten in this volume demonstrates fascinatingly. The
text captures Abelard's barely controlled fury that Bernard would
dare to take exception to the modalities of worship that he, Abelard, had instituted for the nuns of the Paraclete.

Abelard departed from Sens without mounting a public de-

41. On Abelard's followers, see Luscombe, *School of Peter Abelard*, and David E. Luscombe, "The School of Peter Abelard Revisited," *Vivarium* 30 (1992): 127–38.

fense, once it dawned on him belatedly that he would not be allowed to engage with Bernard openly over the points of contention, and once he had realized that far from being a debater, he was to play the role of the convicted at a tribunal with sentencing but with no trial. No doubt he felt compelled to withdraw before suffering an encore of what had befallen him two decades earlier in Soissons. Initially he set off on a trip to lobby Rome in his defense, but even in this measure he was foiled. Because after his departure nineteen propositions ascribed to him were condemned at Sens, and because Bernard managed swiftly to obtain papal support for the condemnation from Innocent II (pope 1130–1143), Abelard abandoned his journey to the Vatican and instead took refuge in Burgundy with Peter the Venerable (1092/94–1156, abbot of Cluny 1122–56). Peter the Venerable acted as an intermediary in bringing about a rapprochement between Abelard and the Church, even with Bernard of Clairvaux himself. Abelard's health soon deteriorated and he died at St. Marcel, a Cluniac priory at Châlons-sur-Saône, on 21 April 1142, as reported by Peter to Heloise in a letter that is still extant.[42] Heloise saw to it that Abelard's body was brought to the Paraclete. After she passed away in 1163 or 1164, she was buried near him there. Eventually, after the destruction of the gravesite during the French Revolution, their remains were transferred in the early nineteenth century to be entombed together in Père Lachaise in Paris, reputedly the most visited cemetery in the world.

Works

As the bouquets of flowers attest that are often tossed upon the statues of Heloise and him that rest upon the tomb in Paris, Abe-

42. On Heloise's letters to Peter the Venerable, see Christopher Baswell, "Heloise," in *The Cambridge Companion to Medieval Women's Writing*, ed. Carolyn Dinshaw and David Wallace, Cambridge Companions to Literature (Cambridge, U.K.: Cambridge University Press, 2003), 161–71, at 162–63.

lard is indebted for his enduring fame above all to the romance and its personal and literary aftermath. But beyond the correspondence with her about their relationship (and much else), he left an impressive panoply of writings that attests to the multiplicity of his interests, versatility of his intellect, and powerful appeal of his self-expression. A decent share of these can now be consulted in translation, and not all will be enumerated here, but most will be found in the bibliography at the end of this volume.[43] In theology and philosophy, his most renowned work is the *Sic et non*, a kind of sourcebook in 158 chapters that collocates excerpts from authoritative Church writers who articulated discordant views on points of biblical interpretation and theological doctrine. Paradoxically, Abelard's *Sic et non* embeds none of its author's own writings or views, with the striking exception of the Prologue, where he educes principles to guide readers in evaluating authorities and in determining which to prefer in cases of such discrepancies.

However salient the *Sic et non* may be today, the theological text Abelard wrote that elicited the fiercest reactions in his own day was undoubtedly his *Theologia*, not so much a single product as a body of thoughts that evolved over many years. This *Theologia* is extant in three different main forms, first the *Theologia "Summi boni,"* then the *Theologia Christiana*, and finally the *Theologia "Scholarium."* To compound the complexities of the *Theologia*, each of these has come down in more than one redaction. Though the word *theologia* was not Abelard's coinage, he imparted to it a distinctive character and infuriated some of his coevals by using it.[44]

---

43. The manuscripts of writings by Abelard and by others who recorded his teachings are not enumerated in the bibliography. For them, see the indispensable, even if now dated, listing in Julia Barrow, Charles S. F. Burnett, and David E. Luscombe, "A Checklist of the Manuscripts Containing the Writings of Peter Abelard and Heloise and Other Works Closely Associated with Abelard and His School," *Revue d'histoire des textes* 14–15 (1984–1985): 183–302.

44. On the slowness with which the noun established itself and on Abelard's role in the process, see Teeuwen, *Vocabulary of Intellectual Life,* 379–81.

In logic Abelard left the *Logica "Ingredientibus"* (Logical Treatise, opening with the phrase "To those beginning") and the *Dialectica,* as well as various other works. In ethics his *Ethica seu Liber "Scito te ipsum"* (Ethics, or the Book "Know Thyself") survives. In addition, he produced biblical commentaries on the six days of creation (the so-called hexaemeron) in Genesis 1–2.25 and on the epistle of Paul to the Romans. Along similar lines, he left analyses (even if not all of them qualify as full-fledged expositions) of liturgical texts, namely, the Athanasian Creed, the Lord's Prayer, and the Apostles' Creed. Finally, he composed and assembled nearly three dozen sermons which are still extant.

Alongside his scholarly writings, Abelard left a spectacular set of writings that could be called (anachronistically) "creative." Closest to his other prose texts would be the *Collationes* (Discussions), formerly known as the *Dialogue between a Christian, a Philosopher, and a Jew,* which could be grouped with his ethical oeuvre, because of its preoccupation with the highest good and with the nature of happiness, but which takes the unconventional expression of two dream debates, one between a Philosopher and a Jew and the other between a Philosopher and a Christian. It may be compared with his *Soliloquium* (Soliloquy), in which a character speaking in the guise of "Peter" discusses matters of faith and reason with an interlocutor designated "Abelard."

From the *Historia calamitatum* and personal letters we infer that Abelard was a celebrated poet and songwriter. Of his early output we possess no certain remnants, but from the phase in his life after Heloise was established at the Paraclete we have poetry that is compellingly varied in form as well as in content. Abelard created a cycle of hymns for the convent; a cluster of six lament poems (*planctus*) in the voices of Old Testament personages (also presumably meant for Heloise and her nuns); the *Carmen ad Astralabium* (Poem to Astralabe), a didactic poem replete with gnomic admonitions and dedicated to his son Astralabe; and the *Carmen figuratum,* a "pattern poem" (verse in which the elements are arranged visually to form a recognizable shape). Numerous other poems have been attributed to Abelard (and Heloise), but often on tenuous grounds.[45]

The Letters, to Heloise and Beyond

Last but not least in Abelard's oeuvre come his prose letters, among which is to be subsumed the autobiographical *Historia calamitatum*, written when Abelard was in his fifties. The most immediately arresting of these letters are the ones to Heloise, which are conventionally split into the personal letters (Letters One through Five) and the letters of direction (Letters Six through Eight). The personal letters in particular have been both blighted and blessed by controversies. As was suggested above, past scholarship is a landscape pocked by sinkholes of disputes over whether the letters were indeed written by the notorious former lovers, whether they were forgeries or even an epistolary novel by a later anonymous, or whether they were all written by Abelard and none by Heloise, but now a consensus holds that the letters by Abelard and Heloise were indeed penned by those two historically attested people.[46] At the same time the questions cannot be reduced to a binary de-

45. Both literature and music supposedly by one or the other have been treated in recent publications that rely substantially on analysis of texts the Abelardian ascriptions of which have not been proven or universally accepted—for examples, see *Poetic and Musical Legacy*, ed. Stewart and Wulstan; David Wulstan, *"Novi modulaminis melos:* The Music of Heloise and Abelard," *Plainsong and Medieval Music* 11 (2002): 1–23; and David Wulstan, *"Novi modulaminis melos:* The Music of Heloise and Abelard," *Plainsong and Medieval Music* 11 (2002): 1–23. For a skeptical assessment of these ascriptions, essential reading is Peter Dronke and Giovanni Orlandi, "New Works by Abelard and Heloise," *Filologia mediolatina* 12 (2005): 123–77, at 123–46.

46. For overviews of the authenticity debate, see John Marenbon, "Authenticity Revisited," in *Listening to Heloise: The Voice of a Twelfth-Century Woman*, ed. Bonnie Wheeler (New York: St. Martin's Press, 2000), 19–33, and John Marenbon, *Philosophy of Peter Abelard*, 82–93. For a philological perspective, see Ileana Pagani, "Il problema dell'attribuzione dell'Epistolario di Abelardo ed Eloisa. Status quaestionis," *Filologia Mediolatina* 6–7 (1999–2000): 79–88.

cision about authenticity or inauthenticity, since the correspondence—even if "real," as is today commonly accepted—has not come down to us without modifications introduced by a reviser, who may have been Heloise, Abelard, or an unknown third party.[47] Furthermore, the present has become enmired in other polemics and uncertainties about the constitution of the correspondence between the two, particularly regarding the so-called *Lost Love Letters of Heloise and Abelard*, whose ascription to the two by some has been roundly rejected by many others.[48] Loosely related to the letters of direction are the *Problemata Heloissae cum Petri Abaelardi solutionibus* (Heloise's Problems, with Peter Abelard's Solutions), a list of forty-two questions about the Bible that Heloise posed to Abelard in her capacity as leader (she styles herself deaconess and abbess in Letter Four) of the Paraclete and that he answered.[49] In their pres-

---

47. This point is expressed lucidly by Peter von Moos, *Abaelard und Heloise*, Gesammelte Studien zum Mittelalter 1, ed. Gert Melville, Geschichte: Forschung und Wissenschaft 14 (Munster, Germany: Lit Verlag, 2005), 210–13 (as well as elsewhere in the volume).

48. The study and English translation that have sparked the controversy are to be found in Constant J. Mews, with Neville Chiavaroli, *The Lost Love Letters of Heloise and Abelard: Perceptions of Dialogue in Twelfth-Century France* (New York: St. Martin's Press, 1999). The best edition of the Latin remains Ewald Könsgen, ed., *Epistolae duorum amantium. Briefe Abaelards und Heloises?*, Mittellateinische Studien und Texte 8 (Leiden, The Netherlands: E. J. Brill, 1974). For an assessment (with references to the burgeoning scholarship on the authorship question) that tends toward rejecting the ascription or at a minimum remaining agnostic, see Jan M. Ziolkowski, "Heloise, Abelard, and the *Epistolae duorum amantium*: Lost and Not Yet Found," *Journal of Medieval Latin* 14 (2004): 171–202.

49. Heloise's use of the term *deaconess* has caused perplexity. Abelard in Letter Seven refers to the history of the words *abbess* and *deaconess* and sees the latter as having come into usage much earlier, which may explain why he switches to it in Letter Eight ("the deaconess, who is now called the abbess"). He cites 1 Timothy 3.10–12, the scriptural basis for the word *deaconess*, and comments upon it in Sermon 31, in *PL* 178: 569C–73B, at 572CD. Heloise herself is nothing if not fiendishly deliberate in her choice of terminology in salutations. Since here she pairs deaconess with a word for a male who fulfills a liturgical function, she may have it in mind to refer to her role as a reader in services. For background, see Mary M. McLaughlin, "Peter Abelard and the Dignity of Women: Twelfth-Century Feminism in Theory and Practice," in *Pierre Abélard—Pierre le Vénérable*, 287–333, at 298–301.

ent contours the *Problemata* in no sense constitute a letter, but they originated in queries from Heloise to which Abelard replied. Furthermore, the *Problemata* cites two passages verbatim from Letter Eight and additionally takes for a given Abelard's promise in Letter Three to respond to queries from Heloise.[50] If the queries and responses were ever sent individually, those documents have disappeared without a trace. The redaction of the *Problemata* as a whole is now thought to have happened in 1137 and 1138.[51]

No one of the twelfth century, with the possible exceptions of Hildegard of Bingen (1098–1179) and Thomas Becket (1118–1170), has captured the emotions and imaginations of people in our day as have Peter Abelard and Heloise. The sheerly human aspects of Abelard's love affair with Heloise and its torturous end, as chronicled in the *Historia calamitatum* and in the so-called personal correspondence, intertwine vigorously with the less romantic but equally persistent intellectual dimensions of his passion for dialectic, which is memorialized in the title of his often invoked *Sic et non*. Yet although the Latin of both the *Historia calamitatum* and the correspondence with Heloise (Letters One through Eight) has been printed and reprinted, and although the texts have been translated repeatedly into English and other European languages, Abelard's other letters (Letters Nine through Fourteen, a letter against Bernard, and other letterlike documents to Heloise's convent and to Bernard) have not garnered the attention that they merit. It is high

50. See Damien Van Den Eynde, "Chronologie des écrits d'Abélard à Héloïse," *Antonianum* 37 (1962): 337–49, at 340–44; Peter Dronke, "Heloise's *Problemata* and Letters: Some Questions of Form and Content," in *Petrus Abaelardus (1079–1142). Person, Werk und Wirkung*, ed. Rudolph Thomas, Trierer Theologische Studien 38 (Trier, Germany: Paulinus-Verlag, 1980), 53–73, repr. in Dronke, *Intellectuals and Poets*, 295–322; Peter Dronke, *Women Writers of the Middle Ages: A Critical Study of Texts from Perpetua (d. 203) to Marguerite Porete (d. 1310)* (Cambridge, U.K.: Cambridge University Press, 1984), 107–43; and Maria Cipolone, "In margine ai *Problemata Heloissae*," *Aevum* 64 (1990): 227–44.

51. Paola De Santis, *I sermoni di Abelardo per le monache del Paracleto*, Mediaevalia Lovaniensia 1/31 (Leuven, Belgium: Leuven University Press, 2002), 167.

time that this omission be remedied by translation, since in their very heterogeneity these other texts open one of the best possible entries into the life and times of Abelard.

Whereas the authenticity of the correspondence with Heloise has been questioned repeatedly, the other letters are unassailably the work of Abelard. And while the exchange with Heloise reflects the perspectives of Abelard during a single period of a few years (1132–1136), the other letters afford insight into his thinking over a longer sweep of time—at least twenty years. Letters Nine through Fourteen, the letter against Bernard, and the other missives may not have the coherence of Letters One through Eight, since they were not directed to a single addressee and were not compiled during the Middle Ages as an integrated correspondence, but they have the appeal of illuminating Abelard's brilliant and willful mind as he trained it upon several of the major confrontations that he and other twelfth-century intellectuals faced. Some of them are interesting because they emanate from controversies or enterprises to which Abelard alludes in the *Historia calamitatum*, while others hold the opposite attraction of introducing us to vicissitudes in his life that fell outside the scope of his autobiographical letter. Having these letters accessible in English translation may enable general readers who are curious about Abelard to transcend the admittedly stirring qualities of the so-called personal letters and to gain an appreciation of Abelard's mind, creativity, and passions as they manifest themselves in dealings at once less revealing and more typical of his life as a whole, when he negotiates not only with Heloise and not only in the kind of intimacy that makes the main body of letters so beguiling.

More than a dozen of the letters that have been associated with Abelard were assigned numbers when they were printed in the nineteenth century in the so-called *Patrologia Latina*, often abbreviated to *PL*. (A more complete title of the series, although still not in all its cumbersome glory, is *Patrologiae cursus completus: Series Latina*.) In the *PL* numbers are given not only to those letters Abelard is alleged to have written but also to those he was supposed to have received, although less exhaustively for the latter. Here the *PL* count is followed for Letters One through Fourteen.[52] Of these Letters One through Eight have been translated in their entirety (with the exception of Letter Seven, which is only summarized) in the Penguin translation by Betty Radice, the paperback that without doubt gives most Anglophone readers nowadays their fullest exposure to the famous lovers, husband and wife, and fellow religious.

The present collection of letters comprises three parts. The first part brings together letters and letterlike texts bound up with Heloise and the Paraclete. The initial one is a lengthy letter to the nuns of the Paraclete, which was probably written after Letters Seven and Eight between the years 1132 and 1135. It is Letter Nine in the *PL* numbering. Although transmitted separately from Letters One through Eight, in many ways it brings the correspondence with Heloise to a logical conclusion (at least from what can be surmised to have been Abelard's perspective). What began as largely personal and retrospective has metamorphosed, or has been redirected consciously by Abelard, into collective and prospective. Thereafter follow the prefaces to the three books of the *Hymnarius Paraclitensis* (The Paraclete Hymnal); the dedicatory letter to his *Expositio in*

52. In that numeration, the personal letters, as has been noted already, comprise Letters One through Five: Letter One, the *Historia calamitatum*, incipit "Ad amicum suum consolatoria" ([Letter] of Consolation to His Friend); Letter Two, Heloise's first letter to Abelard, incipit "Heloisae suae ad ipsum deprecatoria" (Heloise's [Letter] of Complaint to Him); Letter Three, Abelard's first to her, "Dilectissime sorori sue in Christo" ("Rescriptum ipsius ad ipsam," His Reply to Her); Letter Four, Heloise's second to him, "Unico suo post Christum" ("Rescriptum ipsius ad ipsam," Her Reply to Him); and Letter Five, Abelard's second to her, "Sponsae Christi servus ejusdem" ("Ipse rursus ad ipsam," He Again to Her). The letters of direction encompass Letters Six through Eight: Letter Six, Heloise's third letter to Abelard, "Suo specialiter sua singulariter" ("Item eadem ad eundem," Again, She to Him); Letter Seven, Abelard to Heloise, *De ordine sanctimonialium* ("Rescriptum ad ipsam de auctoritate vel dignitate ordinis sanctimonialium," His Reply to Her on the Authority or Worthiness of the Order of Nuns); and Letter Eight, Abelard to Heloise, a letter that leads into the *Institutio seu regula sanctimonialium* (Institution or Rule of Nuns).

Hexaemeron (The Commentary on the Six Days of Creation); and the prologue to the book of *Sermones* (The Sermons).

The hymnal, commentary, and sermons stand on an equal footing in Abelard's corpus in being outfitted with dedications to Heloise. What is more, the texts were very much gifts bestowed upon Heloise by the author, and the prefaces or dedications can be construed as letters to accompany writings he put together (and in some instances composed) with Heloise as the recipient in the forefront of his mind. Whatever generic label we affix to them, these texts are stimulating for both their human and their intellectual complications. They let us glimpse Abelard as he labors to satisfy Heloise's petitions to him for writings—writings by which he aspires to shape the formation, liturgy, and theology of the nuns in the Paraclete, but also writings that Heloise seeks to coax out of him because they gratify her own intellectual predilections, because she intuits they will keep his mind (and vanities) piqued so that he will continue communicating with her and work his way out of the other crises in his life, or all of this at once.

The standard translation of the earlier correspondence may leave an unsuspecting reader with the misimpression that once Heloise has taken the veil, Abelard has no interest in communicating with her. He may come across as being coolly logical and as having no niche for her in his mind and even less in his heart, now that he has been castrated and has turned to religion. Such a construction would be badly misguided. These later letters and the long writings that they accompanied bear witness to an altered but continued devotion to Heloise and thus complicate our understanding of their relationship as it evolved after the affair.

In general the division between "The Personal Letters" and "The Letters of Direction" (as they have been flagged in the Penguin Classics paperback) has had unhappy effects on the reception not only of the latter but also of the even later and more disparate letters to Heloise and the nuns of the Paraclete on the education of nuns (Letter Nine) and on points of liturgy and exegesis.

The distinction between personal and public is at best less applicable to letters from the Middle Ages than to those of our own times, and it may even be downright anachronistic. "The Personal Letters" may have had relevance not just for Heloise but for the other nuns of the Paracelete as well, while "The Letters of Direction" contain strongly personal elements that it would be an error to overlook.[53]

Going beyond both all the correspondence between Heloise and Abelard and the Penguin volume itself, the second part of this volume assembles three letters relating to Bernard of Clairvaux. Letter Ten, dispatched to Bernard himself, conveys fascinating insights into the later frictions between the men, because it shows Abelard defending, very convincingly, his choice of a nonstandard text of the Lord's Prayer for use by the nuns of the Paraclete. His approach entails close textual analysis, at once consistent with his procedures in the *Sic et non* and at the same time not worlds apart from the methods of textual evaluation and constitution applied by philologists even today. Abelard manages to be right while simultaneously displaying an utter unawareness of his correspondent's character and of institutional realpolitik. From a psychological vantage point, it is painful to see how the great logician, though now a eunuch, having laid down the law in liturgy for the female protégée who had been his student, lover, and wife (and who took the veil at his command), bristles in a very masculine way at her reported adulation of a man he contemns as his intellectual inferior. However likely or unlikely the conjecture may be that Bernard and Abelard had met and crossed swords or words earlier in their lives, Letter Ten furnishes the first indisputable tes-

---

53. On the former possibility, see Morgan Powell, "Listening to Heloise at the Paraclete: Of Scholarly Diversion and a Woman's 'Conversion,'" in *Listening to Heloise,* 255–86. On the latter, see Alcuin Blamires, "*Caput a femina, membra a viris:* Gender Polemic in Abelard's Letter 'On the Authority and Dignity of the Nun's Profession,'" in *The Tongue of the Fathers: Gender and Ideology in Twelfth-Century Latin,* ed. David Townsend and Andrew Taylor (Philadelphia: University of Pennsylvania Press, 1998), 55–79.

timony of a personal and intellectual engagement between them, and the incompatibilities between their respective characters, religious outlooks, and casts of mind are already searingly apparent.

Two letters, written ten years later, afford perspectives into Abelard's views on the Council of Sens and on the theological disputes that it brought to a head. Letter Fifteen (not so numbered in the *PL* count, since the letter was not yet known), written a decade later than Letter Ten, is a short call to arms that convokes Abelard's partisans to come support him against Bernard at the Council of Sens. In conjunction with the council, Abelard also produced a much longer document, a full-scale *Apologia against Bernard of Clairvaux* (also translated here). Only fragments survive, but they suffice to allow us to limn the contours of both the prosecution and defense in the trial that never took place but that led nonetheless to a very real sentence.

It is tempting to interpret the *Apologia* as having taken shape originally as a script that Abelard drafted in preparation for the public debate with Bernard in which he never had an opportunity to engage. This *Apologia*, the capstone to the section on Abelard and Bernard, is in essence an open letter in which Abelard strove to refute the nineteen charges of heresy against him that were first sustained in the Council of Sens and later upheld by the pope. It must have been written very close to the time of the events in 1141. The other voice in the polemics between Abelard and Bernard can be heard in the letters of Bernard, which have been put into English.[54]

54. *The Letters of St Bernard of Clairvaux*, trans. Bruno Scott James, Cistercian Fathers Series 62 (Kalamazoo, Mich.: Cistercian Publications, 1998). Since the foregoing was originally produced (1953), a heavily annotated new edition and Italian translation of Bernard's correspondence has appeared: *Opere di San Bernardo*, ed. Ferruccio Gastaldelli, trans. Ettore Paratore, 6:1–2 (Milan, Italy: Scriptorium Claravallense, 1986–1987). It would be valuable to have in English a new translation of the letters connected with Abelard that took into account the Italian commentary. In Italian there exists a now outdated collection along these lines, Bernard of Clairvaux, *Le lettere contro Pietro Abelardo*, ed. and trans. Albino Babolin, Collana di "Testi e saggi" 3 (Padua, Italy: Liviana editrice, 1969).

The third part of this collection is even more variegated than either of its predecessors, in that it draws together letters to four entirely different addressees on four entirely different topics. The addressees include the abbot and monks of St. Denis (Letter Eleven), an unidentified regular canon (Letter Twelve), an equally anonymous ignoramus in the field of dialectic (Letter Thirteen), and the bishop and clergy of Paris (Letter Fourteen). It will be noted that, like the *Historia calamitatum*, two of these letters have unspecified addressees who may be no more than straw men for public (and self-serving) airing of Abelard's views.

Two of the letters in this cluster draw back curtains and throw open windows to let us gaze upon major intellectual, social, and religious preoccupations of the twelfth century. Letter Twelve seeks to determine the essential characteristics that define monasticism and that differentiate monks from members of other religious communities governed by rules. In it Abelard gives utterance to a typically twelfth-century craving to reinstate the apostolic life of early Christians among the cenobites of his day—but how emphatically his idealization differs from those of Bernard of Clairvaux and Norbert of Xanten!

Letter Thirteen, by the best-known exponent of dialectic in the century, elaborates the justifications for the pursuit of aptitude in this discipline. Audaciously, he positions logic as being the study of the *logos*, the word of God. The enterprise that concerns the logician therefore pulses at the heart of philosophy, which with a similar etymological explanation he glosses as a "love for the wisdom" (*sophia*) of God the Father.

Each of the remaining two letters sheds light on events or relationships discussed only fleetingly in the *Historia calamitatum*. In Letter Eleven to Abbot Adam and the monks of St. Denis, Abelard brings to bear his considerable gifts as logician in an endeavor that will be instantly recognizable to many in the humanities, but especially to historians. In Letter Ten to Bernard of Clairvaux, Abelard operated as a philologist would do, by collating different texts with a view toward establishing the best text. In Letter Eleven he quotes his texts, much as he did in the *Sic et non*, before proceeding to weigh them for their superiority as historical sources, in determining which of several Dionysiuses lived when and where. A technical name for what he produces would be prosopography, but it is more immediately and simply recognizable as good old history. In Letter Fourteen, Abelard seeks to defend himself against assaults on him by Roscelin, a former teacher who had become perhaps his most vitriolic foe—no small feat, in the light of the many antagonisms Abelard inspired during the many controversies in which he was embroiled. Roscelin is never mentioned in the *Historia calamitatum*, though his presence can be intuited in its early pages, and the episode to which Letter Fourteen pertains goes altogether unremarked there.

Excluded from this volume are the *Confessio fidei ad Heloisam* (Confession of Faith to Heloise, Letter 17 in the *PL* count) and the *Confessio fidei "Universis"* (Confession of Faith with the First Word "To Everyone").[55] Both of these, which like the *Apologia* date from the last two years of Abelard's life, have some loose claim to be construed in our terms as letters, the one personal and the other public, but to do so would be to distend the definition of letter so far as to render it amorphous and nearly all-inclusive. Since the preface to the *Problemata* is a letter from Heloise to Abelard, his "solutions" to her "problems" could be regarded fairly as *membra disiecta* of letters.[56] But in this instance what matters is not theory but practice:

---

55. The "Confession of Faith to Heloise" is most readily to hand in *The Letters of Abelard and Heloise*, trans. Radice, 211–12. Its Latin text is found with full trimmings in Charles S. F. Burnett, "'Confessio fidei ad Heloisam'—Abelard's Last Letter to Heloise? A Discussion and Critical Edition of the Latin and Medieval French Versions," *Mittellateinisches Jahrbuch* 21 (1986): 147–55. The "Confession of Faith with the First Word 'To Everyone'" can be found in Charles S. F. Burnett, "Peter Abelard, *Confessio fidei 'Universis'*: A Critical Edition of Abelard's Reply to Accusations of Heresy," *Mediaeval Studies* 48 (1986): 111–38.

56. The Latin text, which cries out for a new edition with commentary, is available in Victor Cousin, with Charles Jourdain and Eugène Despois, eds., *Petri Abaelardi*

because the main body of the *Problemata* lacks any salutations or valedictions, and because their content is exclusively exegetic, they are not included here.

For obvious reasons, this book cannot incorporate two letters that do not exist. One, which has been designated the *Epistola ad beati Martini Turonensis ecclesiam* (Letter to the Church of St. Martin), is a letter to the chapter of St. Martin in Tours, which is known only through its mention in a reply to it by Roscelin of Compiègne (discussed in the introduction to Letter Fourteen in this volume). The other is an *Exhortatio ad fratres et commonachos* (Exhortation to His Brothers and Fellow Monks) to which Abelard himself adverts in his *Soliloquium*. This "exhortation" need not have been a letter. In fact, it may have been identical or at least similar to Sermon 33.

A little background is in order to situate Abelard's letters within the context of the epistolary genre in his times. Large letter collections became almost a vogue in the late eleventh and twelfth centuries. Some promoted themselves primarily as models of style (such is the case with the letters of Hildebert of Lavardin, 1056–1134), others for their content (those of Ivo of Chartres served well in the study of law). In occasional instances the authors themselves edited their correspondence for posterity (here John of Salisbury, about 1115/20–1180, and Peter of Blois, about 1130/35–1211/12, suggest themselves as examples). A few of the most important collections were compiled, owing to the prominence of their authors, by teams of devoted editors and scribes; the enthusiasm for this type of initiative was especially lively when the authors were saints who

---

opera, 2 vols., vol. 1 (Paris: A. Durand, 1849), 237–94, as well as in *PL* 178: 677–730. For an English translation, see Elizabeth Mary McNamer, *The Education of Heloise: Methods, Content, and Purpose of Learning in the Twelfth-Century* [sic], Mediaeval Studies 8 (Lewiston, N.Y.: Edwin Mellen Press, 1991). For discussion, see Dronke, "Heloise's *Problemata* and Letters." The most recent treatment is Anne Collins Smith, "The *Problemata* of Heloise," in *Women Writing Latin, Vol. 2: Medieval Women Writing Latin*, ed. Laurie J. Churchill, Phyllis R. Brown, and Jane E. Jeffrey (New York: Routledge, 2002), 173–96.

had behind them the full manpower of a monastery or even a monastic order, as held true for Bernard of Clairvaux and Thomas Becket. As is so often true, Abelard occupies an anomalous place in this regard. Although Letters One through Eight are preserved together as a unity in medieval manuscripts, his other letters survive apart from them. Letter Fourteen appears with Letters One through Eight in Paris, Bibliothèque nationale de France, MS lat. 2923 (thirteenth century), but none of the rest is extant in a medieval manuscript with the main set of letters exchanged by Abelard and Heloise. In other words, Letters One through Eight have been transmitted as a corpus, while the others have come down much more haphazardly. Sometimes (Letter Nine is representative) they are attested in clutches of Abelardiana, but not with the letters.

In the case of the personal letters and the letters of direction, it seems worth speculating that Heloise herself kept her letters as well as copies of his, so as to create if not a systematic correspondence, then at least a miniarchive of his writings. As for the rest, Abelard stood at a disadvantage when compared with either Thomas Becket, who was martyred rather than castrated, or Bernard of Clairvaux, who (like Becket) profited posthumously from having behind him, or after him, the editorial and copying resources of mighty monastic scriptoria. It is a tribute to the allure exercised by Abelard's force of personality and quality of mind that despite the scandals of his life and condemnations of his work, well more than a dozen of his letters have escaped extinction. With the publication of this volume, interested readers without fluent Latin and large libraries will have the chance at last to explore the whole spectrum of Abelard's letters: put together, the Penguin volume and this one comprehend the entire dossier.

A next stage among the many that need to be traversed in Abelardian scholarship would be to complete the translation into English, with commentary, of letters that others in the twelfth century wrote to Abelard and about him. In the first category belong the letter that Prior Fulk of Deuil sent Abelard in 1118 after the castration; the virulent missive that Roscelin dispatched during their final skirmish with each other in 1120 or thereabouts; a courteous letter that Walter of Mortagne (died 1174, bishop of Laon 1155–1174), a fellow dialectician and theologian, composed, probably about 1132–1135, to criticize points in a draft of the *Theologia* and to caution Abelard against the views being ascribed to him by his students;[57] and a letter that Hugh Metel (about 1080–1157), an Augustinian Canon of St. Léon in Toul, wrote him during the brouhaha that peaked in the Council of Sens.[58] In the second group falls, most obviously, the dossier about Sens—not only Bernard of Clairvaux's letters about Abelard but also those of others who took an interest in the Council of Sens, both before and after, such as William of St. Thierry, Thomas of Morigny (1080–1145, abbot of Morigny, 1100–1139), Hugh Metel, Archbishop Samson of Rheims (1140–1161), Archbishop Henry Sanglier of Sens (1122–1142), and Pope Innocent II. The *Apologia* against Bernard of Berengar of Poitiers (born about 1120) belongs in this group.[59]

Notes on Translation Style and Conventions

In the hands of some medieval authors, Latin is a language replete with particles, adverbs, and conjunctions that resonate strangely in today's English and that may be omitted or at least reworded without hazard. The translator may scratch out a "nevertheless" here and a "moreover" there, may globally delete "aforesaid" and "aforementioned," and need lose no sleep afterward. Furthermore, many passages of formal Latin prose take the form

---

57. On Walter, see Southern, *Scholastic Humanism*, 2: 104–12.

58. On Hugh, see Constant J. Mews, "Hugh Metel, Heloise, and Peter Abelard: The Letters of an Augustinian Canon and the Challenge of Innovation in Twelfth-Century Lorraine," *Viator* 32 (2001): 59–91.

59. For bibliography, see Constant J. Mews, "Peter Abelard," in *Authors of the Middle Ages: Historical and Religious Writers of the Latin West*, vol. 2/5, ed. Patrick Geary (Aldershot, U.K.: Variorum, 1995), 45–47 (37–39).

of long sentences or periods, in which dependent clauses fork off one another like branches on a particularly prolific family tree. Fortunately, the person translating into a modern language may often act as a dutiful tree surgeon, who lops and prunes these elaborate ramifications, so that what begins as a centuries-old specimen in danger of tumbling down emerges as a still-living growth, but with much dead wood stacked discreetly on the ground and with many new supporting cables.

The prose style in most of these letters is quintessentially Abelardian and consequently remarkable, and it calls out for special treatment. Abelard is extraordinarily careful with his words, and his Latin style has been characterized as having "exceptional clarity and force."[60] For his prose to have such qualities should take no one by surprise, considering that he devoted his life from his youth until his death to a form of logic that was intensely verbal (and equally intensely Latin). To him the arts of language (*artes sermocinales*) or arts of eloquence (*artes eloquentiae*) were one and the same as the logical arts, in that all were caught up in words (*logoi*). In early drafts of these translations I occasionally opted to omit a small word that seemed superfluous, but almost invariably, when later checking the passage yet again against the Latin, I perceived that whatever had been left out in my English was a signal of one sort or another. The seemingly fusty monosyllables and disyllables all serve a purpose. By the same token, I realized in many cases that by breaking apart long sentences to bring their syntax into closer line with the shorter ones predominant in most twenty-first-century English (even academic prose), I obscured logical relationships Abelard sought to accentuate. As a result, I have endeavored to tamper as little as feasible with Abelard's style. Even so, the two languages are so different that some adjustments have been unavoidable.

---

60. Christopher Brooke, *The Twelfth Century Renaissance* (London: Thames & Hudson, 1969), 28.

What sorts of changes have I made? Abelard sometimes employed short and simple demonstrative pronouns to specify antecedents where exactitude in English would require the use of "the former" and "the latter," but I have tried to minimize such cumbersomeness. The same goes for his characteristically medieval insistence upon adjectives that would most faithfully (but also most stiltedly) be put into English as "abovementioned," "aforesaid," or the like. Furthermore, Abelard's precise use of short words compensated for inconsistencies and lackings in twelfth-century punctuation that have been solved in the meantime. These surrogates for paragraphing or semicolons have been dropped without any ado. Finally, I have made a concession to uniformity and simplicity in rendering many of Abelard's editorial we's as the singular first-person pronoun.

In vocabulary I have striven not to use the English word that is the immediate cognate of the Latin word being translated, but without making an aspiration into a hard-and-fast rule. In general I hope that my translations will be both intelligible to those with absolutely no Latin and that they will function as a helpful and trustworthy commentary to those who wish to wrestle with the original language. If Abelard traveled across time to assess my work, I hope that he would not feel outraged and make me bear the full brunt of his often scathing criticism.

A caveat about the Bible references must be issued. The version of the Bible most often read, cited, and quoted by Abelard and his contemporaries was the Vulgate Latin of Jerome. Accordingly, I have geared the references to it rather than to any of the Bibles more commonly used today. This policy means that the inexperienced should proceed cautiously in pursuing references, notably in the Books of Kings (of which there are four, at Samuel's expense) and in the Psalms. For similar reasons, translations follow the so-called Douay-Rheims Bible, which was put together at nearly the same time (1609–1610) as the King James version (1611) but which unlike it rested upon the text of the Vulgate Latin. However, I have sometimes, when not quoting Scripture, employed more familiar forms of proper names in the Bible. And a smaller word about the seemingly erratic handling of Greek (which is not extensive) is relevant. The policy of the best Abelardian manuscripts and editions determines what I have printed. When they have a Greek word in Greek letters (which is most seldom), the translation follows them. By the same token, when they transliterate, a transliteration appears in my English.

All the letters are translated in their entirety, but I have put square brackets with ellipses [...] to mark points at which Abelard himself has left out (either by choice or by fault of the texts he had at his disposal) portions of texts he quotes. Square brackets that contain other information flag when I have inserted brief explanatory information, such as names, dates, or titles of sources. To avoid clutter, I have not used any brackets in the rare instances when I have supplied an inconsequential word (such as a noun omitted where a neuter adjective suffices in Latin) to make the sense of the original easier to follow. Note numbers signal what would have been more intrusive details. Such additional material ranges from precise information on sources or parallels (with direction to the best Latin edition and often to an English translation as well) to basic background required for the text to be understood and appreciated.

A final note: Letters in collections are regularly designated by Arabic numerals. An exception is made for the letters of Heloise and of Abelard, where the numbers are spelled out. This convention creates occasional incongruities, especially in the notes, where numbers spelled out and numerals may sit somewhat uncomfortably in close proximity. At the same time it allows the text to have a smoother appearance.

PART I

HELOISE AND THE NUNS OF THE PARACLETE

LETTER NINE. TO THE NUNS OF THE PARACLETE

Toward the end of the *Historia calamitatum* Peter Abelard complains of having been cornered into a "damned if he does, damned if he doesn't" stance. Specifically, he tells of the criticisms he endured first for not having been more solicitous of Heloise and her nuns and then for having intensified his attentiveness to the spiritual needs of the community.[1] While delivering these ministrations, and at the instigation of Heloise, Abelard generated a large and heterogeneous array of texts for Heloise and the nuns of her convent (or, to give credit where it is richly due, often *with* Heloise).

Letter Nine belongs to this body of writings, which has been styled collectively as the *Corpus Paraclitense* (Paraclete Corpus), in recognition of the convent named by Abelard and presided over by Heloise. The corpus comprises Letter Nine, *The Paraclete Hymnal,* the lament poems *(planctus),* the *Problemata, The Commentary on the Six Days of Creation,* and *The Sermons.* Whether the correspondence between Heloise and Abelard (Letters One through Eight) fits within this corpus is debatable, partly because of their contents, partly because of their transmission (which is less restricted and less bound to the Paraclete than that of the other texts).

The only major item in the corpus that may have been lost would

---

1. Ed. Monfrin, p. 101, lines 1341–50; trans. Radice, p. 36.

be a commentary on the Song of Songs.[2] In addition, it cannot be determined exactly what the psalter was that Abelard mentions in Letter Three to Heloise. Possibly it contained antiphons he chose. In any case, the reference to the psalter, which is not anticipated by any request for one in Letter Two from Heloise, demonstrates at least that already when writing Letter Three, Abelard was immersed in the Paraclete liturgy. The extended passage at the end of Letter Three makes apparent that he and she tailored the liturgy of the Paraclete sometimes to respond to particularities in Abelard's life and psychological state. Sorting out which of these features owe to him or to her individually would be troublesome under the best of circumstances, but it is all the more difficult because extant manuscripts only record practices from later than Abelard's lifetime, after other influences had made themselves felt.[3]

The array of writings is unparalleled: no other twelfth-century author, male or female, composed for a female religious community anything approaching either the number or the variety of these texts.[4] Making the dossier all the more extraordinary is the extent to which it represents a close engagement of two astounding minds, since Heloise was most definitely an active partner in articulating questions, espousing opinions, and making demands. In fact, the Paraclete corpus (and remember that the name is modern) was the result of her initiative, if anyone's. She solicited from Abelard a history of nuns, a rule designed for women, hymns, sequences, sermons, answers to theological and scriptural questions, and a commentary on the opening of Genesis. Letter Five records her request for the history and rule. Abelard's preface to the first book of *The Paraclete Hymnal* preserves large portions of her request for hymns. Although the dedication letter to *The Commentary on the Six Days of Creation* does not quote

2. See Abelard, Sermon 29, in *PL* 178: 555A, as discussed by Paola De Santis, "Abelardo interprete del Cantico dei Cantici per il Paracleto?" in *Pascua Mediaevalia: Studies voor Prof. Dr. J. M. de Smet*, ed. Robrecht Lievens, Erik van Mingroot, and Werner Verbeke (Leuven, Belgium: Universitaire pers Leuven, 1983), 284–94.

3. On Abelard's role in the liturgy of the Paraclete, the researches of Chrysogonus Waddell have been foundational.

4. See McLaughlin, "Peter Abelard and the Dignity of Women," 287–333.

her letter of petition, it at least refers to it. The same holds true for
the prologue to *The Sermons*. Finally, the *Problemata* opens with the letter from Heloise that laid the groundwork for the subsequent queries
from her and responses from Abelard.[5]

When Abelard obliged Heloise by presenting the women with
these writings, the sisters no longer resided at Argenteuil (on the
Seine northwest of Paris, of which it is now a suburb) but instead
occupied the Paraclete (five miles southeast of Nogent-sur-Seine, on
the road from Paris to Troyes, close to the village Quincey and the
river Ardusson). Abelard had founded the Paraclete as an oratory after leaving the monastery of St. Denis and had transferred it to Heloise and some other of the nuns in their hour of need, after their
eviction from Argenteuil by Abbot Suger.

The text is only implicitly a letter, in that it lacks a formal salutation and valediction. Its abruptness has fostered speculation that it is
actually not a complete letter in its own right, but rather the continuation and completion of Letter Eight, which breaks off abruptly.[6]
Arguing against this theory is the emphasis placed in Letter Nine on
the study of biblical languages, which marks it apart from the earlier
letters as well as from the *Problemata*, even though a few of these texts

---

5. What can be determined of Heloise's standpoint on monasticism, liturgy, exegesis, and other topics has begun to be interrogated intensively only in the past two
decades. Notable studies include Joan M. Ferrante, *To the Glory of Her Sex: Women's Roles
in the Composition of Medieval Texts* (Bloomington: Indiana University Press, 1997), 56–
67; Linda Georgianna, "Any Corner of Heaven: Heloise's Critique of Monasticism,"
Mediaeval Studies 49 (1987): 221–53, repr. in revised form as "'In Any Corner of Heav-
en': Heloise's Critique of Monastic Life," in *Listening to Heloise*, 187–216; and Fiona J.
Griffiths, "'Men's Duty to Provide for Women's Needs': Abelard, Heloise, and Their
Negotiation of the *Cura Monialium*," *Journal of Medieval History* 30 (2004): 1–24. Most
recently, Mews covers some of the same terrain in *Abelard and Heloise*, 145–73.

6. For instance, see John Benton, "A Reconsideration of the Authenticity of the
Correspondence of Abelard and Heloise," in *Petrus Abaelardus*, 41–52, at 43; Chrysogo-
nus Waddell, *The Paraclete Statutes Institutiones nostrae: Troyes, Bibliothèque municipale, Ms. 802,
ff. 89r–90v. Introduction, Edition, Commentary*, Cistercian Liturgy Series 20 (Trappist, Ky.:
Gethsemani Abbey, 1987), 55–56; and Mary Martin McLaughlin, "Heloise the Ab-
bess: The Expansion of the Paraclete," in *Listening to Heloise*, 1–17, at 12, n. 4. Compare
David E. Luscombe, "From Paris to Paraclete: The Correspondence of Abelard and
Heloise," *Proceedings of the British Academy* 74 (1988): 247–83, at 265–66.

(Letter Three, Letter Eight, and the *Problemata*) at least glance at the study and interpretation of the Bible.[7] Whatever decision we reach on the relationship between Letters Eight and Nine, no one would dispute that the two are related closely to each other as well as to the *Problemata*. Yet whether Letter Nine antedated or postdated the *Problemata* has not been established definitively.[8]

Another possibility is that Letter Nine is an integral text but not a letter. Indeed, in the sole surviving medieval manuscript, Paris, Bibliothèque nationale de France, MS lat. 14511 (late fourteenth or early fifteenth century), Letter Nine is heralded: "Incipit sermo magistri Petri Abaelardi ad uirgines Paraclitenses de studio litterarum" (Here begins the sermon of Master Peter Abelard to the virgins of the Paraclete on the study of literature). From the last three words of this incipit derived the title that has sometimes been given to it, *De studio litterarum* (On the Study of Literature). But what are we to make of the second word? In content Letter Nine does in fact show a slight overlap with one of *The Sermons* (Sermon 18), which touches incidentally upon the study of languages while pursuing its larger theme of Pentecost and the gift of tongues.[9]

But there is no call to force Letter Nine upon the Procrustean bed of the sermon genre solely on the basis of the Latin word *sermo*. Taken more generally, *sermo* meant "talk," and in medieval thinking about the epistolary genre letters were regarded as one side of a conversation with a person or people who were absent. Favoring the notion that Letter Nine passes muster as a letter are two facts. One is that the writings with which it is most closely related are all letters (Letters One through Eight) or at least strongly letterlike (*Problemata*). The other is that Letter Nine eluded being absorbed into *The Ser-*

7. De Santis, *I sermoni*, 143.

8. Alcuin Blamires, "No Outlet for Incontinence: Heloise and the Question of Consolation," in *Listening to Heloise*, 287–301, at 297, accepts the arguments in favor of placing Letter Nine after the *Problemata* that were advanced by Van Den Eynde, "Chronologie des écrits," 340–43. Constant J. Mews, "On Dating the Works of Peter Abelard," *Archives d'histoire doctrinale et littéraire du moyen âge* 52 (1985): 73–134, at 131–32, repr. in *Abelard and His Legacy*, has Letter Nine preceding the *Problemata*.

9. Edmé Renno Smits, *Letters IX–XIV: An Edition with an Introduction* (Groningen, The Netherlands: Bouma's Boekhuis BV, 1983), 114–15, and De Santis, *I sermoni*, 142–43.

mons, which Abelard put together for the Paraclete. A perspective that helps in delineating the genre of Letter Nine, as of Letters Twelve and Thirteen, is to consider them as "letter-treatises."[10] Until recently, Letter Nine was roundly ignored. Because it had the misfortune not to have been copied within the principal manuscripts that transmit the earlier letters, it failed to be printed in the editions of the correspondence between Abelard and Heloise that have become modern standards or in the English translations that are the only exposure to the writings of the couple that most people in the Anglophone world receive. Worse still, it has sometimes been judged astringently. One famous scholar who scrutinized it concluded that "[i]t is, by far, the least original" and categorized it as "only a florilegium of extracts from [Jerome's] works and a recollection of his deeds."[11] This denigration of the letter misses the point, since its imposition of Jerome and Marcella upon Abelard and Heloise was deliberate and sophisticated, and its evocation of a Hieronymian education for women is as engrossing now as it was idealistic and unrealistic then.

In Letter Nine Abelard encourages the sisters to apply themselves to biblical studies and, to that end, to delve into the three sacred languages (Hebrew, Greek, and Latin) under the guidance of their leader, Heloise. This threesome, enunciated already by Isidore of Seville (about 560–636), qualified as being sacred because all three were attested in the Sacred Scriptures;[12] Latin passed the test mainly on the somewhat tenuous grounds that the phrase "Iesus Nazarenus rex Iudaeorum" (Jesus of Nazareth, King of the Jews), often reduced to the acronym INRI, or some section of it was identified in the Gospels as having been inscribed on the cross.[13] Additionally, Abelard re-

---

10. The term is used by Marenbon, *Philosophy of Peter Abelard,* 72, n. 62.

11. Jean Leclercq, "'Ad ipsam sophiam Christum': Le témoignage monastique d'Abélard," *Revue d'ascétique et de mystique* 46 (1970): 161–81, at 177. The same article also appeared in German, under the title "'Ad ipsam sophiam Christum.' Das monastische Zeugnis Abaelards," in *Sapienter ordinare. Festgabe für Erich Kleineidam,* ed. Fritz Hoffmann, Leo Scheffczyk, and Konrad Feiereis, Erfurter theologische Studien 24 (Leipzig, Germany: Sankt-Benno-Verlag, 1969), 179–98.

12. *Etymologiae* 9.1.3, ed. Wallace M. Lindsay (Oxford, U.K.: Clarendon Press, 1911).

13. See Matthew 27.37, Mark 15.26, Luke 23.38, and especially John 19.19.

veals in this letter his adherence to a belief, common since Christian antiquity, that Paul wrote the Epistle to the Romans in their language, namely, Latin.

More than once, Abelard asserts that Heloise commanded not only Latin but also Greek and even Hebrew. Jerome, for his grasp of the three sacred scriptural languages, was touted as the *vir trilinguis* (man of three languages); evidently, at least to Abelard's way of thinking, Heloise could be certified as a *femina trilinguis* (woman of three languages). Although Abelard and Peter the Venerable glorified Heloise for her erudition, no other source but Letter Nine claims that she knew any Greek, and only the chronicler William Godel(I) and later sources indebted to him also call her knowledgeable about Hebrew.[14] William was a monk of St. Martial in Limoges who wrote about a decade after Heloise's death; the text ends with the year 1173. Perhaps her Hebraism consisted in the familiarity with the meaning of basic vocabulary and names that was much valued in the etymologically minded Latin Middle Ages.[15] Yet Abelard specifies that she had the capacity to compare biblical texts in the three languages.[16] In any event, the caution has been issued that envisaging the Paraclete as "a kind of Erasmian *collegium trilingue*" was more a dream on Abelard's part than a reality.[17] Above all, the letter espouses a return to an apostolic life, to be achieved through deep study of the Gospels. It is for attaining an understanding of the Bible and

---

14. "Litteris tam hebraïcis quàm latinis adprimè eruditam" (exceedingly learned in Hebrew literature as well as in Latin). For an edition of the text (which in this entry for 1137 presents one after the other Bernard of Clairvaux, Peter Abelard, and Heloise), see *Ex Chronico Willelmi Godelli, Monachi S. Martialis Lemovicensis, Recueil des Historiens des Gaules et de la France*, ed. Léopold Delisle (Paris: Victor Palmé, 1869), 13: 671–77, at 675. The passage was reedited in *Petri Abaelardi opera theologica* 3, ed. Constant J. Mews, CCCM 13 (1987): 291, and translated by Mews, *Lost Love Letters*, 38.

15. For a few pages that trace the pervasiveness of "Etymology as a Category of Thought," see Ernst Robert Curtius, *European Literature and the Latin Middle Ages*, trans. Willard R. Trask, Bollingen Series 36 (Princeton, N.J.: Princeton University Press, 1990), 495–500.

16. Peter Dronke, in a review of Walter Berschin, *Griechisch-lateinisches Mittelalter. Von Hieronymus zu Nikolaus von Kues* (Bern, Switzerland, and Munich, Germany: Francke, 1980), *Romance Philology* 38 (1985): 531–36, at 534–35.

17. McLaughlin, "Abelard and the Dignity of Women," 330.

a fulfillment of it in life that he urges upon the nuns immersion in scriptural languages.

In setting forth a curriculum for the women, Abelard takes as a point of departure Jerome's letter to Laeta (Letter 107, written in 403). Laeta had written to Jerome to request advice on how to raise her infant daughter as a virgin consecrated to Christ. The daughter, named Paula, is sometimes designated "the younger Paula" to differentiate her from Laeta's mother-in-law, Paula. (Laeta's husband and Paula's father was Toxotius, son of the older Paula and brother of Eustochium.) In his reply Jerome delivered lengthy counsel on the education and upbringing of a young girl. Abelard's extensive appropriations and invocations of Jerome's letter serve to bring out the parallels between Jerome and himself in offering spiritual guidance to women, composing texts for them, and suffering slanderous criticism as an outcome.[18]

Simultaneously Abelard presses upon Heloise the place of Jerome's female correspondents and advisees, such as Laeta, the two Paulas, Asella, Eustochium, and other Roman women. Then again, Heloise may have embraced the role of Marcella even before Abelard attempted to cast her as any of the women in Jerome's circle, and she may have given the impetus for his identification with Jerome.[19] In the letter that introduces the *Problemata* she cites Jerome on Marcella, reminding Abelard how greatly Jerome admired the woman not merely for studying the Bible but also for posing questions to him. In any case, in writing this epistle to Heloise and her spiritual daughters, Abelard resorts to more than a dozen quotations from various writings by Jerome, particularly letters to women.[20] The grand design behind this intentionally heavy reliance is to ensure that

18. On Abelard's response to Jerome throughout his writings, see Constant J. Mews, "Un lecteur de Jérôme au XIIe siècle: Pierre Abélard," in *Jérôme entre l'Occident et l'Orient: XVIe centenaire du départ de saint Jérôme de Rome et de son installation à Bethléem, Actes du Colloque de Chantilly (septembre 1986)*, ed. Yves-Marie Duval (Paris: Etudes Augustiniennes, 1988), 429–44 (440 on Letter Nine), repr. in Constant J. Mews, *Abelard and His Legacy*, Variorum Collected Studies CS704 (Aldershot, Hampshire, U.K.: Ashgate, 2001).

19. See especially Blamires, "No Outlet for Incontinence," 287–301.

20. In addition to Letter 107, he relies on Letters 39, 65, 108, 127, and 148.

the idealized monasticism Abelard foresees for the nuns (and for himself as their mentor) will have the validation of the earliest and purest models for a Christian community. In sum, Letter Nine raises intriguing questions about monasticism and the education of women as well as about other narrower topics, such as the knowledge of Greek and the reputation of Hebrew in the twelfth century.

The letter is to be dated between 1132 and roughly 1135, probably after the writing of Letters One through Eight and the *Problemata* but before the assembly of the *The Sermons*.[21] It survives in a single manuscript, Paris, Bibliothèque nationale de France, MS lat. 14511 (toward 1400, copied probably in Paris, from St. Victor), fol. 18r–44v, where it caps an initial section of Abelardiana that encompasses the *Apologia* "*Universis,*" Sermon 14, the commentary on the Athanasian Creed, and the *Problemata,* fol. 44v–50v (for the last of which this manuscript is also our unique witness). The standard edition is that of Smits.

The reason for which Letter Nine failed to be preserved with the letters to Heloise may be that it is not addressed to her and in fact that it epitomizes the turns in their relationship he and not she sought to achieve. These very vicissitudes may have rendered the letter less suited to be stored carefully with the earlier ones, especially the personal letters. The letter is directed to the nuns collectively, of whom Heloise is *prima inter pares* on the strength of her erudition, rather than owing to her past history with him; and yet at the same time that shared past history no doubt contributes to Abelard's evaluation of Heloise, as well as to his extolling of learning as desirable for the women of the Paraclete.

LETTER NINE

Among the other things that blessed Jerome, who is very much concerned with the education of virgins of Christ, writes for their edification, he especially recommends to them the study of sacred literature, and he does not so much encourage them to it by words

21. Smits, *Letters IX–XIV,* 115 and 120. For further details, see Van den Eynde, "Chronologie des écrits," 467–80.

as summon them by example.[22] In fact, mindful of the opinion he uttered when informing the monk Rusticus ("Love the knowledge of the Scriptures and you will not love the sins of the flesh"), he judged love of this study to be all the more needful for women as he perceived them to be weaker by nature and feebler in the flesh.[23] In thus encouraging virgins, he adduces an argument from an analogy that is not derived solely from virgins; for this reason, to achieve a comparison with an element of lesser worth, he takes as an example widows and wives, so that through the matrons of the world he might arouse all the more to study those who are betrothed to Christ and so that by citing the virtue of laywomen he might dislodge or even destroy the sloth of nuns.

And since in accord with that dictum of Gregory's "Everyone starts out from the most modest things so as to arrive at greater ones," it helps to state at the outset with what great steadfastness he desired to steep young virgins in sacred literature.[24] For this reason, to leave out the rest, let that statement now come out into open view which commends to Laeta, in regard to the upbringing of her daughter Paula, instruction in literature, for the teaching of morals:[25]

---

22. The contrast here between words and examples is matched at the end by the characterization of Jerome as being "distinguished in writings as well as in deeds."

23. Jerome, Letter 125.11, ed. Isidor Hilberg, *Sancti Eusebii Hieronymi Epistulae*, 3 vols., CSEL 54–56 (1910–1918), at CSEL 56: 130, also quoted in Abelard, Letter Eight, and in the *Problemata*, in *PL* 178: 678C. Rusticus (died 461), who became an ascetic at Jerome's urging, was by 427 bishop of Narbonne.

24. The dictum appears in Gregory the Great, *Homiliae in Hiezechihelem prophetam*, 2.3, ed. Marcus Adriaen, CCSL 142 (1971): 238, lines 54–55; compare *Moralia in Iob*, 26.6, 29.33, 31.34, 32.12, ed. Marcus Adriaen, CCSL 143B (1985), at 1271, line 29; 1489, lines 8–9; 1602, line 40; 1641, line 38; and elsewhere. Later it is also found in Bede, *In Marci euangelium expositio*, 3.9, ed. David Hurst, CCSL 120 (1960): 427–648, at 549, lines 287–88, and *In Lucae euangelium expositio*, 5.17, ed. David Hurst, CCSL 120 (1960): 1–425, at 309, lines 549–50. Abelard uses it repeatedly: see Sermon 8, in *PL* 178: 439C; Sermon 16, in *PL* 178: 498C; Sermon 26, in *PL* 178: 544D; and Sermon 29, in *PL* 178: 555D.

25. On this and two other uses of the noun *disciplina* (here in the phrase "hanc litterarum disciplinam") in Letter Nine, see David E. Luscombe, "'Scientia' and 'dis-

A soul that is to be a temple of God (he said) must be trained in this way: [. . .] Have a set of letters made for her, of boxwood or of ivory, and let them be called by their names. Let her play with them and let play be her learning. And not only should she hold fast to the sequence of the letters [. . .], but also the sequence should be jumbled frequently and final letters should be mixed up with middle ones, middle ones with initial [. . .]. When she has begun to guide with her hand the stylus upon the wax [. . .], either let her tender fingers be controlled by another's hand or let the rudiments be marked on the tablet so that her own tracings, kept within the margins, may be drawn along the same grooves and may not be capable of straying outside.

Let her spell out syllables for a prize and let her be motivated by the little gifts by which that age is won over. In learning let her have other girls as companions, so that she may envy them and be fretful when they receive praise. She must not be scolded if she should be a little slow, but her talent should be encouraged by praises, so that she both rejoices when she has outdone others and grieves when she has been outdone herself.

First and foremost, care must be taken that she not hate her studies and that a bad association with them acquired in childhood not persist beyond unformed years. Let the very nouns from which she grows accustomed little by little to form sentences not be random but diligently selected and arranged, for example, the names of prophets and apostles; and let the whole list of patriarchs out of Matthew and Luke ensue, going down from Adam, so that as she accomplishes one task, she may also be made ready for future recollection of them.[26]

A tutor of proper age, manner of life, and learning is to be chosen. Not even a learned man can be ashamed to do for a relative or for a virgin of noble kind what Aristotle did for Philip's son, so that in the lowly manner of copyists he might impart to her the rudiments of letters.[27]

---

ciplina' in the Correspondence of Peter Abelard and Heloise," in *"Scientia" und "Disciplina": Wissenstheorie und Wissenschaftspraxis im 12. und 13. Jahrhundert*, ed. Rainer Berndt (Berlin: Akademie Verlag, 2002), 79–89, at 80. Of the other two instances, I translate one as "training in the liberal arts" and the other as "knowledge of their language."

26. The lists are provided in Matthew 1.1–17 and Luke 3.23–38.

27. The Philip in question was the king of Macedonia, whose son was Alexander the Great (356–323 B.C.E.). The philosopher Aristotle was indeed his tutor, after Leonides (whose name is also found as Leonidas).

Things should not be scorned as trifles, if without them great things cannot take form. The very sound of the letters and the first teaching of the instructor are produced in one way by an educated mouth and in another by a coarse one. [. . .] And she should not learn in tender youth what she must unlearn afterwards. [. . .] What unformed minds have absorbed is removed with difficulty. [. . .] Greek history relates that King Alexander [. . .] could not lose the failings of his tutor Leonides in both conduct and bearing with which he had been imbued while still a small boy.[28]

Moreover, so that she might commit to memory Scripture as read aloud, the same [Jerome] also wishes a fixed amount of reading to be stipulated for every single day, and when she completes the recollection of this by rote, he directs that pains be taken not only with Latin but also with Greek literature, since both languages were then used widely in Rome, and especially because of Scriptures translated from Greek into Latin, so that she could understand them better from their original and could discriminate more truly between them.[29] For the Latin world was not yet making use of translations from the true Hebrew version.[30] And so he said:

28. Jerome, Letter 107.4, ed. Hilberg, CSEL 55: 293.

29. The Latin for "discriminate" *(diiudicare)* in the last phrase carries a special charge within Abelard's writings, with earlier attestations in both the *Sic et non* and Letter Eleven. In the first he seems to have been inspired in his choice of the word by a passage in Jerome's letter to Laeta. In both the *Sic et non* and Letter Eleven Abelard employs the verb to denote the evaluation of scriptural or patristic authorities through logical comparison of them. Here he expands its application to include collating Bible texts in different languages, Greek and Latin. Later he adds Hebrew to the mix, to complete coverage of the three scriptural languages.

30. Abelard here employs the Latin phrase *Hebraica ueritas,* which Jerome had applied to the authenticity of the Hebrew Bible over the Greek (and Latin), and elsewhere uses the expression twice in quick succession in commenting on the second day of creation in his *Expositio in Hexameron,* ed. Mary F. Romig, in *Petri Abaelardi opera theologica,* 5, ed. Charles S. F. Burnett and Mary Romig, CCCM 15 (2004): I–III, at p. 24, lines 553–54 (section 76: "Hebraica veritas") and line 555 (section 77: "veritas Hebraica"). For further information on what Jerome meant by the phrase, see Dennis Brown, *Vir Trilinguis: A Study in the Biblical Exegesis of Saint Jerome* (Kampen, The Netherlands: Kok Pharos, 1992), 55–86, and Stefan Rebenich, "Jerome: The 'Vir Trilinguis' and the 'Hebraica Veritas,'" *Vigiliae Christianae* 47 (1993): 50–77.

Let her recite to you daily a fixed portion of Scriptures and let her learn a number of Greek verses. Let her become acquainted with Latin also immediately thereafter. If from the beginning Latin has not set in order the youthful mouth, the tongue is corrupted to a foreign accent and the native language is sullied by flaws belonging to another.[31] Instead of jewels and silk, let her love manuscripts of the Bible, in which she should take pleasure not in sinuous paintings of gold and Babylonian parchment but in faithfully corrected and learned punctuation.[32]

Let her learn first the psalter, let her amuse herself with those songs; in the proverbs of Solomon let her be schooled for life; in Ecclesiastes let her grow accustomed to trample down those things which are of this world; in Job let her follow examples of virtue and patience. Let her pass on to the Gospels, never to set them down from her hands. Let her drink in the Acts of the Apostles and the Epistles with all the will of her heart. And when she has filled the storehouse of her mind with these riches, let her commit to memory the Prophets, and Heptateuch, the books of Kings and Chronicles, and the volumes of Ezra and Esther.[33] In the end she may learn without danger the Song of Songs. If she read it in the beginning, she would not understand that beneath the fleshly literal level it was the wedding song of a spiritual marriage, and she would be injured.

Let her beware of all the apocrypha and if ever she should wish to read them (not for the truth of their doctrines but out of respect for their miracles), let her know that they are not the work of those with whose names they are entitled, and in addition that many faulty things are interspersed in them and that it demands great care to seek out gold in mud.[34] Let her keep Cyprian's works ever in her hand;[35] let her run

31. Jerome, Letter 107.9, ed. Hilberg, CSEL 55: 300.

32. The adjective "Babylonian" implies exotic luxury.

33. The Heptateuch comprehends the first seven books of the Bible, namely, Genesis, Exodus, Leviticus, Numbers, Deuteronomy, Joshua, and Judges. The books of Ezra (Esdras) and Esther figure in the Greek Old Testament and hence in the Vulgate, but not in the Hebrew Bible.

34. Jerome here presents his version of a proverb that enjoyed a long life in Latin after him; see *lutum* 6, in August Otto, *Die Sprichwörter und sprichwörtlichen Redensarten der Römer* (Leipzig, Germany: B. G. Teubner, 1890), 202. Compare *Sic et non*, Prologue, line 62, ed. Boyer and McKeon, 91.

35. Bishop (and St.) Cyprian of Carthage (died 258) left writings, primarily short treatises and letters, that won immediate and lasting popularity.

through the letters of Athanasius and the books of Hilary without stumbling.[36] Let her take delight in the treatises and thoughts of these men, in whose books a devotion to faith does not waver. Let her read others in such a way that she exercises judgment rather than becomes a follower.[37]

You will reply, "How will I, a woman of the world, be able to keep watch over all these conditions amid the great density of people in Rome?" Then do not undertake a burden that you cannot bear but instead, after weaning her, [. . .] send her to her grandmother and aunt; put the precious jewel in Mary's bedchamber and set her in the cradle of Jesus when he was a wailing infant. Let her be raised in a monastery, let her be among troupes of virgins; [. . .] let her be unknowing of the world, let her live as an angel, let her be in the flesh without the flesh; let her think that the entire human race is like her and, though I will remain silent about other things, surely let her free you from the challenge of keeping her safe and the danger of guarding her. It is better for you to long for her when she is absent than to be alarmed at everything. [. . .]

Turn over the little girl to Eustochium.[38] [. . .] Let her admire from her first years that woman,[39] whose speech, style of dress, and bearing are an education in virtues. Let her be in the lap of a grandmother [. . .] who from long experience has learned to raise, teach, and watch over virgins.[40] [. . .] After Hannah offered to the tabernacle the son whom she had pledged to God, she never took him back.[41] [. . .] If you send us Pau-

---

36. Bishop (and St.) Athanasius of Alexandria (about 296–373) is now known better for works other than his letters. Bishop (and St.) Hilary of Poitiers (about 315–367) produced a number of writings, including a treatise on the Trinity and biblical commentaries.

37. This sentence and the two preceding ones are also found in *Sic et non*, Prologue, lines 307–10, ed. Boyer and McKeon, 102.

38. St. (Julia) Eustochium (370–about 419), who along with her mother, St. Paula (347–404), tried to emulate the life of the Egyptian hermits, under the guidance of Jerome. It is after St. Paula that the little girl in question in Jerome's letter is named. Laeta, her mother, is Paula's daughter-in-law.

39. Jerome's phrasing ("illam primis miretur ab annis") is indebted to Virgil, *Aeneid*, 8.517 (". . . primis et te miretur ab annis").

40. The grandmother is Eustochium.

41. Of the four women named Hannah (or Anna) in the Bible, Jerome refers to the mother of Samuel (1 Kings 1–2.21), who remained barren until she vowed that if God blessed her with a son, she would consecrate him as a Nazarite (1 Kings 1.9–11). After her prayer was answered, she weaned the male child she had borne and hon-

la, I promise myself as both tutor and foster father, I will carry her on my shoulders; as an old man I will give shape to her stammering words; more glorious by far than the philosopher of the world, I who will teach not a king of the Macedonians who will die by Babylonian poison, but a bride of Christ who will be offered to the kingdom of heaven.[42]

Ponder thoroughly, sisters who are dearest in Christ at the same time as being fellow servants, how much care such a great doctor of the Church expended upon the education of a single little girl, how he marked out so carefully everything that he judged needful for her instruction, beginning with the alphabet itself. He introduces teaching not only about pronouncing syllables and joining letters but about writing them too, and also he thinks ahead about providing classmates, by envy or praise of whom the girl may be greatly motivated. In addition, so that she may do this of her own free will rather than under duress and so that she may embrace study with a greater love, he advises that she be encouraged by enticements and praises, as well as by little gifts. He also stipulates the very names that are to be garnered from the Sacred Scriptures. By first training herself in pronouncing them, she commits these very much to her memory, in keeping with that dictum of a poet, "A jar will keep for a long time the scent with which it was once imbued when new."[43]

He describes duly also what sort of teacher should be chosen for this purpose, and he does not omit that there ought to be a set amount of reading for her to accomplish daily, held fast in her

---

ored her vow by bringing him to Silo (1 Kings 1.24–28). Abelard refers to her in Letter Seven.

42. Jerome, Letter 107.12–13, ed. Hilberg, CSEL 55: 302–5. Abelard uses parts of this same section in the *Sic et non*, Prologue, ed. Blanche Boyer and Richard McKeon (Chicago: University of Chicago Press, 1977), p. 91, lines 60–62, and p. 102, lines 307–10. The philosopher who needs no further clarification is Aristotle. The king of the Macedonians is Alexander the Great, who died on 13 June 323 B.C.E. after being stricken suddenly by a violent fever that led to a twelve-day illness and culminated in his death. It has been suspected for millennia that he was poisoned.

43. Horace, *Epistle* 1.2.69–70, quoted in Jerome, Letter 107.4, ed. Hilberg, CSEL 55: 295 (and in Abelard, *Collationes* 1.7, ed. and trans. Marenbon and Orlandi, 10–11).

very heart. And because at that time familiarity with Greek literature too existed in abundance in Rome, he does not allow her to be destitute of Greek literature, especially (in my opinion) because the translation of the holy books came down to us from the Greeks. For this reason she could also determine what in our version fell short or was off, and perhaps thanks as well to training in the liberal arts which confer a certain advantage upon those who work toward completeness in learning. He even places this knowledge before the Latin language, as if our mastery began with it.

Moreover, when she has passed from the sound of words to their sense, so that she might wish to understand now what she has learned to pronounce, he specifies for her various texts, from the canon of the two testaments as well as from the minor works of scholars by whose erudition she may advance toward being crowned. Among the canonical Scriptures, furthermore, he recommends to her the Gospels in such a way that he counsels that the virgin never let them part from her hands, as if he might enjoin something more of Gospel reading upon deaconesses than deacons; since those men may have that reading read in church, those women ought never take a rest from reading the Gospels.

Accordingly, writing these things to a mother about a daughter so that the mother might not claim as an excuse that a worldly woman could not accomplish all these things at Rome amid the great density of people, he advises her to free herself of this burden and to commit her daughter to a convent of virgins where she could be raised without danger and be instructed more completely in those things he mentioned. Finally, precluding every chance that the mother should be anxious in the end about a teacher of the sort he had described, he volunteers to be teacher at the same time as foster father of the girl sent from Rome to Jerusalem to the grandmother (namely, the holy Paula) and aunt Eustochium.[44]

---

44. Paula and Eustochium are the grandmother and aunt, respectively, of Laeta (the mother) and not Paula (the child).

And he bursts forth into so great a promise (it is a marvel to say it) that this great scholar of the Church, even though feeble with age, says that he does not disdain to bear the virgin on his shoulders, like a porter. Certainly this would hardly come to pass without suspicion among suspicious people nor without scandal among religious ones.[45] Yet the man, full of God and known to everyone for so long a time on account of the blamelessness of his life, pledged boldly all these things, if only he could instruct one virgin in such fashion that he might leave her as schoolmistress to others and that in her a person who had not seen Jerome might still catch with the eye a glimpse of Jerome.

However, to proceed from the youngest virgins to older ones whom he always challenges very much to the study of literature, as much of course in writing for them what they should read as in praising them for their perseverance in reading or learning, let us hear what he says when writing to the virgin Principia about the forty-fourth Psalm:

Principia, my daughter in Christ, I know that I am reproved by very many people as I sometimes write to women and prefer the weaker sex to males, and on that score I should first respond to my detractors and thus arrive at the little debate you requested. If men should pose questions about the Scriptures, I would not speak to women. If Barak had wished to go to battle, Deborah would not have triumphed over her conquered enemies.[46]

---

45. This aside and the beginning of the next paragraph surely relate to Abelard's indignation about the suspicions he incurred for his ministrations to Heloise and the nuns of the Paraclete. See *Historia calamitatum*, ed. Monfrin, 101–5; trans. Radice, 36–40. Those innuendoes received their bluntest voice from Bernard of Clairvaux, who in a letter (Letter 332) against Peter Abelard addressed to Cardinal Guy (Guido of Città di Castello), the future Pope Celestine II (1143–1144), and a former student of Abelard, capped a sentence that lambasted Abelard as a monk, prelate, and abbot by insinuating that his dealings with boys and women were questionable: "disputantem cum pueris, conversantem cum mulierculis" (debating with boys, dallying with little women).

46. Jerome, Letter 65.1, ed. Hilberg, CSEL 54: 616. According to Judges 4.4–22,

And after some other observations he adds:

Aquila and Priscilla educate and inform Apollo, an apostolic man most learned in the law, about the path of the Lord.[47] If it was not debasing for an apostle to be taught by a woman, why is it debasing for me to teach women too after men? I have touched briefly upon these matters and others of this sort, my daughter, so that you should not rue your sex and so that men, in condemnation of whom the life of women is praised in the Sacred Scriptures, should not become puffed up on account of being called men.[48]

After virgins, it is helpful to pay attention to widows, how much they too may avail in the study of sacred literature according to Jerome's witness and praise. Therefore the same sage, writing to the same virgin Principia on the life of Saint Marcella (as Principia requested), said among the distinguishing features of her virtue:

Her ardent love for divine Scriptures was beyond belief, and she always used to sing: "Thy words have I hidden in my heart, that I may not sin against thee" [Psalm 118.11], and that verse about the perfect man: "And on the law of the Lord he shall meditate day and night" [Psalm 1.2] [. . .] and "By thy commandments I have had understanding" [Psalm 118.104].[49] Finally, when the need of the Church brought me also to Rome together with holy pontiffs[50] [. . .] and I would modestly avoid the gaze of noble-

---

Barak was first summoned by Deborah to wage war against Jabin and then accompanied by her into battle. She gave the signal to attack, whereupon Barak's small company routed Jabin's much larger host. Deborah's role in the episode is mentioned in Abelard, Letter Seven.

47. Aquila was a Jew of Pontus; Priscilla, his wife. She was an early convert to Christianity who is mentioned a half dozen times in the New Testament. Their interaction with Apollo, a Jew born in Alexandria, takes place in Ephesus, where Aquila and Priscilla accompanied St. Paul. See Acts 18.24–28.

48. Jerome, Letter 65.1–2, ed. Hilberg, CSEL 54: 618.

49. The passage that ends with the final quotation from the Psalms is lightly excerpted from Jerome, Letter 127.4, ed. Hilberg, CSEL 56: 148. Compare Letter 65 to Principia. St. Marcella (324–410) was one of the Christian women who had been living an ascetic life of study under Jerome's spiritual direction. Later she was martyred by the Goths when they looted Rome.

50. In the text that Abelard abridges here, Jerome tells that he came to Rome

born women, [Marcella] acted so insistently "in season, out of season" [2 Timothy 4.2] (in the words of the Apostle [Paul]) that her persistence overcame my sense of shame, and because at that time I was held to be of some renown in study of the Scriptures, she never met me without asking something about the Scriptures; nor would she be content at once, but instead would produce questions from the opposing point of view—not so as to be contentious, but so as by asking to learn the answers to these questions which she understood could be raised in objection.

What virtues, what intellect [. . .] I found in her, I hesitate to say for fear that I should exceed the bounds of credulity and should prompt greater sadness in you as you recall how great a boon you have lost. I will say only this, that whatever was assembled in me through long study and turned as it were into part of my nature by unceasing meditation, she tasted it, learned it, and made it her own, in such a way that after my departure, if contention arose about some evidence in the Scriptures, people would go to her to adjudicate. And because she was extremely practiced [. . .], when thus questioned she would reply by saying that even her own words were not hers but either mine or those of any other person at all, so that even in that which she taught, she professed herself a student; for she knew that the Apostle [Paul] said, "But I suffer not a woman to teach" [1 Timothy 2.12], so that she would not seem to commit an outrage against the male sex and sometimes against priests when they posed questions about obscurities or ambiguities.[51]

We consoled ourselves for our separation by an exchange of encouragement, and what we could not maintain bodily, we did spiritually. Always our letters crossed, outdid each other in courtesies, anticipated each other in greetings. Separation, which was healed by constant letters, did not cause much loss. In the midst of this serenity and service of God a storm of heresy arose in these provinces, roiled up everything, and was aroused to such frenzy that it spared neither itself nor anything good, and as if it were a small matter to have stirred up one and all here, it

---

with Bishops Paulinus of Antioch (died about 388) and Epiphanius of Salamis (died 403).

51. Jerome, Letter 127.7, ed. Hilberg, CSEL 56: 150–51. The bishop of Rome in question would be Pope Siricius (384–399). Jerome felt that Siricius treated Rufinus too clemently in 398.

brought a ship filled with blasphemies to the port of Rome. [...] At Rome this poisonous and filthy teaching found people to lead astray. [...] Saint Marcella for a long time held back, so that she would not be thought to do something or other out of rivalry. But after she noted that the faith [...] was being dishonored in many people (such that heresy drew to its support priests as well as some monks and especially laymen and was deluding them in their naïveté), she preferred to please God rather than men, and she took a stand publicly against the bishop, who judged others according to his own character.[52]

She was the beginning of the condemnation of the heretics, when she brought forward witnesses who previously had been educated by them and afterward had been reformed of their heretical mistake, when she showed the great number of people who had been misled, when she forced upon them the impious books *On First Principles* which were on display as amended by the hand of that scorpion, and when heretics, called forth by repeated letters to defend themselves, did not dare to come.[53] And the impact of their consciousness about sinning was so great that they preferred to be condemned when absent rather than to be proven guilty when present. The source of so glorious a victory is Marcella.[54]

You see, dearest ones, how much fruit the praiseworthy study of one woman bore who had been set as head over all the faithful in crushing heresies in the city. And you see with how great a lantern of learning one woman dispelled the darknesses of even the very sages of the Church. As for the studious zeal for sacred literature by which she earned this triumph, the same doctor of the Church [Jerome] thus recalled for your encouragement in his first book on the epistle of Paul to the Galatians:

52. Jerome, Letter 127.8–9, ed. Hilberg, CSEL 56: 152.

53. Jerome adverts here to the *Periarchon*, known in Latin as the *De principiis* (composed 220–230), the most important theological work by Origen (about 185–about 254). It was the first synthesis of Christian dogma that substantially incorporated Platonism. Origen's followers subscribed to a group of theories that have come to be designated as Origenism. Central among these theories was a Trinitarian doctrine that is espoused in this work. The scorpion to whom Jerome refers is his former friend Rufinus (about 345–410), who in 398 published under the title *De principiis* a free Latin translation of Origen's Greek text.

54. Jerome, Letter 127.10, ed. Hilberg, CSEL 56: 153.

Indeed I know that her ardor, I know that her faith, which she has like a flame in her heart, surpasses her sex, forgets humankind, and crosses the Red Sea of this world as the tambourine of the divine tomes rings out.[55] Assuredly when I was at Rome, she never saw me so hurriedly that she did not ask some question about the Scriptures. Nor indeed did she think correct whatever I replied in Pythagorean fashion,[56] nor did any authority hold validity in her eyes which had been determined beforehand without analysis; but she investigated everything and evaluated one and all with her wise mind, so that I felt I had not so much a student as a judge.[57]

At that time so great and studious a zeal for literary learning burned among saintly women, just as also among men, that, not at all satisfied with knowledge of their language, they sought from the very sources the rivulets of the Scriptures that they had, and they believed that the paltriness of one language was not adequate for them.[58] On this topic is also that passage of the aforementioned doctor to Paula on the death of her daughter Blaesilla as he writes thus, among other words, in the highest praise of her:[59]

Who could pass over without sobbing her persistence in prayer, the purity of her language, tight grasp of her memory, shrewdness of her insight? If you heard her speaking Greek, you would think that she knew no Latin. If her tongue turned to the language of the Romans, her speech would smack not in the least of the foreign. Now indeed, as to what Greece ad-

55. This metaphor relates to Exodus 15.

56. The reference to Pythagoras pertains to his reputation not as a man of science but rather as an exponent of mystic doctrines.

57. Jerome, *Commentarii in iv epistulas Paulinas* (Commentary on the Four Epistles of Paul, here the Epistle to the Galatians), Prologue, in *PL* 26: 307–618 (331–656), at 307A–8A (331B–32B). This passage is quoted by Abelard in both the *Sic et non* 1.26, ed. Boyer and McKeon, p. 117, lines 131–41, and the *Theologia "Scholarium"* 2.3, ed. Buytaert and Mews, CCCM 13: 432, lines 767–75. It is also quoted by Heloise in her letter to Abelard at the beginning of the *Problemata*.

58. The metaphor of the sources and rivulets that Abelard develops here in characterizing different sources is also found in Letter Ten.

59. St. Blaesilla was daughter of St. Paula and sister of St. Eustochium. Born about 363, she died in Rome of a fever after having subjected herself to a harsh asceticism.

mires too in the famous Origen, she had surmounted the challenges of the Hebrew language in a few I will not say months but days, to such an extent that she vied with her mother in learning and singing the Psalms.[60]

Certainly the same doctor of the Church does not pass over that her own mother Paula and Paula's other daughter Eustochium, a virgin consecrated to God, were no less engaged in the same study of literature and language. Thus certainly he mentions these things in writing the life of this very Paula and saying about her:

Nothing was more easily instructed than her intellect. She was slow to speak, swift to listen,[61] mindful of the injunction "Listen, O Israel, and be silent" [Deuteronomy 27.9]. She retained the Sacred Scriptures by rote. [. . .] In short, she coerced me to read through both the Old and the New Testament with her daughter as I expounded. Refusing this out of modesty, on account of her perseverance and repeated demands I offered to teach what I had learned. [. . .] If at any point I hesitated and admitted frankly that I had no idea, she did not want at all for me to leave it at that but forced me through unremitting questioning to point out which of the many various opinions seemed likelier to me. I will speak of yet another circumstance which may seem unbelievable perhaps to her rivals. She wanted to learn the Hebrew language, which I learned from adolescence on through much sweat and toil and with tireless practice [. . .] which even now I still do not abandon, lest I be abandoned by it. And she reached the point where she could sing the Psalms in Hebrew and could sound out Greek speech without any telltale characteristic of the Latin language. In fact we perceive this even today in her saintly daughter Eustochium.[62]

To be sure, they knew that the wisdom of Latin texts had come from Hebrew and Greek writings and that the idiom of any language whatsoever could not be maintained by a translator in a for-

---

60. Jerome, Letter 39.1, ed. Hilberg, CSEL 54: 294. On Origen, see note 53 above regarding *On First Principles.*

61. Compare James 1.19: "Let every man be swift to hear, but slow to speak, and slow to anger."

62. Jerome, Letter 108.26 *(Epistula ad Eustochium)*, ed. CSEL 55.344–45.

eign tongue. The Hebrews as well as the Greeks, priding themselves on their perfection, were accustomed sometimes to insult our
translations as imperfect, and to prove their point they adduced
the similar circumstance that any kind of liquid when poured out
in turn into many vessels must be diminished from its full volume,
and its same amount cannot be found in various vessels as it had
in the original one. For this reason too it often happens that when
we strive to refute Jews with some citations, they have the habit of
rebuking us readily for not knowing Hebrew, because (as they say)
of the wrongness of our translations.[63]

Taking careful heed of this, the women who have been mentioned were in their great wisdom not at all satisfied with learning
their own language. As a result they were able not only to instruct
their own coreligionists but also to refute others and to slake their
thirst in the clearest water of the source. Unless I am mistaken, Jerome himself stimulated them greatly to this by his example, being
learned in these languages. In fact, by how much toil and outlay he
gained the perfection of this learnedness, he writes in these words
to Pammachius and Oceanus:[64]

When I was a young man, I was impelled by a marvelous love of learning
and I did not teach myself, as is the presumptuousness of certain men.

63. Disputations between Christians and Jews were a pressing issue when Abelard
made this observation. As this passage illustrates, the tradition of Christian Hebraism originated at least in part as an attempt to refute Jews in disputes; see Anna Sapir Abulafia, *Christians and Jews in Dispute: Disputational Literature and the Rise of Anti-Judaism
in the West (c. 1000–1150)*, Variorum Collected Studies Series CS621 (Aldershot, U.K.:
Ashgate, 1998). There has been controversy, most of it centered upon the *Collationes,*
over the scope of Abelard's familiarity with Hebrew and Judaism. For a review of the
question with up-to-the-date bibliography, see the edition of the *Collationes* by John
Marenbon and Giovanni Orlandi, xlvi–l. The studies that sift the most evidence on
Abelard's knowledge of Judaism are Michel Lemoine, "Abélard et les Juifs," *Revue des
études juives* 153 (1994): 253–67, and Peter von Moos, "Die *Collationes* Abaelards und die
Lage der Juden im 12. Jahrhundert," in Moos, *Abaelard und Heloise,* 327–77.

64. St. Pammachius (about 340–410) was a Roman Christian friend to whom Jerome not only addressed letters but also dedicated commentaries. His wife was the
daughter of St. Paula. Oceanus was the husband of Fabiola (see p. 169 n. 63).

Often I heard the lectures of Apollinarius of Laodicea at Antioch;[65] I studied and although he instructed me in the Sacred Scriptures, I never accepted his controversial teachings on sense. My head was already sprinkled with white hairs and it was more fitting for me to be a teacher than a student. Yet I went to Alexandria and attended the lectures of Didymus.[66] I give him thanks in many regards: what I did not know, I learned; what I knew, I did not forget, as he taught all manner of things. People thought that I had made an end to learning. I came again to Jerusalem and Bethlehem. With great toil and expense I had Baraninas as my teacher by night.[67] For he feared the Jews and represented another Nicodemus to me.[68] I make mention frequently of all these men in my works.[69]

Pondering this zeal for the divine Scriptures that so great a teacher and saintly women have had, I have advised and I wish unceasingly for you to bring about that, insofar as you are able and have a mother superior expert in these three sacred languages, you proceed to this completion of study so that whatever doubt may arise about different translations, a final decision can be reached by you.[70]

65. Apollinarius the Younger (about 310–about 390) became bishop of Laodicea about 360. Apollinarianism, to which Jerome soon alludes, was a Christological heresy that denied that a human soul or mind was present in Christ and that Christ redeemed more than the physical elements of human nature.

66. Didymus the Blind (about 313–398) was an Alexandrian theologian whose students included both Jerome and Rufinus.

67. Baraninas of Tiberias, whose name is sometimes written as Bar-anina.

68. Nicodemus was a Jew who is mentioned in John (3.1–15, 7.50, and 19.39) as having been learned in the Law, as having been well disposed to Christ, and as having helped to bury him.

69. Jerome, Letter 84.3, ed. Hilberg, CSEL 55: 122–23. Part of this passage is cited in Abelard, Letter Eight.

70. At first blush Abelard's aspiration to have Heloise usher the nuns to a mastery of the *tres linguae sacrae* looks wildly improbable and indeed it is most unlikely ever to have been even largely fulfilled. At the same time, Abelard was only trying to have the Paraclete compete with what he would have regarded as rival institutions—competing schools—such as St. Victor, where Andrew of St. Victor (died 1175) took to their height exegetic practices that demanded knowledge of Hebrew and that relied on rabbinic guidance. See Rainer Berndt, "La pratique exégétique d'André de Saint-Victor. Tradition victorine et influence rabbinique," in *L'abbaye parisienne de Saint-Victor au Moyen Age*, ed. Jean Longère, 271–90.

The very inscription on the Lord's cross, written in Hebrew, Greek, and Latin,[71] seems not unfittingly to have prefigured that in his Church the teaching of these preeminent languages should abound, diffused everywhere in the world; for the text of each testament is encompassed in the letters of these languages.[72] You have no need, as blessed Jerome chanced to have, of journeying afar or of many payments to learn these languages, since, as has been stated, you have a mother superior adequate to this pursuit.

After virgins and widows too, let faithfully married women offer you stimulus to learn and either chide your negligence or increase your keenness. To you worthy Celantia offers an additional example, who wishes to live also according to a rule in marriage and who seeks earnestly that a law for marriage be prescribed for her by this very Jerome.[73] At which he writes back to her on this topic and recalls thus:

Summoned by your letter to write [. . .], I hesitated for a long time about replying, with shame enjoining silence upon me. [. . .] For you request, and you request anxiously and passionately, that we delineate for you a rule determined on the basis of the Sacred Scriptures by which you may set in order the course of your life, so that after understanding the will of the Lord amid worldly honors and the enticements of wealth you may cherish instead the trappings of your morals and so that you may be able, while established in a marriage, to please not only your spouse but also him who allowed the very marriage. Not to satisfy so saintly a request and so pious a longing, what else would it be than not to love another's gain? Accordingly, I will obey your entreaties and I will strive to stir you, already prepared to fulfill the will of God, with his opinions.[74]

---

71. On the languages of the inscription, see Luke 23.38 and John 19.20.

72. This thought, reiterated slightly later in this same letter, is also articulated in *Sermo* 18, in *PL* 178.511–12.

73. Celantia was a wealthy noblewoman (fifth century) who took a vow of chastity without obtaining her husband's prior consent. The letter to her was probably by Pelagius (350/4–423/9), a theologian from Britain who taught in Rome in the late fourth and early fifth centuries. Later it was attributed mistakenly to Jerome.

74. Pelagius, *Ad Celantiam* (Pseudo-Jerome, Letter 148.1–2), ed. Hilberg, CSEL 56: 329–56, here 329–30.

Perhaps this matron had heard what the Scripture relates in praise of saintly Susanna.[75] When it had first stated that she was "a very beautiful woman, and one that feared God" [Daniel 13.2], it immediately appended the source from which this fear and true comeliness of soul issued, saying: "For her parents, being just, had instructed their daughter according to the law of Moses" [Daniel 13.3]. Amid the bothers of marriage and disturbances of worldly concerns Susanna was mindful of that instruction, and even when condemned to death she merited to damn her judges themselves and the elders. Indeed, Jerome himself, explicating the passage in Daniel where it is said "For her parents being just, had instructed their daughter" [Daniel 13.3] and so forth, took it appropriately as an occasion for encouragement and said: "This is to be employed as evidence to encourage parents to instruct according to God's law and divine utterance not only sons but also their daughters."[76]

And because wealth is accustomed very much to hinder the pursuit of letters as well as of virtues, let that wealthiest queen of Sheba dispel from you all sloth of heedlessness. This is that queen [3 Kings 10.1–13, 2 Chronicles 9.1–12] who with great toil on account of her weaker sex and with exhaustion from the long route, as well as with extreme perils and expenses, came from the ends of the earth to test Solomon's wisdom and to compare with him what she knew with what she did not.[77] Solomon approved of her

75. Abelard takes for granted that his readers know the story of Susanna, as recounted in the Book of Daniel 13. Susanna, the beautiful wife of Joachim, was spied upon while bathing by two elders who were judges. When they demanded her sexual favors, she cried out for help, whereupon they claimed to have seen her with a young man under a tree. She was sentenced to death, but Daniel halted the execution and asked for the elders to be questioned separately about the tree. When they identified different trees, Susanna was vindicated and the elders were stoned. The *Historia calamitatum* recounts how at the Council of Soissons Thierry (perhaps the famous master, Thierry of Chartres) compares the unjust accusations against Abelard to those against Susanna; see ed. Monfrin, p. 88, lines 882–90; trans. Radice, p. 24.

76. Jerome, *Commentarii in Danielem* 4.13.3, ed. François Glorie, CCSL 75A (1964): 945. Abelard quotes this very passage to comment upon the same Bible passage in *Sermo* 29, in *PL* 178.556–57.

77. Compare Jerome, Letter 65.1, ed. Hilberg, CSEL 54: 617.

scholarship and hard work to such an extent that in reward he gave her everything she asked, except those things which he had offered her of his own accord, following royal custom. Many powerful men flocked together to hear his wisdom, and many of the kings and leaders of the land honored his learning with great gifts; and although he received many gifts from them, it is read that he rewarded for the gifts none of them, except the woman who has just been mentioned. By reason of this he demonstrated openly how much he approved of the woman's saintly scholarship and zeal for learning and how much he judged it to be pleasing to the Lord. As presently the Lord himself and true Solomon (but actually more than Solomon) did not omit to point out in condemnation of men who scorned his learning: "The queen of the south shall rise in judgment with this generation, and shall condemn it" [Matthew 12.42] and so forth.[78]

In this generation, dearest ones, be watchful that your heedlessness not condemn you too. That you may be less readily excused in this, it is not needful for you to undertake the exhaustion of a long journey or to make provision for great expenses. In your mother superior you have guidance which can be adequate for you to all purposes, namely, to exemplify virtues as well as to learn scholarship. Grounded not only in Latin but also in Hebrew as well as in Greek texts, she alone in this age seems to have acquired expertise in the three sacred languages. Of all the ones in blessed Jerome, she is extolled as a unique grace and is commended by him especially among the respectable women who have been mentioned.

The two testaments comprehended in these three (and have no doubt) chief languages have come to our attention. The inscription on the Lord's cross, distinguished by these very languages, which is to say, composed in Hebrew, Greek, and Latin, plainly signals that

---

78. The true Solomon is Christ, since although Solomon is reputed to have been wise (3 Kings 3.12), Jesus is said to have possessed all wisdom and knowledge (Colossians 2.2–3). The same biblical verse is quoted in Letter Seven.

especially in these languages the Lord's teaching and Christ's praises and the mystery of the Trinity itself would be pointed out and
strengthened in the threefold breadth of the world, just as the very
wood of the cross, upon which the inscription was set, was threefold.[79] Certainly it was written: "in the mouth of two or three witnesses every word may stand" [Deuteronomy 17.6 and Matthew
18.16].[80] Consequently, both so that the Sacred Scriptures would be
hallowed by the authority of the three languages and so that the
learning in each language would be bolstered by the witness of the
other two, divine providence ordained that the Old together with
the New Testament be comprehended in these three languages.

It is evident also that the New Testament itself, which surpasses
the Old Testament in worthiness as well as in usefulness, was written first in these three languages, just as that inscription set atop
the cross foretold it would be. In fact, some things written in it
for the Hebrews demanded their language; likewise, it was needful
that others be written in their own languages for the Greeks and
still others be written for the Romans, to whom they were directed. To be sure, first the Gospel according to Matthew, inasmuch as
it was for the Hebrews, was thus first written in Hebrew.[81] So too

79. In referring to "the threefold breadth of the world," Abelard could have in
mind the world visualized as a circle with a cross superimposed upon it, as found in
the maps of the period now called "T-O maps" (because the circumference resem-
bles a letter O and the cross laid over them, with its top more or less transecting the
middle, the letter T). Asia occupies the top half of the map, with Europe and Africa
splitting evenly the semicircle below. Jerusalem stands at the intersection of the two
lines of the T in the center of the map. The cross may be interpreted as being threefold, with a lower vertical limb (sometimes seen as symbolizing matter), a horizontal
one (animal), and an upper vertical one (man).

80. In Letter Eleven Abelard refers to this same verse from Matthew.

81. The tradition that Matthew wrote in Hebrew is very old. It is found already
in Eusebius of Caesarea (about 260–about 340), *Historia ecclesiastica* (Ecclesiastic History) 3.39.16, as translated and continued by Rufinus in Latin, Greek text ed. Eduard Schwartz, Latin translation ed. Theodor Mommsen, *Eusebius Werke* 2/1–3, Die
griechischen christlichen Schriftsteller der ersten drei Jahrhunderte 9/1–3 (Leipzig,
Germany: J. C. Hinrichs, 1897–1941), 3 vols. (1903–1908), 1: 293, line 4, quoting Pa-

it is evident that by the same token the Epistle of Paul to the Hebrews, that of James to the twelve tribes which already were scattered abroad [James 1.1], and that of Peter [1 Peter 1.1], as well as
likewise some others perhaps, were written in Hebrew.[82] In fact,
who would doubt that the three Gospels were written in Greek
to the Greeks, as well as all the Epistles, both of Paul and of the
rest, which were directed to them, and also the Apocalypse sent
by him to the seven churches [Apocalypse 1.11]? But we know one
Epistle of Paul written to the Romans, with the result that we Latin speakers may exult to have a little on our side and that we may
ponder how much the learning of others is needed for us.[83]

If we are eager to know this learning fully, it must be sought
out in the source itself rather than in the rivulets of translations,
especially since the divergent translations of this learning produce
for the reader ambiguity rather than certainty. For, as I recalled
above, it is not easy for a translation to preserve the idiom, which
is to say, the characteristics of every single language, and to adapt
a trustworthy interpretation for every single point, so that we can
thus convey in our own language anything whatever just as it has

---

pias (about 60–130), "Matthaeus quidem scripsit Hebraeo sermone" (Matthew in
fact wrote in the Hebrew language), and Irenaeus of Lyon (about 130–about 200),
Adversus haereses (Against Heresies) 3.1.1, ed. and trans. (German) Norbert Brox, Fontes
Christiani 8/1–5 (Freiburg, Germany: Herder, 1993–2001), 3 (1995): 24, lines 1–2: "Ita
Matthaeus in Hebraeis ipsorum lingua scripturam edidit evangelii" (Thus Matthew,
among the Hebrews, produced the written form of the Gospel in their language). In
addition, it is accepted by Origen and Jerome.

82. The identification of the Epistle of James paraphrases information in the first
verse of its first chapter. Since Abelard uses only a singular to refer to the letter of
Peter, he probably means the First Epistle. In any case, he and other medieval Christians who believed these epistles to have been composed originally in Hebrew were
mistaken; the language was Greek.

83. Just as the medieval belief was erroneous that a few of the Epistles and the
Gospel according to Matthew were composed in Hebrew, so too was the assumption
that the Epistle of Paul written to the Romans would have been in Latin and not
Greek. Abelard expresses the same view about the Epistle to the Romans in *Commentaria in epistolam Pauli ad Romanos*, 1.2.15, ed. Buytaert, CCCM 11 (1969): 86.

been said in the foreign tongue. For often we fail even in one language when we want to explain some word by way of another, since we do not have a word in our own language which can express it more plainly.[84]

We know that even blessed Jerome, among us especially learned in these three languages, sometimes is much in discord with himself in his translations and in the commentaries on them. Indeed he often says in his commentaries thus: "It is rendered in the Hebrew text," which nevertheless is not to be found in his translations made, as he himself asserts, on the basis of the Hebrew.[85] What then is to wonder at if different translators are at odds with each other, if even one is discovered sometimes to be in discord with himself? Whoever wishes therefore to be sure about these matters should not be satisfied with the water of a rivulet but should seek out and take a draft of its cleanness from its source.

For this reason too the translation of blessed Jerome, which was the most recent and carefully researched from the Hebrew or Greek itself (as far as he was able) as if from the wellspring, surpassed the old translations among us, and the old have been cast away with "the new coming on," as has been written in the Law [Leviticus 26.10].[86] On this basis Daniel too said: "Many shall pass over, and knowledge shall be manifold" [Daniel 12.4].[87] Jerome did

84. Here Abelard states succinctly the challenges of translation. For information on translation theory in the Middle Ages, see Jeanette Beer, ed., *Translation Theory and Practice in the Middle Ages*, Studies in Medieval Culture 38 (Kalamazoo, Mich.: Medieval Institute Publications, Western Michigan University, 1997), and *The Medieval Translator* 1– (1989–).

85. The phrase "habetur in Hebraeo" occurs dozens of times in Jerome's writings.

86. This sentence alludes to the displacement of the pre-Hieronymian *Vetus Latina* or Old Latin translations of the Bible by Jerome's version, made at the instruction of Pope Damasus I (366–383), which became the Vulgate (the *versio vulgata*, or "common version").

87. It has been pointed out that here and below Abelard urges upon the nuns of the Paraclete *scientia* not to denote the "science of dialectic" (as it is used in Letter Thirteen) but rather "knowledge of language and literature." Accordingly, I trans-

as he was able to do in his age, and almost alone in his command of the foreign language and not having a Christian but rather a Jewish translator, on whose aid he was very much reliant, as he himself attests, he caused displeasure to many, because he did not believe that the translations which had already been made were adequate; and because he persevered in his project, he prevailed with the help of God, as if heeding and fulfilling that verse of Ecclesiasticus: "Unto the place from which the rivers come, they return, to flow again" [actually Ecclesiastes 1.7]. Like the wellspring of translations are those Scriptures from which those very translations derive; and translations swiftly fail, rejected as false, if they stray from their source and are not shown to return to it in harmony.

But so that we may not believe that this one translator is equipped for everything, as if he had acquired a fullness of expertise about everything, let us hear his own testimony on this, especially when he is said to be paramount among us in Hebrew, so that we may not presume to ascribe more to him than he has. On this topic he writes these words to Pammachius and Marcella and against his accuser:[88] "We, who have at least a modest knowledge of the Hebrew language and yet who are not lacking Latin, can pass judgment more about other matters and set forth in our language what we ourselves understand."[89] Blessed is that soul which, meditating "day and night in the Law of the Lord" [Psalm 1.2], is much occupied in drinking each of the Scriptures like the clean-

---

late the word as "knowledge." See Luscombe, "'Scientia' and 'disciplina,'" 84–85 and 87–88.

88. Writing in 402 from Bethlehem, Jerome addressed a three-book treatise to Pammachius and Marcella, who had urged him to respond to attacks that had been made on him by his former friend, Rufinus. The controversy had many facets, of which a major one was the bitter differences between the two men over Rufinus's free translation, De principiis, of Origen's Periarchon.

89. Jerome, Contra Rufinum (Against Rufinus), known also as Apologia aduersus libros Rufini (Apologia against the Books of Rufinus) 2.28, ed. Pierre Lardet, CCSL 79 (1982): 1–72, at 66.

est water at the fountainhead itself, so that he does not, out of ignorance or for want of another possibility, mistake cloudy rivulets
that run in different directions for clear ones and so that he is not
compelled to vomit forth what he had drunk.

Now for a long time this expertise in foreign languages has
been lacking in men and, with the neglect of literature, knowledge
of it has perished. What we have lost in men, let us recover even
in women and, to the condemnation of men and judgment of the
stronger sex, let the queen of the South again seek out among you
the wisdom of the true Solomon [Matthew 12.42]. You can work
all the harder at it, as nuns have a lesser capacity to sweat in manual labor than do monks and can slip more easily into temptation
owing to the quiet of leisure and the weakness of their nature.
For this reason also the sage who has been cited, distinguished
in writings as well as in deeds, rouses you to toil in literary studies for your learning and encouragement, especially for fear that it
should ever be necessary for men to be brought in for the purpose
of learning or that a mind focused in vain upon the body should
stray outside and after abandoning its spouse fornicate with the
world.

2

PREFACES TO THE THREE BOOKS OF *THE PARACLETE HYMNAL*

Why should a few excerpts from a hymnal by Abelard be accommodated in this volume alongside letters of his? The answer is that Abelard presented many of his nonepistolary works with introductions that are either explicitly letters or else dedications that he and his contemporaries could have readily equated with letters. Although the preface to the second book of the hymnal labels that to the first book explicitly as a "preface," those two and the one to the third have epistolary qualities, and like most of Abelard's letters they are directed to Heloise or to the community of nuns that she headed. Indeed, the preface to the first book goes so far as to quote portions of the note Heloise wrote to Abelard when requesting that he supply hymns to the nuns of the Paraclete, her convent. In other words, it is a reply to her letter.

The scenario is a familiar one. In Letter Three Abelard extended an invitation to Heloise that gave her nearly carte blanche to request writings from him on religious and theological topics. He encouraged her: "If . . . you feel that you have need of my instruction and writings in matters pertaining to God, write to me what you want, so that I may answer as God permits me."[1] Subsequently, Abelard's opening sentences in Letters Seven and Eight both make explicit that they have been composed at Heloise's behest (in Letter Five),

1. Trans. Radice, 56.

as do the dedication letter to *The Commentary on the Six Days of Creation* and the prologue/letter to Heloise that precedes *The Sermons*. All these texts are very fairly to be considered letters.[2] The *Problemata* and "Confession of Faith to Heloise" are both built on the same premise, but in the first instance the text as we have it has been constructed in a question-and-response format, while the second borders on being a creed.

Regrettably, in this case Heloise's letter of request has not come down to us, beyond the quoted excerpts in Abelard's preface, but what survives suffices to document that she shared Abelard's commitment to authenticity in liturgical texts. Abelard's Letter Ten might foster the impression that he was the only or primary one of the two who fretted over establishing the texts most legitimate for use in worship, but Heloise's lengthy observations on hymns bear witness to a mind equal to his own in its bracing candor and lucidity in questioning and analyzing the liturgy.

The hymns belong to the many points in Abelard's writings where his intellectual, spiritual, and personal commitment (or possessiveness) toward Heloise and her direction of a convent intersects with his disagreement (or rivalry) with Bernard of Clairvaux and the Cistercian ideology Bernard promulgated. Abelard wrote the hymns to be sung in the performance of the divine office not just in any monastery whatsoever, but rather in the convent headed by Heloise. This was of course the Paraclete, upon which she had bestowed a grecizing name, devised by Abelard, as unusual as the one she had earlier inflicted on their son. And it was also obviously a foundation that took as its starting point the lands and buildings Abelard transferred to it.

Although the Paraclete was a Benedictine convent, it was in its way as unusual in its Benedictinism as was Peter Abelard himself; but the elements that made it peculiar differed greatly. Heloise's convent appears to have been influenced, at least after 1147, by some Cistercian reforms in its liturgy. At the same time, it owed much to the innovative contributions of Abelard, although despite the special

2. As does Marenbon, *Philosophy of Peter Abelard*, 72.

reverence that was shown him and his works in the convent, his rec-ommendations for their rule and liturgy were by no means accepted wholesale.[3] In a sense the Paraclete as a convent and Heloise as its leader were pinioned between Cistercianism and Benedictinism or, from a more human perspective, between Bernard of Clairvaux and Peter Abelard.

When Bernard of Clairvaux discovered that the nuns of the Para-clete had adopted at Abelard's advice a form of the Lord's Prayer used nowhere else in the Church, Abelard pointed out with all the ferocity his logic could command how his version of the paternos-ter was truer to the texts in Holy Scripture than any other one. Let-ter Ten of this collection, in which Abelard unfolds these arguments (in the strictest sense, his only extant letter to Bernard of Clairvaux), also includes prominently in a list of questionable Cistercian litur-gical innovations the Cistercian hymnary, which he faults for be-ing simultaneously too restrictive and too inclusive of idiosyncratic hymns.[4]

The hymnal is extant in its entirety in no single manuscript, but most of the hymns are present in two manuscripts. One (Brussels, Bibliothèque Royale, MS 10147–10158, fol. 81r–96v), which dates from the last third of the thirteenth century, contains the three pref-

---

3. These conclusions have been reached in various studies by Chrysogonus Wad-dell, especially "Peter Abelard as Creator of Liturgical Texts," in *Petrus Abaelardus*, 267–86; "St. Bernard and the Cistercian Office at the Abbey of the Paraclete," in *The Chimaera of His Age: Studies on Bernard of Clairvaux*, ed. E. Rozanne Elder and John R. Sommerfeldt, Studies in Medieval Cistercian History 5, Cistercian Studies Series 63 (Kalamazoo, Mich.: Cistercian Publications, 1980), 76–121; "Cistercian Influence on the Abbey of the Paraclete? Plotting Data from the Paraclete Book of Burials, Cus-tomary, and Necrology," in *Perspectives for an Architecture of Solitude: Essays on Cistercians, Art and Architecture in Honour of Peter Fergusson*, ed. Terry N. Kinder, Medieval Church Studies 11, Studia et Documenta 13 (Turnhout, Belgium: Brepols, 2004), 329–40; and "Heloise and the Abbey of the Paraclete," in *The Making of Christian Communities in Late Antiquity and the Middle Ages*, ed. Mark Williams (London: Anthem Press, 2005), 103–16. For a compact synthesis of Waddell's findings (apart from the most recent), see Da-vid Luscombe, "Pierre Abélard et l'abbaye du Paraclet," in *Pierre Abélard. Colloque inter-national de Nantes*, 215–29.

4. Chrysogonus Waddell, ed., *Hymn Collections from the Paraclete*, 2 vols., Cistercian Liturgy Series 8–9 (Trappist, Ky.: Gethsemani Abbey, 1987–1989), 1: 88–89.

aces and is divided into three *libelli*, meaning "booklets" or "little books." In this manuscript, the text is missing its end, and the hymns are untitled and total ninety-three. The three prefaces divide the hymns into separate sections, the first being "feriales," hymns for days of the week to praise God in the Trinity and in his creation (numbers 1–29); the second "de tempore," principally for feasts of the Lord; and the third hymns for the feasts of saints. This schema corresponds to the divisions of liturgical books. The breviary was the book containing the Psalms, hymns, lessons, prayers, and so forth that were recited in the office. The temporale was either a section of the breviary or a separate book that provided the parts of offices that varied during the liturgical year. The sanctorale was also either a section of the breviary or a freestanding book that supplied the offices particular to the festivals of given saints.

The other major witness to Abelard's hymns is a liturgical manuscript of the fifteenth century from the Paraclete (Chaumont, Bibliothèque Municipale, MS 31, fol. 9–245). It lacks the three prefaces and contains forty hymns not found in the Brussels manuscript. In it the hymns are arranged to follow the progression of the ecclesiastical year. Two other manuscripts contain only the Marian hymns, while a half dozen codices, all Swiss in both provenance and present location, have the particularly well-known Saturday vespers hymn with the incipit "O quanta qualia" (number 29), in some cases with musical notation. For this one alone of Abelard's hymns has notation been preserved that has allowed a melody to be reconstructed and performed.[5]

When the hymns from the two principal manuscripts are united, they amount to a total of one hundred and thirty-three, a vast repository that Abelard sent to the convent in three consignments. The first group of twenty-nine was accompanied by the first preface, a dedicatory letter to Heloise. At first glance the preface to the second book, of forty-seven hymns, unlike that to the first, betrays

---

5. For transcriptions, see Bruno Stäblein, *Hymnen (I): Die mittelalterlichen Hymnenmelodien des Abendlandes*, Monumenta monodica Medii Aevi 1 (Kassel, Germany: Bärenreiter-Verlag, 1956), 324–25, no. 590, and 592, no. 38, as well as Weinrich, "Peter Abaelard as Musician I," 302–4.

no sign of being a response to a letter from Heloise. It is directed to the nuns of the Paraclete collectively. The same holds true for the preface to the third book, of fifty-seven hymns, which is addressed once again to the sisters of the community. The last two prefaces explain briefly the function of the hymns that Abelard has provided at their entreaty, and they request in return their prayers on his behalf. But both the prefaces to the second and third books contain material that responds to the first preface, which is heavily Heloisan, and thus they too are in a way replies to the letter from her that Abelard quotes extensively (and maybe even in toto) in the first preface.

All three of the prefaces would have been composed between 1132 and 1135, the years in which Abelard wrote the *Historia calamitatum;* corresponded with Heloise in Letters Three, Five, Seven, and Eight; answered her *Problemata;* wrote Letter Nine to the nuns of the Paraclete; and wrote Letter Sixteen, the dedication to *The Sermons.* The preface to the first book is considerably more elaborate than either of the other two and may be outlined as follows:[6]

I. Heloise's Justification of the Need for New Hymns

    A. Then-current hymns were used on the basis of custom rather than authority

    B. Then-current hymns had texts that did not accord with their melodies

    C. Then-current hymns omitted various saints

    D. Then-current hymns forced their singers to engage in a deception

        1. Because they were sung at a time of day in conflict with their content

        2. Because they described within their texts their singers as being in a state of sorrow that would render singing impossible

        3. Because they made overstated claims about the saints they glorify

---

6. My schematization modifies only slightly one of Waddell, ed., *Hymn Collections from the Paraclete,* 1: ccxii.

For those who are not familiar with the times of daily prayer as stipulated in the breviary, these are the canonical hours of prayer:

Matins (from *matutinas*, "pertaining to the morning"; known in earlier usage as *vigiliae*, "vigils"): prescribed for the eighth hour of the night in the Rule of Benedict

Lauds (from *laudes*, "praises," the technical name for Psalms 148–50, always sung at the end of this office): joined to Matins and said overnight by anticipation, as the Night Office

Prime (from *prima* [*hora*], "the first hour"): the first of the "Little Hours" in the Rule of Benedict, said at the first hour

Terce (from *tertia*, "third"): the second of the "Little Hours," said at the third hour

Sext (from *sexta*, "sixth"): the third of the "Little Hours," said at the sixth hour

None (from *nonas*, "ninth"): the fourth and final of the "Little Hours," said at the ninth hour

Vespers (from *vesperas*, "evening"): the evening office, recited before dark

Compline (related to *completorium*): the last of the day-hours, said before retiring

Taken together, the prefaces to *The Paraclete Hymnal* are interesting documents for enabling a deeper appreciation of the evolving relationship between Heloise and Abelard, for gaining insight into his views on poetry and music, and for delving into their thinking about the liturgy in general and hymns in particular. The first preface in particular, encompassing as it does quotations from Heloise, makes apparent that both she and Abelard had a critical perspective on the hymns then being used in the liturgical offices.[7] The hymnal, including the prefaces, has been edited by Chrysogonus Waddell (vol. 2, pp. 5–9, 47–49, and 89–90), whose text is followed here. The closest

---

7. For the backdrop, see Chrysogonus Waddell, "St. Bernard and the Cistercian Office," 102–4.

predecessor to his edition was that of Joseph Szövérffy. The hymnal has been translated in its entirety into English, and the prefaces once again by themselves.[8]

PREFACE TO THE FIRST BOOK

Owing to the insistence of your entreaties, my sister Heloise,[9] once dear in the world and now most dear in Christ, I have composed what are called *hymns* in Greek and *tehillim* in Hebrew.[10] Since in fact you as well as the women of holy calling who live with you very often pressed me to write them, I asked your purpose about this matter. Certainly I considered it redundant for me to draft new ones for you, seeing that you had a wealth of old ones; and it seemed almost blasphemous to promote new songs of sinners before old ones of saints or even to treat them as equal. But when I received different responses from different people, you replied, among other things (as I remember), with this reasoning:[11]

8. For the whole hymn book, see Sister Jane Patricia, trans., *The Hymns of Abelard in English Verse* (Lanham, Md.: University Press of America, 1986). For the prefaces alone, see Constant J. Mews, "Liturgy and Identity at the Paraclete: Heloise, Abelard and the Evolution of Cistercian Reform," in *Poetic and Musical Legacy of Heloise and Abelard,* 19–33, at 30–33.

9. Heloise is addressed as sister by Abelard in Letters One and Three, the dedication letter to *The Commentary on the Six Days of Creation,* and the "Confession of Faith to Heloise."

10. The manuscript reads *tillim,* a form that Abelard would have thought represented the Hebrew and that is attested in manuscripts of Jerome, "Praefatio in libro Psalmorum" (Preface to the Book of Psalms), in *Biblia sacra iuxta Vulgatam uersionem,* ed. Robert Weber and Roger Gryson, 4th ed. (Stuttgart, Germany: Deutsche Bibelgesellschaft, 1994), 768–69, at 768, line 15 (*Thallim*). I have expanded to *tehillim* not to emend the Latin, but rather to provide the modern transliteration of the Hebrew word as we know it now.

11. Here as in many other places in Abelard's writings it is impossible to gauge how accurately he represents Heloise's own expression or how much instead he conjures her up so as to ventriloquize through her his own ideas and words.

We know (you said) that the Latin and especially the Gallican Church cling to custom rather than follow authority in Psalms as also in hymns.[12] Indeed we still consider it uncertain who was the author of this translation of the psalter that our Church, that is, the Gallican, uses.[13] If we want to judge by the statements of those who have revealed to us the variety of translations, the outcome will be greatly dissonant from all other interpretations, and it will not garner any esteem of authority, in my opinion. In this, indeed, the habit of a long-lived custom has prevailed now to such an extent that although in other things we adhere to the texts amended by blessed Jerome, in the psalter (which we use most) we follow noncanonical texts.[14]

To be truthful, there is such disorder in the hymns we now employ that none or only very few of the titles inscribed distinguish who is

12. The Latin Church is that part of the Catholic body that obeys the Latin patriarch, the pope. Within the Latin Church, the Church of what is now France followed the Gallican Rite, which prevailed in France in particular from the earliest times. Heloise's larger motive in invoking the Gallican Church is to criticize it for holding fast to custom in singing anonymous hymns rather than those with authority. In the Middle Ages the connection between *auctor* and *auctoritas* was fundamental. Texts, including hymns, derived the qualities of being "authoritative" and (by a mistaken but pandemic etymology) "authentic" by dint of having known authors. See Waddell, "St. Bernard and the Cistercian Office," 102.

13. Heloise refers to the well-known complication that this all-important book was found in three different Latin versions, all the work of Jerome (supposedly in the first case, definitely in the latter two). The one he produced earliest, which has conventionally been identified with the Roman Psalter, was a revision of the Latin version already in existence (the so-called Old Latin or *Vetus Latina*), which was based on the Greek of the Septuagint. Later (about 392) he composed afresh a new version on the basis of the Hexaplaric text of the Septuagint, which became known as the Gallican Psalter because eventually its circulation radiated out of Gaul, especially out of Frankish Gaul owing to the influence of Charlemagne. Finally (about 400), he made a translation from the Hebrew, which is known as the Hebrew Psalter. Only the first two were widely used.

14. Because the Psalms were so heavily used in the liturgy, the psalter (or book of Psalms) contained most of the divine office. In putting her finger upon the point of friction where authority, custom, and canonicity meet, Heloise (whom Abelard purports to be quoting here) manifests an interest in the very criteria for evaluating texts that he invokes in the Prologue to the *Sic et non* and elsewhere. By apocryphal Heloise (or Abelard?) seems to presume a text that is anonymous and therefore not authoritative, in the sense of having an author.

the author of which; and if some seem to have definite authors, among whom Hilary [about 315–368, saint, bishop of Poitiers] and Ambrose [about 340–397, saint, bishop of Milan 374–397] are believed to have appeared first, then Prudentius [348–after 405] and very many others, the inequality in syllable count is often so great that the songs can hardly accommodate the melody;[15] and without melody a hymn (the definition of which is "praise of God with song") can in no way exist.[16] (You added that) also for very many feasts proper hymns are lacking, for example, those of the Innocents and evangelists or of those female saints who did not have the prominence of being virgins or martyrs.[17]

15. Heloise states that the early hymns, by being structured according to the quantitative principles of classical Latin poetry, failed to achieve the regularity of syllable count that was a prerequisite for the reuse of a melody from one verse or strophe to another. The chief reason for the disjunction in this case between prosody in the two forms of poetry is that in quantitative poetry elision (omission of a sound or syllable) or synaloepha (contraction of two syllables into one by omission of a vowel) was allowed or even required, under specific circumstances, while in rhythmic poetry the need for regularity in syllabic count mostly precluded it. For a definitive exposition of the differences between Medieval Latin quantitative and rhythmic poetry, see Dag Norberg, *An Introduction to the Study of Medieval Latin Versification,* trans. Grant C. Roti and Jacqueline Skubly, ed. Jan M. Ziolkowski (Washington, D.C.: The Catholic University of America Press, 2004).

16. This failure provides the motivation for having Abelard, who was a renowned poet, create a fresh repertoire, on new (rhythmic) principles, for the nuns of the Paraclete. The wording that Heloise and these earlier authors employ rings only a slight change upon the phraseology in Augustine, *Enarrationes in Psalmos* 148.17, ed. Eligius Dekkers and J. Fraipont, CCCL 40: 2177, lines 6–7: "Laus ergo Dei in cantico, hymnus dicitur." After Augustine it is found in Isidore of Seville, *Etymologiarum sive originum libri* 6.19.17, ed. Lindsay, and *De ecclesiasticis officiis* 6.2, ed. Charles M. Lawson, CCSL 113 (Turnhout, Belgium: Brepols, 1989).

The specific wording for the definition of "psalm" that Heloise cites was conventional in Psalm commentaries—for example, it is found in Bede or Pseudo-Bede, *De titulis Psalmorum* (also known as *De Psalmorum libro exegesis*), in PL 93: 477–1098, at 868C; Walahfrid Strabo, *Liber Psalmorum,* in PL 113: 483–1098, at 955D; and Haimo of Auxerre, *In omnes Psalmos pia, brevis ac dilucida explanatio,* in PL 116: 193–696, at 193D.

17. With the last category Heloise betrays an interest in female saints who were neither virgins nor martyrs. She could have had in mind married women, widows, or reformed prostitutes who had achieved sanctity. Those who believe that Heloise cherished a special attraction to Mary Magdalen may sense the presence of that saint in the shadows here; see Constant J. Mews, "Heloise, the Paraclete Liturgy and Mary

Finally, (you contended that) there are some hymns, in which it is sometimes necessary that the people by whom they are sung engage in deception, evidently when owing to the need of the date or to the assertion of a falsehood.[18] Of course, by some chance or by relaxation of a rule the faithful, obstructed in this way very often, either anticipate the fixed times of the canonical hours or will be anticipated by them, and they are forced, at least concerning the time itself, to engage in deception, seeing that (obviously) they sing either night hymns by day or daytime hymns by night. Of course it is resolved, in accord with the authority of the prophets and the institution of the Church, that not even the night itself be devoid of the Lord's praise, as has been written: "In the night I have remembered thy name, O Lord" [Psalm 118.55] and likewise, "I rose at midnight to acknowledge thee" [Psalm 118.62], that is, to praise you; nor are the other seven times of praise, about which the same prophet recalls: "Seven times a day I have given praise to thee" [Psalm 118.164], to be performed, if not during the day.[19] The first of these, in fact, which are called "morning prayers" [matins] (about which it has been written in the same prophet: "I will meditate on thee, Lord, in the morning [Latin, *in matutinis*]" [Psalm 62.7], is to be presented at once in the very beginning of the day as dawn or the morning star first sheds light; this is also indicated in very many hymns. For when it says: "Rising by night, let us all keep vigil" and again, "We interrupt the night in singing," or "We rise to give praise and we break the pauses of night," and elsewhere "Dark night has covered the colors of all things on earth," or "For we rise up from bed in the quiet time of night," and again "As

---

Magdalen," in *Poetic and Musical Legacy of Heloise and Abelard,* 100–112. Heloise's assertion about the Feast of the Innocents overlooks at least two widely used hymns, Sedulius's "A solis ortus cardine" and Prudentius's "Saluete flores martyrum"; see *Hymnarius Paraclitensis,* ed. Szövérffy, 1: 31.

18. The final observation refers first to hymns used for the wrong feast and then to those sung for the wrong saint. On this observation and what follows, see Joseph Szövérffy, "'False' Use of 'Unfitting' Hymns: Some Ideas Shared by Peter the Venerable, Peter Abelard and Heloise," *Revue bénédictine* 89 (1979): 187–99; repr. in Joseph Szövérffy, *Psallat Chorus Caelestium, Religious Lyrics of the Middle Ages, Hymnological Studies and Collected Essays,* Medieval Classics: Texts and Studies (Berliner Reihe) 15 (Berlin: Classical Folia Editions, 1983), 537–49.

19. The "seven times of praise" refers to the canonical hours, listed in the introduction above.

all of us break the hours of the night by singing together," and other words of the same kind, these hymns in themselves give evidence that they are of the night.[20]

So too morning hymns or other hymns sometimes avow the disposition of the particular time in which they are to be pronounced, as for example when it is said "Behold, the shadow of night is already now lessened," and again, "Behold, the golden sun rises," or "Dawn now besprinkles the heavens," or "The dawn of day glows red," and elsewhere "The bird, harbinger of day, foretells that day is near," or "The morning star, having risen, shines bright,"[21] and if they are of this sort, the

20. Heloise's thrust here is that hymns intended for night use had come to be sung at other times, with consequent conflicts between the texts and their contexts. The first quotation is the opening ("Nocte surgentes vigilemus omnes") of a night anthem (possibly early ninth century) for matins that was traditionally ascribed to Gregory the Great, in *AH* 51: 26, no. 24 (Schaller/Könsgen, no. 10283). The second, "Noctem canendo rumpimus," is the third line of a hymn (possibly early seventh century) attributed to Ambrose, 10.3 (incipit, "Consors paterni luminis"), in *AH* 51: 28, no. 26 (Schaller/Könsgen, no. 2649). The third is from a hymn (possibly early seventh century), not for a long time ascribed to Ambrose, that has been used for matins of Wednesday (incipit "Rerum creator optime," strophe 2.3–4: "Ad confitendum surgimus / morasque noctis rumpimus"), in *AH* 51: 28, no. 27 (Schaller/Könsgen, no. 14180). The fourth ("Nox atra rerum contegit / terrae colores omnium") is the opening of a hymn (possibly early seventh century) for Thursday matins, in *AH* 51: 29, no. 28 (Schaller/Könsgen, no. 10621). The fifth ("Nam lectulo consurgimus / noctis quieto tempore") is from another hymn (possibly early seventh century) traditionally ascribed to Gregory the Great (incipit "Tu Trinitatis unus," 2.1–2), in *AH* 51: 29, no. 29 (Schaller/Könsgen, no. 16594). The last ("Ut quique horas noctium / nunc concinendo rumpimus") is from an anonymous hymn (possibly early seventh century) for Saturday matins (incipit "Summae Deus clementiae," strophe 4.1–2), in *AH* 51: 30, no. 30 (Schaller/Könsgen, no. 15810).

21. The first quotation is the opening two lines ("Ecce, iam noctis / tenuatur umbra") of a hymn (possibly early eighth century) for lauds on Sunday that has been traditionally connected with Gregory the Great, in *AH* 51: 31, no. 31 (Schaller/Könsgen, no. 4156). The second is the incipit ("Lux, ecce, surgit aurea") of a hymn in the Roman breviary, to be sung at lauds on Thursday, that was formed by excerpting (with slight modification) lines from a hymn by Prudentius (*Cathemerinon* 2.25 and 93–108), in *AH* 50: 24, no. 24 (Schaller/Könsgen, no. 9114); the opening line of the poem by Prudentius, before the changes, is "Nox et tenebrae et nubila" (*Cathemerinon* 2) in Prudentius, *Carmina*, ed. Maurice P. Cunningham, CCSL 126 (1966): 7 (Schaller/Könsgen, no. 10629). The third ("Aurora iam spargit polum") is the incipit of a hymn (possibly ear-

hymns themselves instruct us as to the time when they are to be sung, so that, if we were not to observe their proper times for them, we would be proven false in the very delivery of them. Yet very often it is not so much that negligence takes away the proper observance as that some necessity or special circumstance prevents it; it is necessary that this happen daily, especially in parish churches or in lesser churches, on account of the occupations of the common people themselves, among whom all things are handled, and almost without cease, by day.[22]

Not only do the right times when not observed produce falsehood, but in addition the composers of certain hymns, either offering incongruous words because of their own soul's remorse or desiring with the zeal of an ill-advised devotion to elevate the saints, have gone so far beyond the measure in some hymns that in them we very often bring forth some of the words against our conscience, as they are in fact far removed from the truth.[23] Indeed there are very few who, while weeping and wail-

ly seventh century) for lauds on Saturday, in *AH* 51: 34, no. 33 (Schaller/Könsgen, no. 1496). The fourth ("Aurora lucis rutilat") is the incipit of an anonymous Ambrosian hymn (fifth or sixth century), in *AH* 51: 89 (Schaller/Könsgen, no. 1498) that has been divided into three separate hymns in the Roman breviary. The first sixteen lines constitute the hymn for lauds during one section of the liturgical year. The fifth is the opening pair of lines in the famous hymn for daybreak by Prudentius (*Cathemerinon* 1.1–2: "Ales diei nuntius / lucem propinquam praecinit"), in *AH* 50: 22 (Schaller/Könsgen, no. 532). The final ("Ortus refulget lucifer") is a line from within another anonymous Ambrosian hymn (possibly early seventh century, incipit "Aeterna caeli gloria," strophe 3.1), which is used for Friday lauds, in *AH* 51: 32 (Schaller/Könsgen, no. 410).

It has been pointed out that all fourteen hymns singled out by Heloise for criticism are present in the hymnal used at Montier-la-Celle in Troyes in the early twelfth century and that would have been followed in St. Ayoul in Provins, the priory where Abelard may well have lodged after taking flight from St. Denis. See Mews, "Liturgy and Identity at the Paraclete," 29. Although this overlap might indicate that Abelard had instituted at the Paraclete liturgical practices followed at St. Ayoul, the hymns are all very well known ones that could have figured in the office at any number of monasteries.

22. In this observation Heloise reveals sensitivity to the practical realities of parish churches, where the necessities of manual labor meant that congregations could not honor the canonical hours.

23. Here Heloise inveighs against exaggerations in certain hymn texts, which if taken literally would render the hymns unperformable. See Waddell, "St. Bernard and the Cistercian Office," 103.

ing in the intensity of their meditation or in the regret of their sins, can sing out in fitting style those words: "Groaning, we pour forth prayers; forgive us, that we have sinned," and again: "Accept with kindness, good Lord, our weeping together with our songs," and other words of the sort, which are appropriate for the chosen, and that means, for the few.[24] Let your discernment decide with what presumption we do not fear in each and every year to sing "Martin, equal of the apostles," or we say, glorifying to an excess individual confessors for their miracles, "Frequently at his sacred tomb the limbs of those ailing, in whatever way they have been oppressed, are brought back now to good health" (and so forth).[25]

With these and similar persuasions from your arguments, respect for your holiness has constrained my spirit to write hymns for the whole circuit of the year.[26] And so, as you entreat me in this, brides and handmaids of Christ, we too in return entreat you to lift up with the hands of your prayers the burden you have placed on our shoulders, so that the one who sows and the one who reaps may take joy in working together.[27]

24. The first two lines of verse ("Preces gementes fundimus, / dimitte, quod peccavimus") are drawn once again from the hymn "Rerum creator optime" (strophe 4.3–4), in *AH* 51: 28. The next two lines ("Nostros pius cum canticis / fletus benigne suscipe") are drawn from the famous hymn "Summae Deus clementiae" (strophe 2.1–2), in *AH* 51: 30, the incipit of which is quoted in Dante, *Purgatorio*, 25.123. The thrust of this sentence, that true compunction belongs to the few, is discussed in Letter Four.

25. "Martine, par apostolis" is the incipit of a hymn for the morning lauds, by Odo of Cluny, in *AH* 50: 266–67 (Schaller/Könsgen, no. 9331). The final lines that Heloise quotes come from a hymn (eighth or ninth century) with the incipit "Iste confessor Domini sacratus" (strophe 3.1–2), in *AH* 51: 134–35, no. 118 (Schaller/Könsgen, no. 8410): "Ad sacrum cuius tumulum frequenter / Membra languentum modo sanitati, / Quolibet modo fuerint gravati, / Restituuntur."

26. Literally, "the holiness of your reverence." The more natural translation, with its reversal of the nouns, was suggested by Waddell, *Hymn Collections*, 1: ccxiii.

27. The final nine words in the Latin reword slightly the second half of John 4: 36: "And he that reapeth receiveth wages and gathereth fruit unto life everlasting: that both he that soweth and he that reapeth may rejoice together." Although Abelard has been castrated and no longer has semen (which means "seed" in Latin), on a spiritual plane he remains capable of sowing seeds in his relationship with Heloise and the other brides of Christ.

PREFACE TO THE SECOND BOOK

In the Epistle to the Ephesians the teacher of the nations [Paul the Apostle: 1 Timothy 2.7] organized the office of divine worship in three parts, saying: "And be not drunk with wine, wherein is luxury; but be ye filled with the Holy Spirit, speaking to yourselves in Psalms, and hymns, and spiritual canticles, singing and making melody in your hearts to the Lord" [5.18–19]. And likewise he says to the Colossians [Epistle to the Colossians 3.16]: "Let the word of Christ dwell in you abundantly, in all wisdom: teaching and admonishing one another in Psalms, hymns, and spiritual canticles, singing in grace in your hearts to God." Certainly the Psalms and canticles, seeing that they were made ready in ancient times on the basis of the canonical Scriptures, do not require attention from us or from anyone to be composed now.

But in fact, although nothing separate about hymns is contained in the above-mentioned scriptural passages (despite the fact that some Psalms have the name of "hymns" or "canticles" written down in their titles), hymns were written subsequently at different points by many people, especially in accord with the variety of appointed times and hours or of feast days, for each of which fitting hymns have been established, and these we now fittingly call *hymns*, although in ancient times some called without distinction hymns as well as Psalms any compositions with rhythm and meter in song of divine praise. For this reason Eusebius of Caesarea in Chapter 17 of the second book of his *Ecclesiastic History*, calling to mind the praises of the most learned Jew, Philo, for the Church of Alexandria under Mark, added, among other things:[28]

---

28. The quotation is from Eusebius, *Historia ecclesiastica* 2.17.13, trans. Rufinus, in *Eusebius Werke* 2/1, ed. Theodor Mommsen, p. 149, lines 1–5. There has been uncertainty over whether to favor the reading *subtilium* (of discriminating men) or *subtilius* (more discriminatingly); see Letter Seven and Hubert Silvestre, "A propos d'une édition récente de l'*Hymnarius Paraclitensis* d'Abélard," *Scriptorium* 23 (1978): 91–100, at 97.

Eusebius (about 263–339) was bishop of Caesarea in Palestine and is now some-

After a few other things he wrote also as follows about the fact that they compose new Psalms: "Thus they not only understand the hymns of discriminating men of old, but they themselves compose new hymns to God, singing them in all meters and tones in a quite beautiful and delightful structure."

Perhaps it is hardly inappropriate that all Psalms composed in the Hebrew style in meter or rhythm and constructed with the sweetness of melody are also called *hymns*, according (it is evident) to the very definition of hymns that we set forth in the first preface.[29] But since Psalms already when translated from Hebrew into another language have been released from the law of rhythm or meter, the Apostle [Paul] in writing to the Ephesians [5.18–19], who are Greek, did well to distinguish hymns from Psalms and also from canticles.

Consequently, seeing that you, most beloved daughters of Christ, have often beseeched our paltry talent with many entreaties about these matters, and have supplied in addition the reasons for which it seems necessary to you, we have now obeyed your entreaties in part insofar as the Lord has granted.[30] In fact, we include in the

---

times styled the father of Church history. Philo of Alexandria (about 25 B.C.E.–after 41 C.E.), also known as Philo the Jew, wrote prolifically in Greek on exegesis, history, and philosophy. Eusebius's reference is to Philo, "On the Contemplative Life," 29, ed. and trans. F. H. Colson, in *Philo*, ed. and trans. F. H. Colson and G. H. Whitaker, 12 vols. (Cambridge, Mass.: Harvard University Press, 1929–1962), 9 (1941): 103–69, at 128–31.

29. Compare in the Preface to the First Book Heloise's definition of hymn as "praise of God with song." The 'we' here may then refer collectively to Heloise and Abelard. The assertion of the definition that hymns may be metrical or rhythmic dates to Jerome, "Prologus in libro Iob" (Prologue to the Book of Job), in *Biblia sacra*, ed. Weber and Gryson, 731–32, at lines 24–36. Jerome was followed in turn by Cassiodorus, *Expositio psalmorum*, "Praefatio" 15, ed. Marc Adriaen, CCSL 97–98 (1958), vol. 97, p. 18, lines 28–30, and Psalm 66.1, vol. 97, p. 581, lines 5–7.

30. In this sentence Abelard resorts to a humility topos, a strategy common in medieval rhetoric whereby an author claims to be less competent than he really is. He makes use of it again in the Preface to the Third Book. For the broad currency of the expression "humility topos," thanks are due to Curtius, *European Literature and the Latin Middle Ages*, 83–85 and 407–13.

preceding book the daily hymns for ferias, which can be adequate for the whole week.[31] You should know that these were composed in such a way that their song is of two types, as is also their rhythm; and there should be one melody common to all the nighttime ones and another for the daytime ones, and so too one rhythm.[32] We also did not omit a hymn of thanks to be offered after meals, according to that which is written in the Gospel: "And a hymn being said, they went out" [Matthew 26.30].[33]

In fact, on the basis of this consideration we arranged the remaining hymns above, so that those which are nighttime should contain the works of their ferias, but the daytime ones should render the allegorical or moral explanation of their works.[34] And it has been done in this way so that the obscurity of the literal may be kept for the night, whereas the light of explanation may be kept for the day.

For me to send along the little gift you have wished, it remains only that I be aided by your prayers.[35]

31. The word *feria* refers to days other than Saturdays and Sundays on which no feast falls. In a sense, the works of the ferias are the works of creation.

32. This statement proves that by possessing the melody for "O quanta qualia" (if we assume that Abelard composed the music as well as the words), we have the melody that was used throughout the hour cycle for the entire day. Since no other melody for the hymns is extant, this circumstance lends a very special importance to this survival. See Waddell, *Hymn Collections*, 1: ccxxii.

To turn from music to prosody, the hymns for the weekly hours conform to only two types of strophes. The pattern for nighttime hymns is four verses, rhymed *aabb*, with two octosyllables followed by two hendecasyllables. The hendecasyllables have a caesura after the fourth syllable. The pattern for daytime hymns is also four verses, rhymed *aabb*, but all four are dodecasyllabic with a caesura after the sixth syllable.

33. Meant here is Hymn 14, "Deus qui corpora."

34. This sentence makes apparent that Abelard planned the nighttime hymns to deal with the historical level of interpretation, which is to say, what happened literally, while the daytime hymns interpret those events ecclesiologically at the allegorical level and in regard to the life experiences of the individual Christian at the moral or tropological level. For further particulars on these three levels, see Dedication Letter to *The Commentary on the Six Days of Creation.*

35. "The little gift" is the final installment of hymns, as Abelard confirms in the first paragraph of the Preface to the Third Book.

PREFACE TO THE THIRD BOOK

In the two books above we put in order daily hymns for ferias as well as hymns befitting the solemn feasts of God. Now, in
truth, for the glory of the heavenly king and for the general encouragement of the faithful it remains to extol too, insofar as we
are able, the very court of the palace on high with the commenda-
tions of hymns that are its due. In this work, in fact, may the very
ones especially aid me with their merits to whose glorious memory
I wish to offer little gifts of any praise whatsoever, in accord with
what has been written: "The memory of the just is with praise"
[Proverbs 10.7] and likewise "Let us now praise men of renown"
[Ecclesiasticus 44.1] and so forth.

Sisters most dear and dedicated to Christ, I beseech you also, at
whose entreaties especially I undertook this work: add the devotion of your prayers, remembering the most blessed lawgiver who
was capable of more by praying than were the people by fighting.[36]
And in order that I may find your charity generous in the supply of prayers, consider attentively how extraordinary your praying
may cause our capability to be. For while we endeavored to hon-
or the praises of God's grace in accord with the measure of our
small talent,[37] we compensated for what is lacking in the rhetorical embellishment with the numerousness of the hymns,[38] namely, in composing fitting hymns for the individual night offices of
the individual feast days, since until now only one hymn preceded
the night offices on feast days as well as on ferias. Consequently
we decided upon four hymns for each feast day, so that the fitting

36. The lawgiver is of course Moses, with particular reference to his praying
against the Amelikites in Exodus 17.8–16.

37. In the Latin text translated here as "in accord with the measure of our small
talent" the Brussels manuscript has a lacuna, which has been filled by a variety of
conjectures, of which *modo* (with the measure)—for which credit is due to Dreves
and which has been followed by Pagani—has the appeal of elegant simplicity.

38. Here Abelard develops a more extensive humility topos than that seen above
in the Preface to the Second Book.

hymn might be sung in each one of the three night offices, and so that in addition a hymn would not be absent from the morning lauds.[39] Of these four again we arranged that two should be joined together in place of one hymn at matins[40] and in the same way that the remaining two should be read out at vespers on the feast day itself; or that they should be divided in groups of two at every single vespers, so that one may be sung with the two preceding Psalms and another with the two following ones.[41] However, I recall, five hymns have been written about the cross, of which the first should be put before every one of the hours, inviting the deacon to lift the cross from the altar and to bring it into the middle of the choir and there to place it, as it were, to be worshiped and greeted, so that in its presence the service may be conducted in its whole solemnity throughout all the canonical hours.[42]

39. This provision for three hymns, together with the single lauds hymn, produces a quartet that Abelard explains can be broken into two sets of two, with one for first and the other for second vespers; for a chart, see Waddell, *Hymn Collections*, 1: ccxxv. The entire arrangement represents a major departure from the traditional office; see Waddell, "St. Bernard and the Cistercian Office," 103.

40. The Latin reads "in vigilia." Matins, which derived from the vigils of the early Church, continued to be called *vigiliae* in the early Middle Ages.

41. Abelard offers two schemata for the use of four hymns; see Waddell, *Hymn Collections from the Paraclete*, 1: ccxxv. In the first scheme, vespers 1 would feature hymns A and B, along with four psalms. Nocturns would have hymn A, with six psalms; hymn B, with six psalms; and hymn C, with three canticles. Lauds would have hymn D, with psalmody. Vespers 2 would have hymns CD, with four psalms. In the second scheme, vespers 1 would have hymn A, with two psalms, and hymn B, with two psalms. Nocturns would have hymn A, with six psalms; hymn B, with six psalms; and hymn C, with three canticles. Lauds would have hymn D, with psalmody. Vespers 2 would have hymn C, with two psalms, and hymn D, with two psalms.

42. On hymns of the cross as a category unto themselves, see Joseph Szövérffy, *Hymns of the Holy Cross: An Annotated Edition with Introduction*, Medieval Classics 7 (Brookline, Mass.: Classical Folia Editions, 1976). In the existing editions of Abelard's *Hymnarius Paraclitensis*, the hymns for the cross are three in number, but the most recent two editions divide the first into three parts, which if counted separately as individual hymns could produce the total of five.

3

DEDICATION LETTER TO *THE COMMENTARY ON THE SIX DAYS OF CREATION*

The *Expositio in Hexameron* (The Commentary on the Six Days of Creation) delivers an explanation of the opening of Genesis that Abelard wrote at Heloise's request. It appears to have been composed before at least one of *The Sermons* (Sermon 29), and it has been dated to the early to mid-1130s, tentatively about 1133, although perhaps with an addition made as late as 1137.[1] In its content and wording it displays a close connection with the hymns in the first book of *The Paraclete Hymnal*.[2] In the commentary Abelard examines the structure of the six days of creation (whence the term *hexaemeron*, simply the Greek for "six days"), the allegories contained in the Genesis account, and the ethical meaning of the creation allegories. The commentary is not complete: even in manuscripts with the fullest extant form of the text, it covers only Genesis 1.1–2.25, breaking off just before the fall of Adam and Eve.

In the very first sentence of the Dedication Letter Abelard identifies three sections of the Bible as posing especial difficulties for prospective interpreters, namely, the opening of Genesis, the Song of

1. See Mews, "On Dating the Works of Peter Abelard," 118–20 and 132, and *Expositio in Hexameron*, ed. Mary F. Romig, in *Petri Abaelardi opera theologica*, vol. 5, ed. Charles Burnett and Mary Romig, CCCM 15 (2004): lxxiv ("early to mid 1130s"). Compare the dating of 1136–1140 previously proposed by Eligius M. Buytaert, "Abelard's *Expositio in Hexaemeron*," *Antonianum* 43 (1968): 163–94, at 182–88.

2. For information, see De Santis, *I sermoni*, 141.

Songs, and the prophecies of Ezekiel. Not one to shy from the difficult, Abelard wrestled as an exegete with each of these three sections
in the Sacred Scriptures, although only *The Commentary on the Six Days
of Creation* is known to survive as an effort (albeit merely partial) at a
full-blown exposition.

As Abelard recounted in the *Historia calamitatum,* he had grappled
already long before with the prophecies of Ezekiel.[3] Upon being
challenged by students of Anselm of Laon not just to carp at the
insufficiencies of their master but instead to show how to do him
better, Abelard had expounded upon the prophet almost by chance
in comments (which he would not necessarily ever have written out
in toto) as his first attempt at exegesis; he claims to have formulated
his lecture from one day to the next. By including Ezekiel here in the
short list of troubling passages in the Bible, Abelard could allude to
a copy of a commentary he had later set down in writing and already
donated to the Paraclete. Alternatively, he could be setting the stage
for a subsequent request by Heloise that he devise one, which would
enable him then to revise for presentation to the nuns whatever ideas
or even whatever old draft (if any) he had retained.

And what of the Song of Songs?[4] Owing to his past affair with
Heloise and also his prospective audience of nuns, it could be imagined that Abelard would have had good reason to avoid the sultry
eroticism of the Song of Songs. Yet such a supposition would be ill-
founded. As can be proven by a glance at the daring and yet subtle
parallels he drew in the *Planctus* (for instance, the *Lament of Dinah*) between biblical episodes and events in his life, Abelard did not hesitate to delve even into matters such as premarital sex and castration.
A greater obstacle than any hypothesized timidity on Abelard's part

---

3. *Historia calamitatum,* ed. Monfrin, pp. 68–70, lines 186–240; trans. Radice, pp.
7–8.

4. The reception of the Song in the Middle Ages, with extensive attention to Lat-
in materials, has been the topic of three books: Ann W. Astell, *The Song of Songs in the
Middle Ages* (Ithaca, N.Y.: Cornell University Press, 1990); E. Ann Matter, *The Voice of
My Beloved: The Song of Songs in Western Medieval Christianity* (Philadelphia: University of
Pennsylvania Press, 1990); and Denys Turner, *Eros and Allegory: Medieval Exegesis of the
Song of Songs,* Cistercian Studies Series 156 (Kalamazoo, Mich.: Cistercian Publications,
1995). Only the second gives much coverage to Peter Abelard.

owing to his sexual past with Heloise could appear to be that the
Song of Songs was conventionally reserved for the most advanced
learners, as Jerome stated in a passage quoted in Letter Nine. However, this impediment vanishes when one realizes that Abelard's writings for the Paraclete show him trying to pervade the existence of
the nuns, insinuating his ideas and words not merely into the cycli-
cal patterns of the liturgy as it repeated itself over the hours of the
days, days of the week, and seasons, but even into the passage of the
nuns through the stages of life, as they grew spiritually from girl-
hood or young womanhood to (as he hoped) ever greater spirituality
and wisdom. It would have been natural for him eventually to proffer
his thoughts on the Song to the most advanced sisters, who need not
have been the eldest. Finally, Abelard could have also realized that
Bernard of Clairvaux was composing sermons on the Song, which
were to form the cornerstone of a substantial Cistercian literature
devoted to this book of the Bible, and an awareness of this other
project could have been an incentive rather than a disincentive to trying his own hand at interpretation of the Song. In fact, Abelard cites
the Song of Songs repeatedly in *The Sermons,* even in ones addressed
to women.[5] In the former of these two sermons, the citation is preceded by a passing remark that may refer to a lost commentary on
the Song of Songs.[6] But all of these speculations do nothing to rem-
edy one fact: we do not have Abelard's commentary on the Song of
Songs, if in fact he ever wrote one.

5. Examples would be Sermons 29, "De sancta Susanna, ad hortationem virgin-
um" (On Holy Susanna, to the Encouragement of Virgins), and 31, "In natali sancti
Stephani, vel caeterorum diaconorum, qui ab apostolis derivati sunt obsequio sancta-
rum viduarum" (On the Birthday of Saint Stephen, or of Other Deacons), in *PL* 178:
555A–64A and 569C–73B. Sermon 31 contains an internal address to *fratres* (brethren)
which may indicate that it was earlier addressed to the monks of St. Gildas.

6. The sentence of Sermon 29 in question reads, in *PL* 178: 555A: "Audistis, cha-
rissimae, atque utinam exaudissetis beatam illam sponsae sollicitudinem in Cantico canticorum, ad exhortationem vestram diligenter descriptam" (Dearest ones, you
have heard [and if only you have hearkened to it!] that blessed attentiveness of the
bride in the Song of Songs, carefully described for your encouragement). On this
passage, as well as on other evidence for Abelard's interest in the Song, see De Santis,
"Abelardo interprete del Cantico dei Cantici," 284–94.

Whatever the status of Abelard's thinking and writing about Ezekiel and the Song of Songs, the suggestion from Heloise that Abelard explicate the six days of creation was well calculated to pique his appetite for difficulty. It would be an understatement to observe that literature on the hexaemeron preexisted Abelard. To look at only a few of the many examples, the first preserved example of hexaemeral literature was Philo of Alexandria's *On the Creation of the Cosmos According to Moses.*[7] Among the fourth-century attempts to grapple with it were Basil the Great's (about 329–379) *Homilies on the Hexaemeron*, translated by Eustathius (about 400) from Greek into Latin, and Ambrose of Milan's (about 333–397) *Hexaemeron*, with both of which Abelard was familiar.[8] The exegetic works of Bede (673–735), the authority whom Abelard discusses with care in Letter Eleven, comprehend a substantial *Hexaemeron;* Abelard knew this text as well.[9]

Probably unknown to both Heloise and Abelard and written after his commentary was that of Thierry of Chartres (about 1100–about 1155), dated to 1130–1140.[10] Though Abelard may not have been acquainted with the commentary in written form, he knew Thierry and is said in an anecdote from the twelfth century to have had Thierry as a teacher.[11] The commentary ascribed to Clarembald of Arras, who flourished between 1150 and 1170, is argued to have been written in the late 1160s and thus falls too late to have been a possible influence.[12]

7. Trans. David T. Runia, Philo of Alexandria Commentary Series 1 (Leiden, The Netherlands: Brill, 2001).

8. See Basil the Great, *Homélies sur l'Hexaéméron,* ed. and trans. Stanislas Giet, 2d ed., Sources chrétiennes 26 bis (Paris: Éditions du Cerf, 1968), and Ambrose, *Hexameron, De paradiso, De Cain, De Noe, De Abraham, De Isaac, De bono mortis,* ed. Carolus [Karl] Schenkl, CSEL 32/1 (1896): 3–261.

9. See Bede, *Libri quatuor in principium Genesis usque ad nativitatem Isaac et eiectionem Ismahelis adnotationum,* ed. C. W. Jones, Opera exegetica 1, CCSL 118A (1967).

10. See Thierry of Chartres, *De sex dierum operibus,* in *Commentaries on Boethius by Thierry of Chartres,* ed. Nikolaus M. Häring, Pontifical Institute of Mediaeval Studies and Texts 20 (Toronto: Pontifical Institute of Mediaeval Studies, 1971), 555–75; on the dating, see 46–47.

11. Mews, "In Search of a Name and Its Significance," 172.

12. *Tractatulus super librum Genesis* (Little Tractate on the Book Genesis), in *Life and Works of Clarembald of Arras, a Twelfth-Century Master of the School of Chartres,* ed. Nikolaus

But more than any of these other commentaries, the efforts that made the greatest impression on Heloise were those of Augustine, another thinker whom Abelard held in high esteem. Augustine left three different explications of the hexaemeron (to say nothing of books eleven through thirteen of the *Confessions!*), each of them ostensibly to explain the six days in a literal sense, but all of them containing much that employs allegorical interpretation to arrive at a spiritual meaning.[13] No wonder that, according to what Abelard reports, Heloise professed to have trouble following the interpretations ventured by the bishop of Hippo.

In the letter-preface Abelard presupposes a threefold exposition of Scripture, with literal-historical, moral, and allegorical interpretations.[14] He proposes to concentrate upon the first mentioned, the *expositio historica* (literal-historical explication), but he scarcely overlooks the *moralitas* (moral interpretation) and *allegoria* (allegorical interpretation).[15] Whether deliberately or not, Abelard in his commentary sidesteps the pitfall of seeking global answers to global questions. Instead, he focuses on one question at a time, isolating the difficulties, presenting alternative clarifications, rejecting some, and corrob-

---

M. Häring, Pontifical Institute of Mediaeval Studies Studies and Texts 10 (Toronto: Pontifical Institute of Mediaeval Studies, 1965), 226–49 (text) and 20–23 (dating).

13. *De Genesi contra Manichaeos, PL* 34: 173–220; *De Genesi ad litteram liber imperfectus,* ed. Joseph Zycha, CSEL 28/1 (1894): 457–503; *De Genesis ad litteram libri XII,* ed. Joseph Zycha, CSEL 28/1: 1–435; and *Confessions,* ed. James J. O'Donnell, 3 vols. (Oxford, U.K.: Clarendon Press, 1992).

14. On the development of such exposition, see Henri de Lubac, *Exégèse médiévale: Les quatre sens de l'Ecriture,* 4 vols. (Paris: Aubier, 1959–1964); English (partial), *Medieval Exegesis: The Four Senses of Scripture,* vol. 1, trans. Mark Sebanc, and vol. 2, trans. E. M. Macierowski (Grand Rapids, Mich.: W. B. Eerdmans, 1998–2000). For a treatment of threefold interpretation that was written in the late 1120s at Paris, see Hugh of St. Victor, *Didascalicon de studio legendi* 5.2 and 6.3–5, ed. Charles Henry Buttimer, Catholic University of America Studies in Medieval and Renaissance Latin 10 (Washington, D.C.: The Catholic University Press, 1939), 95–96 and 113–23; *The Didascalicon: A Medieval Guide to the Arts,* trans. Jerome Taylor, Records of Civilization 64 (New York: Columbia University Press, 1961), 120–21 and 135–45.

15. For the fullest study of Abelard's techniques in the commentary, see Eileen F. Kearney, "Peter Abelard as Biblical Commentator: A Study of the *Expositio in Hexaemeron,*" in *Petrus Abaelardus,* 199–210.

orating others. Not unpredictably, his theological procedures bear the stamp of the *quaestio* format employed in formal logic, as it was taught in his times (and indeed as he pioneered it).[16] Even so, Abelard does not follow here the *quaestio* format thoroughgoingly, probably because he is writing exegesis for a convent of nuns rather than a treatise on logic for an audience of Parisian masters and students. Nonetheless, the principles that he set forth as a logician for application to theology in the prologue to the *Sic et non* come to the fore here too in at least a small way. Thus the invocation of Aristotle and the quotation of Boethius's comment on the *Categories* that he interjects here in order to explain Augustine are familiar from the prologue.

One attraction of commenting upon the days of creation would have been the opportunities to explore nature and to apply the resources of physics as it was conceived in the twelfth century. These opportunities were part of what elicited a commentary from Thierry of Chartres, who partook of the curiosity about nature and physics that is a hallmark of the so-called Chartrian Neoplatonists. Drawing inspiration from Plato's *Timaeus* as translated by Calcidius (fourth or fifth century C.E.), Thierry explains the creation after the first day as relying on the operation and interaction of the four elements (in the sequence air, water, fire, and earth). But by and large Abelard's explication holds fast to the verbal analysis typical of the *trivium* (grammar, rhetoric, and dialectic) rather than venturing deeply into the sciences of the *quadrivium* (geometry, arithmetic, music, and astronomy).[17]

The exegetical format is not so bluntly evident as in the *Problemata*, but it tends in the same direction. If there is an overarching moral interpretation, it emphasizes the goodness demonstrated by the Holy Spirit in the creation. In the allegory the stress falls upon the parallels between the six days of creation and the six ages of the world

16. G. R. Evans, *Language and Logic of the Bible: The Earlier Middle Ages* (Cambridge, U.K.: Cambridge University Press, 1984), 127–28, and Marenbon, *Philosophy of Peter Abelard*, 76.

17. For a couple of remarks in this connection, see Jolivet, *La théologie d'Abélard*, 105–10.

(*sex aetates mundi*). The six ages of the world were conceived of as follows:[18]

First: from Adam (the first man) to Noah (who constructed the ark at the flood)

Second: from Noah to Abraham (the father of all nations)

Third: from Abraham to David

Fourth: from David to the Babylonian Captivity

Fifth: from the Captivity to the Advent of Jesus Christ

Sixth: from the Advent on through the Present

Although Abelard proceeds day by day through the hexaemeron, he devotes much more space to the sixth day than to any of the others. This disproportion enables him to deal comparatively with the basic natures and traits of men and women, who were created on the sixth day. It also allows him more readily to draw Christological connections. Last but not least, it permits him to align the six ages of the world with the six ages of human life (*sex aetates hominis: infantia, pueritia, adolescentia, iuventus, gravitas, senectus*), as they had been coordinated ever since Augustine.[19]

To return to the preface, it takes the form of a letter in which the conventional schema of an opening salutation has been jumbled or at least deferred.[20] It opens with a paragraph on the three most

18. These parallels were suggested already by Augustine, *De catechizandis rudibus* (On the Catechizing of the Uninstructed) 17.28 and 22.39, ed. J. B. Bauer, CCSL 46 (1969). The fullest information on early sources will be found in Hildegard L. C. Tristram, *Sex aetates mundi: Die Weltzeitalter bei den Angelsachsen und den Iren: Untersuchungen und Texte*, Anglistische Forschungen 165 (Heidelberg, Germany: C. Winter, 1985).

19. On the connection of the six ages of the world with the six ages of life, see J. A. Burrow, *The Ages of Man: A Study in Medieval Writing and Thought* (Oxford, U.K.: Clarendon Press, 1988), 55–94. On Augustine's *De diversis quaestionibus LXXXIII* 1.58 (in *PL* 40: 11–100) in particular, see 80–85 and (for text and English translation) 199–200.

20. The same surprising placement of the salutation occurs in Letter Eight. On the customary placement and content of the greeting, see Carol Dana Lanham, *Salutatio Formulas in Latin Letters to 1200: Syntax, Style, and Theory*, Münchener Beiträge zur Mediävistik und Renaissance-Forschung 22 (Munich, Germany: Arbeo-Gesellschaft, 1975).

challenging parts of the Bible. After listing the sections, Abelard proceeds to quote passages from two early ecclesiastic writers, Origen and Jerome, that support his contention about the difficulty of Genesis. Origen, who castrated himself so as to be able to preach to women without risk of scandal, was a personage whom Abelard invoked often for various reasons, one of which needs no saying. Jerome, who took a special interest in the education and religious life of women, became a fitting model for Abelard as he became more and more immersed in laying out the life to be led and the devotions to be performed by Heloise and the nuns of the Paraclete. Like Jerome, Abelard had been subjected to rumors because of having demonstrated an attentiveness to religious women that was perceived by some to be unseemly.

The second paragraph finally unveils a salutation, of the sort familiar to those who have read the so-called personal letters between Heloise and Abelard. Two words, "sister Heloise," recur in three other letters from Abelard to her.[21] The greeting as a whole plays upon the changed status of their relationship and requests her prayers for him in his moment of need, in this case because he is embarking on a difficult exegetic undertaking. The third paragraph returns to the topic of decoding the hexaemeron. After referring to moral and allegorical/mystical interpretation, Abelard professes a goal of privileging the literal-historical, as Augustine did, but he goes on to quote the *Retractationes* (Reconsiderations), where the bishop of Hippo offered retrospectively a candidly critical assessment of his accomplishments in the commentary on Genesis. In this passage Abelard draws parallels first between Augustine and Aristotle and then between Augustine and himself.[22] In the final paragraph, Abelard contends that if his own interpretative effort founders, Heloise warrants responsibility for having asked him to undertake it.[23]

21. Letter Three, ed. Muckle, 76; Preface to Book 1 of *The Paraclete Hymnal*; and Prologue to *The Sermons*.

22. Beryl Smalley, "*Prima clavis sapientiae:* Augustine and Abelard," in *Fritz Saxl 1890–1948: A Volume of Memorial Essays from His Friends in England*, ed. D. J. Gordon (London: Thomas Nelson and Sons, 1957), 93–100, at 97.

23. By this quotation Abelard "covers himself with a Pauline variation of the humility topos"; see Ferrante, *To the Glory*, 60. On the humility topos as a concept in

The text is extant in four twelfth-century manuscripts: Avranches, Bibliothèque municipale, MS 135, fol. 75r–90v (twelfth century, Mont Saint-Michel); Copenhagen, Det Kongelige Bibliotek, MS E don. var. 138 quarto, fol. 9r–16v and 19r–25v; Paris, Bibliothèque nationale de France, MS lat. 17251, fol. 33v–46r (twelfth century, La Meilleraye-de-Bretagne, Nantes); and Vatican, Biblioteca apostolica vaticana, MS Vat. lat. 4214, fol. 1r–30v (twelfth century).[24] The critical edition is *Expositio in Hexameron*, ed. Romig, in *Petri Abaelardi opera theologica*, vol. 5, ed. Burnett and Romig, CCCM 15 (2004): I–III, at 3–5, which is followed here.

DEDICATION LETTER

There are three sections in the Old Testament that experts in the Holy Scriptures have judged to be very difficult to understand, namely, the beginning of Genesis, according to the literal account itself of God's activity [Genesis 1–2]; the Song of Songs; and the prophecy of Ezekiel, especially in the first vision about animals and wheels [Ezekiel 1] and in the last about the building established on the hill [Ezekiel 40–48].[25] For this reason (they say) it has been established among the Hebrews that the explication of those writings is on account of its extreme difficulty to be entrusted only to the ripened insights of elders, as Origen himself recalls in the first homily on the Song of Songs, saying:

They say too that among the Hebrews it is observed no one is allowed to hold this book in his hands except he who has arrived at a full and ripe age. But from them we have received that practice to be maintained, that among them all the Scriptures are handed down by teachers to boys but

---

medieval rhetoric, see above, note 30 to the introduction to the prefaces to the three books of *The Paraclete Hymnal.*

24. The Avranches manuscript is the closest to Abelard and in fact one of the three scribes may have been the *magister* himself. See Romig, CCCM 15 (2004): xx–lxx, as well as Buytaert, "Abelard's *Expositio*," 163–94.

25. Abelard refers to the difficulty of at least one prophecy in Ezekiel in the *Historia calamitatum*, ed. Monfrin, 202–3; trans. Radice, 8.

that four books are kept to the end, that is, the beginning of Genesis in which the creation of the world is described [Genesis 1]; the beginning of the prophet Ezekiel in which a report is given about the cherubim [Ezekiel 1] as well as the end in which is contained the construction of the temple [Ezekiel 40–48]; and this book of the Song of Songs.[26]

Hence also that statement of Jerome in the prologue of his commentary on Ezekiel:

I will undertake the prophet Ezekiel, whose difficulty the Hebrew tradition attests. For if a person among them has not reached the age of priestly ministry, that is, the thirtieth year, he is not allowed to read the beginning of Genesis, the Song of Songs, or the beginning and end of this book, that the full time of human experience may bring its supplement to complete wisdom and figurative understanding.[27]

Thus you demand in entreating and entreat in demanding,[28] sister Heloise,[29] once dear in the world, now dearest in Christ, that I attend in the explication of these sections all the more zealously as it is apparent that an understanding of them is the more difficult, and I will bring this to fruition especially for you and your spiritual daughters. For this reason I ask you (just as you ask) that because you compel me to this by asking, you obtain fulfillment for me by praying to God. And since, as is often said, we must begin from the head, may your prayers help me at the opening of Genesis the more fully, in proportion as it is evident that its dif-

---

26. Origen, *In Canticum canticorum*, Prologue, in *Patrologiae cursus completus: Series Graeca*, ed. Jacques-Paul Migne, 161 vols. (Paris: J.-P. Migne, 1857–1866), 13: 62–84, at 63D–64A.

27. Jerome, *Commentarii in Ezechielem*, Prologue, ed. François Glorie, CCSL 75 (1964): 3–4, lines 24–30.

28. Abelard himself uses this same wording in the first person in Letter Three: "Supplicando itaque postulo, postulando supplico." Compare Heloise, in the letter to Abelard that forms the prologue to the *Problemata*: "supplicando rogamus, rogando supplicamus" ("we ask in entreating, we entreat in asking").

29. Abelard uses the same manner of address elsewhere; compare Letter Three, ed. Muckle, *Mediaeval Studies* 15 (1953): 76; the first line to *The Paraclete Hymnal*, Preface to Book 1; and the first line to Letter Sixteen: Prologue to *The Sermons*.

ficulty is greater than the rest, as the very rarity of commentaries testifies.

Indeed, although many men put together many allegorical or moral interpretations of Genesis, among us [Latin Christians] the insightful intellect of most blessed Augustine alone undertook to explicate the literal-historical in this matter.[30] He acknowledged this as being so difficult that the things he said there on the basis of opinion rather than by assertion of thought, he brought forth, if you will, by investigating them as matters of doubt rather than demarcating them as certainties. It is as if he heeded that counsel of Aristotle's:

Perhaps (he said) it may be difficult to make confident pronouncements on matters of this sort, unless they have been studied often. Furthermore, it will not be without benefit to waver in judgment about individual points.[31]

Consequently the aforesaid doctor of the Church said in the second book of his *Retractationes* [Reconsiderations], as he was about to reconsider his twelve books *On Genesis According to the Letter:*

---

30. Bede, *Libri quatuor in principium Genesis usque ad nativitatem Isaac,* Preface, ed. C. W. Jones, CCSL 118A (1967): 1, uses the wording "multi multa dixere" ("Many [men] have said many [words]") before singling out Augustine for special acknowledgment. Compare Thierry of Chartres, ed. Häring, 555.

31. Aristotle, *Categoriae vel praedicamenta* 1.1–5, trans. Boethius, 8b21–8b24, ed. Laurentius Minio-Paluello, *Corpus philosophorum Medii Aevi: Aristoteles Latinus* 1/1 (Bruges, Belgium: Desclée de Brouwer, 1961), 23 = Boethius, *In categorias Aristotelis libri IV,* 2, in *PL* 64: 159–294, at 238D.

As can be seen throughout his established oeuvre, Abelard demonstrates a remarkable propensity to reuse the same quotations, and the present passage is a case in point. These two sentences can be found in the *Logica "Ingredientibus,"* ed. Geyer, *Peter Abaelards philosophische Schriften,* 2 (1921): 223, where Abelard glosses it, and in the conclusion to the Prologue to the *Sic et non,* ed. Boyer and McKeon, 103, where he also rephrases the gloss. In the *Sic et non,* as here, Abelard invokes Aristotle's name without explaining that the passage appears in Boethius's commentary on his translation of Aristotle's *Categories.* On Abelard's comparison between Augustine and Aristotle here, see Smalley, *"Prima clavis,"* 96–97.

In this work more matters have been examined than discovered, and fewer of those which have been discovered have been substantiated. In truth, the remaining matters should be set down in such a way as though they must still be investigated.[32]

But seeing that the statements of this work also seem obscure to you, to the extent that the very explication of it is regarded as needing to be explicated again, you entreat our opinion too in explicating the beginning of Genesis. In fact, you should recognize how at the instance of your prayers I am now undertaking this explication in such a way that when you see me fail, you may await from me the excuse of the Apostle [Paul]: "I am become foolish: you have compelled me" [2 Corinthians 12.11].[33]

---

32. *Retractationes* 2.24, ed. Almut Mutzenbecher, CCSL 57 (1974): 109, lines 8–11. The *Retractationes* was an extremely important text to Abelard, as can be gauged from his mention of it in the final sentence of the Prologue to the *Sic et non* (p. 104, lines 348–50). This capping mention and the subsequent quotations from the *Retractationes* in the body of the *Sic et non* are implicit reminders of the quotation from the same Augustinian text earlier in the Prologue (pp. 92, line 86–93, line 96), which established the principle of analysis that when analyzing conflicting authorities, the reader must determine if any of them was subsequently retracted by its author.

33. The closing statement from the Bible appears repeatedly in exegesis and also, coincidentally, near the close of two letters by Bernard of Clairvaux, Letter 244.3, in *Sancti Bernardi opera*, 8 vols. (Rome: Editiones Cistercienses, 1957–1977), vols. 7–8, ed. Jean Leclercq and Henri Rochais (1974–1977), 8: 135, line 29; and Letter 448, 8: 425, line 10.

4

LETTER SIXTEEN. PROLOGUE TO *THE SERMONS*

Near the close of the *Historia calamitatum* Abelard avers that he began frequenting the Paraclete after the neighbors faulted him for not having helped the nuns in the hard times after they took up residence in his former hermitage. He specifies that these unnamed detractors carped at him, since he could have easily given the women counsel "if only through my preaching."[1] The following text is the preamble to a collection that draws together the preaching Abelard eventually did for the nuns, as well as sermons originally addressed to other audiences.

The authenticity of this very brief letter is unimpeachable.[2] It responds to an earlier missive from Heloise, no longer extant, in which she requested that Abelard send her sermons for her "spiritual daughters," the nuns of the Paraclete.[3] It serves as a preface to a collection, now totaling thirty-four sermons, that he furnished in response to her request, and presumably it survives thanks to having been preserved in the holdings of the Paraclete. The Paraclete codex

1. "Nostra saltem predicatione," ed. Monfrin, p. 101, lines 1343–44; trans. Radice, p. 36.

2. Paola de Santis, "Osservazioni sulla lettera dedicatoria del sermonario di Abelardo," *Aevum* 55 (1981): 262–71.

3. Abelard used the same phrase to describe the nuns in the Dedication Letter to *The Commentary on the Six Days of Creation*.

of the sermons is likely to have been the basis for the most influential early printed edition, after which time the manuscript disappeared. At least six extant manuscripts transmit isolated sermons, in no case more than a handful, all of which are also found in the collection as a whole. One manuscript that contained two sermons was destroyed in the Second World War.[4] Finally, one additional sermon, discussed in the General Introduction and not in the collection, has been attributed definitively to Abelard.[5]

The sermon book was put together, and the preface was written, between 1132 and 1135, when (as has been pointed out before) Abelard wrote the *Historia calamitatum;* corresponded with Heloise in Letters Three, Five, Seven, and Eight; answered her *Problemata;* wrote Letter Nine to the nuns of the Paraclete; and wrote the prefaces to *The Paraclete Hymnal.* It should be noted that not all the sermons need to have been composed during this period. In fact, near the end of the preface Abelard appears to acknowledge that his achievement in producing *The Sermons* lay in arranging them rather than in writing them.[6] The implication would be that the individual sermons had existed already. Many of them may have been tailored for delivery by Abelard before either the nuns of the Paraclete or the monks of his monastery of St. Gildas, where he was abbot, but others could have been pronounced before other audiences and could have been written years earlier.[7] Thus, for example, it has been reasoned that three

4. De Santis, *I sermoni,* x.

5. L. J. Engels, *"Adtendite a falsis prophetis* (Ms. Colmar 128, ff. 152v/153v). Un texte de Pierre Abélard contre les Cisterciens retrouvé?" in *Corona gratiarum. Miscellanea patristica, historica et liturgica Eligio Dekkers O.S.B. XII lustra complenti oblata,* vol. 2 (Bruges, Belgium: Sint Pietersabdij / The Hague, The Netherlands: Martinus Nijhoff, 1975), 195–228 (1–34).

6. I translate "in his ... scribendis seu disponendis" as "when writing *or* rather arranging these," whereas De Santis, *I sermoni,* 87 and 97, construes the phrase instead as "Nello scriverli *e* nel disporli" (my emphases). Waddell, "Peter Abelard as Creator," 278–79, sees Abelard as having composed sermons afresh for the book of sermons, which he regards as having differed substantially in its contents from the sermons we have, which is "the fusion of a homogeneous collection with a great many disparate and occasional pieces."

7. Engels, *"Adtendite a falsis prophetis,"* 199–203, 210, and 223, presents arguments in support of the idea that Sermon 33 was originally meant for the monks of St. Gildas.

of *The Sermons* were at least drafted before the core of sermons that Abelard prepared for the nuns.[8]

Other medieval sermons were composed, delivered, and dedicated by male writers for female religious communities, but Abelard's collection is remarkable for its girth and (insofar as the extant manuscripts allow us to gauge) structure.[9] As such, it forms a worthy constituent of the so-called *Corpus Paraclitense,* as has been called the extraordinary body of writings that Abelard designed for the Paraclete at the instance of Heloise. It follows logically upon Letter Eight, which mentioned en passant that the daily round should include the reading and explication of either a sermon or a part of the monastic rule.[10] Such sermons, which would be read aloud in the refectory during mealtimes as well as before compline, would allow Abelard to project his words and (through a feminized ventriloquism) his voice within the Paraclete.

In the prologue Abelard makes cursory but clear reference to the organization of *The Sermons.*[11] In arranging the sermons he reenacts the chronology of Christ's life, starting with the Feast of the Annunciation and the Incarnation (25 March), proceeding to Christmastide, and moving forward eventually to Easter season, Rogation Days, Ascension, and Pentecost. At that point he shifts to salvation history as it proceeded after Christ, with a few sermons connected with the apostles; he caps this section with a sermon on the Assumption of the Virgin Mary. Thereafter the collection as we have it offers a few

---

De Santis examines in detail which sermons harbor clues that their audiences were nuns, which monks.

8. On Sermons 27, 30, and 33, in *PL* 178: 547B–50D, 564A–69C, and 582B–607A, see Damien Van den Eynde, "Le recueil des sermons de Pierre Abélard," *Antonianum* 37 (1962): 17–54, at 52–54.

9. For information on other sermons, see De Santis, *I sermoni,* xi, n. 2, and 87–88, n. 19.

10. Letter Eight, ed. T. P. McLaughlin, "Abelard's Rule for Religious Women," *Mediaeval Studies* 18 (1956): 241–92, at 264: "Ubi postmodum vel aliquo sermonis edificio fiat vel aliquid de regula legatur et exponatur" (In that place then either there should be some edifying sermon or something from the Rule should be read and expounded upon).

11. The foundational study of the order in which the sermons would have originally been arranged is Van den Eynde, "Le recueil des sermons," 17–54.

other sermons, mostly designed for topics or circumstances that he seems to have deemed particularly well suited to the sisters of the convent. *The Sermons* conclude with four (two on St. Stephen and one each on St. John the Baptist and the Holy Innocents) that bring the calendar full circle to the Christmas season (26–28 December). As it stands, the collection amounts to thirty-four sermons, a total that, perhaps by sheer happenstance, embeds numerologically the Christological spread of *The Sermons,* since Christ was thirty-three years old but in the thirty-fourth year of his life when he died.[12]

The salutation and valediction of the prologue are characterized by the same beautifully delicate complexity as are those of the more famous personal letters. In the Latin of the salutation, the word order of the vocative has an ambiguity that vanishes in English: "veneranda in Christo et amanda soror Heloissa" could be translated most literally as "sister to be revered in Christ and loved" but more appropriately (in terms of medieval Christian values) as "sister to be revered and loved in Christ." In the valediction Abelard plays upon Heloise's past ties to him and her present duties toward God, upon flesh and spirit, and, at greatest length, upon her bonds to him as wife, sister, and, most daringly, consort. The last word may evoke the spousal relationship Heloise once had with Abelard as well as the status they share in their new vocations as nun and monk. As a whole, the valediction reflects as great a level of comfort with the whole spectrum of relationships Abelard has had with Heloise as emerges in any of the letters. He has passed far beyond the direct emotional engagement that she once coveted (and still may have done so), but in counterbalance he lavishes his intellectual, scholarly, and literary skills upon the needs of the Paraclete as she defines them.

In this preface Abelard refers tantalizingly to a "libellus hymnorum vel sequentiarum" (small book of hymns and/or sequences) that he had earlier completed at Heloise's bidding. The hymns would presumably be Abelard's hymnal for the Paraclete. If here he used se-

12. For a thumbnail sketch of the number symbolism, see Heinz Meyer and Rudolf Suntrup, *Lexikon der mittelalterlichen Zahlenbedeutungen,* Münstersche Mittelalter-Schriften 56 (Munich, Germany: W. Fink, 1987), column 706.

quences as an alternative description of hymns ("hymns or sequences"), then *The Paraclete Hymnal* is the only work under discussion. This
interpretation has the advantage of fitting better with what *vel* usually
means, but it would strain all usual senses of *sequentia* to have it apply
to the forms of poetry found in the hymnal. Another possibility is
that Abelard means the two nouns to designate two different genres
and that the *libellus* comprised not only all or part of the hymnal but
also other songs in the form known technically as the sequence.

   Although the last word in the phrase is too vague to permit certainty, the mention of "sequences" could pertain to the six *planctus,*
or laments, by Abelard that are still extant.[13] The *planctus* have come
down to us without an accompanying dedication, but it is hard to
imagine that they were devised and sent to anyone other than Heloise and the nuns of the Paraclete.[14] All six are in the voices of Old
Testament figures and lament other Old Testament figures. *Planctus
One* is by Dinah, daughter of Jacob, for Shechem (Genesis 34); *Planctus Two* is by Jacob for his sons (Genesis 42.36, 43.14, 37.7–9, 35.18);
Planctus Three is by the virgins of Israel for the daughter of Jephthah
the Gileadite (Judges 11.29–40); *Planctus Four* is by Israel for Samson
(Psalm 35.7, Judges 13–16); *Planctus Five* is by David for Abner, son of
Ner, whom Joab slew (2 Kings 3.26–39); and *Planctus Six* is by David,
for Saul and Jonathan (2 Kings 1.17–27). These sequences survive as
a group in only one manuscript (Vatican, Biblioteca Apostolica Vaticana, MS Reginensis latinus 288, fol. 63v–64v), although *Planctus Six*
is preserved separately in two others as well. Beyond the six *planctus,*
it has been argued that Abelard should be credited with three other

---

   13. See Marenbon, *Philosophy of Peter Abelard,* 80. On p. xviii Marenbon gives information on the best separate editions and treatments of individual *planctus.* The chief
advantage of two Italian editions is that they present all six *planctus* as a group; see
Giuseppe Vecchi, ed., *Pietro Abelardo, I "Planctus": Introduzione, testo critico, trascrizioni musicali,* Istituto di filologia romanza della Università di Roma: Collezione di testi e manuali 35 (Modena, Italy: Società tipografica modenese, 1951), and Massimo Sannelli,
ed. and trans. (Italian), *Pietro Abelardo: Planctus,* Littera 3 (Trento, Italy: La Finestra,
2002). A new edition, with English translation and accompanying studies, has been
announced as forthcoming by Juanita Feros Ruys and John O. Ward, to be entitled
The Repentant Abelard (Palgrave MacMillan).
   14. Dronke, *Women Writers,* 134.

sequences, but the ascription of these to him has been contested. If
these other sequences were authentically Abelardian, they could also
be the ones to which he makes reference in this letter.[15]

The term "sequence" requires a bit of explanation. In much lyric
poetry the text is the primary element, to which the music is merely
an adjunct. The opposite holds true for the trope and sequence, two
musico-poetic forms that (in the view of many) emerged mainly
from liturgical chant. In fact, one could even argue that the sequence
is really only an elevated prose set to music.

The classical liturgical sequence had a specific location in the
mass. The alleluia served as a conclusion to the gradual (the anti-
phon sung after the Epistle) and as a preamble to the Gospel. It was
delivered in the following way: after the cantor sang the alleluia, the
choir repeated it with a long vocalization of the -a (the *iubilus*). Then
the cantor recited the versus. Finally, the choir repeated the alleluia with the *iubilus*, which was expanded considerably in its musical
form. This prolonged melody (which is called a melisma) came to
be known as the *sequentia* of the alleluia, since the sequence "follows"
the alleluia. By the middle of the ninth century people had begun to
supply the music of the *sequentiae* with texts. They called such a composition *sequentia cum prosa, prosa ad sequentiam*, or, simply, *prosa*.

Although the thousands of surviving sequences display considerable variety, all of them are characterized by two features. First, the
text is set syllabically to the music (although the music is not always
extant). Under ideal circumstances, the text is preserved with the medieval equivalent of a musical note or melodic phrase above each syllable. Second, the text is constructed in couples of isosyllabic lines,
with each pair sharing the same melody. Thus the typical sequence is
distinguished by its structure, which is designed to lend itself to performance by a double choir. Because the two choirs sing versicles in

15. Chrysogonus Waddell, "*Epithalamica:* An Easter Sequence by Peter Abelard,"
Musical Quarterly 72 (1986): 239–71, at 241–42, has proposed that Abelard wrote *Epi-
thalamica*, in *AH* 8: 45–47; *De profundis ad te clamantium*, *AH* 10: 54–55; and *Virgines castae*,
AH 54: 133–35. These ascriptions have been questioned or rejected more than once by
Peter Dronke, who sets out fully the many grounds for doubt in Dronke and Or-
landi, "New Works by Abelard and Heloise?" 123–46.

alternation, the sequence must be composed of carefully paired versicles. Single lines were often but not always used to begin and end the composition. Often the word *alleluia* remained in the text of the sequence; if not, its melody dictated that the first stanza open with a four-syllable word and its pronunciation suggested (mainly to French composers) that the lines of the sequences end in *-a.*

In constituting the text of the preface Paola De Santis relied not only on the 1616 *editio princeps* (which was based on at least one lost manuscript, from the Paraclete, and possibly also on another from the Sorbonne), but also on a transcription printed in 1577 that formed part of a report on a manuscript then preserved at the Sorbonne. This report, by the humanist Jean-Papire Masson (1544–1611), was published in his *Annalium libri quatuor: Quibus res gestæ Francorum explicantur* (Paris: apud N. Chesneau, 1577), 260. The Sorbonne manuscript used by Masson is likely to have been the same as that consulted in preparation for the *editio princeps* of *The Sermons* by François d'Amboise and André Du Chesne, editors, *Petri Abaelardi . . . et Heloisae conivgis eivs . . . Opera* (Paris: Sumptibus Nicolai Bvon, 1616). Nonetheless, there are significant variations between the texts offered by Masson, on the one hand, and d'Amboise and Du Chesne, on the other. See De Santis, *I sermoni,* 85 (for the Latin text), 85–86 (for an Italian translation), and 86–97 (for commentary on the text), as well as 35–36 and 85–86 (on the lost manuscripts and early editions).

LETTER SIXTEEN

Having completed recently a small book of hymns and sequences at your entreaty, Heloise, sister to be revered in Christ and loved, I have hurried more than is my custom to write in addition as best as I can some minor works of sermons at your request, for you as well as for your spiritual daughters who are assembled in our oratory.[16]

16. In some instances the first-person plural as used in Abelard's letters in this volume is mainly a variation on the first-person singular, but here the "our" probably serves to include Heloise in addition to Abelard himself. The word "oratory" is also

Certainly, given more to lecturing than to sermonizing, I devote myself to explanation, striving for plainness, not construction of verbal art—for literal meaning, not rhetorical embellishment.[17] Perhaps a clean rather than an embellished style, as it is plainer, will be more suited to the understanding of simple people; and, in proportion to the nature of the listeners, the very roughness of unadorned speech will be a kind of cultivated embellishment, and the ready understanding of little women will be a kind of dash of good taste.[18]

complex, in that it is a place at once of prayer and (when sermons are given) of oratory in the rhetorical sense. The salutation merits comparison with the openings of Letter Seven, Letter Eight, the preface to the first book of *The Paraclete Hymnal*, and the Dedication Letter to *The Commentary on the Six Days of Creation*.

17. The sentence is freighted with words that may seem straightforward or even banal at first but that upon closer study reveal complications. *Lectio*, translated here as "lecturing," could also refer to reading. If Abelard were not giving the preamble to a collection of sermons, it would be feasible to construe *sermo* as 'talking,' in contrast to *lectio*, which could then mean '(meditative) reading' in a monastic sense. *Expositio* is similarly ambiguous, since it could refer to explanation in the technical sense of biblical exegesis or in a variety of other ways.

Abelard is indebted to Boethius, *De syllogismo categorico libri duo*, Prologue, in *PL* 64: 793–832, at 794C: "Non enim eloquentiae compositiones, sed planitiem consectamur: qua in re, si hoc efficimus, quamlibet incompte loquentes, intentio quoque nostra nobis perfecta est" (For I do not pursue constructions of verbal art, but plainness: in this endeavor, if I achieve this, even though speaking in unadorned style, I have fulfilled my aim). Within Abelard's own writings the closest parallel to the aesthetic judgment expressed here comes in the *Carmen ad Astralabium*, 869–70, ed. José M. A. Rubingh-Bosscher, *Peter Abelard—Carmen ad Astralabium* (Groningen, The Netherlands: n.p., 1987), 155: "Planiciem quemcumque sequi decet expositorem, / quantumcumque rudis sermo sit eius in hoc" (It is proper for a commentator to use a simple style, / however rough his language might be in this matter). Compare 12–14, p. 107: "et sensus verbis anteferendus erit / ornatis animos captet persuasio verbis / doctrine magis est debita planicies" (and the sense will have to be preferred to the words. / Yet persuasion seizes minds with ornate words: / for instruction, plainness is required instead). For context, see L. C. Engels, "Abélard écrivain," in *Peter Abelard: Proceedings*, 12–37, at 23–26.

18. This sentence too is packed with terminology that carried heavy charges in Medieval Latin. On the words here translated as "roughness" and "cultivation," see Michael Richter, "*Urbanitas—rusticitas*: Linguistic Aspects of a Medieval Dichotomy," *Studies in Church History* 16 (1979): 149–57. The expression *condimentum saporis* (a certain

Moreover, in maintaining the sequence of the feast days when writing or rather arranging these,[19] I have begun at the very beginning of our redemption.[20] Farewell in the Lord, you who are his handmaiden, once dear to me in the world, now dearest to me in Christ; then wife in flesh, now sister in spirit and consort in the profession of a sacred way of life.

---

dash of good taste) appears in apposition to the "salt of the earth" (Christ's metaphor in Matthew 5.13) in a number of sources, with pseudo-Augustine, *Sermo* 222 *De sanctis apostolis* (= Hrabanus Maurus, *Homilia* 35), being the earliest: *PL* 39: 2156–58, at 2157. In addition, Abelard himself dishes out a broader food metaphor in Letter Eight.

In discussing this passage, De Santis, *I sermoni di Abelardo*, 86, points out that the word *paruula* (little woman, young woman, mere woman) is frequent in Jerome, Letter 107, and that as a consequence it appears three times in Abelard, Letter Nine, which quotes heavily from Jerome. She also observes, 91, that there were young women at the Paraclete at this time, and she takes the word as connoting relative youth.

19. If Abelard has in mind the same structure as he follows in the second book of *The Paraclete Hymnbook*, he means by the phrase *ordo festivitatum* the feast days *de tempore*, taken separately from those of the saints. Alternatively, he could have in mind a distinction to mark apart the feast days of saints from other solemnities. This other possibility would gain weight from *Sermo* 13, in *PL* 178: 486. See Van den Eynde, "Chronologie des écrits," 21, 31, 47, and 52.

20. He refers here to the Feast of the Annunciation, which, by commemorating the Incarnation, celebrates the beginning of redemption.

PART II

BERNARD OF CLAIRVAUX

5

LETTER TEN. TO BERNARD OF CLAIRVAUX

In the last two years of his life Abelard found himself under mounting criticism from Bernard of Clairvaux and his allies for allegedly heretical writings and teachings. The aspersions escalated rapidly into full-scale attacks. Both of them egged on by their respective camps, Abelard and Bernard engaged in a bitterly polemic campaign of letter writing and political maneuvering. The skirmish between them peaked at the Council of Sens in 1141, which condemned Abelard as a heretic and prompted the pope to place him under a sentence of perpetual silence. The excommunication and ban of silence were not lifted formally until after a reconciliation was arranged by Peter the Venerable shortly before Abelard's death about 1142.

Had there been bad blood between Abelard and Bernard before the Council of Sens, or, to put the question less cagily, for how many years had there been bad blood between them? Many circumstances could have set the two on a collision course. One is ideological. Abelard embodied a new outlook that is often summed up in the word "Scholasticism," as opposed to the monasticism of Bernard.[1] According to this dichotomy, Abelard could be seen to represent the

1. For fuller context, see Ferruolo, *Origins of the Universities*, 47–92, and Matthew A. Doyle, *Bernard of Clairvaux and the Schools: The Formation of an Intellectual Milieu in the First Half of the Twelfth Century*, Studi 11 (Spoleto, Italy: Fondazione Centro italiano di studi sull'alto Medioevo, 2005).

schools, teaching, reason, and logic, Bernard the cloisters, preaching, authority, and faith.

Another dimension to the conflict was political, in that some key supporters of Bernard were rivals or opponents of Abelard, and vice versa. Thus William of Champeaux, whom Abelard's pressure had encouraged to leave Notre Dame for St. Victor, was not merely the bishop who had installed Bernard as abbot of Clairvaux but also the teacher and personal counsellor who had saved Bernard's life by persuading him to moderate the harsh asceticism that had nearly killed him. Later Bernard lashed out against the royal chaplain and chancellor Stephen of Garlande, who backed Abelard at key moments in his life. Beyond these two celebrities, lesser figures whom Abelard had antagonized tended to gravitate toward Bernard.[2] In the end, the patrons and clients of both Bernard and Abelard may have been spoiling for them to fight more than they were themselves—but the operative verb is *may,* since the evidence permits speculation but not conclusion.

Years before Sens Abelard may have disliked Bernard and his loyalists or at least rejected their conception of an apostolic life, if the anti-Cistercian diatribe-sermon (dated tentatively 1127–1128) known after its incipit as "Adtendite a falsis prophetis" is indeed Abelard's.[3] Five years later, Abelard still refrained from naming names, but he came closer to revealing personal disregard for Bernard. In the *Historia calamitatum* (dated 1132–1133) he referred to "new apostles," one of whom "boasted that he had reformed . . . the life of the monks."[4]

And what of Bernard's views on Abelard and pronouncements about him prior to Sens? Bernard's *Apologia for Abbot William* (1124 or

2. Peter Dinzelbacher, *Bernhard von Clairvaux. Leben und Werk des berühmten Zisterziensers* (Darmstadt, Germany: Wissenschaftliche Buchgesellschaft, 1998), 102 and 236–37.

3. Smits, *Letters IX–XIV,* 127–28. For the text and an introduction to it, see L. J. Engels, "'Adtendite a falsis prophetis,'" 195–228. For a translation and study, see Chrysogonus Waddell, "Adtendite a falsis prophetis: Abaelard's Earliest Known Anti-Cistercian Diatribe," *Cistercian Studies Quarterly: An International Review of the Monastic and Contemplative Spiritual Tradition* 39 (2004): 371–98.

4. "novos apostolos . . . quorum . . . alter monachorum se resuscitasse gloriabatur": ed. Monfrin, p. 97, lines 1201–4; trans. Radice, p. 32. For fuller discussion, see the introduction to Letter Twelve.

1125), a text esteemed among historians of medieval art for the light it casts on attitudes toward images during the Middle Ages, was addressed to none other than William of St. Thierry, a close intimate of Bernard's and a onetime friend of Abelard's as well, who had been involved in the Council of Soissons and who spearheaded the later one at Sens.[5] The *Apologia* launched a frontal assault on non-Cistercian monks for their failings—but although Abelard could have imagined that it was inspired at least in part by him, it never identifies him or even makes what could be taken as a glancing reference to him.[6] Similarly, Bernard's *Letter on Baptism* (1127 or 1128) was written in response to a request from Hugh of St. Victor (died 1141), a theologian at the school associated with one of Abelard's main rivals, namely, William of Champeaux. Furthermore, it was prompted by Hugh's questions about a series of *sententiae* that an unnamed contemporary had employed in teaching.[7] Although it lies within the realm of possibility that the nameless teacher was either Abelard himself or one of his followers, Bernard left the person unidentified and displays no evident antagonism as he brought forth patristic citations in framing his responses.[8]

To move from the quicksands of speculation to surer ground, Letter Ten (probably composed in 1131) offers rich insights into the relations between the men at a stage in their lives and careers a decade before the Council of Sens. In brief, the background of the letter is that Abelard writes to Bernard of Clairvaux and takes is-

5. On the *Apologia ad Guillelmum abbatem* (Apologia to Abbot William), see Conrad Rudolph, *The "Things of Greater Importance": Bernard of Clairvaux's "Apologia" and the Medieval Attitude toward Art* (Philadelphia: University of Pennsylvania Press, 1990), who provides an edition and a translation, as well as information on the correspondence between Bernard and William.

6. Clanchy, *Abelard*, 245.

7. The letter-treatise *Epistula de baptismo* is *Epistula 77*, edited in *Sancti Bernardi opera*, 7: 184–200. The introduction in the *PL* edition (*PL* 182: 1029–46) presents as unlikely the notion that the anonymous teacher would have been Abelard, on the grounds that Hugh would have been sure to identify Abelard by name rather than to leave the matter murky. Bernard speaks with impenetrable vagueness of "quemdam . . . nescio quem (nam non nominas)" (some man . . . I know not whom [for you do not name him]): *Sancti Bernardi opera*, 7: 185.

8. Dinzelbacher, *Bernhard von Clairvaux*, 112.

sue with him on a point of liturgy. Through Heloise Abelard has learned that Bernard had found fault with the wording of the Lord's Prayer followed by the nuns of the Paraclete. Abelard first seeks to prove that the Paraclete wording is preferable to that followed by almost all other Latin Christians. Then he blasts aspects of the liturgy employed by the monks of Bernard's own order, the Cistercians. But the circumstances and contents of the letter merit a fuller exposition.

Once, when Abelard is staying at the Paraclete, Heloise tells him with excitement about the long-desired visit that the quasi-angelic Bernard of Clairvaux, the future saint and the present notability of the Cistercian order, has paid to the convent. In her report she lets drop to Abelard how disapproving Bernard was in a private interview with her that in the recitation of the Lord's Prayer at lauds and vespers the nuns used an unconventional text, particularly because it contained the word *supersubstantialem* (supersubstantial) instead of the word *quotidianum* (daily) as the adjective that normally modified "bread." Since Abelard supplied Heloise and her nuns with their Lord's Prayer (and since Bernard must have been cognizant that the version the women followed emanated from him), and since Abelard claims to have enjoyed a special *caritas*, or love, from Bernard, the older man feels obliged to explain his rationale in following a text that differs from the usual one. He writes a response that illuminates his modus operandi as a philologist, his relations with Bernard, his attitudes toward the Cistercian order, and his erudition as a liturgiologist. Although the letter is devoted to minutiae of scriptural wording and liturgy that could seem narrowly and hopelessly medieval, the theoretical issues Abelard raises and the procedures of analysis he applies come across as strikingly modern—a quality that is also salient in the *Sic et non*.[9]

Although Abelard and Bernard are coupled most memorably in the confrontation that culminated in the Council of Sens, Letter Ten is the only surviving letter addressed by Abelard to Bernard. Rather than dealing with one of the major theological controversies in which the two men became enmired, Letter Ten zeroes in upon a

9. See Rizek-Pfister, "Die hermeneutischen Prinzipien," 484.

seemingly picayune point of liturgy. The interaction did not matter enough to either of the parties for them to mention it afterward in any extant writings. Abelard makes no reference to it in the *Historia calamitatum*, nor does Bernard in his correspondence. Indeed, had the two men not differed over the text of the prayer, and had Abelard not sent off this piece, we might well never have known of Bernard's visit to the Paraclete.

The letter was probably composed in 1131, and certainly before 1135, but after 20 January 1131, when Abelard had traveled from St. Gildas in Brittany to Morigny (south of Paris, near Étampes, in the diocese of Sens) to be in attendance when Pope Innocent II consecrated an altar to St. Lawrence in the abbey church. Also present at the ceremony, alongside eleven cardinals and many bishops of the Paris region, was Bernard. By a curious chance, those attending included, in addition to Abelard himself, a half dozen figures who would come together against him at the Council of Sens a decade later.[10] To sharpen the coincidence, the log of those present that is recorded in the *Chronicle of Morigny* juxtaposes none other than "Bernard, abbot of Clairvaux, who at that time was the most renowned preacher of God's Word in Gaul" and "Peter Abelard, monk and abbot, and himself a man of religion, a director of most outstanding schools, into which men of letters streamed together from almost the whole of the Latin-speaking world."[11] But the trouble of Sens that would pit the two men against each other lay a decade in the future.

At this juncture in his life, Abelard's greatest worries may well have been bound up with the practicalities of monastic living and administration, particularly both the disastrous situation at St. Gildas and the happier but equally preoccupying need to achieve official recognition and stability for Heloise and her nuns at the Paraclete. In

10. Clanchy, *Abelard*, 207–10.

11. *Chronicon Mauriniacense*, 2.14, ed. Léon Mirot, *La chronique de Morigny (1095–1152)* (Paris: Alphonse Picard et fils, 1909), 54: "Bernardus, abbas Clararum Vallium, qui tunc temporis in Gallia divini Verbi famosissimus predicator erat, Petrus Abailardus, monachus et abbas, et ipse vir religiosus excellentissimarum rector scolarum, ad quas pene de tota latinitate viri literati confluebant." Compare *A Translation of the Chronicle of the Abbey of Morigny, France, c. 1100–1150*, trans. Richard Cusimano, Mediaeval Studies 22 (Lewiston, N.Y.: E. Mellen Press, 2003), 103.

the second connection, it has been speculated that Abelard may have invited Bernard to stop at the convent on this trip and that the visit may have had a formal sense, as being an inspection—not a casual visit but an official visitation, on behalf of the pope, to determine whether or not the Paraclete merited accreditation.[12] At this time the Paraclete was in the process of seeking affirmation from the pope of its status. Not much later, Heloise received the papal privilege "Quotiens illud" (dated 23 November 1131) to confirm the convent's holdings and to grant it the right to retain future gifts.[13]

Letter Ten comes to a halt without a valediction, but that abruptness is likelier to reflect a loss in transmission than intentional curtness.[14] Even without the missing farewell, scholars would have been polarized over the tenor of the letter. Some, who see it as being even-tempered and lacking any personal edge, can point both to Abelard's claim to have been held in special affection (*caritas*) by Bernard and to his choice of the superlative *dilectissimus* in addressing Bernard. Others, who regard it as dripping with sarcasm and hostility, can adduce reasons for supposing that Abelard had ample motives for feeling distrust or even antipathy toward Bernard from 1115 on.[15]

Whether the letter is sarcastic or neutral, Abelard's expenditure of effort on it betokens the seriousness with which he regarded negative comments from Bernard upon the liturgy of the Paraclete. Although the Paraclete was not a Cistercian foundation, few ecclesiastic institu-

12. Smits, *Letters IX–XIV,* 129–30, who recapitulates the speculations of Pietro Zerbi, "'Panem nostrum supersubstantialem.' Abelardo polemista ed esegeta nell'*Ep. X*," in *Raccolta di studi in memoria di Sergio Mochi Onory,* 2 vols. (Milan, Italy: Editrice Vita e Pensiero, 1972), 2: 624–38.

13. The bull addresses her as prioress, whereas she termed herself deaconess and abbess. See McLaughlin, "Abelard and the Dignity of Women," 295, n. 14.

14. In the personal correspondence Letter Four, from Heloise, also lacks a valediction.

15. For references, see Smits, *Letters IX–XIV,* 120–36. Two who perceived the relations between Abelard and Bernard as having been cordial are Arno Borst, "Abälard und Bernhard," *Historische Zeitschrift* 186 (1958): 497–526, at 500–509, and Edward Little, "Relations between St. Bernard and Abelard before 1139," in M. Basil Pennington, ed., *Saint Bernard of Clairvaux: Studies Commemorating the Eighth Centenary of His Canonization,* Cistercian Studies Series 28 (Kalamazoo, Mich.: Cistercian Publications, 1977), 155–68. But their stance seems not to have secured proponents lately.

tions would not have felt vulnerable to criticism from as powerful a churchman as Bernard of Clairvaux. Such susceptibility would have been especially keen at the oratory of the Paraclete, which (as noted already) received apostolic privilege only toward the end of 1131.

According to Abelard's account, the Lord's Prayer is attested in the New Testament in the two versions of the Sermon on the Mount. The Gospel of Matthew records the prayer as heard by the evangelist himself, whereas the Gospel of Luke preserves a form of the Lord's Prayer that the Gospel writer, who was a disciple of Paul and not of Jesus himself, received through others. Abelard, citing both versions in their entirety, shows that Matthew has seven petitions, Luke only five. He interprets seven as carrying greater numerological weight than five, since it is a perfect number associated with sevenfold mercy rather than an imperfect one bound up in the five senses. Because of its greater perfection, the Fathers had preferred the Lord's Prayer as Matthew transmitted it to the wording in Luke. Yet the Lord's Prayer in the liturgy of Abelard's day (and of today) describes the bread as being *quotidianum* (daily, the adjective in Luke) rather than *supersubstantialem* (supersubstantial, as in Matthew). Abelard sees the resulting text as being a presumptuous pastiche, true to neither Jesus Christ nor any one of the Gospel writers, and he views his alternative not as being newfangled but on the contrary as clinging more faithfully to the Greek original from which the Latin of the Vulgate Gospel of Matthew was translated. (As a point of fact, the discrepancy in the adjective between Matthew and Luke is not detectable in the Greek, which has ἐπιούσιν—the equivalent of *supersubstantialem*—in both passages. It was Jerome who rendered the word in two different fashions in the Latin. Thus Abelard is tripped up by his lack of skill in the very scriptural languages and texts that he singles out in Letter Nine as being essential objects of study.)[16]

16. In Sermon 14 (*PL* 178: 489A–95D, at 493D–94D), Abelard reiterates the argument that he advances here to justify his insistence on using the adjective *supersubstantial* in place of *daily* in the Lord's Prayer. He also deals with the question in his *Explication of the Lord's Prayer, with the Incipit "We have read the prayers of many"*; see Charles S. F. Burnett, ed., "'Expositio Orationis Dominicae'—*Multorum legimus orationes*—Abelard's Exposition of the Lord's Prayer?" *Revue bénédictine* 95 (1985): 60–72.

Abelard's Letter Ten not only delivers a stout defense of his Lord's Prayer but also modulates into a critique of the Cistercians for themselves being too innovative in their liturgy. This counter-charge, backed by mentions of six specific innovations, would have been irksome to as prominent a Cistercian as Bernard, since the over-riding aim of the Order was not to *innovate* but instead to *renovate*— to reinvigorate the spirit of early monasticism in general and of Benedict in particular.[17] Furthermore, on the conceptual spectrum of Christian and Latin tradition, renewal and novelty stood at oppo-site poles.[18]

The new, in contradistinction to the renewing, was likely to result from pride and to lead to heresy. Thus Bernard of Clairvaux's letters against Peter Abelard, both before and after the Council of Sens, are replete with striking phrases that tax the controversial teacher with all the wrong sorts of newness. Two letters addressed to Pope In-nocent II before the council are cases in point. In the first Bernard charges that "[a] new Gospel is being forged for the peoples and na-tions, a new faith is being proposed, a foundation different from what has been laid is being set."[19] In the second Bernard first rails at Abelard as a *new* theologian and then accuses him, among many other misdeeds, of having heaped *new* heretical dogmas atop his old ones and of having brought forth *new* profanities in both words and meaning.[20]

In the end Bernard has demonized Abelard into being a heretical viper, filled with the venom of newness.[21] Was Bernard giving tit for tat? Here, ten years earlier, it is Abelard who addresses Bernard and the Cistercians as being "newly arisen"—and Abelard's later refer-

17. See Chrysogonus Waddell, "Peter Abelard's *Letter 10* and Cistercian Liturgical Reform," in John R. Sommerfeldt, ed., *Studies in Medieval Cistercian History* 2 (Kalama-zoo, Mich.: Cistercian Publications, 1976), 75–86.

18. Beryl Smalley, "Ecclesiastical Attitudes to Novelty, c. 1100–1250," *Studies in Church History* 12 (1975): 113–31.

19. Letter 189.2, in *Sancti Bernardi opera*, 7: 13, line 21. Compare Letter 190.12, 8: 27, line 11, and Letter 330, 8: 267, line 9.

20. Letter 190.1.1–2, in *Sancti Bernardi opera*, 8: 17, line 14; 8: 17, line 18; 8: 18, line 25. Compare Letter 192, in *Sancti Bernardi opera*, 7: 43, line 17, and Letter 332, 8: 271, line 11.

21. Letter 331, in *Sancti Bernardi opera*, 8: 270, line 8.

ence in the *Historia calamitatum* to "new apostles" should perhaps be put in the backdrop as we strive to sort out the implications of this characterization. It is Abelard who comes up with a new conception of *novitas* itself, one that Bernard may have found abhorrent.

In reviewing the Cistercian liturgy, Abelard evidences a surprisingly minute acquaintance with their worship. It seems unlikely that he could have become conversant with Cistercian worship solely from secondhand information, although he had to have done so in his remarks about the rite of Milan, a city he had never visited. The extent of his familiarity with Cistercian practices raises the question of where he could have engaged in the industrial espionage necessary to acquaint himself with the ins and outs of their office. The White Monks were often taxed with being secretive about their liturgical practices, to the extent of not permitting visiting monks from other orders to witness their forms of worship. Possibly the Paraclete itself was the venue of his "on-site" experience, if the nuns of the convent had been allowed the means to try out elements of the Cîteaux rituals.[22]

Whatever his source of knowledge, Abelard accuses the White Monks of being aberrant first of all in their hymnal—for rejecting traditional hymns, for introducing other unfamiliar ones, and for reusing the "Aeterne rerum conditor" (Eternal Creator of the World) throughout the year for the vigils—and for not having special devotions for the saints, even the Virgin. His roll call of other deviancies in the Cistercian liturgy includes the near absence of processions, the presence of the alleluia (which was usually set aside during Lent as a token of mourning) all the way to Easter, and other tamperings with the liturgy of Holy Week. With a backhanded magnanimity, he volunteers to be tolerant of the Cistercians for their odd practices if in turn they allow him to be true to the words and spirit of Christ in his version of the Lord's Prayer. According to him, diversity is good so long as its practitioners remain aware that common practice (*usus*) counts for less than logical method (*ratio*), and custom (*consuetudo*) less than truth (*veritas*). He comes out with a crystal-clear statement

22. Waddell, "Saint Bernard," 105.

of principle: everyone should ensure "that usage not be preferred to logic nor custom to truth." These final assertions make the letter consonant with Abelard's own method for resolving contradictions between authorities as set forth in the Prologue to the *Sic et non*. Seeing that Abelard relied to some degree in the *Sic et non* on Ivo in both methodology and specific content, it comes as no surprise to find that in this section of Letter Ten he taps heavily Ivo's *Decretum* for quotations.[23]

How did Bernard react to Letter Ten? No reply is extant—unless the Council of Sens itself embodies the response that Bernard felt was obligatory to restrain Abelard from applying his powers of reasoning as an individual to matters of consequence to the entire Christian community. Abelard, *magister* par excellence, epitomized the problems of accountability and authority that masters posed to the Church.

Letter Ten survives in a single, postmedieval paper manuscript, Paris, Bibliothèque nationale de France, MS lat. 13057 (last quarter of the sixteenth or first quarter of the seventeenth century). The codex is devoted to Abelardiana, with Prior Fulk of Deuil's letter to Abelard, Abelard's Letters Two through Seven, Abelard's Letter One, Abelard's *Confessio fidei "Universis,"* and finally Abelard's Letter Ten.[24]

Abelard's Letter Ten has been translated into Italian, in an edition with few but useful notes that have helped me to supplement my own and Smits's: *"Dacci oggi il nostro pane." Sermo 14 e Lettera 10*, trans. Edoardo Arborio Mella, Testi dei padri della chiesa 49 (Magnano, Italy: Edizioni Qiqajon, Monastero di Bose, 2001), 25–35.

23. Waddell, "Peter Abelard's Letter 10," 79.

24. Fulk's (or Fulco's) letter is edited in *PL* 178: 371–76. The omissions in the *PL* text of Fulk's letter can be filled by the text edited by Damien Van den Eynde, "Détails biographiques sur Pierre Abélard," *Antonianum* 38 (1963): 217–23, at 219. The letter reconstituted on this basis has been translated into English and can be consulted at *http://www.fordham.edu/halsall/source/fulk-abelard.html* (accessed 1 July 2006). A French translation of Fulk's letter exists in Yves Ferroul, *Héloïse et Abélard: Lettres et vies* (Paris: GF-Flammarion, 1996), Appendix 2, 197–205.

LETTER TEN

To Bernard, venerable and most dearly beloved brother in Christ, abbot of Clairvaux, his fellow priest Peter [sends greeting].

When recently I had come to the Paraclete under the press of certain business matters to be handled there, your daughter in Christ and my sister, who is called abbess of that place,[25] related to me with the highest exultation that you, after having been desired for a long time, had come there for the sake of a holy visitation and that you, not so much a human being but (as it were) an angel, had strengthened her as well as her sisters with encouragements to holiness.[26]

Yet privately she indicated to me that you were somewhat distressed in the charity with which you embrace me in particular, because in the daily offices the Lord's Prayer was not customarily recited there in that oratory in the same way as it is usually recited elsewhere, and since you believed that this was done on my account, that I seemed in this regard remarkable (as if for some sort of innovation).[27] Having heard this, I decided to write you my justification in this regard (for what it is worth), since I was especially sorry, as is appropriate, at offending you, more than at offending all others.

It is evident, as you know, that we hold this Lord's Prayer for a certainty to have been committed to writing by Matthew and

25. The phrase "who is called abbess of that place" may well allude to the fact that when Abelard wrote the letter, Heloise was not yet officially the abbess, since the status of the Paraclete as a convent had not been confirmed by the pope.

26. The suggestion that Bernard is perceived as being an angel rather than a human being is not necessarily entirely complimentary. In a passage in Letter Twelve, Abelard likens to angels those who deliberately surround themselves in the world with the attractions of the opposite sex.

27. The phraseology may imply that Abelard believed Bernard to accord him a special affection, but then again the wording may assume that Bernard showed *caritas* to everyone and that he was distressed specifically in the *caritas* that he extended to Abelard individually.

Luke alone, of whom Matthew, apostle as well as evangelist, was present for this prayer when it was handed down; for which reason there is no doubt that he wrote it more fully and completely, like the whole sermon held on the mount in which it is included.[28] But Luke, the disciple of Paul, was not present at this sermon and did not write what he heard from the Lord's mouth, but what he learned through the report especially of Paul (who it is a fact was not present at the sermon). In addition, he writes not that more complete speech of the Lord, which he held on the mount with the apostles, but that which he made to the throngs on the plains.[29] For the Lord, when he was going to choose the apostles, went out upon a mountain, as is written [Matthew 5.1 and Luke 6.12]; but when he was going to teach the throngs, he returned to the plains [Luke 6.17]. In fact, he ascended to the mountain and descended to the plains, so that he might show openly how much higher that teaching was by which he taught the teachers themselves. In short, as Saint Jerome attests, we know, just as self-evident truth holds, that "things that have been heard are told in one way, things that have been seen in another, and what we understand better, we also bring forth better."[30]

Matthew drank from the very source, Luke from the stream of the source. We do not accuse Luke of lying, nor does he grow angry at us, if we should place Matthew before him, or if we should

28. The Sermon on the Mount, which begins with the Eight Beatitudes ("Blessed are the poor in spirit" and so forth), contains the Lord's Prayer in its middle. In the Synoptic Gospels Mark makes no mention of the sermon. As Abelard elucidates, Matthew devotes three successive chapters (5–7) to it, whereas Luke divides this material into parts.

29. The tradition that Luke was the disciple of Paul dates at the latest to Irenaeus of Lyon, *Adversus haereses* (Against Heresies) 3.1.1, ed. and trans. (German) Brox, 3 (1995): 24, lines 5–7: "Et Lucas autem sectator Pauli quod ab illo praedicabatur evangelium in libro condidit" (And Luke also, companion of Paul, recorded in a book the Gospel preached by him).

30. Jerome, "Prologus in Pentateucho," in *Biblia sacra*, ed. Weber and Gryson, p. 4, lines 38–39, quoted in his *Contra Rufinum* (known also as *Apologia aduersus libros Rufini*) 2.25, ed. P. Lardet, CCSL 79 (1982): 1–72, at 63, lines 61–62.

prefer the Lord's Prayer which was rendered collectively to all the apostles and written by an apostle to the one which was spoken to a certain disciple, especially since it is obvious that the one of Matthew is preeminent in authority as in completeness. However, so that we may judge better about each of the two when it is (as it were) set before our eyes, it is useful to include each of the two in the present passage.

Just as Matthew writes, therefore, when he [Jesus] handed down the aforesaid prayer to the apostles, he [Jesus] said:

Thus therefore you will pray: "Our Father who art in heaven, hallowed be thy name. Thy kingdom come. Thy will be done on earth as it is in heaven. Give us this day our supersubstantial bread. And forgive us our debts, as we also forgive our debtors. And lead us not into temptation. But deliver us from evil" [Matthew 6.9–13].

Luke in fact says as follows:

And it came to pass, that as he was in a certain place praying, when he ceased, one of his disciples said to him: "Lord, teach us to pray, as John also taught his disciples." And he said to them: "When you pray, say: 'Father, hallowed be thy name. Thy kingdom come. Give us this day our daily bread. And forgive us our sins, for we also forgive every one that is indebted to us. And lead us not into temptation'" [Luke 11.1–4].

Thus it is obvious that Matthew wrote more completely, as I recalled above, than Luke, since plainly the former put seven petitions in the prayer and the latter only five. Indeed Matthew's prayer was transmitted more completely to the apostles, as was fitting, and was established in that number of petitions, whereby the fullness of the sevenfold grace is signified, concerning which Paul avows that the apostles themselves received the first and superior gifts, saying: "ourselves also, who have the firstfruits of the Spirit" [Romans 8.23] and so forth.[31] But Luke's prayer, which he reports

31. Isaiah 11.2–3 lists seven kinds of spirit that will rest upon the one who flowers from the root of Jesse. These seven spirits became the basis for the tradition of the seven gifts of the Holy Spirit.

was rendered by the Lord to one of the disciples who requested it long after the sermon held on the mount, not without cause indicates the import of its incompleteness in the very fivefold number of the petitions. For the senses of the body are five, just as the gifts of the spirit are seven. For this reason this number well suits those senses, which inasmuch as fleshly are to such a degree inferior to spiritual ones.

I think that this is not to be doubted about that one disciple, who it is apparent was not present among the disciples on the mount when the Lord handed down to them the New Covenant, in which (as we said) he included also the very prayer that that same apostle had not yet heard. Likewise, when he said "Lord, teach us to pray, as John also taught his disciples" [Luke 11.1] in calling to mind John [the Baptist], who was less than Christ in all ways and more incomplete, he acknowledged also that very incompleteness of his own understanding. It is often evident too that the law, which consists of five books, and was given to a fleshly people led more by its senses than by reason and avid for bodily goods more than for spiritual, was expressed figuratively through John.[32] For this reason it happened fittingly that he who sought from Christ the instruction of a prayer of the sort that John had given should be obliged to receive one more incomplete than that of the apostle. Indeed, on account of its incompleteness, it was rightly foreseen by the holy fathers that in its stead that prayer which is written more completely by Matthew would come into use and would be practiced regularly in the offices of the Church.

The person who can should say (if, in spite of what has been said, he has the capacity to do so) what cause therefore existed, that we should change one word alone of Matthew but keep the rest, to wit, saying *daily* instead of *supersubstantial.* For this word *dai-*

32. The remark about the five books of course relates to the Pentateuch, while the closing reference is to John 1.17: "For the law was given by Moses: grace and truth came by Jesus Christ."

ly does not seem to convey so well the superiority of this bread as does *supersubstantial*. In addition, it seems to be immoderately presumptuous to amend the words of an apostle and thus to put together out of two Gospel writers one prayer, in such a way that in it neither of the two alone seems to be adequate, and to bring it forth in a form in which it was neither spoken by the Lord nor written by any one of the evangelists. This is especially the case, since in all the rest of the texts which are recited from their writings in the Church, their words are not intermingled, no matter what the extent to which they differ in completeness or incompleteness.

If consequently anyone should censure me for innovation in this regard, let him consider whether that man is more to be censured who had the presumption to compose one new prayer from two written in ancient times—a prayer to be called not so much the Gospel writer's as his own. In sum, the discernment of the Greeks, whose "authority is greater" (as Ambrose says), brought into customary use only Matthew's prayer for the reasons that have been stated (in my opinion), saying, namely, *arton imon epiousion*, which is rendered "our supersubstantial bread."[33] For although Luke wrote in Greek and Matthew in Hebrew, the Greeks decided nonetheless instead to favor the use of the more ancient and complete prayer of the foreign language and to follow the translation rather than the written version in their own language.[34]

Accordingly, unless I am mistaken, by these principles as well as by these authorities, I seem to demand censure for being old-fashioned rather than newfangled and I seem less to be criticized for presumption, I who in this matter follow particularly the Lord as well as the apostles and the obvious foresight of the Greeks. For it is beyond doubt that the apostles regularly practiced this prayer

33. Ambrose, *De incarnationis dominicae sacramento* 8.82, ed. Otto Faller, CSEL 79 (1964): 225–81, at 265.

34. On the notion that Matthew wrote in Hebrew, see note 81 to Letter Nine.

handed down to them by the Lord and first written by the apostle in the same words in which they had received it from the Lord and in which the apostle had transmitted it in writing. For who would not judge that those who live in common and in so doing live a most apostolic life ought likewise to insist especially upon the teaching of the apostles?[35]

In short, since the Lord transmitted this prayer, either in these words according to Matthew or in those according to Luke, and enjoined that it be said as he transmitted it, who would not see that they are more than a little presumptuous, who say it in such a manner as it was never transmitted by the Lord himself or written by someone? For how great is the presumption in this prayer neither to follow something written nor to hold fast to the precept of the Lord, but rather to dare to emend what is written as well as the Lord himself, if by chance this presumptuousness can be called emendation?

All the same, I enjoin no one, I urge no one to follow me in this and to depart from customary usage. "Let every man abound in his own sense" [Romans 14.5]. Yet let that person, whosoever he may be, pay heed to that dictum, and pay heed that usage not be preferred to logic nor custom to truth. Indeed, the laws of the world as well as the teachings of the holy fathers saw fit to commend this very much to us. Book 8, Chapter 1 of the Code [of Justinian] states: "The authority of longstanding practice and distinguished use is not beneath contempt, but in and of itself it is not going to be for a moment capable of prevailing over either reason or law."[36] Augustine, in *On Baptism* Book 4, says: "In vain do

35. The notion that those who live in common live an apostolic life is a convention attested as early as John Cassian (about 360–435), *Conlationes* 18.5, ed. Michael Petschenig, CSEL 13 (1886): 509, lines 19–20, which opens with the sentence "Itaque coenobiotarum disciplina a tempore praedicationis apostolicae sumpsit exordium" (And so the system of coenobites took its rise in the days of the preaching of the apostles).

36. Emperor Justinian I (483–565) produced the *Corpus iuris civilis* (529–534), a

those who are overcome by reason raise custom as an objection to us, as if custom were greater than truth or as if what had been revealed for the better by the Holy Spirit were not to be followed in spiritual matters. This is plainly true, inasmuch as reason and truth must be preferred to custom."[37] Gregory VII wrote to Wimund, bishop of Aversa:[38] "If perhaps you adduced custom, what the Lord says should be pointed out: 'I am,' he said, 'the truth' [John 14.6]; he did not say, 'I am custom.'"[39] What is more, blessed Gregory, writing about the different customs of Churches to Bishop Augustine of the English, leaves to his foresight to choose in divine offices or in the celebration of the mass from the various uses

codification of Roman law in three parts. One part is the *Codex*, conventionally known as *Justinian's Code*. The statement Abelard quotes is found in the *Codex*, Book 8.52(53).2 (Emperor Constantine to Proculus), in *Corpus juris civilis*, ed. Paul Krueger, Theodor Mommsen, Rudolf Schöll, and Wilhelm Kroll, 3 vols. (Berlin: Weidmann, 1963–1965), vol. 2, ed. Paul Krueger, p. 362. But Abelard's immediate source for this and the following two quotations is Ivo of Chartres, *Panormia* 2.163, in *PL* 161: 1041A–1344D, at 1120C. Ivo's *Decretum* in particular was a resource with which Abelard, had he not known it already, could have become conversant during his studies with Anselm of Laon; see Mews, *Abelard and Heloise*, 37.

37. Augustine, *De baptismo contra Donatistas libri vii* 4.5.7, ed. Michael Petschenig, CSEL 51 (1908): 143–375, at 228. This passage is substantially a quotation from Cyprian, Letter 73.13.1, in *Epistulae*, ed. G. F. Diercks, CCSL 3A–D (1996–1999), at 3C. This passage too is quoted by Ivo of Chartres, *Decretum* 4.235, in *PL* 161: 48–1022D, at 315AB. Last but not least, it is quoted by Abelard himself in Letter Eight, trans. Radice, p. 168.

38. St. Gregory VII was pope from 1073 to 1085, while Wimund was a supporter who later became bishop of the south Italian diocese of Aversa.

39. *Epistola 69 extra registrum*, in *PL* 148: 713CD. Although this letter has been traditionally ascribed to Gregory VII, it could also be the work of Urban II (1088–1099). On the lineage of this observation on custom, see André Gouron, "'Non dixit: Ego sum consuetudo,'" *Zeitschrift der Savigny-Stiftung für Rechtsgeschichte. Kanonistische Abteilung* 105 (1988): 133–40.

This passage was quoted three times by Ivo of Chartres, *Decretum* 4.213 and 4.234, in *PL* 161: 311BC and 315A, and *Panormia* 2.166, in *PL* 161: 1121A. Abelard uses it in Letter Eight as well, where he quotes it from Augustine, *De baptismo*: it appears in Augustine's treatise at both 3.6.9 and 6.37.71, ed. Petschenig, CSEL 51: 203 and 334. In the Latin *opponas* does not here mean "oppose," but instead "adduce (in support of a position)."

of others whatever he decided, and in such matters not to follow so much even the very mother Church of Rome as that which he deemed worthy to maintain:[40]

Your brotherhood knows (he said) the custom of the Roman Church, in which it recalls having been raised. [. . .] But I decree that you choose carefully if you have found something that can please omnipotent God more, whether in the Roman, Gallican, or some other Church, and that you instill into the Church of the English (which is still newly come to the faith) whatever you have been able to gather from many Churches by way of special usage. For you do not correct things on behalf of places but places on behalf of good things. Therefore choose from every individual Church those traits which are pious, religious, and right, and set these down, gathered as it were into a sheaf, as a custom among the minds of the English.[41]

But if it be permitted us in such matters to choose from among the customs of the Churches, it does not seem that our choice must be rejected. In this our choice even imitated the provident care of the Greeks, from whom we have received much learning, so that the very authority of custom should not be lacking from so self-evident a principle. Thus we see plainly that you insist upon this principle and that you are adamant about it in such fashion that you dare to hold and maintain it against the custom of all Churches in divine offices. To be sure, you, as if newly arisen and rejoicing greatly in your newness, contrary to the custom held by all clerics as well as monks far in the past and enduring now too, established by certain new decrees that the divine office should be conducted otherwise among you. And yet you consider that you

40. St. Gregory I (the Great) was pope from 590 until his death in 604. St. Augustine was the first bishop of Canterbury and apostle of the English (died 604).

41. Gregory the Great, *Registrum epistolarum* 11.56a, ed. Paul Ewald and Ludwig Hartmann, Monumenta Germaniae Historica: Epistolae 1–2, 2 vols. (Berlin: Weidmann, 1887–1899), 2: 334 = 11.64 in *PL* 77: 1187AB. This letter, the authenticity of which has been controverted, is quoted in Bede, *Ecclesiastical History of the English People*, 1.27, ed. and trans. Bertram Colgrave and R. A. B. Mynors (Oxford, U.K.: Clarendon Press, 1969).

are not to be faulted then, if this novelty or uniqueness of yours departs from the old habit of others, seeing that you believe it to accord very much with the principle and tenor of the Rule, and you do not care with however much astonishment others are disturbed concerning this and mutter, so long as you obey your principle (as you think it).

To call to mind a few of these matters, with all due respect to you, you have rejected the usual hymns and you have instituted certain ones unheard of among us, unknown to almost all the Churches, and less adequate.[42] For this reason you content yourselves with one and the same hymn throughout even the whole year on the vigils of ferias as well as of feast days, even though in accordance with the difference of the ferias and feast days, the Church employs different hymns, just as in the case of Psalms too and other texts which are known to relate to these, as self-evident reason also demands. For this cause those who hear you always singing the same hymn (namely, "Aeterne rerum conditor") on Christmas Day, Easter, or Pentecost and other holidays are stopped in their tracks, stunned with the highest stupefaction, and they are stirred not so much to wonderment as to mockery.[43]

42. Although not all the hymns used traditionally in Benedictine monasteries were absent from Cistercian ones, many were indeed omitted from the practices of Cîteaux. Furthermore, the Cistercian rite included hymns taken from the Ambrosian rite (followed in Milan and a limited number of other locations), which would have been unfamiliar to many monks elsewhere.

43. The famous *Regula Benedicti* (Rule of Benedict, the work of Benedict of Nursia [about 480–543]), the basis for Western monasticism, stipulates that the night office should include "an Ambrosian hymn" or "the Ambrosian hymn," which in either case could be construed (as it was often in the twelfth century) to mean a hymn by Ambrose (9.4 "Inde sequatur ambrosianum"): ed. Hanslik, CSEL 75: 54. The Rule uses the noun *ambrosianum* three more times: 12.4, ed. Hanslik, CSEL 75: 60; 31.11, ed. Hanslik, 75: 62; and 17.8, ed. Hanslik, 75: 67. Later the Rule refers to the "Te Deum laudamus" (11.8), which at the time of Benedict was commonly ascribed to Ambrose, and to the "Te decet laus" (11.10). Although Benedict uses the word *ambrosianum* only in connection with matins, lauds, and vespers, these references sufficed to instill in the Cistercians their insistence on using throughout all the canonical hours noth-

You have forbidden altogether to be performed by us prayers that are everywhere celebrated by the Church after supplication and the Lord's Prayer, and those which are called the litanies of the saints, as if the world had less need of your prayers or you of the litanies of the saints.[44] And, what is a source of wonder, although you establish all your places of prayer in memory of the Lord's mother, you practice no commemoration of her, just as you do not do so of the other saints there.[45] You have excluded from yourselves almost the whole celebration of processions.[46] You do not leave off in Septuagesima the alleluia in the usual way, but you retain it into Lent.[47] The creed which is called the Apostolic Creed, which has been repeated from ancient times by clerics as well as monks at prime and likewise at compline, has been removed from your custom[48]—you who nevertheless decided that the Athana-

---

ing but a single Ambrosian hymn, such as the "Aeterne rerum conditor." (Note that the White Monks restricted themselves to hymns supposedly composed by St. Ambrose, and preserved in the Milanese repertory, not merely to hymns conforming to the metrical scheme favored by Ambrose.) The first Cistercian hymnal contains only thirty-four hymns, sung to only nineteen melodies, all drawn from Ambrosian sources; see Waddell, "St. Bernard," 101.

44. These litanies could be called suffrages, a somewhat less-known term to designate the assemblage of antiphons, versicles, and collects to honor especially important saints.

45. All Cistercian churches were dedicated to the Virgin Mary. The commemoration of a saint usually took place on his or her memorial day, in most cases the day of martyrdom or death.

46. When Abelard wrote Letter Ten, the Cistercians restricted themselves to processions on Candlemas Day and Palm Sunday; see Waddell, "Peter Abelard's *Letter 10*," 81.

47. Septuagesima was the ninth Sunday before Easter and the third before Lent. Despite the implications of its Latin name (which means "seventieth"), it fell sixty-four rather than seventy days before Easter. In any event, it signaled the start of changes in the liturgy (such as the wearing of purple vestments and the setting aside of the alleluia) that intensified in Lent and reached a peak in Holy Week. For the Cistercians to keep the alleluia in their office into Lent marked them very much apart from not merely other monks but even other churchgoing Christians.

48. The Apostolic or Apostles' Creed (*Symbolum Apostolorum*) was so named because it was legendarily ascribed to the twelve apostles. An encapsulation of the fun-

sian Creed be recited only on Sundays.[49] You sing the "Gloria"
only with the responsories of vigils.[50] You have done away altogether with ancient custom on the days of the Lord's burial; at the
same time you established, against every practice of the Church
and against (as people say) logic, that you say with the "Gloria"
both the invitatory and hymn together with only three lessons and
responsories. For since this three-day period, as the funeral rites
of the Lord, is conducted in mourning and since for this reason
the vigils of these days are commonly called Tenebrae [a Latin
word meaning "darkness"], that this sorrow may be conveyed by
the lamps which are extinguished there and then, it seems not a
small cause for wonder for either the invitatory, hymn, or "Gloria"
(which are in contrast expressions of joy) to be sung then.[51]

---

damental tenets in Christian belief, it comprises a set of brief articles pertaining to
God, Jesus Christ, and the Holy Spirit. For further information, refer to J. N. D. Kelly, *Early Christian Creeds*, 3rd ed. (London: Longman, 1972), 368–434. The practice of
reciting the Creed upon awakening and upon going to bed is mentioned already by
Augustine, Sermon 58.11.13, in *PL* 38–39: 332–1638, at 38: 399.

49. The Athanasian Creed, known also from its incipit as the "Quicunque vult,"
is no longer ascribed to the famous archbishop of Alexandria but instead is thought
to have originated in the Latin West, probably in southern Gaul. It offers a succinct
exposition of the doctrines of the Trinity and the Incarnation. For further information, refer to J. N. D. Kelly, *The Athanasian Creed* (New York: Harper & Row: 1964).
As was mentioned in the general introduction, Abelard himself wrote expositions on
both the Apostolic Creed and the Athanasian Creed.

50. The "Gloria" designates "Gloria in excelsis Deo" (Glory to God on high),
the greater doxology in the mass. (A doxology is a short formula of praise to God.)
Since it begins with the words sung by the angels at Christ's birth (Luke 2.14), it is
often referred to as the *hymnus angelicus* (angelic hymn). The Latin "Gloria," which derives from an ancient Greek hymn modeled on the Psalms, was customarily sung after
the "Kyrie" on Sundays and solemnities, except during the Advent and Lent seasons.

51. During the last three days of Holy Week which are known technically as the
Sacred Triduum, the Cistercians were unique in still chanting the night office with
the invitatory psalm (Psalm 94, which "invited" the celebrants to sing praise to
God), hymn, and a responsory with doxology, as was done in the conventional week-
day form of the office; see Waddell, *Hymn Collections*, 1: 91, and Waddell, "St. Bernard,"
100. Tenebrae is the name for the service of matins and lauds (but to be anticipated
and sung shortly after compline) during the Triduum.

All these matters come as a source of great wonderment to everyone, which is to say, why this innovation of yours should be preferred among your people to the usage of the whole Church. Even so, you do not on this account retreat from your practice nor do you care what others mutter, because you have confidence that you are doing it logically—you whom the establishment of a rule compels "to make a new work of an old," just as Jerome recalls about himself.[52] For the Apostle [Paul] does not forbid "novelties of words" [1 Timothy 6.20], but only novelties that are "profane" [1 Timothy 6.20] and contrary to faith. Otherwise we would not prefer the New Law to the Old and we would reject in the manner of heretics many words devised, after the canonical Scriptures, out of need for the faith. Indeed, to reject a new heresy a new word *homoousion* was invented, and the words *Trinity* and *person* were not included in the canonical Scriptures.[53]

In short, who does not know the differing and countless customs of the Church present among even clerics themselves in divine offices? Certainly not even the city of Rome itself holds to the ancient custom of the Roman see, but only the Lateran Church, which is the mother of all, holds to the ancient office, with none of her daughters following her in this, not even the very basilica of the Roman palace.[54] In matters of this kind the metropolitan Church of Milan diverges from all, in such fashion that none even

52. Jerome, "Praefatio in Evangelio," in *Biblia sacra*, ed. Weber and Gryson, p. 1515, line 2.

53. The term *homoousion* (of the same essence or substance) was used in the Nicene Creed (325) to ward off Arianism by expressing the relations of the Father and the Son within the Trinity. It corresponds to the Latin *consubstantialis*. The Christian Latin neologism *trinitas*, translating the slightly earlier Greek *trias*, is attested first in Tertullian (flourished 197–220), *De pudicitia* 21.16 (line 77), ed. and trans. Charles Munier, 2 vols., Sources chrétiennes 394–395 (Paris: Editions du Cerf, 1993), 1: 274, before coming into general usage in the third century. *Persona* existed in Classical Latin, but not in the senses that the word acquired among Christians.

54. The Latin for the final phrase is "Romani palatii basilica," which refers to St. Peter's, the basilica that lies at the foot of the Vatican Hill. In the twelfth century the popes had a residence, known as a *palatium*, located adjacent to the basilica.

of her dependent churches seeks to resemble the practice of the mother Church.[55] So too Lyon, the first see of the Gauls, alone persists in its office.[56]

And although so great a variety has come about in these matters, no censure for innovation occurs, no matter what one Church after another has established in a new fashion, because there was nothing contrary to the faith. For this variety in the divine rite has a measure of attractiveness, because, as Cicero recalls, "in all things monotony is the mother of boredom."[57] Therefore he who wished to be preached in all kinds of tongues enjoined that worship be done in different manners of offices.[58] Since he also com-

55. For "dependent churches," Abelard uses the word *suffraganeae* (suffragan), which designates churches subordinate to a metropolitan or archiepiscopal see.

56. The Church of Lyon maintained its own rites throughout the Middle Ages, as Bernard himself acknowledged in a letter (Letter 174.1, in *Sancti Bernardi opera*, 7: 388, lines 5–8) to the canons of the city that betrays intriguing parallels to Abelard's Letter Ten:

> Inter ecclesias Galliae constat profecto Lugdunensem hactenus praeeminuisse, sicut dignitate sedis, sic honestis studiis et laudabilibus institutis. . . . Praesertim in officiis ecclesiasticis haud facile umquam repentinis visa est novitatibus acquiescere, nec se aliquando iuvenili passa est decolorari levitate ecclesia plena iudicii.

> Among the Churches of France, it is established that that of Lyon has until now held ascendancy, as much for the dignity of its see as for its honorable studies and praiseworthy institutions. . . . Especially in the divine offices this judicious Church has never seemed readily to acquiesce in sudden novelties, and has never suffered to be stained by the inconstancy typical of youth.

57. Cicero, *De inventione* 1.41.76. Evidently Abelard much valued the saying, since he also uses it in the Prologue to the *Sic et non*, ed. Boyer and McKeon, p. 89, lines 14–15; in the *Theologia "Summi boni"* 2.77, ed. Buytaert and Mews, CCCM 13: 140, lines 693–94; in the *Theologia Christiana* 3.133, ed. Buytaert, CCCM 12: 245, lines 1621–22; and in the *Theologia "Scholarium"* 2.90, ed. Buytaert and Mews, CCCM 13: 452, lines 1348–49. On Abelard's use of Cicero in general, see Gabriella d'Anna, "Abelardo e Cicerone," *Studi medievali*, 3rd series, 10 (1969): 333–419. In the present collection of letters Cicero is also quoted in the *Apologia* against Bernard of Clairvaux and twice in Letter Twelve (once being the *Rhetoric to Herennius*, which from a modern vantage point qualifies only as pseudo-Ciceronian).

58. The wording "omnium linguarum generibus" may owe to "genera linguarum" in 1 Corinthians 12.10, 12.28, and 14.10. Even without this allusion, it would be clear that the subject of this and the following sentence is Jesus Christ.

posed the aforementioned prayer in different manners and commanded that the praying in it be done in each of two ways, how will we fulfill his command, if we presume to remove some word and if we never profess it in the manner in which he said it?

In sum, so that I may satisfy everyone, I say now even as further above, "Let every man abound in his own sense" [Romans 14.5]. Let him say it as he wishes. I prompt no one to follow me in this. Let him change the words of Christ as he wishes. However I will retain unaltered those words, as too their meaning, insofar as I am able.

6

LETTER FIFTEEN. TO HIS COMRADES,
AGAINST ABBOT BERNARD

The present letter relates to the famous collision between Peter
Abelard and Bernard of Clairvaux at the Council of Sens, which
was ostensibly concerned with Abelard's *Theologia* but which had
motivations and implications that transcended this one treatise and
the teachings associated with it. The chronology of this council has
been the object of copious analysis.[1] If an *opinio communis* now builds
and holds around a dating of the council in 1141, the sequence of
events would take the following shape. (If not, then in most cases a
year would need to be subtracted from most of the following dates,
since previously the prevailing tendency was to peg the council on
Sunday and Monday, 2–3 June 1140.) In Lent of 1140 Bernard of
Clairvaux receives from his close friend William of St. Thierry a
letter-treatise. In it William impugns thirteen allegedly mistaken

1. The fullest and most recent stocktaking in English, together with a presentation of the council in a broad sociohistorical context, can be had in Constant J.
Mews, "The Council of Sens (1141): Bernard, Abelard and the Fear of Social Upheaval," *Speculum* 77 (2002): 342–82. Other important studies that have appeared lately
are Peter Godman, *The Silent Masters: Latin Literature and Its Censors in the High Middle Ages*
(Princeton, N.J.: Princeton University Press, 2000), 61–103; Wim Verbaal, "Sens: Une
victoire d'écrivain. Les deux visages du procès d'Abélard," in *Pierre Abélard. Colloque international de Nantes*, 77–89; and Pietro Zerbi, *"Philosophi" e "Logici": Un ventennio di incontri
e scontri: Soissons, Sens, Cluny (1121–1141)*, Istituto storico italiano per il medio evo: Nuovi studi storici 59 (Rome: Nella sede dell'Istituto, Palazzo Borromini, 2002).

doctrines of Abelard, who was once (but is no longer?) a friend of his.[2]

Even if Bernard nurses no hidden grudges against Abelard for past injuries to himself or to his supporters, the climate is bound to be tense. The boundaries between teachings and writings look hazy, as do those between a master's teachings and his students' reports of them. It is not possible always to differentiate emphatically between what a teacher teaches and what his listeners understand. As a consequence masters are often held accountable for the impressions (and misimpressions) their followers take away from lectures, in notes, in memories, or in both. The issue of responsibility would be particularly problematic in the case of Abelard, who has been testing the patience of conservatives in the Church by his readiness, when confronting questions or uncertainties in doctrine, to apply logical analysis rather than to content himself with citing authorities.

Matters are not helped by the fact that Bernard is able to present Abelard as being in an unholy alliance with a former student of his, Arnold of Brescia (about 1090–1155). For rebelling against his bishop in Brescia and for speaking out against the policy of allowing the Church to own property, the canon and abbot Arnold has been ex-

2. On William's relationship with Abelard and knowledge of his writings and thought, see Jean Châtillon, "Guillaume de Saint-Thierry, le monachisme et les écoles: À propos de Rupert de Deutz, d'Abélard et de Guillaume de Conches," in *Saint-Thierry: Une abbaye du VIe au XXe siècle: Actes du Colloque international d'histoire monastique, Reims-Saint-Thierry, 11 au 14 octobre 1976,* ed. Michel Bur (Saint-Thierry, France: Association des Amis de l'Abbaye de Saint-Thierry, 1979), 375–94; Thomas Michael Tomasic, "William of Saint-Thierry against Peter Abelard: A Dispute on the Meaning of Being a Person," *Analecta Cisterciensia* 28 (1972): 3–76; and Piero Zerbi, "Guillaume de Saint-Thierry et son différend avec Abélard," in *Saint-Thierry, une abbaye du VIe au XXe siècle, Actes du colloque international d'histoire monastique, Reims-Saint-Thierry, 1977* (Saint-Thierry, France: Association des Amis de l'Abbaye de Saint-Thierry, 1977), 395–412, repr. in Pietro Zerbi, *Ecclesia in hoc mundo posita: Studi di storia e di storiografia medioevale raccolti in occasione del 700 genetliaco dell'autore,* ed. Maria Pia Alberzoni, Bibliotheca erudita: Studi e documenti di storia e filologia 6 (Milan, Italy: Vita e pensiero, 1993), 549–76. On his correspondence with Bernard, see Jean Leclercq, "Les lettres de Guillaume de Saint-Thierry à saint Bernard," *Revue bénédictine* 79 (1968): 375–91, at 375–82, and M. Basil Pennington, "The Correspondence of William of St. Thierry," *Studia monastica: Commentarium ad rem monasticam investigandam* 18 (1976): 353–65.

pelled from Italy by Pope Innocent II (1130–1143), and he has come
not just to Paris but indeed to Mont Ste. Geneviève, where he is a
master at the church of St. Hilary. (It is conceivable, but far from
provable, that Abelard also teaches there and that their stays overlap.)
At Sens he is reputed to have defended Abelard against Bernard. In
a metaphor that manages to allude simultaneously to Abelard's actual noble birth and his combativeness as a disputant, Bernard casts
Abelard as Goliath, Arnold as his squire.[3] One of Innocent II's letters to condemn Abelard prescribed the same punishments for both
him and Arnold. About fifteen years later Arnold, who has by now
been expelled from France after denouncing Bernard, is captured
and put to death as a rebel with the assent of both the Holy Roman
Emperor, Frederick Barbarossa (1122–1190), and the pope, Adrian IV
(1154–1159).[4]

Against this strained backdrop, Abelard and Bernard meet twice
in the winter of 1140–1141 and discuss Abelard's allegedly mistaken
creeds. From Bernard's perspective, these rendez-vous follow both
the letter and the spirit of Gospel-certified procedures for dealing
with a wayward fellow Christian (Matthew 18.15–17), which escalate
from what could be termed *correctio fraternalis* (fraternal correction) to
denuntiatio evangelica (open denuntiation before the Church):

But if thy brother shall offend against thee, go, and rebuke him between
thee and him alone. If he shall hear thee, thou shalt gain thy brother. And if
he will not hear thee, take with thee one or two more: that in the mouth of

---

3. See Letter 189.3, in *Sancti Bernardi opera*, 7: 14, line 1: "Procedit Golias procero
corpore, nobili illo suo bellico apparatu circummunitus, antecedente quoque ipsum
armigero eius Arnaldo de Brixia" (Tall Goliath walks forward, defended on all sides
by all that war-gear of his, with his squire Arnold of Brescia walking before him).

4. On Arnold and Abelard, see Romedio Schmitz-Esser, "Arnold of Brescia in
Exile: April 1139 to December 1143," in *Exile in the Middle Ages: Selected Proceedings from
the International Medieval Congress, University of Leeds, 8–11 July 2002*, ed. Laura Napran
and Elisabeth van Houts, International Medieval Research 13 (Turnhout, Belgium:
Brepols, 2004), 213–31, at 217–20 and 229–30. On Arnold himself, the classic but dated biography in English remains George William Greenaway, *Arnold of Brescia* (Cambridge, U.K.: Cambridge University Press, 1931), while a definitive treatment is given
in Arsenio Frugoni, *Arnaldo da Brescia nelle fonti del secolo XII*, Istituto storico italiano per
il Medio Evo: Studi storici 8–9 (Rome: Nella sede dell'Istituto, 1954).

two or three witnesses every word may stand. And if he will not hear them: tell the Church. And if he will not hear the Church, let him be to thee as the heathen and publican.

These meetings appear to be cordial, but Abelard does not cede ground on the central points of his doctrine. Afterward, Bernard is entitled to believe that he has shown charity and restraint by trying to persuade Abelard to renounce his heterodox beliefs.

Abelard's reactions differ, especially after he learns from his supporters that Bernard has denounced his writings and teachings (though maybe not naming him) before the students of Paris, who would have included some loyal to Abelard, and has asked them to turn from the Babylon of student life in Paris to the Jerusalem of monasticism, as indeed a number have done by joining the Cistercian Order. It has been hypothesized that Bernard's attack before the students in Paris is preserved, in a reworked form, in his sermon *Ad clericos de conversione* (On Conversion, to Clerics).[5] Whatever the exact contours and contents of the sermon may have been, to Bernard it would have been the *denuntiatio evangelica*, the public denunciation that the Gospel according to Matthew stipulated. To Abelard it would have appeared a Judas-like betrayal from a hypocrite who had simulated friendliness in earlier encounters but who had in mind all along to undercut him or worse.

In addition, Abelard has read or heard that Bernard has referred contemptuously to his *Theologia* as the *Stultilogia* (Stupidology). In fact, in a letter that survives Bernard makes this very mockery, which also appears in a colophon in the manuscript of another contempo-

5. The Latin text is in *Sancti Bernardi opera*, 4: 59–116; the English is in G. R. Evans, trans., *Bernard of Clairvaux: Selected Works* (New York and Mahwah, N.J.: Paulist Press, 1987), 65–97, and in *Bernard of Clairvaux, Sermons on Conversion: On Conversion, A Sermon to Clerics and Lenten Sermons on the Psalm "He Who Dwells,"* translated by Marie-Bernard Saïd, Cistercian Fathers 25 (Kalamazoo, Mich.: Cistercian Publications, 1981), 31–79. In favor of the hypothesis, see Borst, "Abälard und Bernhard," 512–13, and against it, Pietro Zerbi, "San Bernardo di Chiaravalle e il concilio di Sens," in *Studi su s. Bernardo di Chiaravalle nell'ottavo centenario della canonizzazione: Convegno internazionale, Certosa di Firenze: 6–9 novembre 1974*, Bibliotheca Cisterciensis 6 (Rome: Editiones Cistercienses, 1975), 49–73, at 57.

rary text directed against Abelard's allegedly heretical doctrines.[6] The same letter by Bernard deals at length with the errors of Abelard.[7]

However Abelard became aware of Bernard's hostility, he feels both betrayed and threatened. The letter translated in the present section speaks to Abelard's sense that Bernard has been two-faced, in first meeting amiably with him and then publicly chastising him. Furthermore, Abelard suffers from a paranoia to which he is richly entitled, as far as the attitudes of the Church toward his writings and teachings are concerned. Consequently, he decides that his best defense is a good offense and that he will compel Bernard to debate him in public.[8] In this instance he knows that a group of bishops will assemble in Sens, after Pentecost, for a solemn exposition of the relics of St. Stephen, and accordingly he requests that Archbishop Henry Sanglier of Sens (1122–1142) convert this gathering into a synod. Thereafter Bernard writes to the bishops of France to rally them in defense of the faith,[9] while Abelard distributes a letter exhorting his friends and students to muster at Sens on the Sunday after Pentecost, when Abelard has proclaimed that he will stand ready to defend himself point by point against Bernard's accusations.

Though Abelard rarely displays much shrewdness about political realities, in this instance he must have realized that it could redound to his advantage to have his followers present in large numbers as a counterweight to all the Church officials involved in the proceedings, since (to put it mildly) not all of the ecclesiastics would be predisposed toward him. To whom Abelard would have sent the let-

6. See Bernard, Letter 190.4, to Pope Innocent II, in *Sancti Bernardi opera*, 8: 24, line 24. On the colophon, see the anonymous *Capitula haeresum Petri Abaelardi*, ed. Eligius M. Buytaert, *Petri Abaelardi opera theologica 2*, in CCCM 12 (1969). The *Capitula* are edited on 473–80; the colophon is discussed in the introduction on 457: "Haec sunt capitula Theologiae, immo Stultilogiae Petri Abaelardi" (These are the chapters of the *Theology*, or rather of the *Stupidology*, of Peter Abelard).

7. Bernard's other letters against Abelard (Letters 187–90, 192–93, 330–38) survive and are available in translation.

8. The decision is no departure from the reflexes he had displayed in the past, as can be seen in the remarkably similar way he tried to proceed twenty years earlier in a skirmish with Roscelin that Letter Fourteen allows us to glimpse.

9. Letters 187–88, in *Sancti Bernardi opera*, 8: 9–10.

ter initially cannot be determined, but may be irrelevant: the letter is a circular that was meant to go round (or the contents of which were intended to be bruited about) among the largest possible circle of friends and students. Similarly, where Abelard is staying when he writes the letter is unknown, but evidently he must not be too near to Paris or else he would not need to circulate his request in writing. As was the case in Letter Fourteen, Abelard does not identify his opponent. In that instance the omission was a rhetorical ploy not to dignify a heretic by naming him. Here, although there can be no doubt that the enemy is Bernard of Clairvaux, it may be a slight instinct for self-preservation that prompts Abelard to refrain from setting in writing the name of the most powerful churchman of his day.

The Council of Sens does indeed take place on 25 May 1141, but it turns out to be a far cry from the public disputation Abelard envisages. Although Abelard's supporters do come, neither they nor their master is able to sway the course of events. Rather than allowing for a debate, the proceedings are stage-managed to be the equivalent of the sentencing hearing after a court trial. Or, to draw a more extreme comparison, they even resemble a show trial, in which a list of Abelard's supposed heresies is proclaimed and condemned. This outcome must have been a nightmare for Abelard, whose *Historia calamitatum* indicates that he had an undimmed and unmitigated recollection of the Council of Soissons in 1121, where he was forced to consign one of his books to the flames.[10] Whatever Abelard's motivations, he refuses to take part even by responding, preferring instead to appeal directly to Pope Innocent II in Rome.

Despite the fact that Abelard is known to have enjoyed the backing of various clergymen in the papal curia, the pope receives a fusillade of letters with Bernard's heated rhetoric and alarming allegations to put forward his side of the story. Swayed by these communications, Innocent II issues on 16 July 1141 a rescript in which he condemns Abelard and Arnold of Brescia for heresy, orders the master's books (and those of Arnold, though he is not known to have written any) to be burned, excommunicates his disciples, and

10. Ed. Monfrin, p. 87, line 838–p. 89, line 909; trans. Radice, pp. 20–25.

commands that Abelard himself be confined in perpetual silence.[11] Probably not long after the council, Abelard addresses a "Confession of Faith" to Heloise.[12] For reasons that require no explaining, he ceases teaching. Instead, he sets out to defend himself in Rome, but en route he stops and takes refuge in the monastery of Cluny. Later, thanks to the mediation of Abbot Peter the Venerable (about 1092–1156), Abelard and Bernard are reconciled, and the pope's rescript is lifted.[13]

Abelard postures himself often in his works as being saintlike, martyrlike, and even Christ-like.[14] In the *Historia calamitatum* he writes, "And, to draw a comparison between a flea and a lion or an ant and an elephant, my rivals persecuted me with no gentler a spirit than heretics once did St. Athanasius."[15] In the present letter Abelard also establishes an explicit analogy between himself and a saint. He opens the text

11. A rescript is a response in which a pope (or another ecclesiastic superior) replies to a question concerning doctrine or discipline.

12. This is the *Confessio fidei ad Heloisam*, ed. Burnett, 152–55; trans. Betty Radice, *The Letters of Abelard and Heloise*, 211–12.

13. Possibly it was not Pope Innocent II but Pope Celestine II who restored Abelard. Celestine II, the former Master Guy of Città di Castello, had been well disposed toward Abelard (a onetime master of his) and had retained copies of the *Theologia* and *Sic et non* even after Innocent II had ordered all copies burned. On the manuscript, see Mews, "The Council of Sens," 366.

14. On his identification with Christ, see Donald K. Frank, "Abelard as Imitator of Christ," *Viator* 1 (1970): 107–13. He was encouraged in this identification by Heloise; see Heloise, Letter Six, ed. Muckle, *Mediaeval Studies* 17 (1955): 252; trans. Radice, 109. A very powerful moment of *imitatio Christi* not merely in his writings but in his actual life would be his refusal to speak at the trial of Sens, if we accept the suggestion advanced by C. Stephen Jaeger, "Peter Abelard's Silence at the Council of Sens (1140)," *Res publica litterarum* 3 (1980): 31–54.

15. Ed. Monfrin, p. 97, lines 1218–1221; trans. Radice, p. 33. The two passages are very close, since both involve saints. Even in other contexts, Abelard displays his precision as a logician in his self-conscious analysis of the similes he deploys. For example, see in Letter Nine the elaborate sentence: "In thus encouraging virgins, he adduces an argument from a likeness that is not derived solely from virgins; for this reason, to achieve a comparison of lesser worth, he takes widows and wives as an example, so that through the matrons of the world he might arouse all the more to this study those who are betrothed to Christ and so that by citing the virtue of laywomen he might dislodge or even destroy the sloth of nuns."

with a reference that likens his travails to the passion of the Spanish protomartyr Vincent, deacon of Saragossa, who died in 304 C.E. (22 January) during the persecutions of the Roman emperors Diocletian (284–305) and Maximian (286–305), and later includes a comparison of Bernard with Dacian, the Roman governor of Spain who oversaw Vincent's grisly martyrdom.

Among the details of the martyr's life, Abelard may have found particularly relevant to his own situation both that Vincent suffered as a consequence of having accepted the commission of preaching (which he did because his bishop had a speech impediment) and that during his martyrdom he was offered release from prison but refused when the condition was stipulated that he should consign the sacred texts to the fire: Abelard was haunted by the memory of having had to deposit one of his own books in the flames at Soissons. In art Vincent is often represented holding a codex. Abelard could have known the details of Vincent's legend from many sources, foremost among which would have been Prudentius's (348–405) *Peristephanon* and Augustine's *Sermons*.[16]

In this letter Abelard interjects a quotation that fuses lines from two classical poets. He draws the first line from Ovid, *Remedia amo-*

---

16. See Prudentius, *Peristephanon*, Poems 4 (Hymn in Honor of Ten Saints and Eight Martyrs of Saragossa) and especially 5 (The Passion of the Holy Martyr Vincent). In Sermon 275, in *PL* 38: 1254–1255, Augustine indicates that the Acts of Vincent were read in the churches of Africa at the end of the fourth century. Also in his sermons, Augustine testifies that the cult of Vincent extended everywhere in Christendom. The strength of popular attachment to Vincent can be gauged from the evidence of other, recently discovered sermons by Augustine, in which he gives a vivid portrayal of the overexcited congregation. See Augustine, *Sermo eiusdem de oboedientia* [Dolbeau 2, Mainz 5 = Sermon 359b] (preached at Carthage, the day after the feast day of St. Vincent), in *Augustin d'Hippone: Vingt-six sermons au peuple d'Afrique retrouvés à Mayence*, ed. François Dolbeau, Collection des études augustiniennes Série Antiquité 147 (Paris: Institut d'Études augustiniennes, 1996), 328–44, which reprints *Revue des Études Augustiniennes* 38 (1992): 50–79, at 63–79; English, *The Works of Saint Augustine: A Translation for the 21st Century: Sermons III/11. Newly Discovered Sermons*, trans. E. Hill (Hyde Park, N.Y.: New City Press, 1997), 331–53. For extensive information on the legends and cult of Vincent up to the millennium, see Victor Saxer, *Saint Vincent, diacre et martyr: Culte et légendes avant l'An Mil*, Subsidia hagiographica 83 (Brussels, Belgium: Société des Bollandistes, 2002).

ris 369–70. Abelard also quotes it in his *Carmen ad Astralabium* (lines 327–28). He takes the second line from Horace, *Odes* 2.10.11–12, two bits of a Sapphic strophe that he also cites in the *Historia calamitatum*, where it is featured in a speech allegedly pronounced by Bishop Geoffrey of Chartres at the Council of Soissons.[17] Last but not least, the later twelfth-century Gerald of Wales (Giraldus Cambrensis, about 1146–about 1223) incorporated into one of his many writings an anecdote that he had heard while a student at Paris. As Gerald tells it in a text written in 1191, Abelard resorted to the same two lines in a sharp debate with a Jew, which took place in the presence of King Philip (which would have to mean King Philip I, the Amorous, reigned 1060–1108).[18]

The hybrid couplet from Ovid and Horace deals with a recurrent topic in Abelard's writings, namely, envy. Abelard announces this theme in the very first sentence of this letter. According to his understanding of his life, it is partly his own pride in his renown but mainly his opponents' envy at that same fame that lead again and again to his ruin. This outlook comes to the fore repeatedly in the *Historia calamitatum*.[19] In the *Collationes* (also known as the *Dialogue between the Philosopher, the Jew, and the Christian*), Abelard has the Philosopher refer to the envy that could not destroy the *Theologia* and to the increased fame that the work acquired through the attempts of envy to persecute it.[20]

The "Letter of Peter Abelard against Abbot Bernard" is extant in a single manuscript, Heidelberg, Universitätsbibliothek, Codex Heidelbergensis 71, fol. 14v–15v. It has been surmised to have belonged

17. Ed. Monfrin, p. 86, lines 803–4; trans. Radice, p. 22.

18. *Itinerarium Kambriae,* Book 1, chapter 12, in *Giraldi Cambrensis opera,* ed. James F. Dimock, 8 vols. (London: Longman, 1861–1891), Rolls Series, 6 (1868): 3–152, at 95; English in Gerald of Wales, *"The Journey through Wales" and "The Description of Wales,"* translated by Lewis Thorpe (London: Penguin Books, 1978), 153.

19. On *livor, emuli,* and *invidia,* see ed. Monfrin, p. 70, lines 236–40; p. 83, line 708; and p. 85, line 791–p. 86, line 809; trans. Radice, pp. 8, 20, and 22.

20. *Collationes,* Praefatio 4, ed. Marenbon and Orlandi, 4–5. See also *Dialectica* 4.1, ed. Lambertus Marie De Rijk, *Petrus Abaelardus, Dialectica, First Complete Edition of the Parisian Manuscript,* Wijsgerige Teksten en Studies 1, 2d ed. (Assen, The Netherlands: Van Gorcum, 1970), p. 469, lines 5–6.

to a German cleric in the third quarter of the twelfth century who took an interest in the correspondence of Bernard of Clairvaux and Pope Eugenius III about the Second Crusade. The other items in the manuscript are mainly letters of Bernard, together with one by Pope Eugenius III.

The letter has been edited twice: Jean Leclercq, "Études sur Saint Bernard et le texte de ses écrits," *Analecta sacri ordinis Cisterciensis* 9 (1953): 1–247, at 104–5; and Raymond Klibansky, "Peter Abailard and Bernard of Clairvaux. A Letter by Abailard," *Mediaeval and Renaissance Studies* 5 (1961): 1–27, at 6–7. Klibansky's edition, which is followed here, is flanked on one side by a terse discussion of Abelard's epistolary activity in general and a full consideration of the unique twelfth-century manuscript in which the text is preserved, and on the other side by a detailed evocation of the context in which Abelard produced the letter. Among the many other places where the letter has been considered, see Clanchy in the introduction to the Penguin translation of *The Letters of Abelard and Heloise*, xli–xlii.

LETTER FIFTEEN

To his most beloved comrades their most beloved servant [*sends*] *greeting.*[21]

It is quite demonstrably to the glory of the martyr Vincent that after his deeds had been described, the enemy envied his fame.[22] Something of the sort is happening to me also now, to extend in an analogy a comparison from the greatest to the least. Certainly that man, for a long time now a secret enemy, who has pretended until this point to be a friend, even the greatest of friends, has now blazed out into such great envy that he could not bear the

---

21. By using the term *socius* Abelard avoids *discipulus*, which had been the conventional word to designate the students who followed a *magister*; see Teeuwen, *Vocabulary of Intellectual Life*, 75 and 135–36. *Socius* could designate a colleague as well as a student and need not have been restricted to an academic or even an ecclesiastic context.

22. The enemy is Satan, whose very name in Hebrew denotes his role as the adversary of God and mankind.

fame of my writings, by which he believed his glory to be debased the more as he thought that I was elevated the more.[23]

For a long time moreover I heard that he groaned heavily, because I had entitled with the name *Theologia* that work of mine about the sacred Trinity, insofar as the Lord granted it to be composed by me. In the end, hardly able to bear it, he offered the opinion that it should be called the *Stultilogia* rather than the *Theologia*.[24] Thanks be to God, that the toil of this work of mine could be esteemed so great that it should become worthy of prompting to such shameless and overt envy first the teachers of France, then the monks and those endowed with the esteem of still greater sanctity![25] The Lord will watch over his work, so that what I wrote under his inspiration will not suffer to be obliterated through the ill will of the wicked. The more often he rages against it, we trust that with the approval of God, he will avail not so much to suppress as to exalt that work:

> Envy seeks what is highest; winds blow upon the highest heights
>   and lightning strikes the tops of mountains.

You should know furthermore that, before seeing the message of your affection, I had heard already through the report of certain people how many venom-filled reproaches that Dacian of mine spewed out against me:[26] he belched them out from the

23. Compare Letter Ten, with its reference to "the charity with which [Bernard] embrace[d him] in particular."

24. Bernard's neologism substitutes the element "foolish" for "God": taken etymologically, the words could be contrasted, roughly, as "Fool-Teaching" and "God-Teaching."

25. Although this statement is too vague to allow for definite conclusions, Abelard could here have in mind that his writings on the Trinity were questioned first by the Schoolman Walter of Mortagne and then later by the monks William of St. Thierry and Bernard of Clairvaux. Walter's letter to Abelard on the topic survives; see *Epistola Gualteri de Mauritania episcopi ad Petrum Abaelardum*, in *Sententiae Florianenses*, ed. Heinrich Ostlender, Florilegium Patristicum tam veteris quam medii aevi auctores complectens 19 (Bonn, Germany: Peter Hanstein, 1929), 34–40.

26. Dacian was the Roman governor who had St. Vincent and Bishop Valerius

depths of his wickedness first at Sens, in the presence of the lord archbishop and many of my friends, and later at Paris, before you and others.[27]

And so the lord archbishop, in accordance with my request, sent a letter to him: If he wished to persist in accusing me, I would hold myself ready on the octave of Pentecost to respond concerning the propositions that he found objectionable.[28] In truth, I have not yet heard what sort of response he has given to that letter. You should know, however, that, the Lord willing, I will come on that day, and I wish and request that you be present. Farewell.

---

dragged in chains to Valencia and imprisoned there. After banishing Valerius, Dacian had many torments inflicted upon Vincent, who eventually died in his cell.

27. The archbishop is Henry Sanglier of Sens.

28. In ecclesiastical usage the octave is either the eighth day after a feast day (with the feast day itself being included in the count) or the entire period from the feast day through the eighth day after it. Here it is the former, 25 May 1141.

7

APOLOGIA AGAINST BERNARD OF CLAIRVAUX

The work discussed and translated here has been known in Latin both after its intended target as the *Apologia contra Bernardum* (Apologia against Bernard) and after its opening words as the *Apologia "Ne iuxta Boethianum"* (Apologia [with the Opening Words] "In Keeping with That Dictum of Boethius"). The *Gesta Frederici imperatoris* (Deeds of Emperor Frederick), which the Cistercian Otto of Freising (after 1111–1158) composed shortly after Abelard's death, refers to the text as the *Apollogeticum (sic)* of Abelard and quotes its opening words.[1] Thomas of Morigny refers to it both as the *Apologia* and the *Apologeticum*.[2] Most emphatically not to be confused with Abelard's *Apologia* is another against Bernard and others who condemned Peter Abelard, the earliest known writing by Berengar of Poitiers, an extremely satirical text written soon after the Council of Sens, which Berengar had himself witnessed.[3]

1. Otto of Freising, *Gesta Frederici*, 1.52, ed. Schmale, pp. 234, line 28–236, line 11; *Deeds of Frederick*, 1.51 (49), trans. Mierow, 87–88. On Otto's observations on Abelard, see Robert Folz, "Otton de Freising, témoin de quelques controverses intellectuelles de son temps," *Bulletin de la Société historique et archéologique de Langres* 13 (1958): 70–89, at 77–78, and Fiorella Vergani, "'Sententiam vocum seu nominum non caute theologiae admiscuit': Ottone di Frisinga di fronte ad Abelardo," *Aevum* 63 (1989): 193–224.

2. For references, see *Apologia contra Bernardum*, ed. Buytaert, 359.

3. Ed. Rodney M. Thomson, "The Satirical Works of Berengar of Poitiers: An Edition with Introduction," *Mediaeval Studies* 42 (1980): 89–138, at 111–38. For fundamental analysis, see Luscombe, *School of Abelard*, 29–49.

Around the time of the Council of Sens Abelard undertook to
rebut the list of his alleged heresies that Bernard of Clairvaux and
his allies had compiled.[4] Bernard and Abelard's other critics took
unanimous offense at Abelard's methods in theology in general as
well as at specific doctrines they believed him to hold.[5] For his information about Abelard's methods and doctrines, Bernard relied on a
compilation of *capitula* ("headings," "sections," or "counts" of an in-
dictment) that William of St. Thierry, his fellow Cistercian, assembled.[6] William drew in turn on a culling that was accomplished by an
unidentified excerptor from a lost work known as the *Liber sententiarum* (Book of Sentences or Book of Opinions).[7] Other collections
of sentences are extant, which seem to rest (directly or indirectly) on
notes of students who heard his lectures.[8] Insofar as the nature of
the *Liber sententiarum* can be determined, it seems to have been an altogether different sort of work from run-of-the-mill "sentences" or
opinions. Although Bernard and his party held it to be representative
of Abelard's teaching and thinking, Abelard staunchly denied authorship of it.

Bernard directed a letter to Pope Innocent II (which circulated among a wider audience than even the curia alone) as a broadside against the heretical doctrines he accused Abelard of having espoused.[9] To defend himself, Abelard eventually wrote an apologia in
which he sought to parry one by one each of the nineteen charges

4. Otto of Freising reports that Abelard wrote the *Apologia* much later, while at
Cluny, but Otto makes mistakes on other details of Abelard's life and there is good
reason to infer that this dating is inaccurate.

5. Luscombe, *School of Peter Abelard*, 110.

6. On the relationship between Abelard and William of St. Thierry, see Jean-Marie Dechanet, "L'amitié d'Abélard et de Guillaume de Saint-Thierry," *Revue d'histoire
ecclésiastique* 35 (1939): 761–74.

7. On the excerptor, see Luscombe, *School of Peter Abelard*, 107–8. All that survives
of the *Liber sententiarum* are twenty-five excerpts quoted against Abelard by his opponents; see Constant J. Mews, "The *Sententie* of Peter Abelard," *Recherches de théologie ancienne et médiévale* 53 (1986): 159–84, at 174–83.

8. For lists of these *sententiae* with bibliography, see Marenbon, *Philosophy of Peter
Abelard*, xviii–xix, and *Cambridge Companion to Abelard*, ed. Brower and Guilfoy, 339.

9. Letter 190, in *Sancti Bernardi opera*, 8: 17–40, discussed by Mews, *Abelard and Heloise*, 9–11.

of heresy (the *capitula*) that had been leveled against his theology, in particular as presented in his *Theologia "Scholarium"* but also in another source, probably the anonymous *Liber sententiarum*. Abelard quotes these accusations word for word in the second section of the *Apologia*. In the third section he points out that the wordings have not been taken verbatim from his own writings and that they are therefore based on an inauthentic work. Even so, Abelard seeks to answer and refute all the charges.[10]

The *Apologia* survives in fragments in only two manuscripts. One codex, Munich, Bayerische Staatsbibliothek, clm 28363, fol. 132v–35r (twelfth century, French), is a fragment offering only the opening section. The other, Budapest, Országos Széchényi Könyvtár, MS Széchényi 16, fol. 1r–48v (twelfth century, Clairvaux), has quotations, two of which coincide with what is preserved in the Munich manuscript, incorporated by Thomas of Morigny in his *Disputatio contra Petrum Abaelardum* (also known as the *Disputatio catholicorum patrum*).[11] Thomas wrote at the instance of Hugh of Amiens (1085–1164, archbishop of Rouen 1130–1164). Although as a young man Thomas may have frequented the schools, by the time he formulated his "disputation" he had been a monk for more than forty and an abbot for more than thirty years. From 1140 to 1144 he lived in Paris at the Benedictine priory of St. Martin-des-Champs, while suspended from his abbacy by Archbishop Henry Sanglier of Sens. During his sojourn there he wrote the "disputation," probably in 1141.

It is impossible to calculate exactly what fraction of the whole *Apologia* we possess, but it is worth noting that the fragment in the Munich codex comprises an introduction, a rebuttal of Bernard's first charge, and a small piece of the arguments against Bernard's second charge. Fifteen fragments in the Budapest codex do not overlap with the one in the Munich codex. Thomas of Morigny identifies four of them (fragments 8–11) as taken from Abelard's refutation

10. For two very different, systematic discussions of the propositions, see Luscombe, *School of Peter Abelard*, 103–42, and A. Victor Murray, *Abelard and St Bernard: A Study in Twelfth Century 'Modernism'* (New York: Barnes & Noble, 1967), 49–88.

11. Ed. Nikolaus M. Häring, "Thomas von Morigny, *Disputatio catholicorum patrum adversus dogmata Petri Abaelardi*," *Studi Medievali*, 3rd series, 22 (1981): 299–376.

of the fifth charge. Seven (fragments 1–7) would seem to come from the proof against a third charge, which differs from the wording and count of the charges as given in Abelard's own second section. Three (fragments 13–15) appear to be drawn from the rebuttal of the seventh charge. Put together, this information suggests that we have full or partial information about Abelard's defense against charges 1–3, 5, and 7, but nothing whatsoever about 4, 6, and 8–19.

As far as dating is concerned, Thomas's *Disputatio* was itself a reply to the *Apologia*, which lends the *Apologia* the air of having been an open letter of sorts to Bernard. Since in the *Disputatio* Thomas fails to mention the Council of Sens or the condemnation of Abelard, and since the fragments of the *Apologia* make no reference to Sens either prospectively or retrospectively, it has been argued that both the *Disputatio* and the *Apologia* must be dated before the council. To be precise, the *Disputatio* would have been composed around Easter of 1141 and the *Apologia* against Bernard during the second half of 1140 or, at the latest, during the early winter of 1140–1141.[12] Still, it is conceivable that the *Apologia* could have been written after Sens. The twofold evidence of other lists of heresies imputed to Abelard and of Bernard's correspondence gives the impression that the nineteen charges to which the *Apologia* responds resulted from a merging of documents, such as could have occurred at the council itself just as well as (or even rather than) beforehand.[13]

Closely related to the *Apologia* is the "Confession of Faith to Heloise," which has been preserved only because it is quoted by Berengar of Poitiers, a student and supporter of Abelard, in his own *Apologia*, a blistering diatribe against Bernard of Clairvaux and other critics of

12. This argument, advanced by Eligius M. Buytaert and accepted by John Marenbon, contradicts earlier scholarship, which held that the *Apologia* was written after Sens; see Buytaert, ed., *Petri Abaelardi opera theologica* 1, CCCM 11 (1969): 352–55, and Marenbon, *Philosophy of Peter Abelard*, 69, n. 54. In presenting the dating, I have honored the sequence of events that they advocated, but I have shifted forward most dates by roughly a year, to be consonant with the dating of 1141 for the Council of Sens, which Marenbon is now inclined to accept; see Marenbon, "Life, Milieu, and Intellectual Contexts," 17 and 39, n. 2.

13. On the lists, see Constant Mews, "The Lists of Heresies Imputed to Peter Abelard," *Revue bénédictine* 94 (1985): 73–100, reprinted in Mews, *Abelard and His Legacy*.

Abelard who participated in the Council of Sens. Although Berengar intimates that what he quotes of the "Confession of Faith to Heloise" is only a fragment, it appears to be complete.

The "Confession of Faith to Heloise" is not to be confused with the "Confession of Faith *Universis*," which is a public document addressed to the Church rather than a personal statement directed to Heloise. This "Confession of Faith *Universis*" appears if not to recant, then at least to contradict, basic positions that in the *Apologia* and "Confession of Faith to Heloise" Abelard had either defended or interpreted as misrepresentations of his true views. More remains to be pieced together about the original contents and respective dating of all these texts.

About 1142 Abelard died. While his passing occurred too long after Sens to have been a direct consequence of it, it is hard not to infer that the stress surrounding both the council and the subsequent condemnation to perpetual silence were not conducive to good health and longevity. Peter the Venerable referred to Peter Abelard as a man who had attained the philosophy of Christ, but the title by which the abbot of Cluny designated him was *magister* rather than *monachus*.[14] Abelard was a teacher first and foremost, and to have been silenced may have truly been the death of him.

This translation of the *Apologia* follows the Latin of Buytaert, ed., *Petri Abaelardi Opera Theologica*, 1, CCCM 11 (1969): 357–68. Buytaert's paragraph numbering has been maintained within square brackets. At the risk of cluttering the English with too many Arabic numerals, I have also supplied (without brackets) further numbers to designate each of the nineteen propositions within the second paragraph.

---

14. Letter 98, to Pope Innocent II, and Letter 115, to Heloise, in *The Letters of Peter the Venerable*, ed. Giles Constable, 2 vols., Harvard Historical Studies 78 (Cambridge, Mass.: Harvard University Press, 1967), 1: 258–59, at 258, and 1: 303–8, at 306; trans. Radice, pp. 215–16 and 217–23.

APOLOGIA

[1] In keeping with that dictum of Boethius, "Time should not be wasted in prologues that accomplish nothing," it is needful to come to the matter at hand, so that the truth of the facts rather than a superfluity of words may establish my blamelessness.[15] First the charges are to be recorded which seem to have been brought forth from my writings against me; then responses will be appended on the basis of which the logic of truth may refute the ill will of falsehood.

[2] Thus you say that I wrote concerning God:

1. "That the Father is full power, the Son a certain power, the Holy Spirit no power."[16]

2. "That the Holy Spirit is not of the Father's substance but rather the world soul."[17]

3. "That Christ did not take on flesh to free us from the devil's yoke."[18]

---

15. Boethius, *De syllogismo categorico libri duo*, Prologue, in *PL* 64: 794C. Choosing to cite this text as an *auctoritas* shows Abelard defiantly, and typically, asserting the supremacy of dialectic in reaching (and maybe even in constructing) determinations of truth.

16. This heading seemingly contradicts the Athanasian Creed on the equal power of the three persons in the Trinity. For the wording, see William of St. Thierry, *Disputatio aduersus Petrum Abaelardum*, ed. Leclercq, "Les lettres de Guillaume de Saint-Thierry," 377–78; Bernard of Clairvaux, Letter 190, in *Sancti Bernardi opera*, 8: 39, line 2; and section 5 of Abelard's *Apologia* against Bernard. Henceforth I will not list all the parallels either internally within the *Apologia* or to William and Bernard, for which the interested reader should consult the *apparatus fontium* in Buytaert's edition.

17. The foundational study of the identification of the Christian Holy Spirit with the Platonic World Soul is Tullio Gregory, *Anima mundi. La filosofia di Guglielmo di Conches e la scuola di Chartres*, Pubblicazioni dell'Istituto di filosofia dell'Università di Roma 3 (Rome: G. C. Sansoni, 1955), 133–54. For Abelard's views, see Marenbon, "Life, Milieu, and Intellectual Contexts," 35–38.

18. This charge suggests that Abelard denied the Redemption or at least the need for the Redemption and that the Passion took place to display Christ's love rather than to redeem humankind from sin.

4. "That neither 'God and man' nor 'this person' which is Christ is the third person in the Trinity."

5. "That free will in and of itself suffices for some good."

6. "That God can do only the things that he does, or renounce the things he renounces, either only in that way or at that time and not another."

7. "That God neither ought to nor can forestall evils."

8. "That we did not contract from Adam guilt but only punishment."

9. "That those who in ignorance crucified Christ did not sin."

10. "That whatever is done through ignorance is not to be considered a cause for guilt."

11. "That the spirit of the fear of God was not in Christ."

12. "That the power of binding and loosing has been given only to the apostles and not to their successors."[19]

13. "That a man is not made either better or worse on account of his actions."

14. "That omnipotence relates to the Father properly or specially, because it comes from no other, but that neither wisdom nor kindness do so."[20]

15. "That even chaste fear is excluded from the afterlife."[21]

16. "That the devil implants suggestions through the application of stones or herbs."

17. "That the coming at the end of the world could be ascribed to the Father."

---

19. This statement would deny the Church the power to excommunicate or to free people from sin by pardoning them.

20. The identifications of the Son as the wisdom of God and of the Holy Spirit as his love, benignity, or kindness, which did not originate with Abelard, are made passim in the *Theologia "Scholarium."*

21. *Castus timor* could be translated less literally as "the reverence of love"; see Luscombe, *School of Abelard,* 128. The expression owes to Augustine, *Enarrationes in Psalmos, Sermo* 22.6 (Psalm 118), ed. Dekkers and Fraipont, CCSL 40: 1740, lines 8–9, and 40: 1752, lines 24–25 and 34, and *Sermo* 1.7 (Psalm 127), 40: 1871, lines 3–4.

18. "That the soul of Christ did not descend to the underworld as such but only potentially."

19. "That neither action nor will nor desire nor the delight that occasions desire is a sin, and that we ought not to want it to be extinguished."

[3] Finally, in drawing to a close the aforementioned charges, the accuser says by way of conclusion: "These charges have been found partly in the book *Theology* of Master Peter, partly in the *Book of Sentences* of the same, and partly in the book entitled *Know thyself.*" By which person or persons they have been found, he did not add, because he could not indicate a finder of things that do not exist. Thanks be to God, however, as to what he claims is found in these books, where since such writings either cannot be found or were not mine, the writings themselves prove him wrong without my saying even a word.

[4] But seeing that, as blessed Augustine recalls, "he is cruel who neglects his reputation," and according to Cicero "silence is tantamount to a confession," let me give as I proposed some response to every single charge in order.[22] Thus evidently I will maintain the policy according to which blessed Gregory instructed the faithful against the tongues of detractors, with these words:

It is to be known that just as we ought not in our zeal arouse the tongues of detractors, for fear that they perish, so too we ought to endure them, when aroused by their ill will, with calmness, so that our merit may increase; but sometimes also we ought to restrain them, that while spreading ill words about us they not corrupt the hearts of the blameless who could hear us to good effect.[23]

---

22. The quotation from Augustine is to be found in *Sermo* 355, in *Sancti Aurelii Augustini Sermones selecti duodeviginti*, ed. Cyrille Lambot, Stromata Patristica et Mediaevalia 1 (Utrecht, The Netherlands: Spectrum, 1950), 123–31, at 124 (=) *PL* 39.1569: "qui confidens conscientiae suae neglegit famam suam, crudelis est." Abelard also quotes it in other writings, as in *Historia calamitatum*, ed. Monfrin, p. 102, line 1391; Sermon 33; *Theologia Christiana* 2.102; and *Confessio fidei "Universis."* The other quotation is Cicero, *De inventione* 1.32, also paired with the quotation from Augustine in the *Confessio fidei "Universis."*

23. Gregory the Great, *Homiliae in Hiezechihelem prophetam*, 1.9.17, ed. Adriaen, CCSL

Moreover, heeding this advice of one who was saintly and distinguished in the assessment of morals, I endured for a long time your unendurable accusations with which you have been afflicting me, waiting to see if maybe, either for fear of sin or for respect of decency, you would leave off persecuting me in my innocence or if you would lessen the persecution you had begun. But now, because it is evident that your plan is to persist even more shamelessly in what you began shamelessly enough, I am forced to turn back against you your own barbs so that, because you aim arrows against your neighbor, you may receive them loosed against you, and thus may be fulfilled in you the words of the comic playwright: "If you set out to say what you wish, you will hear things you do not wish."[24]

Martial grows indignant against Fidentinus, who recited his book, that he recites his words poorly and makes them his own, rather than the author's. He grows indignant, I say, and he declares, "What you recite is mine, O Fidentinus, but when you recite poorly, it begins to be yours."[25] The devil is held to blame who, interpreting the Scriptures wrongly, said to the Savior "that he has given his angels charge over you" [Matthew 4.6, quoting Psalm 90.11] and so forth. Yet the devil, even if he interprets the Scriptures wrongly, does still cite the words of the Scriptures, to whatever meaning he may twist them back.[26] But you, diverging

---

142 (1971): 132, lines 331–37; compare *The Homilies of St. Gregory the Great on the Book of the Prophet Ezekiel*, trans. Theodosia Gray, ed. Juliana Cownie (Etna, Calif.: Center for Traditionalist Orthodox Studies, 1990), 101. This quotation follows those from Augustine and Cicero in the *Confessio fidei "Universis."*

24. The source of this saying is Terence, *Andria* 920 (5.4.17).

25. Abelard quotes Martial, Epigram 1.38.1–2, with the omission of the word *libellus* at the end of the first line in the couplet. The Latin poet Martial lived from 38/41–101/104. Fidentinus is probably a fictitious name.

26. The saying in English, "The devil can cite Scripture for his purpose," originates with Shakespeare, *Merchant of Venice*, 1.3.98 (Antonio, speaking of Shylock). The Latin "diabolus male Scripturas interpretatur" appears in Haimo of Auxerre (died 855), *Homilia* 28, in *PL* 118: 190C–203B, at 198A; "male interpretatur diabolus Scripturas" in Otfrid of Weißenburg (about 800–about 870), *Glossae in Matthaeum* 4.6, ed.

from my words as well as my meaning, endeavor to make arguments on the basis of your fancies rather than my statements, and as you boast that you condemned my writings together with their author, you promulgate a sentence against yourself and your own writings instead. As charges you also bring against me some [of my words] as if heretical, which can be refuted by neither reason nor authority.

[5] Therefore, making a beginning with that first charge, I ask you first in which passage I said or wrote what you reprove: "That the Father is full power, the Son a certain power, the Holy Spirit no power." Produce the text if you can, and you may convict me as a heretic; but if you cannot do this, you undo yourself utterly by fabricating such great wrongs against your neighbor. But perhaps you will say that I did not write or deliver these words in fact but that I implied the same opinion albeit in different words. But if only you would express my opinion in such a way that you did not distort it in words, so that nothing of your slander would be left under discussion!

[6] I think that you were led particularly to this opinion, that you should believe evidently I said that the Son was a certain power and the Holy Spirit no power, because of certain words of mine in which, to differentiate between the begetting of the Son and the going forth of the Holy Spirit, I call the Son himself (as is sure) "the wisdom of God" and the Holy Spirit his "love" or "kindness."[27] For this reason I said that the wisdom of God was called a certain power of his (which is to say, the capacity of discerning all

---

Cesare Grifoni, CCCM 200 (2003), p. 77, lines 58–59; and "Diabolus scripturas sanctas quidem bene intellegit sed eas falso semper interpretatur," in Heiric of Auxerre (841–876/877), *Homiliae per circulum anni* (written 865–870), 28, ed. Riccardo Quadri, CCCM 116 (1992), p. 236, lines 242–43.

27. See Eileen F. Kearney, "*Scientia* and *Sapientia*: Reading Sacred Scriptures at the Paraclete," in *From Cloister to Classroom: Monastic and Scholastic Approaches to Truth*, ed. E. Rozanne Elder, Spirituality of Western Christendom 3, Cistercian Studies Series 90 (Kalamazoo, Mich.: Cistercian Publications, 1986), 111–29, at 111 and 123, n. 2.

things truly), by which he can evidently discern or distinguish all things, so as to be unable in any case to go astray out of not knowing, because "all things are noted and open to his eyes" [Hebrews 4.13].[28] I also said that his love relates to the affection of kindness rather than to the capacity of power, so that this love plainly should be called the "will" rather than the "power" of God; that best will of God, I say, by which he wills or arranges all things to be done, in the way in which they accord better, and also, to the best end to which he wishes all things to be done, to be brought into conformity, and in the way in which every single thing turns out as best it can. And so the love of God or goodness is his best will of doing or arranging all things in the best way, as I said, not the power of doing or arranging them. Never indeed ought love or kindness, in us or in God, to be called a "power," since to love or to be kind are not at all some power, seeing that often those who love more or who are kinder are less able to fulfill what they want, and those who have better wishes are less powerful, rich in affection but without resources in effect.

[7] Therefore, just as the wisdom of God, which we understand to be his Son, is a certain power or capacity of God—and that is to say, a power or capacity to discern or distinguish all things so that he is unable to go astray in anything out of not knowing—so his love or kindness, which we call the Holy Spirit, is his best will rather than power, as we have determined. For even if he who wishes something should also have the power, nonetheless the wish must not on that account be called the "power," since (it is evident) wishing something is not at all having that power. Certainly he who is animate and corporeal is not animateness or corporeality. And, to return to God, he who is eternal and incarnate is not eternity and incarnation.

28. Such a statement is found in the *Theologia "Scholarium,"* 1.31, 2.113–14 (with the quotation of Hebrews 4.13), and 2.139. Further parallels to the *Theologia "Scholarium"* may be found in Buytaert's edition.

[8] Thus although I said that the wisdom of God is a certain power of his, that is, the power of recognizing and discerning all things, and again that his love is not some power but will, I think, brother, that you arrived at that opinion because you believe me on this basis to assert that the Son of God, who is called his wisdom, is a certain power and that the Holy Spirit, which is believed to be his love, is no power. You are manifestly mistaken, brother, as if in no way comprehending the import of the words, and as if you did not have a share of that teaching which is the mistress of debate and which not only teaches to understand words but is able to discuss them once they have been understood.[29] So know what you did not know, and learn what you have not learned, because although "the wisdom of God" may be in some way the same as "the Son of God," or "the charity of God" the same as "the Holy Spirit," yet that is not the same as saying or understanding that "the Son of God is some power of God" and "the wisdom of God is some power of his," or "the Holy Spirit is in no way the power of God" and "the charity of God (or his love) is in no way his power." For indeed it happens often that some words, when taken on their own, may be entirely of a given meaning, yet when placed in a construction and joined with the words of the construction, they change meaning, so that this sense of the construction may be true but that one false.

[9] It is clear that this is to be ascribed to creation, as well as to the creator himself. Of course "sitting" and "who sits" are the same in meaning, and likewise "father" and "having a son," or "having paternity," are not different in meaning. Although nevertheless it may be true of the person who is not sitting that he "will be sitting," all the same it is not true that "he will be who sits." Or, although it may be true about this man that he "is that one's father," nevertheless it is not true that he "is having a son of that one" or "having paternity of that one."

---

29. The teaching in question is of course logic or dialectic. See Letter Thirteen.

[10] And therefore concerning God there are some words with the same meaning which change sense when juxtaposed to the same words. To be sure, "God" is nothing other than "divinity" itself, and this noun "God" signifies nothing other than this noun "divinity." If, however, I were to say "God is man" and "divinity is human," "God has suffered" and "divine nature has suffered," the meaning is then far different. One of them is accepted and the other is rejected. Likewise, although "God" is nothing other than "a divine substance" or "the substance of God," nevertheless we do not say that the substance of God is crucified, suffers the Passion, dies, or is born of the Virgin, even though we do not shrink to say this about God. Or although "God" is nothing other than "substance of God," nevertheless it is not the same to say "to be from God" or "to be in God" as "from the substance of God" or "to be in the substance of God." Certainly the Apostle [Paul], acting on account of God, said, "of whom [are] all things, by whom [are] all things, in whom [are] all things" [1 Corinthians 8.6: compare Romans 11.36], and according to John "of God many were born" [John 1.12–13]. Nevertheless, in no way can they be said to be born of divine substance. In addition, since God himself is spirit (that is, uniform spiritual substance and nothing else), man in fact is a corporeal and constructed thing.[30] Surely it is not possible that just as we say "God is a man," so we grant that "the Holy Spirit is a man" or "the spiritual substance is corporeal," or "a uniform thing is also composite," or the Holy Spirit, who is God, has flesh and bone because "God is man," and in fact man has flesh and bone?[31]

[11] In sum, as God is called his power and not another, and indeed his justice and not another, is it really possible that when he is said to be wisdom or charity, he must be denied to be his wis-

---

30. See John 4.24: "God is a spirit."

31. Compare Luke 24.39: "For a spirit hath not flesh and bones, as you see me to have."

dom or charity? But if God the Father is his wisdom and charity, is it possible that on this account we assume his Son or his Spirit to exist, since clearly the Son of God is the wisdom of God, or the Holy Spirit is his charity itself? Or although absolutely the same wisdom or charity belongs to the three persons, and the Son as well as the Holy Spirit has the wisdom of the Father and the love of the Father, although they know and love altogether the same, is it possible that the Son too or the Holy Spirit has the Son of the Father, as if born of him, or the Holy Spirit of the Father as if emanating from him? In any case, it is not fitting that this be granted on that basis, though the wisdom itself may be the Son of God and the charity of God the Holy Spirit.

[12] Thus even when we assume that the wisdom of God is a certain power of his, that is, the capacity of seeing everything, and even when we state that his love is his will rather than his power, nevertheless we are not compelled on this account to grant either that the Son of God is a certain power of his or that the Holy Spirit is none. For though the three persons may be wholly of the same substance or power, just as entirely of the same substance and worthiness—for which reason too each one is called all-powerful, just as we set forth in the *Theologia* itself[32]—it is not at all fitting that the Son rather than the Father be called a certain power or that the Holy Spirit be called none, since each of the three persons is equally powerful as the other two, equally wise, and equally kind, although the power is especially divine in the word "of the Father," just as the wisdom is divine in the name "of the Son," or the goodness of divine charity is expressed in the name "of the Holy Spirit."

[13] And thus the meaning of words, in the same matters as well as in different ones, is to be weighed carefully, so that the truth of a sentence may be differentiated from the truth itself. And thus when "the wisdom of God is a certain power of his" is

32. *Theologia "Scholarium"* 1.44, ed. Mews, CCCM 13: 124, lines 482–84.

said, that is, the power of discerning everything, it is as if we were
to say that he was wholly God, that he was wise, and that God has
this capacity of discernment—and this is true. But if however it
should be stated "the Son of God is a certain power" as though
on this basis he could be inferred to be able to do certain things
but not everything, the meaning is altogether false. For in equal
measure the power of the Son, like that of the Father, is able to do
everything, and in equal measure the Father, like the Son, knows
everything.[33]

[14] To respond in this manner also to the objections relating
to what we taught about the Son and the wisdom of God, the solution about the Holy Spirit and the love of God will be easy, in
that plainly when we say "the love of God is not some power," we
do not however say "the Holy Spirit is in no way a power." On this
account certainly love is to be called "power" neither in God nor
in us, but "will," seeing that it must never be said that "to love" is
"to be able to do something" but rather "to have good will in regard to something." Indeed, the Holy Spirit is to be called power
or powerful in equal measure with the Father or Son, because this
power can accomplish whatever it wants no less than those.

[15] I think that I have answered your first objection adequately
with these words, my accuser, brother Bernard. Now let us proceed
to the remaining charges.

[16] The second of your accusations was when you take me to
task for having said "that the Holy Spirit is not from the substance of the Father." To this I answer first that I assert openly in
the same book, where you claim to find this, that the Father, Son,
and Holy Spirit are utterly of the same substance or essence, that
they are altogether the same substance or essence, and that the Son
as much as the Holy Spirit are from the Father, the Son in fact

33. Compare John 16.30: "Now we know that thou knowest all things and thou
needest not that any man should ask thee. By this we believe that thou camest forth
from God."

as born, the Holy Spirit indeed as proceeding [from him]; and that I do not stray from Catholics in any way in faith, even if by chance in words I seem different from, not inimical to, some one of them.

[17] But to answer you more fully on the basis of my work as well as my thinking, you may not have at all any reason why you should object . . .

Fragments from the Lost Portion of Abelard's *Apologia* Conserved by Thomas of Morigny

From Abelard's Response to Proposition Number Two, "That the Holy Spirit is [. . .] the world soul."

[1] I call "the grace of God" anything that God parcels out of himself for the salvation of man, and anything that bestows upon him what he has not earned himself. Indeed, the Apostle [Paul] says: "There is a remnant saved according to the election of grace. And if by grace, it is not now by works: otherwise grace is no more grace" [Romans 11.5–6]. Therefore the grace of God is in his chosen, because he has marked them out beforehand from eternity, and because in them he has inspired faith, merits which certainly antedate our own and without which we could not love him so as to earn the right to be saved. For the love which he brings about in us first through what has been said, is itself either the effect of God himself or his gift, and must be imputed to his grace before we can earn even the least bit of salvation. For this reason too the Apostle [Paul] says: "What hast thou that thou hast not received?" [1 Corinthians 4.7].

[2] Therefore, too, free will itself, because it is a boon, is the gift of divine grace, and it is the very principle in which free will consists.

[3] Both free will and the principle in which it consists are common to the chosen and the wicked alike.

[4] Therefore, since the Lord confers reason upon the wicked as upon the chosen, may he also show the way by which one must attain blessedness, and may he summon us perpetually toward a perception of the same, which he offers to all, by his precepts and exhortations. Some men hearken to him in regard to these and comply with his precepts by living virtuously, that they may be accorded the rewards held out to them; others despise him and, lingering in their idleness, take flight from the toil of obedience.

[5] He has readied in advance the wicked, like the chosen, for virtuous living, that is (it is evident), by teaching, by advising, and by offering that capacity, so that no further preparation remains.

[6] But you say that God has not put good will in the wicked as in the chosen.

[7] The wicked are not to be blamed if they do not live righteously as do the chosen, since that grace for the righteousness of life, without which they can in no way live righteously, has been denied them.

From Abelard's Response to Proposition Number Four,
"That neither 'God and man' nor 'this person' which is Christ
is the third person in the Trinity."

[8] When you rebuke me for not saying that God and man are a single person in the Trinity, clearly you admit that you think it. I wish to recognize your error, because it is so much contrary to sound faith. For God and man, being of two natures, cannot be called a single person in the Trinity, whether they are understood individually or together.

[9] Therefore, the humanity assumed by the Word must not be said to be some one among the three persons in that everlastingness, but rather the Word itself, to which it has been joined. Furthermore, if it must not be said of God and man as separate beings that they are some one person therein, it is much less fitting for it to be said

about those two natures at once. For those two natures cannot be an everlasting thing, since one of them lacks everlastingness.

[10] That alone which was once in that Trinity, remains in the same person forever, and nothing new comes into the same Trinity, because it is not lawful to conceive of God as new.

[11] We must be on guard in all ways, that we not assert any such a thing to exist as has not been there forever, or posit something temporal in that timelessness, or something composed in that simplicity, or something corporeal in that incorporeality, or anything new in that antiquity.

[12] And because these two natures cannot be something everlasting since one of them lacks everlastingness, "God and man" are not a person in the Trinity.

From Abelard's Response to Proposition Number Six "That God can do in one way only the things which he does, or omits in one way only what he omits, either in that manner only, or at that time and no other."

[13] It is generally and without doubt to be maintained that whatever good God has in himself cannot either increase or diminish in him in any way. In fact, just as his power and his wisdom are coeternal in him, so the will that he has, in creating or disposing any things whatever, is coeternal with him.

[14] For it is not one thing to be powerful and another to be well disposed in God, in whom it is the same thing to be and to be God, as the preceding words make evident; and his will and his power are nothing other than himself. Augustine, in the seventh book of his *Confessions* [7.4.6], says: "And you will not be compelled against your will to anything, because your will is not greater than your power. However it would be greater, if you yourself were greater than you yourself. For the will and the power of God is God himself."[34]

34. Abelard uses this same passage from the *Confessions* in the *Theologia "Summi boni"*

[15] Therefore, if he can do only that which it is fitting for him to do or to will, truly he can do and can will to do only that which he wants at any time, and in that way only and likewise in that time in which he does it, because clearly it is not fitting for him either to do or to will to do this in any other way or at any other time.

2.33; *Theologia Christiana* 3.73; *Theologia "Scholarium"* 2.72; and *Sic et non*, 13.3–4, lines 14–17, ed. Boyer and McKeon, 142.

PART III

OTHER CONTROVERSIES

8

LETTER ELEVEN. TO ABBOT ADAM AND THE MONKS OF ST. DENIS

Letter Eleven is addressed to the abbot and monks of St. Denis (whose name in Latin is Dionysius), the royal abbey to which Abelard had withdrawn not long after his defeat at the Council of Soissons in March 1121. It must have been written between then and 19 February 1122, when Abbot Adam of St. Denis, the first-mentioned addressee of the letter, died.[1] This span of time likely coincides with the period when Abelard began to compile the *Sic et non,* and it offers a nice demonstration in practice of the methods he outlines theoretically in the prologue to his famous treatise. To our eyes the procedures he follows in the letter may seem reminiscent of historical criticism.

The backdrop to Letter Eleven can be reconstructed from the *Historia calamitatum,* written about a dozen years later and much less diplomatic in tone, which relates how Abelard noticed that a passage in the Venerable Bede's (died 735) *Super Acta apostolorum expositio* (Commentary on the Acts of the Apostles) conflicted with a passage in Hilduin's (died 855) *Historia* or *Gesta Dionysii* (History or Deeds of St. Denis, commissioned in 835) about where Dionysius the Areop-

---

1. February is the death date as given by Clanchy, *Abelard,* 337; 9 January 1122 by Hubert Silvestre, "Aratus pour Arator: un singulier lapsus d'Abélard," *Studi medievali,* 3rd series, 27 (1986): 221–24, at 221.

agite had been bishop.[2] Though in his autobiographical letter Abelard tried to pass off his discovery of the contradiction and his announcement of it to the monks as having happened casually and even jokingly ("quasi jocando monstravi"), he had to have been entirely aware of the enormous weight that the seemingly small discord between two sources carried. Indeed, the inconsistency led Abelard to express the doubt that St. Denis/Dionysius (after whom the abbey was named, and around whose tomb it was built), the apostle of France, and Dionysius the Areopagite, an Athenian convert of St. Paul (Acts 17.34), were one and the same. By pointing out this contradiction, Abelard drove a wedge not only explicitly between Denis/Dionysius and Dionysius the Areopagite but also implicitly between Denis/Dionysius and the fifth-century figure now known as Pseudo-Dionysius the Areopagite. Pseudo-Dionysius was the author of the Corpus Areopagiticum, which encompassed a number of famous texts (such as *The Divine Names, Mystical Theology, Celestial Hierarchy,* and others) that helped to transmit Neoplatonism to the Middle Ages.[3]

To lessen the prestige of St. Denis by dissociating him from the biblical Dionysius and from the pseudonymous author of the same name was to insult not merely the abbey named in his memory but also the very kingdom that (and king who) took him as patron saint. Though Abelard was essentially correct in his sifting of the evidence,

2. See *Historia calamitatum,* ed. Monfrin, pp. 89–91, lines 941–81; trans. Radice, pp. 26–27. For the first source, see Bede, *Super Acta apostolorum expositio,* 17.34, ed. M. L. W. Laistner, CCSL 121 (1983): 1–99, at 68, lines 1–6; English: *Commentary on the Acts of the Apostles,* trans. Lawrence T. Martin, Cistercian Studies 117 (Kalamazoo, Mich.: Cistercian Publications, 1989), 145. For the second, see Hilduin, *Vita s. Dionysii, sive Areopagitica,* in *PL* 106.9–50.

3. See Édouard Jeauneau, "Denys l'Aréopagite, promoteur du néoplatonisme en Occident," in *Néoplatonisme et philosophie médiévale: Actes du Colloque international de Corfou, 6–8 octobre 1995 organisé par la Société internationale pour l'étude de la philosophie médiévale,* ed. Linos G. Benakis, Société Internationale pour l'Etude de la Philosophie Médiévale: Rencontres de Philosophie Médiévale 6 (Turnhout, Belgium: Brepols, 1997), 1–23, and Adolf Martin Ritter, "Die Absicht des Corpus Areopagiticum," in *Christian Faith and Greek Philosophy in Late Antiquity: Essays in Tribute to George Christopher Stead, Ely Professor of Divinity, University of Cambridge (1971–1980) in Celebration of His Eightieth Birthday, 9th April 1993,* ed. Lionel R. Wickham, Caroline P. Bammel, and Erica C. D. Hunter, Supplements to Vigiliae Christianae 19 (Leiden, The Netherlands: E. J. Brill, 1993), 171–89.

his brethren in the monastery of St. Denis understandably took no pleasure in being enlightened by his new perspective. On the contrary, unhappy to find the historicity of their patron undermined by a new arrival who had plainly already not ingratiated himself with them (among other things, by insisting on continuing to teach), the monks alerted their abbot, Adam. In turn, Abbot Adam threatened to notify the king so that he could punish Abelard, on the grounds that a sally against Denis was ipso facto an act of lèse-majesté, since the saint was the patron of the royal family. Although in the *Historia calamitatum* Abelard may have overstated his panic, he reports that he left the abbey stealthily by night and took refuge outside the kingdom of France, in the territory of Count Thibaud (Theobald) of Champagne. In the end the story sorted itself out to Abelard's advantage, since not too much later Abbot Adam passed away and his successor, Abbot Suger, permitted Abelard to leave St. Denis so long as he did not submit to another abbot.[4]

Beyond the hornet's nest of questions surrounding Denis/Dionysius, Abelard stirred up a problem that to be resolved might require questioning the authority of either the Venerable Bede or, even more troublingly for the monks, Hilduin, a former abbot of St. Denis (814–840); Hilduin had written his "Deeds of St. Denis" at the instigation of no less than Emperor Louis the Pious (778–840). It was Hilduin who had first promulgated the view—or, to be less mealymouthed, the confusion—that St. Denis and Dionysius the Areopagite (and, by extension, Pseudo-Dionysius the Areopagite, although Abelard does not mention the pseudonymous author in Letter Eleven) were identical.

Here as in the examination of the Lord's Prayer and of the Cistercian liturgy that he wrote to Bernard about a decade later (Letter Ten), Abelard shows his consistency in articulating and practicing principles for the critical study and comparison of texts. In this case he addresses himself to the third question raised in the prologue to the *Sic et non*, that of homonymy or synonymy:

---

4. Ed. Monfrin, p. 91, lines 976–89; trans. Radice, p. 27.

The greatest barrier to our understanding is the unusual style and the fact that very often the same words have different meanings, when one and the same word has been used to express now one meaning, now another.[5]

One Dionysius is not automatically identical with another.

History has proven Abelard right in the basic line of his reasoning, namely, that we are dealing with a conflation of more than one Dionysius. First, Dionysius the Areopagite was a pagan Athenian philosopher who was converted by St. Paul, according to Acts 17.34: "But certain men, adhering to him, did believe: among whom was also Dionysius the Areopagite and a woman named Damaris and others with them." A second-century tradition held that this Dionysius was the first bishop of Athens. Second, Bishop Dionysius of Corinth (about 170), mentioned by Eusebius of Caesarea (263–339) in the *Historia ecclesiastica* (Ecclesiastic History), a Greek work available in Latin as translated and extended by Rufinus of Aquileia (345–410), is not said to have been a martyr. Third, the Dionysius who has become known as St. Denis was placed by the oldest extant sources in the mid-third century, when he was supposedly martyred under either the Roman emperor Decius (249–251) or Aurelian (270–275). Only later did it become believed that he had been sent by Pope Clement I (88–97) to Gaul, where he suffered martyrdom with his companions under the Roman emperor Domitian (81–96). Last but not least is the author who is known now as Pseudo-Dionysius—and who is known now not to have been who he claimed to be.[6] Named only once as Dionysius (with no qualifications), he is not referenced by any Church writer before the first half of the sixth century. He appears to have been a Christian Neoplatonist of Greece or Egypt

---

5. Ed. Boyer and McKeon, p. 89, lines 11–13, "Ad quam nos maxime pervenire impedit inusitatus locutionis modus ac plerumque earundem vocum significatio diversa, cum modo in hac modo in illa significatione vox eadem sit posita"; trans. A. J. Minnis and A. B. Scott, *Medieval Literary Theory and Criticism, c. 1100–c. 1375: The Commentary-Tradition* (Oxford, U.K.: Clarendon Press, 1988), 87.

6. See David E. Luscombe, "Denis the Pseudo-Areopagite in the Middle Ages from Hilduin to Lorenzo Valla," in *Fälschungen im Mittelalter. Internationaler Kongreß der Monumenta Germaniae Historica, München, 16.–19. September 1986*, ed. Wolfram Setz, Schriften der Monumenta Germaniae Historica 33/1–5, 5 vols. (Hannover, Germany: Hahn, 1988), 1: 133–52 (147–48 on Abelard).

who wrote at the end of the fifth or beginning of the sixth century but who presented himself as having lived in the apostolic age.

In Letter Eleven, Abelard attempts methodically to sort out the evidence for and against identifying St. Denis/Dionysius with Dionysius the Areopagite. The letter represents a practical application of the techniques for logical evaluation set forth in the Prologue to the *Sic et non*. First the passages in question (in medieval terms, the "authorities") are quoted, then they are dissected with an eye to determining whether they contradict each other or whether they merely diverge from each other without demonstrating fundamental incompatibilities. In this case Abelard quotes three passages, one from Eusebius's *Ecclesiastic History*, a second from Jerome's *De uiris inlustribus* (On Illustrious Men), and a third from Bede's commentary on the Acts of the Apostles.[7] Abelard shows that the first two passages, which are pulled from more authoritative texts, subvert the third. In the end he advances three possible explanations for Bede's divergence from the other two sources. One is that Bede was misled by the identity of the names (in Latin) and erred; another is that he was repeating the views of others, who should be held accountable for the mistake; and the third is that Bede knew of two Dionysiuses who were both bishops of Corinth. Incidentally, apparently even Abelard sometimes slipped, since at one point in this letter he appears to conflate the ancient Greek poet Aratus of Soli (about 315–about 245 B.C.E.) with the sixth-century Christian Latin poet Arator.

Letter Eleven is a genuine letter in that it opens with a salutation and closes with a valediction. Its transmission suggests that it was intended for public consumption, as was commonly the case with letters in the Middle Ages. It survives exclusively in manuscripts not with other items from Abelard's correspondence, but rather with writings concerning St. Denis.[8] In what seems an irony, Letter Eleven may owe its existence to the wrongheaded surmise of the monks at

---

7. Jerome, *De uiris inlustribus* 27, ed. Aldo Ceresa-Gastaldo (Florence, Italy: Nardini Editore, Centro internazionale del libro, 1988), 122; *On Illustrious Men*, trans. Thomas P. Halton, Fathers of the Church 100 (Washington, D.C.: The Catholic University of America Press, 1999), 50–51.

8. Smits, *Letters IX–XIV,* 28–29.

St. Denis that it supported the identity of St. Denis and Dionysius the Areopagite.[9] Such an inference has scant basis in fact. Though conciliatory, the letter is absolutely unyielding in emphasizing the need to face the realities of the testimony about Dionysius in Bede.

Four codexes transmit Letter Eleven: Paris, Bibliothèque nationale de France, MS lat. 356 (third or fourth quarter of the twelfth century); Paris, Bibliothèque nationale de France, MS lat. 2445A (fourth quarter of the twelfth century); Paris, Bibliothèque nationale de France, MS lat. 2447 (second half of the thirteenth century); and Paris, Bibliothèque nationale de France, MS nouv. acq. lat. 1509 (second half of the thirteenth century). Two further manuscripts were copied from the last mentioned. The edition followed is that of Smits.

LETTER ELEVEN

To Adam, his most beloved father, abbot (by the grace of God) of the monastery of the most glorious martyrs Dionysius [= St. Denis], Rusticus, and Eleutherius[10] who rest there bodily, and at the same time to his dearest brothers and fellow monks, Peter, in habit a monk and in life a sinner, wishes "Grace to you and peace" (as the Apostle [Paul] said) "from God our Father and the Lord Jesus Christ" [Romans 1.7].

Often the error of one person engulfs many, and people inclined to evil are dragged more easily through one man into falsehood than through many into truth. Moreover, I say this for the reason that many are accustomed to set up the authority of Bede alone against the truth which I hold concerning Dionysius the Areopagite, minimizing either through ill will or perhaps through ignorance the weightier authorities which support me. For a certainty Bede avows that Dionysius the Areopagite was bishop of the Corinthians, although others whose authority is by far more

9. Smits, *Letters IX–XIV,* 153.

10. Bishop Dionysius, or Denis, was sent in the third century with five other bishops to convert Gaul. He was supposedly imprisoned together with his companions, the priest Rusticus and the deacon Eleutherius, before being beheaded.

powerful assert instead that he was bishop of the Athenians, and they demonstrate by their declarations that Dionysius the Areopagite was one altogether distinct person, Dionysius the bishop of the Corinthians another.

Accordingly, let us set down the words of each one, and then consider if they are not only different, but even mutually opposed and entirely contradictory to each other. If we have ascertained this, let us differentiate between the authorities themselves so that, since they cannot all be preserved, that one which rests upon a lesser merit may be put to the test.[11]

About this matter it has been written in [Eusebius's] *Ecclesiastic History* Book 4, Chapter 23 in the following words:

We must come at length to recall blessed Dionysius, bishop of the Church of the Corinthians. Not only these peoples whom he had undertaken to guide, but also those people located far away to whom he accorded his presence through letters enjoyed his instruction and the grace that he had in the word of God. In fact, these survive, his epistle written to the Lacedaemonians about the Catholic faith [. . .] and another to the Athenians, in which he summons and stirs the more sluggish to belief in the Gospel. [. . .] And in the same epistle he indicates the fact that Dionysius the Areopagite, who after being instructed by the apostle Paul believed in Christ (according to what is indicated in the Acts of the Apostles [17.34]), was ordained by the same apostle as the first bishop at Athens.[12]

---

11. As noted in connection with Letter Nine, Abelard uses the verb *diiudicare* (to discriminate) in the Prologue to the *Sic et non*, just before he quotes Jerome's letter to Laeta (which itself uses the word): "So too, blessed Jerome, although he put some teachers of the Church before others, advised us to read them in such a way as to discriminate between them rather than to follow them."

12. The quotation is from Eusebius, *Ecclesiastic History* 4.23.1–3, as translated and continued by Rufinus in Latin, ed. Schwartz and Mommsen, *Eusebius Werke* 2/1, Die griechischen christlichen Schriftsteller der ersten drei Jahrhunderte 9/1, 1: 375, lines 1–15. The only one of Dionysius's letters from which extracts have survived is his letter to the Romans, which (although not mentioned in this passage) is quoted earlier in Eusebius at 2.25.8, ed. Mommsen, 1: 179, lines 10–14.

In addition, Jerome, that outstanding doctor of the Church, as I say, thus recalls about this same matter in the book *On Illustrious Men* [27]:

Dionysius, the bishop of the Church of the Corinthians, was of such eloquence and industry that he instructed in his letters not only the peoples of his city and province, but also those of other provinces and cities. Of these letters one is to the Lacedaemonians and the other to the Athenians

and so forth.[13] And after a few words: "He came to fame under Emperor Marcus Antoninus Verus and Lucius Aurelius Commodus."[14]

Now let us set down the words too of Bede himself who, in explaining the Acts of the Apostles (in the passage where it is said "Among whom Dionysius the Areopagite" [Acts 17.34]), stated as follows:

This is the Dionysius who, having been ordained to the episcopacy, guided the Church of the Corinthians gloriously and who, taking a nickname from the place which he oversaw, left many volumes marked by his talent which relate to the utility of the Church and which remain even today. For Areopagus is the court of Athens, deriving its name from Mars, inasmuch as in Greek Mars is called *Arios*, village is called *pagos*.[15]

Consequently, now that the authorities have been introduced as we proposed, let us consider their difference or inconsistency as we promised. The two authorities cited above which are consonant with each other seem however entirely contradictory to the authority of Bede. On the basis of those two authorities it is plainly demonstrated that Dionysius the Areopagite was one person, Dionysius the bishop of the Corinthians another. For according to

13. *De uiris inlustribus* 27, ed. Ceresa-Gastaldo, 122.

14. Marcus Aurelius and Lucius Verus reigned together from 161 to 169.

15. Bede, *Super Acta apostolorum expositio*, 17.34, ed. Laistner, CCSL 121 (1983): 93, lines 1–11; *Commentary on the Acts of the Apostles*, trans. Martin, 145. A more correct etymology would be "Hill of Ares," in reference to a promontory northwest of the Acropolis, which was used by Athenians in preclassical times for sittings of the council of elders and in classical times for the highest judicial court of the city.

the *Ecclesiastic History* Dionysius the bishop of the Corinthians is reputed to have written about Dionysius the Areopagite, and in the same source Dionysius the Areopagite is imputed to have been bishop of the Athenians. And it is no less evident from the words of Jerome that the first was different from the second, since plainly he says that Dionysius the bishop of the Corinthians won fame under Marcus Antoninus and Lucius Aurelius.

It is established for a certainty that Dionysius the Areopagite, who was converted by the preaching of Paul, lived in the time of Christ and the apostles, and that he was already an adult man, to the point that it is established that he already then had a wife Damaris, about whom recollection is made, together with him, in the Acts of the Apostles.[16] For this reason it is also found written there that "certain men adhering to Paul did believe; among whom was also Dionysius the Areopagite, a woman named Damaris, and others with them" [Acts 17.34].

Moreover, from the time of Tiberius Caesar [14–37] under whom the Lord suffered, up until the times of those emperors under whom Dionysius of the Corinthians is said to have been renowned, the reckoning of the chronicles assigns more than one hundred and sixty years. As a result, the lifetime of the man who has been mentioned could in no way be sufficient for so great a time. Indeed it is written in the Psalms: "But if in the strong [they be] eighty years: and what is more of them is labor and sorrow" [Psalms 89.10].

From this passage one can clearly gather that Dionysius the Ar-

---

16. *Mulier,* the word used to qualify Damaris in Acts 17.34, can mean either woman or wife. The fact that Damaris, identified as *mulier,* was named in the passage together with Dionysius ("Dionisius Ariopagita et mulier nomine Damaris") has sometimes led interpreters to assume, understandably but probably erroneously, that the two were husband and wife. The assumption is found (for example) in Ambrose, *Epistola* 14 (63), section 22, lines 236–37, in CSEL 82, no. 3: 247 (= *PL* 16: 1196A) "cum Damali uxore sua," as well as in Hilduin of St. Denis, *Prolegomena (Rescriptum ad serenissimum imperatorem, dominum Ludovicum),* in *PL* 106: 16A "cum . . . Damari uxore sua," and *Passio s. Dionysii,* Chapter 8, in *PL* 106: 28D "cum . . . Damari uxore sua."

eopagite was one person, Dionysius the bishop of the Corinthians another. And so, by the statements of the authors who have been mentioned, we refute the opinion of Bede, especially also since their authority is by far weightier, and since it is more appropriate for a word to stand in the mouth of two [Matthew 18.16] than of one.[17] For certain, Bede as well as other ecclesiastic writers resort to the *Ecclesiastic History* as the first and greatest basis of ecclesiastic history. What, then, does it seem to you that Bede can respond, if you have pointed out that those writings, by the authority of which he frequently defends himself, are opposed to him? In my opinion nothing is more correct than that verse of a wise man: "He who is in conflict with himself will agree with no one."[18]

However, so that no one should take it badly and should recoil strongly from [thinking] that Bede is sometimes mistaken and that he produced certain statements through his own rather than divine inspiration (evidently for the reason that the Latin Church has especially frequent recourse to his commentaries), he should recall to memory the prophet Nathan who was mistaken about the building of the temple,[19] and the baneful pretense of the very prince [Peter] of the apostles that was corrected by his fellow apostle

17. Abelard frequently makes repeated use of the same quotation in different writings of his own. In this case, his partial quotation of Matthew 18.16 calls to mind a similar appearance of the verse in Letter Nine.

18. Abelard's source is the *Distichs of Cato* 1.4 (in Latin, *Disticha Catonis, Catonis disticha,* or simply *Cato*), a poem of short moral observations that was wrongly believed in the Middle Ages to have been written by Cato the Elder or Cato the Younger. Since the poem, which began with a section of monostichs and proceeded to the more numerous and famous distichs, was often one of the first readings assigned to a pupil learning Latin, Abelard needs not identify it in any way: the quotation would have been immediately recognizable to any reader.

19. The prophet Nathan, who succeeded Samuel, lived in the reigns of David and Solomon. He comes on the scene when David is considering building a temple to the Lord (2 Kings 7). First he assures David of the Lord's support, but then he is directed by the word of God to discourage the king from erecting the temple on the grounds that the honor of doing so was to be reserved for Solomon (2 Kings 7 and 1 Chronicles 17.1–15).

Paul, "because" he said "he was to be blamed" [Galatians 2.11], and as well the venerable doctor Augustine who was not embarrassed to reconsider, of his own free will, his own errors in correcting almost all his writings.[20] And let him think back to that old saying of Elijah: "For I am no better than my fathers" [3 Kings 19.4]. And then in truth when he has recalled the errors of such great men, he will cease to wonder at Bede's mistake.

Indeed, as blessed Gregory asserts in his first homily on Ezekiel, sometimes to maintain humility the Holy Spirit withdraws itself from the minds of the faithful and permits them to slip into error, so that (as it is clear) they may recognize how useless they are when the Holy Spirit departs.[21] Even when it exercises control over the minds of the saints, it thus reveals some things so that it may keep others hidden. It is not a cause of great worry if we assert sometimes that saints made mistakes in literal matters or in such matters as do not lead to the endangerment of the Catholic faith, since obviously Augustine can be confirmed by Jerome to have been mistaken about the literal meaning of the Seventh Psalm, in the title of which, it is plain to see, is read: "For the words of Chusi son of Jemini" [Psalms 7.1];[22] inasmuch as Augustine was completely ignorant of the Hebrew language.[23]

If, however, anyone should strive to salvage the authority of Bede too, so that he may satisfy everyone, perhaps it will be per-

20. In 428 Augustine (354–430) wrote a work entitled *Reconsiderations* (Latin *Retractationes*), in which he passed a final judgment upon his earlier writings to correct what he deemed to be misleading or wrong.

21. *Homiliae in Hiezechielem*, 1.1.15, ed. Adriaen, CCSL 142 (1979): 12; *Homilies*, trans. Gray, ed. Cownie, 18–19.

22. The title will not be found in the King James Version and its relatives, but it is counted as the first verse of the psalm in the Douay-Rheims version (as well, of course, as in the Vulgate).

23. In his commentary on this verse Augustine concludes by stating that "Chusi should be interpreted silence"; see *Enarrationes in Psalmos*, 7.1, ed. Eligius Dekkers and Johannes Fraipont, CCSL 38 (1956): 35–36. This assertion contrasts with Jerome's *Liber interpretationis Hebraicorum nominum* (Book on the Intepretation of Hebrew Names), in which Jerome interprets the name Chusi as meaning Ethiop or Ethiopia; see *Liber in-*

mitted to say that in this passage Bede followed the view of others rather than that he established his own opinion. Indeed often, so that we may protect undamaged the authoritative statements of the saints, we attribute to the opinion of others rather than to their own views those things that they write. Thus let us say in this passage too that Bede introduced the opinion of others, who having been misled by the equivocality of the name believed that Dionysius the Areopagite and Dionysius of Corinth were the same person. For a certainty we see that even blessed Ambrose went so far astray from literal truth in a certain passage owing to the equivocality of a name as to assert that James, the brother of John whom the Lord took up apart from the rest at his transfiguration together with his brother John and with Peter [Matthew 17.1], was the James "who first mounted the priestly throne."[24] This fact, it is established, must be understood about the other James, who both was called "the brother of the Lord" [Galatians 1.19] and was first ordained into the Church of Jerusalemites, so that clearly in this way this other James should be understood first to have mounted the priestly throne. If therefore so great a doctor may have been permitted to deviate from literal truth in the explication of the Gospels through the ambiguity of the name of James, what is the wonder if the ambiguity also of the name Dionysius deceived Bede and many others, especially in that commentary on the Acts of the

---

terpretationis hebraicorum nominum, ed. Paul de Lagarde, CCSL 72 (1959): 63, line 14; 99, lines 3–4; 107, line 12; and 119, line 14.

The final phrase, translated here as "the Hebrew language," is *Hebraica ueritas* in Abelard's Latin. It could be put literally into English as "the Hebrew truth," but Jerome (with whom it originated) applied it in reference to the authenticity of the Hebrew Bible texts. For further information, see Letter Nine.

24. *Expositio euangelii secundum Lucam*, 7.9, ed. Marcus Adriaen, CCSL 14 (1957): 1–400, at 218; *Commentary of Saint Ambrose on the Gospel According to Saint Luke* 7.9, trans. Íde M. Ní Riain (Dublin: Halcyon Press/Elo Publications, 2001), 195. In Catholicism the two apostle Jameses are both saints, often differentiated as James the Greater, the son of Zebedee and brother of John; and James the Less, the son of Alpheus and brother of Jesus.

Apostles which it is certain was reconsidered afterward by Bede himself? In fact, so that we might understand briefly his words in the short preface of his reconsideration, he began thus:

We know that the distinguished doctor [. . .] Augustine [. . .] produced books of *Reconsiderations* about certain works [. . .] of his. [. . .] It has suited us too [. . .] to imitate his industry, so that, after the commentary on the Acts of the Apostles which we wrote many years [. . .] previously, now we should set down a brief work of reconsideration about that same volume, above all out of a desire either to add to things that were said too briefly or to emend things which seemed to have been said differently from what I wanted.[25]

In that commentary he also frequently introduces verses of Aratus, some of whose mistakes we know, although clearly Jerome in the book *On Illustrious Men* shows that he erred about the same day on which Peter and Paul suffered their passions.[26] Indeed, Aratus

25. Bede, *Retractatio in Acta Apostolorum*, preface, ed. M. L. W. Laistner and D. Hurst, CCSL 121 (1983): 93, lines 1–11.

26. Abelard states that Bede knew in some form the verse of Aratus and used it frequently, which is a problematic assertion. The Stoic poet Aratus wrote a didactic epic entitled *Phaenomena* (about 270 B.C.E.), on the constellations and weather, which was highly regarded in the ancient world. St. Paul even cited a hemistich of it in his Areopagus speech (Acts 17.28). The poem was translated into Latin by Cicero. It is to the translation by Cicero that Jerome refers in his preface to Eusebius's *Chronicle, Epistula praefatoria in Chronicis Eusebii*, ed. Rudolf Helm, *Eusebius Werke* 7/1–2, Die griechischen christlichen Schriftsteller der ersten drei Jahrhunderte 24 and 34 (Leipzig, Germany: J. C. Hinrichs'sche Buchhandlung, 1913–1926), 1: 1–7, at 1, column 1, line 20–column 2, line 4. In the early Middle Ages the Greek of Aratus, translated in an abridged form, was supplemented with other material to form the *Aratus Latinus*.

Although the works of Bede contain citations of Aratus here and there, a poet of the third century B.C.E. cannot very well have discussed the death dates of Peter and Paul. A poet whom Bede does in fact cite in his commentary on the Acts of the Apostles is the altogether different but similarly named poet Arator, who wrote in Latin verse a biblical paraphrase *De actibus apostolorum* (On the Acts of the Apostles). This so-called Bible epic indicates an adherence to the theory that Peter and Paul died on the same day, but one year apart; see *De actibus apostolorum*, 2.1246–50, ed. Arthur Patch McKinlay, CSEL 72 (1951): 148–49, and *Arator's On the Acts of the Apostles*, trans. Richard J. Schrader, Joseph L. Roberts III, and John F. Makowski, Classics in

as well as Bede, who in the *Martyrology* trusted in Aratus's authority, accept the day as being exactly the same, unless the span of a year had passed [between them], since Jerome pronounces that Peter as well as Paul suffered their passions on the very same day in the fourteenth year of Nero.[27]

To conclude, so that we may be able to lay to rest completely with a most serene conclusion this disagreement of different opinions, perhaps easily if we hypothesize that there existed two Dionysiuses who were bishops of the Corinthians, we will be able to maintain that Bede too was truthful and to take nothing by way of opinion, in such a way that one of the Bishop Dionysiuses of the Corinthians and Dionysius the Areopagite were the same as the one about whom Bede writes, and that at different times the same man was in charge at Athens and Corinth as bishop and that afterward he was ordained as apostle of Gaul by St. Clement, but that another of the Bishop Dionysiuses of the Corinthians was that Dionysius whom the *Ecclesiastic History* and Jerome call to mind;[28] and so I judge that the whole contention could be resolved. Therefore, of all the things that we have advanced by way of resolving it, this is the summation: either we should concede that Bede was misled, or that he proffered the opinion of others to us, or that there existed two Bishops Dionysius of the Corinthians. Most beloved brethren, farewell in the Lord.

Religious Studies 6 (Atlanta, Ga.: Scholars Press, 1987), 94. On Abelard's confusion between the two poets, see Silvestre, "Aratus pour Arator," 221–24.

27. The relevant passage in the most recent edition of Bede's *Martyrology* contains no reference to either Aratus or Arator, but is clear in indicating that Paul died "on the same day as Peter"; see 29 June: III Kalendas Julii, in *Edition pratique des Martyrologes de Bède, de l'anonyme Lyonnais et de Florus,* ed. Jacques Dubois and Geneviève Renaud (Paris: Editions du Centre National de la Recherche Scientifique, 1976), 116–17. Jerome refers to Peter and Paul's having died on the same day in the same year in his *De viris illustribus,* 1.5, in PL 23: 607–718, at 617A. Nero reigned from 54 to 68. In placing the death of Peter in 68, Jerome followed Eusebius. The likelier date is 64, when there was a persecution.

28. This is the Pope Clement I (88–97) who was credited with having dispatched the future martyr Denis to France.

9

TO A REGULAR CANON

The practice of canonical life had taken root long before the twelfth century, but during Abelard's time it grew up and ramified in directions and fashions that inevitably occasioned tensions between canons and monks. Viewed from afar, the two groups as they were then constituted may seem to resemble each other intimately, and in fact they have for a long time been treated as being nearly synonymous. Nonetheless, they can be differentiated.

Monachus (monk) was a term that usually designated a man who lived celibate and who was devoted to contemplation and the performance of religious duties, especially song and prayer. The exact feminine equivalent, *monacha,* was far less commonplace in the High Middle Ages than *monialis.* Although the last-mentioned form is sometimes said to be an abbreviation of *sanctimonialis,* all these words derive from a Greek adjective for "single, unique, solitary," and in Letter Twelve Abelard cites Jerome to this effect. In a striking paradox, however, a medieval monk dwelled much more often within a particular religious community than in solitude. The communities tended to be separated from the world, to be governed by a rule, and to require of their members adherence to vows, with those of poverty, chastity, and obedience being especially important within the Benedictine order.

A canon was a cleric who resided with others in a cloister or in a house within the precinct of a cathedral or collegiate church.[1] Canons were so called because they ordered their lives according to canons of the Church. The word *canon* was a Latin importation from Greek, meaning "rule." Different groups of canons followed different rules. Canons whose rule required them to renounce private property were known as Regular Canons (designation that is pleonastic, from an etymological standpoint), whereas others were called Secular Canons. The Regular Canons were also designated Augustinian or Austin Canons, since Augustine had referred to this practice, and as Black Canons, from the color of their garb.[2] In 1120–1121 a new group evolved from the Regular Canons. Because they conformed to a stricter rule that was established by Norbert of Xanten (about 1080–1134, bishop of Magdeburg 1126–1134) and his followers in their community at Prémontré, they became known as the Norbertines or the Premonstratensian Canons.[3] They were also called the White Canons, in reference to the hue of the clothing they wore.

Eventually canons and monks grew so similar in the rigor of the lives they led as to seem indifferentiable. Both were tonsured, wore habits that set them apart from secular folk, lived in common, and followed rules. Yet in Abelard's lifetime, many people—above all, monks—would have distinguished sharply between the two groups, and it is not surprising that monks fought hard to accentuate the differences between themselves and the canons. Once again, it warrants remark that Abelard was, despite the difficulties he caused and the failings he experienced in both capacities, a monk and an abbot. During his monastic career he belonged to four abbeys (St. Denis,

1. For an introduction to canons and what they represented, see Jean Châtillon, *Le mouvement canonial au moyen âge: Réforme de l'église, spiritualité et culture,* ed. Patrice Sicard, Bibliotheca Victorina 3 (Paris: Brepols, 1992).

2. A straightforward account of the Augustinians can be found in John C. Dickinson, *The Origins of the Austin Canons and Their Introduction into England* (London: S.P.C.K., 1950).

3. The standard biography of Norbert has not been translated into English, although an English summary is printed at the end of the German translation; see Wilfried Marcel Grauwen, *Norbert, Erzbischof von Magdeburg (1126–1134),* trans. Ludger Horstkötter, 2d ed. (Duisburg, Germany: Selbstverlag der Prämonstratenser-Abtei St. Johann, 1986).

the Cluniac St. Médard, the unreformed St. Gildas, and Cluny itself)
and spent time in several other cells, priories, oratories, and hermit-
ages (such as the unlocalized cell where he moved from St. Denis to
teach; St. Ayoul in Provins, the Carthusian priory in which he took
refuge after fleeing St. Denis; his hermitage at Quincey; and St. Marcel at Châlons-sur-Saône, where he died).[4]

At the same time, Abelard's itinerary of abbeys, priories, and as-
sorted other facilities argues that he had little knack for the *stabilitas*
(fixity in a given place, in a given community, or both) that is one of
the promises a professing monk must make according to the Rule of
Benedict.[5] On the contrary, he passed from being a "peripatetic Palatine" to being a peripatetic monk. Bernard of Clairvaux had equal
claim to the latter title, except that he was not tainted by an association with the schools that would render his movements suspect as
vagabondage.[6] Abelard was a far better contender to be classed, however wrongly, as a wandering scholar.

During a few of his sojourns as a monk, Abelard knew monastic
retreat. Yet such interludes of withdrawal from the world, and particularly from the world of teaching, came almost only under constraint.[7] Despite Abelard's avowals of reverence for monastic solitude,
he was apparently unable to withstand on a permanent basis the enticements of his natural calling as a *magister.* In seeking to combine
life as a monk with life as a master, and in striving to coordinate the
cloister with the school, Abelard was swimming against the tide of

4. His experience in the latter class of institution did not induce him to exempt
from his criticism the small cells or priories known as "obediences"; see Sermon 33,
in *PL* 178: 589BC.

5. 4.78; 58.4, 9, 17; 60.9; and 61.5.

6. In a famous letter to Pope Eugene III (1145–1153), one in which he refers to
himself as "the chimera of my age," Bernard reveals that he recognized in himself
this inconsistency. See Letter 250.4, in *Sancti Bernardi opera,* 8: 147, lines 1–3: "Ego enim
quaedam Chimaera mei saeculi, nec clericum gero nec laicum. Nam monachi iam-
dudum exui conversationem, non habitum" (For I am a kind of chimera of my generation, and I do not conduct myself as a cleric or a layman; for I have long shed a
monk's way of life, not his habit). For astute analysis, see Godman, *Silent Masters,* 93.

7. Here too the circumstances under which Abelard himself turned to monasticism do not prompt him to be less critical of others who retreated to solitude out of
a constraint, such as fear; see Sermon 33, in *PL* 178: 584AB.

his times. The experiment of the oratory he built in the wilds was a utopian alternative to teaching in a town. At the Paraclete Abelard could be a master to his retinue of students, but he could do so only out of the public eye, in a monastic institution of his own devise. The initiative was too radical.

The irony is that Abelard could have had his cake and eaten it too, by leading a regular life and by teaching—but as a canon, not as a monk. In the end it speaks volumes that while Abelard obsessed over the rivalry between monks and canons, Bernard of Clairvaux came to see the paramount competition almost as a war between the forces of light and darkness, except that the combatants were monks and scholars.[8] Ultimately both Abelard and Bernard were enlisted on the losing sides of their respective campaigns. As far as Abelard's position goes, first canons and later friars only grew in strength in the teaching world at the cost of monks. But the bigger picture is that not even Bernard could arrest the ascent of the schools.

To complicate matters further, it must not be overlooked that Abelard had been a canon before his entrance into monastic life. In the *Historia calamitatum* he has Heloise, in her harangue to him against marriage, refer to him as being "clerk and canon."[9] He dismisses his entry into religion as having been dictated "by shame and confusion . . . rather than any devout wish for conversion," but was the necessity to escape from the world the only incentive for becoming a monk as opposed to a canon?[10] His students, when trying to dissuade their master from remaining cloistered in St. Denis after his castration, interpreted his choice as one for wealth over poverty, since by remaining in the royal abbey, he would be ministering to the wealthy rather than educating poor students. They wanted him instead to be a philosopher of God by teaching, which is what he attempts both to achieve in reality at the Paraclete with his students and to promote as an ideal in parts of many later writings.[11] In sum, it can be readily understood both why Abelard would consider himself a monk

---

8. Ferruolo, *The Origins of the University*, 49.

9. *Historia calamitatum*, ed. Monfrin, p. 78, line 530; trans. Radice, p. 16.

10. *Historia calamitatum*, ed. Monfrin, p. 80, lines 623–24; trans. Radice, p. 18.

11. *Historia calamitatum*, ed. Monfrin, p. 81, lines 642–54; trans. Radice, p. 19.

in good standing and yet why Bernard of Clairvaux would view him as "Master Peter Abelard, a monk without a rule, a prelate without commitment, [who] neither holds to an order nor is held by one."[12] To Bernard, Abelard is master first, monk later; master first, abbot still later.

The most fundamental question in weighing monks and canons against each other was to determine the truest manner of leading an apostolic life.[13] Was it by leading a communal life of worship, as monks did, or was it by emphasizing poverty and pastoral work, such as preaching, as canons did? The conception of their ministry that the canons held differed sharply from that of the monks. To the canons, the model was the communal life that early Christians shared, first in Jerusalem and later in the household of Bishop Augustine of Hippo. Their ministry was a kind of public apostolate, a matter of teaching, by both word and example: *docere verbo et exemplo*.[14] This self-conception could have been very threatening to a monk as thoroughgoingly committed to teaching as was Abelard, and to one who set as much stock by the example of his own life as mediated through his own words as he did.[15] To some extent Abelard's discomfort vis-à-vis the canons may have resulted partly from an unspoken contention over whether the roles of a *magister* were more compatible with those of a *monachus* or a *canonicus*.

---

12. Bernard, Letter 193.7, ed. Leclercq, 8: 44, line 16: "Magister Petrus Abaelardus, sine regula monachus, sine sollicitudine praelatus, nec ordinem tenet, nec tenetur ab ordine." Compare Letter 332, in *Sancti Bernardi opera*, 8: 271, line 7.

13. For the broad background, see Marie-Humbert Vicaire, *L'imitation des apôtres. Moines, chanoines, mendiants IVe–XIIIe siècles*, Tradition et spiritualité 2 (Paris: Editions du Cerf, 1963).

14. The classic study of this view among the canons is Caroline Walker Bynum, *Docere verbo et exemplo: An Aspect of Twelfth-Century Spirituality*, Harvard Theological Studies 31 (Missoula, Mont.: Scholars Press, 1979). When revisiting the topic later, she situated it within the larger context of the spirituality of canons in the twelfth century; see *Jesus as Mother: Studies in the Spirituality of the High Middle Ages*, Publications of the Center for Medieval and Renaissance Studies, UCLA, 16 (Berkeley and Los Angeles: University of California Press, 1982), 22–58.

15. For confirmation of the latter point one need look no further abroad than the inaugural sentence of the *Historia calamitatum*, ed. Monfrin, p. 63, lines 1–2; trans. Radice, p. 3.

For the past few decades it has become routine to envisage the early Middle Ages as having had a tripartite social structure, which subsumed people into three categories: those who prayed (*oratores*), those who bore arms (*bellatores*), and those who worked the soil (*laboratores*).[16] From the vantage point of a twelfth-century monk, the more compelling three-part classification may have been monks, canons, and laymen.[17]

In Letter Twelve Abelard enters the fray by taking to task a Regular Canon who contends that the way of life of his peers is superior to that of monks. In Letter Seven to Heloise and in *The Sermons* Abelard dealt more than a half dozen times with the topic of "the dignity of women," specifically in the context of religious life.[18] Over the course of this letter he manifests a similar intentness on delineating the "dignity of monks" and their way of life, a topic to which he devotes considerable effort also in Sermon 33 (dated 1127–1128), addressed to the monks of St. Gildas on John the Baptist. In particular, he advocates both the special dignity of monks in comparison with clerics and Regular Canons and a contemplative life in contrast to an active one.[19]

First Abelard seeks to elucidate whether his opponent means dignity in the eyes of men or of God, since only the latter is of moment. Then he points out that often those who attain heights in the world enter monasteries later, so as to make amends for the worldly wrongs

16. The classic exposition of this perspective is Georges Duby, *The Three Orders: Feudal Society Imagined*, trans. Arthur Goldhammer (Chicago: University of Chicago Press, 1982).

17. See Giles Constable, *Three Studies in Medieval Religious and Social Thought: The Interpretation of Mary and Martha; The Ideal of the Imitation of Christ; The Orders of Society* (Cambridge, U.K.: Cambridge University Press, 1995), 249–360, especially 295–304.

18. Letter Seven is entitled "On the Authority and Dignity of the Nun's Profession." The relevant passages are identified in a rich study, McLaughlin, "Peter Abelard and the Dignity of Women," 291, n. 1. Further information about Abelard's thoughts on women's weakness and dignity is presented in Fiona J. Griffiths, "Brides and *Dominae*: Abelard's *Cura Monialium* at the Augustinian Monastery of Marbach," *Viator: Medieval and Renaissance Studies* 34 (2003): 57–83, at 71–74.

19. In Sermon 33, he takes particular pains to elevate monks over bishops, as the avatars of the secular clergy; for a few key passages, see *PL* 178: 585D ("Considerate, monachi dignitatem vestram"), 594B, 595C, 598D, and 599B.

they committed as clerics. Those who become monks may not return to secular life. If they are assigned ecclesiastic offices outside
the monastery, they retain their monastic habits. Monks may be appointed bishops, but clerics may not become abbots. The basic difference between monks and clerics is that monks have *religio* (religious
or ascetic life, religious order) whereas clerics have *officium* (a charge,
duty).[20] The *religio* of monks consists in the liturgy of prayers and
hymns.

To turn to authoritative statements by Church Fathers that but-
tress one or the other side in the debate, Abelard clarifies that one
passage may leave a misimpression that Jerome supposed clerics to
be superior to monks. In fact Jerome, drawing parallels between the
desert fathers, on the one hand, and the holiest prophets and sons of
prophets, on the other, held monastic life in higher regard than clerical life. Pseudo-Chrysostom established a similar analogy between
John the Baptist and a monk. At this juncture Abelard proceeds to
find instances in the New Testament of figures who show the prefer-
ence of Christ for the contemplative over the active life. He interprets the bride in the Song of Songs and Rachel in Genesis to the
same effect.

The choice of female examples may not be dictated entirely by
the conventions of medieval allegory: it bears remembering that in
Letter Six of the correspondence Heloise compares nuns with others who follow an apostolic life. Furthermore, Letter Twelve itself
invokes in its final sentences nuns as role models: if even rich noble-
women have been able to habituate themselves to the asceticism required by the monastic life, then men should be capable of learning
from them.

In the end Abelard leaves off defending monks and instead goes
on the attack against canons. Since Regular Canons build convents

---

20. Once again, Abelard covers the same ground in Sermon 33, where (at *PL* 178:
586A, 593B, 597A, 598CD, 603ABC, and 604A) he rates the *religio* of monks above the
officia of preachers, priests, bishops, and their Old Testament precursors. He draws
the distinction most bluntly at 598C: "Monachus, fratres, seu eremita, nomen est reli-
gionis. Episcopus autem sive clericus vocabulum est officii et operis, magis quam de-
votionis" (Brothers, monk or hermit is a noun for religious life. But bishop or cleric
is a word for duty and work, rather than devotion).

so as to avoid the world, they should complete their "regulariza-
tion" by conforming to monastic rules (and the Latin for rule is *regula*). Authoritative citations from the Church Fathers and from Christ
confirm that the contemplative life is to be preferred to the active,
and that consequently the monastic life surpasses the canonical.

There has been speculation, beguiling but unprovable, that Abelard composed Letter Twelve directly in reaction to one of two specific historical events. One would be the founding of the canonical
community at Prémontré, about twelve miles west of Laon, by Norbert of Xanten (died 1134), the other the publication of the treatise *De dignitate clericorum* (On the Dignity of Clerics), perhaps around
1140, by another Premonstratensian, Philip of Harveng(t) (about
1100–1183), abbot of Bonne-Espérance (1157–1182), near Binche in the
diocese of Tournai.[21] The hypothesis about Norbert of Xanten is
more plausible for three reasons. First, because the date when Philip
is hypothesized to have composed his work would seem to fall too
late for when Abelard could have and would have drafted his letter-
treatise. Second, because in any event Abelard claims to be responding not to texts but to speech. Third, because whereas Abelard never
names Philip elsewhere in his writings, he makes what is generally
agreed to be a critical reference to Norbert in the *Historia calamitatum*,
when he mentions that his onetime rivals whetted on against him:

some new apostles in whom the world had great faith. One of these boasted
that he had reformed the life of the Regular Canons, the other the life of
the monks.[22]

---

21. The treatise is less properly known as *De institutione clericorum* (On the Institution of Clerics); see Norbertus Iosephus Weyns, "A propos des Instructions pour les
clercs (De Institutione clericorum) de Philippe de Harveng," *Analecta Praemonstratensia*
53 (1977): 71–79.

22. "novos apostolos, quibus mundus plurimum credebat . . . quorum alter regu-
larium canonicorum vitam, alter monachorum se resuscitasse gloriabatur": ed. Monfrin, p. 97, lines 1201–4; trans. Radice, p. 32. On Abelard's attitude toward Norbert,
see Wilfried Marcel Grauwen, "Het getuigenis van Abaelard over Norbert van Gennep," *Analecta Praemonstratensia* 63 (1987): 5–25, and "Nogmaals over Abelard, Bernard
en Norbert," *Analecta Praemonstratensia* 65 (1989): 162–5.

The reformer of the Regular Canons is taken to be Norbert, that of the monastic life Bernard of Clairvaux. Corroborating this inference is that Norbert and Bernard were paired by others who wrote in the first half of the twelfth century, such as Herman of Tournai (abbot 1127–1136, died 1147) and Laurence of Liège.[23] In a sermon written several years earlier, Abelard identified Norbert and a "coapostle" called Farsitus as having endeavored to no avail to revive the dead:

I should come to weightier matters and those highest miracles that were essayed in vain in connection also with the raising of the dead. We marveled in fact, and we laughed, that Norbert and his hench-apostle Farsitus recently presumed to do this. For a long time they lay, stretched out in like manner in prayer before the people and thwarted in their presumption. When, disconcerted, they left off their plan, they began shamelessly to rebuke the people, that its faithlessness worked against their devoutness and unremitting faith.[24]

Perhaps not coincidentally, Abelard uses the same verb in Sermon 33 to describe the revival of the dead as he does in the *Historia calamitatum* to qualify the revival of monasticism.

Yet it is also undeniable that throughout his career Abelard evinced hostilities toward not just Norbert but numerous other canons as well, such as William of Champeaux, Roscelin, and, last but not least, Fulbert (the uncle of Heloise who had him castrated). Beyond such personal animosities toward individual canons, already before marrying Heloise Abelard may have nurtured reservations about the very status of canons. Whereas he reports that in the antinuptial

23. Grauwen, "Het getuigenis van Abaelard," 21.

24. Sermon 33, in *PL* 178: 605BC: "Ad majora veniam, et summa illa miracula de resuscitandis quoque mortuis / inaniter tentata. Quod quidem nuper praesumpsisse Norbertum, et coapostolum ejus Farsitum mirati fuimus, et risimus: qui diu pariter in oratione coram populo prostrati, et de sua praesumptione frustrati, cum a proposito confusi deciderent, objurgare populum impudenter coeperunt, quod devotioni suae et constanti fidei infidelitas eorum obsisteret." There has been dispute over the identification of the Farsitus named here. Norbert's longtime companion and his successor as abbot of Prémontré was Hugh of Fosses (ca. 1093–1164). A Regular Canon named Hugo Farsitus of Soissons delivered the funeral oration for Norbert in 1143. Quite possibly Abelard's Farsitus and these other two personages are one and the same.

speech in the *Historia calamitatum* she sang to him the advantages to a philosopher of being a canon,[25] he opted shortly after his castration not to remain a canon as he had been but instead to enter a monastery.

Abelard also makes mention of Regular Canons (once qualifying them as Augustinian Canons) twice in Letter Six. Elsewhere in Abelard's oeuvre, Sermon 33 frames the saint as the prototype of the contemplative life and therefore of monasticism.[26] (For this reason it is à propos that Bernard of Clairvaux, in a letter to Cardinal Ivo of Asbach, taxes Abelard with being "Herod on the inside, John on the out.")[27] The main thrust of the sermon is not to attack canons but rather to critique the monastic life of Abelard's day. Its conception of monasticism overlaps with that in the foreground of Letter Twelve, and like Letter Twelve (and Letter Nine) it taps Jerome heavily as a source. Indeed, Letter Twelve goes so far as to present Elijah, John the Baptist, and Jerome as almost the founding fathers of monasticism.

Many motives for Abelard's invocation of Jerome emerge in Letter Nine, as also in the correspondence with Heloise. Elijah and John the Baptist, who make cameo appearances in a number of Abelard's other works, need to be explained differently. At the risk of oversimplifying matters, they are both pre-Christians who nonetheless came with a scriptural imprimatur and could be used to legitimate the conception of the monklike philosophers that Abelard strove to realize in his own living and that he held out for emulation, first by his students at the Paraclete and later by the nuns there.

Other parallels to Letter Twelve can be seen in Letter Eight and Sermon 35 (with the incipit "Adtendite a falsis prophetis"), which

25. *Historia calamitatum,* ed. Monfrin, p. 78, lines 528–35; trans. Radice, pp. 15–16.

26. For a full examination, see Grauwen, "Het getuigenis van Abaelard," 8–18. On the use of John the Baptist as a model in medieval monasticism, see Gregorio Penco, "S. Giovanni Battista nel ricordo del monachesimo medievale," *Studi monastica* 3 (1961): 7–32.

27. Letter 193, in *Sancti Bernardi opera,* 7: 44, line 17: "Homo sibi dissimilis est, intus Herodes, foris Ioannes, totus ambiguus, nihil habens de monacho praeter nomen et habitum."

has been attributed to Abelard.[28] Additionally, Sermon 24 contains an overt statement on the superior merits of monks and nuns over prelates and laymen.[29] Finally, in the second book of the *Theologia Christiana* Abelard conveys his views on the qualities necessary to a monk when he extols the lives of ancient philosophers. His *Exhortatio ad fratres et commonachos* (Exhortation to Brothers and Fellow Monks) may be lost, or it may be extant as Sermon 33. Yet even without it, a goodly pool of information remains that can elucidate Abelard's ideals about monasticism.[30] Taken in combination, Abelard's antagonisms toward specific canons and his tendencies to philosophize about monasticism suggest that Letter Twelve, even in the event that it was addressed to a particular canon such as Norbert of Xanten, was meant for a more extensive audience than a single recipient. It was an open treatise-letter.

Since no medieval manuscript survives, in constituting the text of Letter Twelve Edmé Smits and his predecessors were forced to rely on the 1616 editio princeps. Like so much connected with Abelard's letters, this earliest edition has a peculiarity pertaining to authorship. It survives in two versions, both dated 1616, both having nearly identical texts, but each having different title pages and preliminary matter that ascribe the edition to different editors, the earlier to André Du Chesne (1584–1640) and the later to François d'Amboise (1550–1619). It has been supposed that d'Amboise began the edition, that Du Chesne completed it, and that Du Chesne took primary credit until the hazards of printing works by an author on the Index (as Abelard was) made expedient the tactic of attributing editorship to the more established d'Amboise. In any event, the mystery of the

---

28. On such parallels to other works within Abelard's oeuvre, see Smits, *Letters IX–XIV,* 155–72.

29. Sermon 24, in *PL* 178: 529B–36B, at 534D–35A. See Van den Eynde, "Le recueil des sermons," 38–39.

30. For further information on the last two sentences, see David E. Luscombe, "Abélard et le monachisme," in *Pierre Abélard—Pierre le Vénérable,* 271–76, at 272, and "Monasticism in the Lives and Writings of Heloise and Abelard," in *Monastic Studies: The Continuity of Tradition,* ed. Judith Loades (Bangor, Gwynedd, Wales: Headstart History, 1990), 1–11.

editorship in the early seventeenth century is happily irrelevant to the constitution of the Latin text.[31]

LETTER TWELVE

Through the reports of many people it has come to our ears that the status of our order (that is, the monastic one) has been injured quite often to no small degree by you in the presence of many. We believe that this has been undertaken for no other reason, than that you can thus endeavor to exalt clerics in your calling, whom you call Regular Canons, by humiliating ours. What is more, we are filled with wonder if that is the explanation, but we are filled with all the more wonder if it is not, since we can discern no other cause. You say, as people report, that our order is by far inferior to yours and that monks are very far removed from the dignity of clerics. In which regard indeed we wish to inquire of you first on the basis of which dignity you understand this, whether of eminence among men or of religious life in the sight of God. Certainly this dignity of religious life is the truest which commends us especially to God and adorns us with virtues and makes us all the more glorious among the heavenly, as we are considered humbler among the earthly.

But indeed you should say if you can (or you should go on to state why you cannot) by what reason or on what authority clerics are able to claim dignity for themselves. For who would not know, as we are instructed by daily experiences, that even these clerics who are prominent in a very high rank elect the monastic life, as they take pains to mend faultlessly the shortcomings they had in clerical life, and that when it is permitted them to make a transition to monkhood, they are in no way allowed to return to the clerical life? Or if sometimes, through the outstanding quality of

---

31. Smits, *Letters IX–XIV,* 59–60.

their religious life, ecclesiastic persons elected from the monasteries are put in charge over the offices of clerics, the monastic habit itself also is distinguished by such great dignity that once taken up it must not be set down; for this monastic habit not only secular but even clerical garb is to be cast aside. Why is it indeed that nevertheless monks, having been made bishops, are often put in charge of clerics or are assigned to any ecclesiastic offices whatsoever? Why does the opposite not hold, that abbots in monasteries should not be made of clerics or that they should undertake care for monastic offices? Why, I say, why, I ask, if not that it is considered most unworthy that a less strict life should be preferred to the rule of that life, for which it is to be held of no value and through which, as we said, it is to be mended? Why else do even you yourselves and the entire Church say in the prayer of the litanies, "All holy monks and hermits, all holy virgins, all holy widows and chaste people pray on our behalf" and not "All holy clerics or holy priests or holy bishops?"[32] Certainly because the latter names are rather of office, just as the former are of religious life. Why is it also that no mention of you is made, as it is made of monks and virgins in those hymns of the Feast of All Saints in which the good offices of the saints are sought as much by you as by the rest?[33] For certainly it has been written thus:

> Chorus of saintly virgins
> and of all monks,
> together with all saints,
> make [us] companions of Christ![34]

---

32. Litanies are responsive petitions (or prayers) used in both public liturgical services and private devotions. With a few small but interesting discrepancies, this sentence is nearly identical to one in Sermon 33, in *PL* 178: 599A.

33. All Saints' Day is a solemnity celebrated on 1 November to honor (as the name would lead one to infer) all the saints.

34. This stanza is from a hymn (early ninth century) for All Saints' Day, with the incipit "Christe, redemptor omnium," in *AH* 51: 150, no. 129 (Schaller/Könsgen, no. 2220).

Likewise:

> May the good offices of the monks
> and all the citizens of heaven
> assent to the desires of suppliants
> and demand [for them] the reward of life.[35]

I hear nevertheless that you are accustomed to present to us as conflicting evidence also what our Jerome wrote: "If a monk has fallen, a priest will pray for him. Who will there be to pray for the lapse of a priest?"[36] Certainly you could say this with some justification, if it happened that monks were in no way priests. When indeed he says "monk and priest," assuredly that differentiates from the authority of a priest the monk who is not a priest. For thus when we say "king and knight" or "bishop and priest" or "priest and deacon," although in fact kings may be knights, bishops priests, or priests deacons, we understand him to be a knight who is not a king, a priest who is not a bishop, and a deacon plain and simple. Also, when [Jerome] says "The priest will pray for him," he understands specifically that prayer is the mass which is proper to a priest, not that which suits any just man whatsoever. The Apostle [James], commending the just generally, said, "For the continual prayer of a just man availeth much" [James 5.16]. For whoever is more just deserves to be heeded by him who weighs not

35. This stanza is from another hymn (ninth or tenth century) for All Saints' Day, with the incipit "Iesu, salvator saeculi," in *AH* 51: 152, no. 130 (Schaller/Könsgen, no. 7666).

36. This passage appears in Jerome, Letter 14.9 (to the monk, Heliodorus: 373 or 374), ed. Hilberg, CSEL 54: 59. Abelard's quotations of the letter here and later underpin his general argument well. Heliodorus was formerly a soldier, is at the time of the letter a presbyter, and will eventually become a bishop. After accompanying Jerome to the East and finding life as a solitary in the desert unsatisfactory, he returned to Aquileia and resumed his clerical duties. In the letter Jerome takes Heliodorus to task for abandoning the fulfillment of ascetic life. For the whole letter in English, see *The Letters of St. Jerome*, trans. Charles Christopher Mierow, vol. 1, Ancient Christian Writers: The Works of the Fathers in Translation 33 (Westminster, Md.: Newman Press, 1963), 59–69.

so much words as works and considers not so much the tongue as the life. Moreover, how much the same doctor [of the Church = Jerome] prefers to yours the monastic life on account of its perfection, he asserts overtly to the monk Heliodorus, writing in these words:

Interpret the word "monk"; this is your name. What are you who are alone doing in a crowd?[37] [. . .] "What then? Are any people who are in the city not Christians?" You do not have the same motives as the others do. Hear the Lord saying, "If thou wilt be perfect, go sell what thou hast, and give to the poor and come, follow me" [Matthew 19.21]. You however have promised that you are perfect. For when, after having left behind the worldly army, you castrated yourself for the sake of the kingdom of heaven, what else did you follow but a perfect life?[38]

And after some words he said, "As I mentioned before, the motivation of the monk is one and that of clerics another," which is to say that their calling and way of life differ greatly from one another and that their aim tends toward different ends, "As," he said, "I mentioned before."[39] Indeed, when he did this cannot be determined, unless it was when he distinguished monastic perfection from the life of the faithful who dwell in the city, saying, "What then? Are any people who live in cities not Christians?" In writing to Paulinus (who was at once a priest and a monk), he also asserts overtly that clerics ought to dwell among people rather than hold to the perfection of monastic solitude:

37. Abelard quotes this same pair of sentences from Jerome in Letter Eight. References to the etymology of *monachus* were conventional; see Jean Leclercq, *Etudes sur le vocabulaire monastique du moyen âge*, Studia Anselmiana 48 (Rome: "Orbis Catholicus" Herder, 1961), 8–9.

38. Jerome, Letter 14.6, ed. Hilberg, CSEL 54: 52–53. Abelard quotes the first two sentences of this passage from Jerome in Letter Eight as well as in Sermon 33, in *PL* 178: 589A and 596D (where he also separately incorporates the same verse from Matthew); he modifies the first sentence lightly in quoting it in his "solution" to the fourteenth of Heloise's *Problemata*, in *PL* 178: 698C.

39. Jerome, Letter 14.8, ed. Hilberg, CSEL 54: 55.

Therefore, since you enquire as a brother by which path you ought to proceed, I will speak with you with my face unconcealed.[40] If you wish to perform the duty of a priest, if either the work or honor of the episcopacy perhaps entices you, live in cities and castles and make the salvation of others into the profit of your soul. But if, however, you wish to be what you are called, a monk, that is "alone," what are you doing in cities which in point of fact are the dwelling-places not of solitaries but of multitudes? Each way of life has its leaders [. . .] and, to come to ours, bishops and priests should hold as their example the apostles and apostle-like men; and when they possess the rank of these others, they should strive also to have their merit. However, we should have as leaders of our way of life the Pauls, Anthonies, Julians, Hilarions, [and] Macariuses, and, to return to the authority of the Scriptures, our leader [is] Elijah, our [leader] Elisha, our guides the sons of the prophets, who dwelt in fields and solitary places and made for themselves tents near the running waters of the Jordan.[41] Among these are also those sons of Rechab who did not drink wine and cider, who dwelt in tents, who were praised by the voice of God through Jeremiah, and it is promised them that there will not be wanting a man from their stock who stands before God.[42]

Among our leaders wonder not only at Elijah, who shone forth so greatly among people of old that while still living he deserved to be elevated into heaven, but also at John, coming in his spirit and like another Elijah, to whom the Lord gave so much power of witness that in proportion to the distinction of his life he called him a very angel by reason of the prophet's power of wit-

---

40. "With my face unconcealed" means "openly."

41. The Paul invoked here is known as both Paul the Hermit and Paul of Thebes (died about 347). Anthony the Hermit (about 251–356) has often been viewed as the founder of cenobitism. Julian is Julian the Hospitaller ("the Poor Man": no known dates). Hilarion, another hermit, was the first solitary in Palestine (about 291–about 371). Macarius the Elder was a desert monk, the father of Egyptian monasticism (about 300–about 390). Elijah, who appears in 3 Kings, was one of the foremost prophets in the Hebrew Bible. Elisha succeeded him (3 and 4 Kings).

42. Jerome, Letter 58.5 (to Paulinus of Nola, written around 395), ed. Hilberg, CSEL 54: 533–34. Abelard quotes this letter twice in his Letter Eight and three times in Sermon 33, in PL 178: 585BC and 597A. On the Rechabites, see Jeremiah 35.6–7.

ness and preferred him over not only prophets but all other men too.[43] About him John Chrysostom comments in Homily 23 on the Gospels,[44] which begins thus "About John it is said: 'There was a man sent from God' [John 1.6]":

He was named John. Grace is encompassed in the name; for John is interpreted as "God's grace," [. . .] inasmuch as he received a greater grace. Therefore he teaches wisdom in the wilderness and holds himself for the arrival of Christ, because he was to announce Christ. At once he is nourished in the wilderness, at once he grows there; he does not wish to dwell with men, he moralizes in the wilderness with angels. [. . .] Consider, monks, your excellence. John, the originator of your doctrine, is himself a monk. As soon as he is born, he lives in the wilderness, he is nourished in a solitary place, he awaits Christ in a solitary place. [. . .] In that time when John was born and was in the wilderness, how many riches, what gold, and what silver this temple (which we see was destroyed) contained. [. . .] Josephus [. . .] describes how many gems, how much silk, how many priests, scribes, and offices of all kinds there were.[45] [. . .] Christ is not known in the temple and is preached in the wilderness. [. . .] Why do I say all of this? That I may show the founder of your doctrine to be John the Baptist.[46]

43. On Elijah's elevation to heaven, see 2 Kings 2.11. Matthew 11.7–9 (compare 11.11) and Luke 7.24–26 refer to John the Baptist as being more than a prophet. On the likeness of John to Elijah, see Matthew 11.12–14 (compare 17.12–13) and Mark 9.12–13.

44. St. John Chrysostom lived from about 347 to 407. The epithet that follows his first name means "Golden Mouth" and was bestowed upon him in recognition of his power as a preacher, which remains (along with his exegesis) his best-known attainment.

45. Flavius Josephus (born about 37–38 c.e.) was a Jewish priest who left extensive historical writings in Greek. Jerome refers in particular to *Jewish War* (about 75–79), 6.9.3. For other descriptions of the Temple, see the *Jewish War*, 5.5.1–8, and *Jewish Antiquities* (published in 93/4), 15.11.1–7.

46. The homily is in fact not by John Chrysostom but rather by Jerome, *Homilia in Ioannem Euangelistam* (Homily on John the Evangelist), 1.1–14, ed. Germain Morin, CCSL 78 (1958): 517–23, at 517–18. For an English version of the entire homily, see *The Homilies of Saint Jerome*, no. 87, translated by Marie Liguori Ewald, 2 vols., The Fathers of the Church (a new translation) 48 and 57 (Washington, D.C.: The Catho-

You have heard, brothers, the founders of our order and like-wise of yours invoked above so that the difference of each of the two may be apparent. If you rejoice that the apostles too are num-bered among your founders and the priests of the Old as well as the New Testament (which is to say, from Aaron himself down to Annas and Caiaphas), do not, I beg of you, grieve that Elijah and John who are greater than these are the leaders of our order.[47] There is no doubt that John exchanged a clerical for a monastic state. Since he was the son of a priest, priestly dignity was owed him by hereditary right at that time; he held the city of less ac-count than solitary places, the priest than the monk, and he put perfection of life ahead of ecclesiastic preferment.

Jerome, writing about him to the monk Rusticus, said:

I hear that you have a religious mother, a widow of many years' stand-ing, who nursed and reared you as an infant.[48] John the Baptist too had a saintly mother and was the son of a priest, and yet he was convinced by neither his mother's affection or father's wealth to live at the risk of chastity in his parents' house.[49] He lived in the wilderness and deigned to gaze upon nothing else with his eyes longing for Christ. [. . .] The sons of the prophets,[50] whom we read in the Old Testament were monks, built

---

lic University of America Press, 1964–1966), 2: 212–20. Abelard relies on part of this same passage in *Sermo* 33, in *PL* 178: 585D.

47. Aaron, the eldest brother of Moses, was the first high priest, named repeat-edly in the Pentateuch. Annas was a high priest in the time of Christ, while Joseph Caiaphas was the high priest at the trial of Jesus; both are mentioned in the Gospels and the Acts of the Apostles.

48. Jerome, Letter 125.6, ed. Hilberg, CSEL 56: 123.

49. The life of John the Baptist is described in the canonical Gospels, especially that of Luke. John's father, the priest, was named Zachary, while his mother was Eliz-abeth, cousin of Mary (Luke 1.36). The element upon which both Jerome and Abe-lard focused was the ascetic life John led in the desert.

50. The Old Testament expression "sons of the prophets" could be glossed less metaphorically as "disciples of the prophets." The expression is used particularly of-ten in 4 Kings, sometimes in close proximity to "man of God." Both turns of phrase are tied closely to Elijah and Elisha. Their diet of pottage and wild herbs in a time of famine is mentioned in 4 Kings 4.38–39.

hovels for themselves near the waters of the Jordan and, having left behind the throngs of the cities, subsisted upon pottage and wild herbs.[51]

Elsewhere he recalls of them, "Elijah was a virgin, Elisha a virgin,
the sons of the prophets virgins."[52] Why is it, I beg of you, brother, that the Lord as he was about to elect apostles did not summon
John from the desert, nor did he when to be baptized by him call
him back from solitary places even for an hour, but like other people came to him among the others, even he himself to be baptized
by the monk, as it was written, "Now it came to pass, when all the
people were baptized, that Jesus also being baptized" [Luke 3.21] and
so forth. Why is it, I say, unless that, as he said, he reckoned Mary's
portion to be preferred to Martha's, which is to say, the repose of
contemplation to the care and frequent disturbances of the world?[53]

In truth, preoccupied by these cares the Apostle [Paul] groans,
saying: "Besides those things which are without: my daily instance,
the solicitude for all the churches. Who is weak, and I am not
weak? Who is scandalized, and I am not on fire?" [2 Corinthians
11.28–29].[54] The Lord himself taught openly, when he determined

51. Jerome, Letter 125.6–7, to Rusticus, ed. Hilberg, CSEL 56: 125. The passage was
one to which Abelard resorted often for quotations or to which he (and Heloise, as
reported by him) referred without quoting it verbatim: twice in the *Historia calamitatum*, ed. Monfrin, p. 77, lines 501–503, and pp. 93–94, lines 1084–1090; trans. Radice,
pp. 15 and 29–30; once in Letter Seven; once in Letter Eight; and once in Sermon 23,
in *PL* 178: 525C. Once again, the letter Abelard has chosen lends itself well to the case
he is building. In the letter, Jerome counsels the young monk Rusticus not to become
a hermit but to remain a cenobite. In addition, Jerome proposes rules for monastic
life and indicates what characterizes a good and what a bad monk.

52. Jerome, Letter 22.21, ed. Hilberg, CSEL 54: 172.

53. Martha, sister of Mary and Lazarus of Bethany (Luke 10.38–42 and John 12.1–
8), afforded a type for the practical life, as opposed to the contemplative life of her
sister. Abelard employs the pair to stand for these two kinds of life in Sermon 8, in
PL 178: 436B–44D, at 438D–439C, and Sermon 33, in *PL* 178: 582B–607A, at 595A and
598B. In Bethany Christ visited the house of Martha and Mary. At table Mary anoint-
ed Jesus' feet and wiped them with her hair, while Martha busied herself in serving. Jesus singled out Mary for praise. For information on the appearances and functions of
the two women in twelfth-century thought, see Constable, *Three Studies*, 1–141.

54. The Douay-Rheims translates thus. Smits presents the Latin with commas

to wash the feet of the apostles, how difficult it is amidst preoccupations and annoyances to maintain cleanness of heart and to frequent earthly routes without some pollution of dust.[55] The bride
in the Song of Songs, attending dutifully to this, excuses herself
with foresight in these words to the betrothed who knocks at her
door and asks that she arise from bed and open to him, "I have put
off my garment, how shall I put it on? I have washed my feet, how
shall I defile them?" [Song of Songs 5.3]. For what is the bed of the
bride, if not the repose of a soul that is contemplative and removed
from the concerns and cares of the world? Indeed, the more fully it
devotes itself to God in the cloisters like the bride in the bedchamber and the more tightly it is bound to him in complete desire, the
further it is removed from worldly preoccupations, and already in
the secrecy of celestial chambers it is so joined to him through contemplation that the spirit is one with God, in accordance with what
is read of blessed Martin: "He compelled his limbs as they grew
tired to do service to the spirit; and reclining on his bedding he
deigned not to see the earth and was wholly avid for heaven."[56] For
such repose of the bed and secrecy of contemplation the betrothed
as he comes asks that the door be opened to him [Song of Songs
5.2], [in the same way] as the Christian people entreats whoever is
of contemplative soul, that in undertaking their direction he may
thus grant them entrance to [the bridegroom] himself.[57]

around "instantia mea," which would presume the alternative: "my instance, the daily
solitude."

55. The washing of the disciples' feet before the Last Supper is related in John 13.

56. The quotation is based upon Sulpicius Severus (around 360–around 420–425),
Letter 3.14, ed. Jacques Fontaine, *Vita S. Martini episcopi*, 3 vols., Sources Chrétiennes
133–35 (Paris: Editions du Cerf, 1967–1969), 1: 316–44, at 340. Sulpicius's various texts
on St. Martin of Tours (about 316–397), including the letters, enjoyed considerable
favor in the Middle Ages. St. Martin is best known for the episode in his legend in
which he bestowed half his cloak upon a beggar and experienced afterward a vision
of Christ that summoned him to baptism and religion, but here Abelard turned to
the saint's asceticism, a feature of the life that better suited his preoccupation with
the contemplative life. It is of course also apt to invoke Martin in this light, owing to
his standing as the father of monasticism in France.

57. Commentaries on the Song of Songs sometimes counterpoise the repose of

What Christ himself is said to do in his members,[58] it is done through his inspiration and is entreated in his name and authority. Indeed, so long as that perfect soul, passionately loving its repose, shuns toil (lest for the profit of others it should incur damage to its perfection), it refuses to rise from bed and says to the persistent betrothed, as has been said, "I have put off my garment" [Song of Songs 5.3], that is, "I have because of a vow disregarded the external care of worldly actions." Indeed the inner and more refined garment is a shift, the outer and coarser one a tunic.

For this reason the first adornment is to be called contemplative, but the second habit active. To be sure, these people, shutting themselves away in monastic cloisters, contemplate all the more subtly and perfectly the splendor of the highest light as they are the more fully distanced from outer cares of the world. Indeed, when the bride agrees in no way to return from contemplation to action, she avoids taking up again like a tunic this occupation of cares which Martha expends upon the needs of a neighbor and which those who oversee the people practice. For this reason, supplying a motive, the bride says, "I have washed my feet, how shall I defile them?" [Song of Songs 5.3]. To be sure, our states of mind, by which we are drawn to whatever must be done, are (as it were) feet by which we are led. He washes off these feet who restrains his mind from worldly concerns; for it is difficult that a soul spread thin by these in different directions should not be spattered at least by some stains of thoughts or should not yield at some times to temptations. The bride, considering this, fears to set her feet from the bed to the ground, that is, to embroil herself again in cares, so long as she believes that no place outside her bed is free from con-

---

the contemplative soul (associated with monks) with the action of the apostolic Church. For an allegorical reading of Song of Songs 5.2–7 that may inform Abelard's presentation here, see Bede, *In Cantica canticorum*, section 3, ed. David Hurst, CCSL 119B (1983), 165–375, at 274–82.

58. Since the Church may be viewed as the body of Christ, his members are metaphorically equivalent to those of the Church; see Romans 12.5, 1 Corinthians 12.27, and Ephesians 4.25 and 5.30.

tagion. At length she is compelled at the instance of the betrothed to arise from bed and to open for him, just as he demanded.

About him it has been added that when she wished to hold him and embrace him, as she was accustomed: "But he had turned aside, and was gone" [Song of Songs 5.6]. For God cannot be discovered in public just as in private, nor can the devotion of Martha, as she is crowded about with many concerns, attend constantly to Christ [Luke 10.38–42], nor can a mind attentive to worldly concerns keep watch quietly in God. For this reason the beloved himself advises that the chamber door be closed, so that we may pray more devoutly. Otherwise he turns aside and goes on from us, because the less we are free for him, the more we are abandoned by him and the more fully we are left destitute of the gifts of his grace. Even his spouse, having passed out into the public from the privacy of the bedchamber, finds how much for the profit of others she is diminished concerning her perfection; and the more the danger develops, the more the reckoning to be rendered remains with him for the souls committed to him.

Pay heed, brother, I entreat, to the dignity of your order and the state of your office, in which both merit is diminished and peril is imminent. See what the profit of dignity is, when the perfection of religious life is taken away, when he who is greater in the world becomes lesser in the face of God and endures a serious loss of himself. You rejoice that Leah, whom you married, is fertile, but you grieve when you see that she is bleary-eyed [Genesis 29–30].[59] Leah had a marriage by night, as if such a bond were not worthy of daylight. So long as Rachel remained sterile, she lived in safety. Afterward, having become fertile, she expired through her own childbirth. From this event it is plainly indicated how hazard-

---

59. Rachel and Leah (or Lia) were sisters. Leah, the elder and less attractive, was Jacob's first wife. She bore him six sons and a daughter. Rachel, the younger and more beautiful, was at first barren. The two were interpreted figuratively in various ways, with Rachel being associated with contemplation and Leah with activity or work. See Constable, *Three Studies*, 10–11 and 48–52.

ous it is to receive that in which you glory, and that this glory is to be called ruin or degradation rather than exaltation.

According to that statement of the Psalmist "When they were lifted up, thou hast cast them down" [Psalm 72.18], blessed Jerome in fact paid heed to their easy fall and hazardous ascent and wrote in a certain passage to the monk Heliodorus with these words: "But if the pious allurements of the brothers win you over to the same order, I will rejoice for the elevation, but I will fear for the fall."[60] In commending the security of solitary (which is to say, monastic) life in *Against Vigilantius*, the same man says:[61]

"Why," you will say, "are you going to the desert?" It is plainly that I may not hear you, see you, be moved by your wrath, suffer your hostilities; that the eye of a prostitute not capture me; that a most beautiful form not lead to unlawful embraces. You will respond: "This is not to fight but to flee. Stand in the battle line, stand armed and resist adversaries, so that you may be crowned after you have vanquished." I admit my weakness. I do not wish to fight in hope of victory, for fear that at some time I might lose victory. If I flee, I have avoided the sword; if I stand, I must either win or fall. But why is it necessary to part with sure things and to strive for unsure ones? Death must be avoided either with a shield or with the feet. You who fight can be both overcome and victorious. When I flee, I do not vanquish in fleeing, but I flee so that I may not be vanquished. There is no safety in sleeping with a serpent nearby. It can happen that it might not bite me; nevertheless it can happen that at some time it might bite me.[62]

The same man wrote to Oceanus about the death of Fabiola:[63]

60. Jerome, Letter 14.8, ed. Hilberg, CSEL 54: 56.

61. Jerome and Vigilantius (born 370), a presbyter from Aquitaine, had a quarrel that eventuated in Jerome's polemical invective, which attacked Vigilantius for many shortcomings, including failings in celibacy and monastic discipline.

62. *Contra Vigilantium* 14.8, in *PL* 23: 339–52 (353–68), here 367a. This text by Jerome is cited by Heloise in Letter Four, ed. J. T. Muckle, *Mediaeval Studies* 15 (1953): 82, and another part of it by Abelard in his solution to the fourteenth of Heloise's *Problemata* in *PL* 178: 700A (ed. Cousin, p. 262, line 2); in Sermon 33, in *PL* 178: 603A; and in Sermon 35 "Adtendite a falsis prophetis," ed. Engels, p. 226, line 46.

63. Letter 117.3, ed. Hilberg, CSEL 55: 425–26. St. Fabiola (died 399) was a Roman

A religious man should beware of living there where he may have the necessity daily of either perishing or winning. For it is safer not to be able to perish than not to perish in the proximity of danger.

Seneca, that greatest moral philosopher, who also held this opinion and advised his Lucilius to philosophize in this fashion, said in the fifty-third of the letters which he wrote to him:[64]

We must choose a place that is healthy not only for the body but also for the morals. [. . .] We must do this so that we may shun as long as possible the incitements of vices. The soul must be hardened and kept far from the enticements of pleasures. One winter weakened Hannibal, and the pampering in Campania debilitated that man untamed by snows or the Alps.[65] He conquered with weapons, he was conquered by vices. We must also serve as soldiers and in a certain manner of soldiery, by which leisure is never granted. [. . .] First of all, pleasures must be overcome which, as you see, have also captured for themselves even savage natures. If anyone imagines how great a task he has approached, he will know that nothing must be done gently, nothing softly.

But perhaps to these counsels of holy fathers as well as of philosophers you will respond in truth that it is dangerous to undertake church administration and most difficult to toil in it, as much as is necessary; but for a fact it is certain that the greater the rewards are, the greater the difficulty weighs upon this labor. To which I reply first of all with that statement of Cicero, "Even if it

matron who went in 395 to Bethlehem, where she stayed with Paula and Eustochium under the direction of Jerome. Eventually she returned to Rome. The passage also appears (with wording closer to what Abelard cites) in Pseudo-Jerome, *Homilia ad monachos*, in *PL* 30: 311–18, at 315A.

64. Seneca the Younger (Lucius Annaeus Seneca) was forced to commit suicide in 65 C.E. Among his extant works are the *Epistulae morales*, one hundred and twenty-four letters divided into twenty books. Their addressee is nominally Lucilius (Gaius Lucilius Iunior). Although Abelard cites Letter 53, in the numbering of standard modern editions the passage quoted is Letter 51.4–6.

65. After the Carthaginian general Hannibal (247–183/2 B.C.E.) wintered with his troops in southern Italy (216–215 B.C.E.), his campaign against Rome (217–202 B.C.E.) met with less success. "Post hoc, ergo propter hoc" reasoning has attributed the subsequent failures of the Carthaginians to "the debauch of Capua."

be laborious, it is not necessarily excellent" [Pseudo-Cicero, *Rhetorica ad Herennium* 4.4.6]. Otherwise in the Church of God those who are entangled in the daily bothers of marriage and in incessant cares would have to be preferred to those who in leading a celibate life are less oppressed by the weight of the world and on this account are devoted more freely and purely to God, as if having obtained the repose of bed.[66] In sum, if for the increase of merits you extol those who, trusting in their virtues, have resolved to endure rather than flee fights of temptations and enticements of the world, consider whether it should be counseled to those who have taken vows of chastity that they should strive to preserve this virtue in brothels or where they see frequent fornications and that exposing themselves voluntarily to perils, but, as if attending closely to angels rather than human beings, they should presume to test God through so great a complacence about themselves.

Why indeed are clerics prohibited from having women in their dwelling place, except such persons of close blood relationship about whom no suspicion of baseness could be held? Augustine, your instructor most particularly (as you say), also decreed that these women should be avoided to such an extent that he did not allow even his most saintly sister to dwell with him, saying: "Those who are with my sister are not my sisters."[67] Why, even you yourselves, newly called "Regular Canons" by yourselves, just as you are newly arisen, do you not remain separated from the enticements and temptations of the world, hedging your cloisters about with a great circumference of walls in the manner of monks?[68] If

66. The phrasing of the "bothers of a marriage" comes close to that used in the description of Susanna in Letter Nine. "The repose of bed" refers to Abelard's explication of Song of Songs 5.2 earlier in Letter Twelve.

67. Smits, *Letters IX–XIV*, 267, has pointed out that although this anecdote appears in Possidius's *Vita Augustini (Life of Augustine)* 26, in *PL* 32: 55, it does not appear in Augustine's own writings. Abelard's likely source is Ivo of Chartres, *Decretum* 6.77, in *PL* 161: 462B, a text on which Abelard often relied.

68. This sentence holds at least twofold interest. On the one hand, Abelard presents himself in it tacitly as defending against innovation, a stand that he also took in

therefore, as you also teach and as is evident to one and all, it is more fitting for human frailty to be protected from dangers than to oppose itself to them willingly, indeed the advice is to avoid all temptations to the extent that we can, especially if we should choose that life which both is of greater merit and lies less open to temptation. This is declared by the authority of the fathers as well as by certain examples of deeds.

It is apparent that the life of contemplation and repose were preferred by the Lord to the tumultuous activity of the faithful, and it is certain that the part of Mary (which he called the best [Luke 10.42]) was preferred to the part of Martha. For although Martha refreshed the Lord, Mary was more blessedly refreshed by the Lord; and the Lord administered refreshment better by far than did Martha. The ministration of Martha is to see to the body's needs, to distribute the word of preaching, to take care of others by virtue of one's own office rather than of oneself. For the pastors of the Church, in that they are shepherds (*pastores*), are obliged to think not so much about their own nourishment as about that of those subject to them, and in this they benefit not so much themselves as others. For this reason the Lord, when he established Peter in this office, did not say at all "Feed yourself" but "Feed my sheep" [John 21.17] or "my lambs" [John 21.15–16], that is, instruct them or bolster them with the bread of spiritual teaching or encouragement. About the bread of God's word it has in fact been written elsewhere: "Not in bread alone doth man live, but in every word that proceedeth from the mouth of God" [Matthew 4.4].

But if in this time you compare the toil and hardness of life of clerics and monks, what becomes evident through daily experiences need not be discussed in a long debate. Compare bishops with abbots, archpriests of churches with priors of monasteries, clerics

---

Letter Ten. On the other, it confirms that he viewed both the name and the institution of Regular Canons as being new. The newness could be merely relative to monasticism or could conceal another, more specific reference.

with monks, and ask whomever you wish who among them lead a harsher or more toilsome life than who. The result will be that if you should ponder the toil, you would find far superior in merit us, to whom you yourselves ascribe a life not other than that of penitents, and you call our cloisters not places of worthiness but prisons of penance. Blessed Jerome, differentiating this from the life of clerics, also writes to Heliodorus on the death of Nepotian in these words:[69]

If anyone, having forsaken the clergy, should hand himself over to monastic rigor, let him be incessant in prayers, watchful in devotion, offering tears to God and not to men.[70]

Certainly if the life of clerics were more bounded and if those who are preeminent in worthiness within the Church also stood out for the severity of their lives, not at all would monks be sought after with such great desire to become bishops nor would spiritual fathers solicit clerics with such great anxiety to the monastic way of life. Of this sort too is that passage from the same teacher [Jerome] when exhorting the deacon Praesidius:

Deacon, you will say, "I cannot safely forsake the Church. I fear to commit sacrilege, if I abandon the altars." But consider, I beg you, that it is quite difficult to fill the place of Stephen or Paul, to stand in the ministry of an angel and to look down from above in bright vestments upon the people who lie below.[71] The pearl is precious, but it is readily broken, and once broken, it cannot be restored.[72]

69. Bishop Heliodorus of Altinum has suffered the loss of his nephew Nepotian, a presbyter who died of fever in 396.

70. Jerome, Letter 60.10, ed. Hilberg, CSEL 54.561.

71. Stephen was one of the Seven (Acts of the Apostles 21.8), a group that has been taken as the archetype of the order of deacons. Paul the Apostle was a great missionary and preacher (also discussed passim in the Acts of the Apostles).

72. Jerome, *Epistula ad Praesidium*, ed. Germain Morin, *Bulletin d'ancienne littérature et d'archéologie chrétiennes* 3 (1913): 51–60, at 57.

Likewise,

When they tear to pieces the good life in cities, what will you do, brother, caught in the middle? Either you will seek out things that are contrary to continence or, if you do not wish to do them, you will be condemned yourself. I pass over various enticements by which even the most unyielding minds are softened. Now I assert this because, even if matters were not so, you would have been obliged to forsake things that are lesser in comparison with so enormous a good.

Add that you are a deacon, but by your withdrawal the churches will not experience losses. Elijah lived in the desert, a chorus of prophets followed Elisha. John, the harbinger of the Lord, having been nurtured in a solitary place, came down to the banks of the Jordan for this reason only, that he might rebuke the peoples flowing together and, understanding the Pharisaical clerics of the Jews, might designate them as broods of vipers [Matthew 3.7]. Recently you have seen the deserts of Egypt, you have gazed upon the angelic family. How many flowers are there? How are the meadows verdant with spiritual jewels? You have seen the garlands with which the Lord is crowned.[73]

Likewise,

You will have a little cell that holds you alone. But you will not be alone; an angelic throng will live with you. However many comrades, that many saints. You will read the Gospel, Jesus will converse with you. You will repeat again and again the words of apostles and prophets. Will you be able to have any other such companion for your words? Let us at least strive to imitate little women; may the weaker sex instruct us. However much they prospered in riches as well as in nobility, they then (in fact, I do not wish to say the words for fear that I seem to be fawning), by abandoning material goods and spurning close relations, rated as easy to do what you thought difficult, owing to your own fear.[74]

73. Jerome, *Epistula ad Praesidium*, ed. Morin, 57.
74. Jerome, *Epistula ad Praesidium*, ed. Morin, 57.

10

LETTER THIRTEEN. TO AN IGNORAMUS IN THE FIELD OF DIALECTIC

The most common and fundamental schema of learning in the Middle Ages was the seven liberal arts, which comprehended the trivium of the verbal or logical arts (grammar, rhetoric, and dialectic or logic) and the quadrivium of the so-called mathematical arts (arithmetic, geometry, astronomy, and music).[1] Grammar enabled correct speech and writing, together with interpretation of poetry; rhetoric was the art of persuasion; and dialectic or logic imparted the skills necessary for distinguishing between truth and falsehood. Although from one period to another the arts within the trivium shifted in relative importance, grammar was always the first to be studied for the obvious reason that a working knowledge of Latin was essential before any other formal higher learning could be approached. In late antiquity rhetoric held the highest standing, as can be sensed from Augustine's *Confessions*. In the early Middle Ages grammar predominated. In the twelfth century both dialectic, or logic, and rhetoric gained prestige at the expense of grammar. Although we must not force our own terms upon the twelfth century, to an extent the rivalry between dialectic and grammar corresponds to a friction between theory and practice.

---

1. In the *Didascalicon* (2.20) Hugh of St. Victor touches upon similar matters of relevance to the worldviews of Peter Abelard and other twelfth-century contemporaries.

From what has been said about the trivium, it is evident that dialectic was not far from being an altogether new area of study. A revolutionary development of the twelfth century, associated above all with Peter Abelard himself, was to transform dialectic from being a discipline concerned with identifying and rejecting false arguments to one that encompassed much more than that. Even in Abelard's most restrictive understanding of the craft he made his own, dialectic stood preeminent among the liberal arts. In his *Dialectica* he gave the following definition: "Dialectic, to which all judgement of truth and falsehood is subject, holds the leadership of all philosophy and the governance of all teaching."[2] Beyond philosophy and teaching lay theology and faith itself. Here dialectic constituted a means of reasoning that could enable its practitioner to determine or even construct the elements of faith on the basis of rational argumentation. In other words, dialectic became in Abelard's eyes no longer merely a weapon with which to defend faith from the outside against the falsities of flawed or even heretical doctrines. In his view it could actually be a force within faith, a component in its inner workings.

Letter Thirteen is addressed to an unidentified and possibly imaginary recipient who is ignorant in dialectic. Still worse, from Abelard's point of view, his addressee is hostile to dialectic and thinks it bad that others should study it. In this letter Abelard rails that some of his contemporaries in the world of learning are like the fox in the fable about sour grapes; his version has sour cherries instead of grapes, but the moral is the same. Unable to achieve a mastery of dialectic, they denigrate its methods as being mere sophistries and fallacies. (In two versions of his *Theologia*, Abelard refers to opponents of another sort, those who lay claim to proficiencies in dialectic they truly lack, as pseudodialecticians.)[3] Since the critics being rebutted here have no training or aptitude in dialectic, Abelard must combat

2. *Dialectica*, ed. De Rijk, p. 470, lines 3–4, trans. Constant J. Mews, "Peter Abelard on Dialectic, Rhetoric, and the Principles of Argument," in *Rhetoric and Renewal in the Latin West 1100–1540: Essays in Honour of John O. Ward*, ed. Constant J. Mews, Cary J. Nederman, and Rodney M. Thomson, Disputatio 2 (Turnhout, Belgium: Brepols, 2003), 37–53, at 43.

3. *Theologia "Summi boni"* 2.5–26, pp. 115–23, and in the *Theologia Christiana* 3.1–58, pp. 194–219.

their accusations by employing the method of argumentation with which they are familiar. Accordingly, he adduces Scripture and patristic authorities such as Augustine and Jerome to prove that dialectic is necessary for interpretation of the Bible, refutation of heresy, and other purposes. By implication, the practitioners of dialectic (the logicians) are themselves also indispensable.

Abelard differentiates resolutely between dialectic and sophistry, which resemble each other in employing logical arguments but differ in that the logical arguments in dialectic are true while those in sophistry are false. He cites authorities from both the Bible and the Church Fathers to confirm that knowledge of dialectic is required for avoiding the pitfalls of sophistry. While on this topic, Abelard makes a point of emphasizing both how logic underpins New Testament revelation, since in Greek the Word (as "In the beginning was the Word" [John 1.1]) is *logos*, from which the word *logic* derives, and how logic is fundamental to philosophy, which is love of Christ as the Father's wisdom (*sophia*).[4]

Although Abelard's works contain many considerations of philosophy, the excursus on logic and *logos* in Letter Thirteen seems to be the most sustained treatment of them he produced.[5] After this sec-

---

4. Elsewhere, Abelard deals with Christ as wisdom itself in Sermon 33, in *PL* 178: 582B–607A, at 592B, and in the *Soliloquium*, ed. and trans. Charles S. F. Burnett, "Peter Abelard *Soliloquium*: A Critical Edition," *Studi Medievali*, 3rd series, 25 (1984): 857–94, at 886–87.

For discussion of this convention, see Leclercq, "Ad ipsam sophiam Christi," pp. 161–81. Other monastic authors identified Christ with *sophia* and *philosophia*: see Henri Rochais, "Ipsa philosophia Christus," *Mediaeval Studies* 13 (1951): 244–47. In monastic use the term *philosophia* often designated the monastic life as a whole: see Leclercq, *Etudes sur le vocabulaire monastique*, pp. 39–67 and 156–57.

Abelard, when describing his entry into monasticism in the *Historia calamitatum*, describes his aspiration to be "nec tam mundi quam Dei vere philosophus" (a true philosopher not of the world but of God): 653–4, ed. Monfrin, p. 81; trans. Radice, p. 19. The fusion Abelard sought to bring about between the two forms of *philosophia* seemed unreachable to a contemporary such as Bernard of Clairvaux: see Gianni Festa, "San Bernardo di Chiaravalle tra *ipsa philosophia Christi* e *philosophorum ventosa loquacitas*," *Divus Thomas: Jahrbuch für Philosophie und spekulative Theologie* 96 (1993): 207–38.

For a distillation of findings on the semantic range of *philosophia* in Medieval Latin, see Teeuwen, *Vocabulary of Intellectual Life*, pp. 395–99.

5. Zerbi, *"Philosophi" e "Logici,"* 31–34.

tion Abelard explicates the descent of the Holy Ghost at the Feast of Pentecost as a conversion of the disciples into philosophers and logicians.[6] Christ used reasoning and miracles to bring to the faith Greeks and Jews, respectively. As miracles have become less useful in guiding people to faith, reasoning has grown all the more important. Finally, it is true that poor logic can result in error. Quoting Augustine, Abelard sees this liability as an additional incentive to ensure that scholars be trained in logic and motivated to employ it correctly.

Dialectic instructs in how to distinguish truth from falsehood, how to attain truth, and how to avoid falsehood. It teaches not only how to learn but even how to teach, according to a turn of phrase Abelard appropriates from Augustine. Beyond learning and teaching, dialectic is tied to religion: logicians are bound up more than merely etymologically with the Word of God, the *logos*. In their study of the word of God the logicians belong to the enterprise of philosophy, which is itself devoted to the wisdom (*sophia*) of the Father.

With an unnamed addressee and without any references to specific controversies in Peter Abelard's life, Letter Thirteen has proved difficult to date. Smits leaned toward a date around 1130, while Jolivet inclined toward dating it perhaps around 1132. See Jean Jolivet, *Arts du langage et théologie chez Abélard*, 2d ed. (Paris: J. Vrin, 1982), 269–72.

Since no manuscript survives, in constituting the text Edmé Smits and his predecessors were constrained to rely on the 1616 editio princeps. For information on the earliest printed edition, see the introduction to Letter Twelve above. The letter has been translated into French: Jean Jolivet, *Abélard ou la philosophie dans le langage: Présentation, choix de textes, bibliographie*, Vestigia 14 (Fribourg, Switzerland: Éditions universitaires, 1994), 150–56.

6. As Peter von Moos summed up this aspect of Letter Thirteen, "To the founder of the monastery of the Paraclete, the miracle of Pentecost was the decisive entry of God into the human history of language and the point of revaluation of all values in the theory of speech"; see "Literary Aesthetics in the Latin Middle Ages: The Rhetorical Theology of Peter Abelard," in *Rhetoric and Renewal*, 81–97, at 86–87.

LETTER THIRTEEN

A certain fable with a hidden meaning that tells of a fox has been taken into common usage as a proverb.[7] "The fox," they say, "after seeing cherries on a tree began to creep onto it so that it could nourish itself with them. When it could not reach them and, having slipped back, fell down, it said peevishly, 'I do not care for cherries; their taste is terrible.'"[8] In the same way too certain teachers of our own time, since they cannot attain the capacity of dialectical reasoning, curse it in such a way that they reckon all its teachings to be sophisms and deceptions rather than consider them to be forms of reason. These "blind leaders of the blind" [Matthew 15.14] knowing not, as the Apostle [Paul] said, "the things they say, nor whereof they affirm" [1 Timothy 1.7], damn that which they do not understand, and accuse that of which they have no knowledge. They judge deadly the taste that they have never attained. Whatever they do not understand, they say is stupidity; whatever they cannot comprehend, they regard as madness.

Because in fact we cannot refute by principles of reasoning people who lack reason, at least let us restrain their presumption through the testimonies of the Sacred Scriptures, on which they profess that they rely very much. Therefore let them recognize how much the art (which is to say, dialectic), which they so vehemently detest as being opposed to the Sacred Scriptures, is commended

7. "Mystica quaedam . . . fabula" could also be translated as "a certain allegorical fable."

8. In the Latin fabular tradition this fable, which usually features grapes instead of cherries and which remains entrenched in the English expression "sour grapes," is attested first in the fables of Phaedrus (first century C.E.), Book 4, Fable 3, in *Babrius and Phaedrus*, ed. and trans. Ben Edwin Perry, Loeb Classical Library 436 (Cambridge, Mass.: Harvard University Press, 1984), 302–5. Though Phaedrus's verse fables were themselves not widely known in the Middle Ages, they exercised a powerful indirect influence through prose adaptations that went under the name of Romulus (and hence these versions are sometimes entitled *Romulus*) and that were often joined with the *Distichs of Cato* as components of the most basic textbook for the study of Latin (and simultaneously for the acquisition of rudimentary ethical principles).

by the doctors of the Church and is judged by them to be necessary to the Sacred Scriptures.[9]

Certainly, blessed Augustine dared to extol this type of knowledge with such great praise that in comparison with the other arts he acknowledges it to be the only one leading to knowledge, as if it were the only one that should be called knowledge. For this reason in the second book of *On Order* he refers to it thus:

They call dialectic the discipline of disciplines. It teaches to teach, it teaches to learn. In it reasoning itself makes itself evident and reveals what it is, what it intends. It alone knows; it not only intends to make people knowledgeable but also can do so.[10]

In the second book of *On Christian Doctrine* the same man professes that among all the arts dialectic and arithmetic in particular are needed for reading Scripture, the first to resolve questions and the second to analyze the transcendent secrets of allegories which we often examine in the natures of numbers. In doing so, he extolled dialectic so much the more as he judged it necessary, obviously, for putting an end to all manner of dubieties expressed in questions. Moreover he said as follows:

Those things remain which do not relate to the bodily senses but to mental reasoning, where the discipline of disputation and number prevails. But the discipline of disputation avails greatly at delving into and

9. In this long passage Abelard appears to use the terms *ars* and *scientia* interchangeably to designate dialectic, but at the same time he "makes the point that dialectic is the only true 'scientia' because it alone enables us to have knowledge ('scire')"; see Luscombe, "'Scientia' and 'disciplina,'" 87. In the sentence that follows, it could be translated as "science," but at the cost of its association with the Latin verb "to know."

10. *De ordine* 2.13.38, ed. William M. Green, in *Aureli Augustini opera*, part 2, vol. 2, CCSL 29 (1970): 128. Abelard makes use of this passage elsewhere in the *Theologia "Summi boni,"* 2.5, "Laus dialectice," ed. Buytaert and Mews, CCCM 13: 115, lines 38–41; *Theologia Christiana* 2.117, ed. Buytaert, CCCM 12: 184–85, lines 1785–89; *Theologia "Scholarium,"* 2.19, ed. Buytaert and Mews, CCCM 13: 415, lines 262–66; and *Collationes*, 2.76, ed. and trans. Marenbon and Orlandi, 96–97. For context, see Jolivet, *Arts du langage et théologie*, 269–72, and Jolivet, "Doctrines et figures," 115.

resolving all sorts of questions which arise in the Sacred Scriptures. The only dangers there are excessive pleasure in quarreling and a certain childish showiness in misleading an opponent. For there are many things which are called sophisms, conclusions in reasoning which are false and which very often mimic true conclusions in such a way as to mislead not only the slow-witted but also the clever who are less sedulously attentive. In my estimation, the Scripture expresses loathing for this sort of fallacious conclusions in that passage where it is said: "He that speaketh sophistically, is hateful" [Ecclesiasticus 37.23].[11]

It is plain that the arts of dialectic and sophistry are very distinct from each other, since the first consists in the truth of reasoning and the second in the appearance of such truth; the second imparts false lines of argument and the first resolves them and teaches that they can be detected as false through the discernment of true argumentation. And yet each of the two disciplines, dialectic as well as sophistic, relates to the discernment of arguments, and no one will be able to be discerning in arguments, other than by having the capacity to distinguish false and deceptive lines of argument from true and consistent ones.

Accordingly, writers on dialectic have not failed to produce a treatise on this art, since the very prince of the Peripatetics, Aristotle, also communicated this art, writing the *Sophistical Refutations*.[12] For as knowledge of evil is also needed for a just man, not so that he should do evil but so that he should be able to guard against

11. *De doctrina Christiana* 2.31.48, ed. Martin, CCSL 32: 65–66. Abelard deploys this same passage in the *Sic et non* 1.29, ed. Boyer and McKeon, pp. 117–18, lines 150–62; *Theologia "Summi boni"* 2.5, "Laus dialectice," ed. Buytaert and Mews, CCCM 13: 115–16, lines 44–54; *Theologia Christiana* 2.117, ed. Buytaert, CCCM 12: 185, lines 1789–1800; *Theologia "Scholarium"* 2.19, ed. Buytaert and Mews, CCCM 13: 415, lines 272–83; and *Collationes* 2.76, ed. and trans. Marenbon and Orlandi, 96–97.

12. The works from Aristotle's (384–322 B.C.E.) *Organon* (a collective term for his writings on logic) that had been translated into Latin by Porphyry and Boethius and that circulated in the early Middle Ages were known as the *ars vetus* or *logica vetus*. The *Sophistical Refutations* belonged instead to the other parts of the *Organon*, such as the *Prior Analytics*, the *Posterior Analytics*, and the *Topics*, which were translated in the twelfth century and later and which were designated as the *ars nova* or *logica nova*.

evil after recognizing it,[13] so too a dialectician cannot be lacking experience in sophisms, so that he may be able to protect himself from them. Nor will he have discernment in the principles of arguments, unless having recognized falsities as well as truths, he has the capacity to distinguish the second from the first and to differentiate each of the two thoroughly.

For this reason too, just as blessed Jerome attests, Solomon himself encourages us very much to recognize false as well as true forms of argument. For writing against the slanders of Magnus, an orator of the city Rome, just as we too now write against very much the same types, Jerome spoke thus, amid other words about that most wise Solomon:[14]

In the opening of Proverbs [Proverbs 1.1–6] he reminds that we should understand words of prudence and verbal artifices, parables and obscure speech, sayings of the wise and riddles, which are properly the realm of dialecticians and philosophers.[15]

For what does he understand by words of wisdom and verbal artifices, if not the incompatibility of true and false forms of argument? As we have said, these are so connected to each other, that a person who is ignorant of the false cannot be discerning in the true, since for the understanding of anything whatsoever, the

13. Abelard expresses the same thought in similar words in *Theologia "Summi boni"* 2.7, ed. Buytaert and Mews, CCCM 13: 116, lines 70–72; *Theologia Christiana* 3.6, ed. Buytaert, CCCM 12: 196, lines 61–63; *Theologia "Scholarium"* 2.29, ed. Buytaert and Mews, CCCM 13: 421, lines 438–40; and *Dialectica*, ed. De Rijk, 469.

14. Magnus, a professor of rhetoric in Rome, was also the addressee of Jerome, Letter 70 (dated 397), ed. Hilberg, CSEL 54: 700–708, which contains the famous defense of retaining profane literature so long as it is treated like the captive woman in Deuteronomy 21.10–14 (by removing from it all that is earthly and idolatrous).

15. Jerome, Letter 70.2, ed. Hilberg, CSEL 54: 701. In the *Theologia Christiana* 1.102, 2.2, and 2.119-a, ed. Buytaert, CCCM 12: 113–14, lines 1312–16; 132, lines 19–23; and 186, lines 2–5; and in the *Theologia "Scholarium"* 1.162, 2.2, and 2.20, ed. Buytaert and Mews, CCCM 13: 384, lines 1872–76; 406, lines 20–23; and 416–17, lines 313–17, Abelard adverts repeatedly to the idea expressed in this sentence, quoting it or closely paraphrasing it.

knowledge of its opposite is needed. For no one will know virtues thoroughly who is ignorant of vices, especially since some vices are so close to virtues that because of their similarity they easily mislead many people, just as false argumentations entice very many into fault because of their similarity to true ones. Out of this arises not only the variety of propositions in dialectic, but also the multiplicity of errors in the Christian faith, since by the snares of their assertions wordy heretics entice into all manner of sects many naïve people, who, not at all trained in argumentations, take a likeness for the truth and a fallacy for reasoning.

The doctors of the Church themselves also remind us to train in disputations against this plague, so that what we do not understand in Scriptures, we may not only seek from the Lord by praying, but also search out from each other by disputing. From this concern comes also that observation of Augustine in his treatise *On Mercy* when he explicated those words of the Lord "Ask, and it shall be given you; seek, and you shall find; knock, and it shall be opened to you" [Luke 11.9]. "Ask," he said, "by praying, seek by disputing, knock by questioning," that is, by interrogating.[16] For we are not equipped to rebut the attacks of heretics or of any infidels whatsoever, unless we are able to unravel their disputations and to rebut their sophisms with true reasonings, so that falsity may yield to truth and dialecticians may crush sophists. As blessed Peter cautions, dialecticians are "always ready to satisfy everyone that asks us the reason for that hope (or faith) which is in us" [1 Peter 3.15]. To be sure, when we have refuted those sophists in this disputation, we will display ourselves as dialecticians, and we will be truer disciples of Christ, who is the truth, by that much more as we attain greater power in the truth of reasoning.[17]

16. Pseudo-Augustine, *Tractatus de oratione et eleemosyna*, in *PL* 40: 1225–28, at 1227. This passage also influenced Abelard in the *Sic et non* 1.28, ed. Boyer and McKeon, p. 117, lines 149–50; *Theologia "Scholarium"* 2.40, ed. Buytaert and Mews, CCCM 13: 427, lines 615–16; and *Collationes* 2.75, ed. and trans. Marenbon and Orlandi, 96–97.

17. The interplays between Christ as the truth, wisdom, or word; logicians as fol-

To come to the point, who would not know the art of disputation, by which term it is established that dialecticians as well as
sophists are known without distinction?[18] Indeed the very Son of
God, whom we call "the Word," the Greeks name *logos,* which is
the conception of the divine mind or God's wisdom, or reasoning.
On this basis too Augustine says in the forty-fourth chapter of
the book *On Eighty-Three Different Questions,* "'In the beginning was
the Word' [John 1.1], which is called *logos* in Greek."[19] In the book
Against Five Heresies the same author says: "'In the beginning was the
Word' [John 1.1]: the Greeks do better to say *logos,* inasmuch as *logos*
signifies word and reasoning."[20] So too Jerome wrote in his letter
to Paulinus on the Sacred Scriptures:[21]

"In the beginning was the Word" [John 1.1]: *logos* signifies many things in
Greek. For it is the *word, principle, calculation,* and *cause* of everything whatsoever, by which all things which exist are. Rightly we understand all of
them in Christ.[22]

---

lowers of the word; and philosophers as lovers of wisdom are also elaborated in Abelard's *Soliloquium,* ed. Burnett, 889.

18. Smits marked the final clause as a crux because the passage appeared to him to
be faulty. If something has indeed been omitted, the gist could be that both dialecticians and sophists are known for the art of disputation, which Abelard goes on to
identify (with the backing of the Gospel of John) as logic.

19. *De diversis quaestionibus LXXXIII,* 53, in *PL* 40: 11–100, at 54. Other quotations of
this passage will be found in Abelard, *Theologia Christiana* 16-a and 66-b, ed. Buytaert,
CCCM 12: 78, lines 1–2, and 295, lines 10–11; *Theologia "Scholarium"* (short redaction)
67, ed. Buytaert, CCCM 13: 428, lines 796–98; and *Theologia "Scholarium"* 1.59, ed. Buytaert and Mews, CCCM 13: 341–42, lines 651–52.

20. The text is now ascribed not to Augustine but to Quodvultdeus (died 454),
Adversus quinque haereses, ed. René Braun, CCSL 60 (1976): 288. Abelard quotes it in
the *Theologia Christiana* 1.21 and 4.66-b, ed. Buytaert, CCCM 12: 80, lines 254–57, and
295, lines 12–13; *Theologia "Scholarium"* (short redaction) 67, ed. Buytaert, CCCM 12:
428, lines 803–5; and *Theologia "Scholarium"* 1.60, ed. Buytaert and Mews, CCCM 13: 342,
lines 656–58.

21. The addressee is Paulinus (353/4–431), bishop of Nola and future saint, who
was taught early by Ausonius and became later a friend of Jerome, Augustine, and
others.

22. Jerome, Letter 53.4, ed. Hilberg, CSEL 54: 449.

Therefore, since the Word of the Father, Lord Jesus Christ, is called *logos* in Greek, just as it is named the *sophia* of the Father, this knowledge seems to relate very much to him which is connected with him also by name and which is by a certain derivation from *logos* called logic; and just as Christians seem properly to be so called from Christ, so is logic from *logos*.[23]

In addition, lovers of logic are all the more truly called philosophers as they are truer lovers of that higher *sophia*. Indeed, when that highest wisdom of the highest Father assumed our nature so that it might illuminate us with the light of true understanding and turn us from love of the world toward love of itself, it made us at once Christians and true philosophers.[24] When he promised to the disciples that capacity of wisdom by which they might be able to rebut the arguments of those who contradicted them, and when he said "For I will give you a mouth and wisdom, which all your adversaries shall not be able to resist" [Luke 21.15] (indeed after love [*philo-*] of him [*sophia*], on account of which philosophers are truly so called), obviously he promises them an arsenal of reasoning by which they may be made the highest logicians in disputing.[25]

That hymn of Pentecost "Beata nobis gaudia" (Blissful Joys to Us) carefully differentiates those two (which is to say, about this love and its teaching by which philosophers as well as highest logicians are produced), when it is said: "So that they may be fluent in words and aflame with charity."[26] For that arrival of the heavenly

23. Compare *Soliloquium*, ed. Burnett, 889.

24. The wisdom of God is of course Christ (1 Corinthians 1.24: "Christ, the power of God and the wisdom of God").

25. At the opening of the *Historia calamitatum* Abelard employed metaphors of weapons and warfares to characterize his commitment as a young man to dialectic; see ed. Monfrin, pp. 63–64, lines 25–28; trans. Radice, p. 3. On the pervasiveness of such metaphorics in his writing and on its meaning, see Andrew Taylor, "A Second Ajax: Peter Abelard and the Violence of Dialectic," in *The Tongue of the Fathers*, 14–34.

26. The hymn (early tenth century), which remains the hymn for lauds on Pentecost and throughout the octave, is sometimes wrongly ascribed to Hilary (Schaller/

Spirit, having been revealed in fiery tongues, conferred upon them these two things especially, that through love it should produce philosophers and through the power of reason the highest logicians. On this basis the Spirit was aptly made apparent in the likeness of fire and tongues, so that it might confer upon them love and eloquence in all manner of tongues.

To come to the point, who could not know that even the Lord Jesus Christ himself refuted the Jews in repeated disputations and crushed their slanders in writing as well as in reasoning, that he increased the faith very much not only by the power of miracles but also by the strength of words? To accomplish these ends, why did he not use miracles alone, by which the Jews particularly, who seek signs, would be motivated, if not because he decided to instruct us by his own example as to how through reasoning we might entice to faith even those who search for wisdom? The Apostle [Paul], differentiating between these two, said, "For the Jews require signs, and the Greeks seek after wisdom" [1 Corinthians 1.22], which is to say, that the Greeks are moved to faith very much by reasons, just as the Jews are especially by signs. Since, however, miraculous signs have now run short, one means of combat remains to us against any people who contradict us: that we may overcome through words, because we cannot do so through deeds, especially since among people of discernment reasoning carries greater force than miracles; it is easy to be uncertain whether or not a diabolic illusion produces miracles. On this basis the truth says, "There shall arise false prophets and [they] shall show great signs and wonders, insomuch as to deceive (if possible) even the elect" [Matthew 24.24].[27]

Könsgen, no. 1617). The most commonly used English version of the hymn begins with the words "Round Roll the Weeks." For the Latin text, see Arthur S. Walpole, ed., *Early Latin Hymns* (Cambridge, U.K.: Cambridge University Press, 1922; repr., Hildesheim: Olms, 1966), 365–67, no. 115 (as well as *AH* 2: 50, no. 51, 27: 99, no. 42, 51: 97, no. 91). The hymn would have had special meaning to Abelard because it names the Paraclete prominently: "Beata nobis gaudia / anni reduxit orbita, / cum spiritus paraclitus / effulsit in discipulos."

27. "The truth" designates Jesus Christ (John 14.6: "I am the way, and the truth,

But in fact you will say that even in logical reasoning error intrudes very much, so that when the reasons for arguments are advanced, it is not easily determined which should be accepted as reasonable and which should be rejected as sophisms. Thus, I say, it happens to those who have not acquired expertise in arguments. So that this will not chance to happen, care must be expended upon the principle of reasoning (which is to say, of the teaching of logic), which as blessed Augustine recalls "is very valuable in delving into all types of questions which occur in sacred literature."[28] And certainly this is needed among those teachers who, trusting that they are adequate in resolving questions, hardly escape them.

---

and the life"). Abelard's text of Matthew 24.24 differs slightly from the Vulgate. Additionally, the Douay-Rheims translates loosely the clause "ut in errorem inducantur."

28. *De doctrina Christiana* 2.31.48, ed. Josef Martin, CCSL 32 (1962): 65–66. As noted above when Abelard employed the same passage, he also uses it the *Sic et non, Theologia "Summi boni," Theologia Christiana, Theologia "Scholarium,"* and *Collationes.*

LETTER FOURTEEN. TO BISHOP G[ILBERT] AND THE CLERGY OF PARIS

Addressed to a bishop who is identified only by the initial *G* and to the clergy of Paris, Letter Fourteen deals with the rivalry between Abelard and Roscelin of Compiègne, his former teacher, a logician and theologian.[1] Roscelin is not named outright in the letter, but there has never been the shadow of a doubt that he is the heretical antagonist about whom Abelard is quite exercised.[2] As for the addressee, the most plausible candidate for *G* is Bishop Gilbert of Paris (1116–25 January 1124).[3] In the letter Abelard complains that he has been accused falsely by Roscelin of teaching heresy. To set the record straight, Abelard asks that a debate be scheduled between him and Roscelin.

Letter Fourteen can be dated to about when the *Theologia "Summi boni"* was composed, a treatise that Abelard wrote as his first major

1. The only book on Roscelin more recent than the early twentieth century is not one that supersedes its predecessors; see Heinrich Christian Meier, *Macht und Wahnwitz der Begriffe. Der Ketzer Roscellinus* (Aalen, Germany: Ebertin, 1974), especially 157–85.

2. On the light Letter Fourteen sheds on the relationship between Abelard and Roscelin, and on the close relationship between this letter and the *Theologia "Summi boni,"* see Constant Mews, ed., *Petri Abaelardi opera theologica* 3, Theologia "Summi boni," CCCM 13: 39–46.

3. Another possibility that has been advanced is Bishop Galo of Paris (1104–23 February 1116). Accepting this hypothesis would require shifting backward by a few years many events in Abelard's biography; see Werner Robl, *Heloïsas Herkunft: Hersindis Mater* (Munich, Germany: Olzog, 2001), 237.

venture into theology sometime after 1118. (In the *Historia calamitatum* he refers to his treatise by the title *De unitate et Trinitate divina,* whereas in Letter Fourteen he calls it *De fide sancte Trinitatis.*) At that moment in his life Abelard, having entered St. Denis after his castration, had resumed teaching in a *cella* (probably meaning a priory) of the abbey. The location of the priory has been placed variously in Paris or its environs, not far from Argenteuil; in Troyes or elsewhere in Champagne; or in the area of Nogent-sur-Seine.[4] The letter seems to have been composed in about 1120, in an attempt to rally Gilbert to choose capable judges who could hear out Abelard and Roscelin and decide which of them was right in their difference of opinions.[5]

Roscelin's only surely attested extant text is also a letter, to none other than Peter Abelard, written around the same time. In it, more than twenty years after the fact, Roscelin himself asserts that he taught Abelard for a long time as a boy and youth (evidently sometime in the stretch from around 1093 to around 1099) at Tours and Loches.[6] Roscelin would have come to Loches after having been accused of heresy by a council in Soissons and after having stayed for a year or two in England. Otto of Freising (1111/15–1158) corroborates Roscelin's assertion by identifying him as having been Abelard's first teacher;[7] but Abelard makes no reference to Roscelin in the *Historia*

---

4. Clanchy, *Abelard: A Medieval Life,* 229–30, and Smits, *Letters IX–XIV,* 201.

5. On the date, see Smits, *Letters IX–XIV,* 195 and 197, and Mews, "On Dating," 130–31.

6. The letter, designated Letter Fifteen in the *PL* edition of Abelard's correspondence (*PL* 178: 357–372A), is edited in an appendix by Josef Reiners, *Der Nominalismus in der Frühscholastik. Ein Beitrag zur Geschichte der Universalienfrage im Mittelalter,* Beiträge zur Geschichte der Philosophie des Mittelalters: Texte und Untersuchungen 8/5 (Munster, Germany: Druck und Verlag der Aschendorffschen Buchhandlung, 1910), 62–80. The reference to Tours and Loches is at p. 65, line 26. The text can also be found, conveniently assembled with other letters to Roscelin, passages pertaining to him elsewhere in the writings of Abelard, and related materials, in François Picavet, *Roscelin, philosophe et théologien d'après la légende et d'après l'histoire. Sa place dans l'histoire générale et comparée des philosophies médiévales* (Paris: Félix Alcan, 1911), 112–43, at 128–29. A partial French translation is presented in Ferroul, *Héloïse et Abélard,* Appendix 2, 191–96. Werner Robl has made available a rough German translation at http://www.abaelard.de/abaelard/Main.htm (accessed April 2007).

7. Otto of Freising, *Gesta Frederici,* 1.50, ed. Schmale, p. 224, line 29; *Deeds of Frederick,* 1.49 (47), trans. Mierow, 83.

calamitatum.[8] A twelfth-century source indicates that Abelard lost interest in the accused heretic's teachings after Roscelin enjoined him to follow his lectures for a year.[9]

Abelard seems as a rule to have behaved mutinously toward his former *magistri,* but beyond his innate rebelliousness major differences both philosophically and theologically could have induced him to gloss over his relations with Roscelin. For one thing, Roscelin advocated an extreme nominalism, or, perhaps more accurately, vocalism, which led him to interpret texts (both logical and theological) as being about words rather than things.[10] More important, he was forced to recant for the heresy of tritheism at a council held in Soissons in 1092, and as a consequence he was expelled first from the kingdom of France in 1092 and later from England around 1093. Tritheism is a heretical teaching that denies the unity of substance in the three persons of the Trinity. Roscelin had the dubious distinction of being the foremost figure to be accused of this doctrine since the Monophysites of the sixth century. His particular belief was that God the Father had not become incarnate in Christ. Whatever the precise nature of Roscelin's heterodoxy, Abelard was following a long-established convention in not deigning to mention the name of a heretic.

The chronology of the dispute between Roscelin and Abelard in 1120 is open to different interpretations.[11] One outlook would be that Abelard intended his *Theologia "Summi boni"* from the outset

8. Hubert Silvestre, "Pourquoi Roscelin n'est-il mentionné dans l'"Historia calamitatum'?" *Revue de théologie ancienne et médiévale* 48 (1981): 218–24, explains the lack of acknowledgment as supporting his theory, which he unfurled in successive articles and notes, that the *Historia calamitatum* was a forgery.

9. Munich, Bayerische Staatsbibliothek, clm 14160, ed. Ludwig Hödl, *Die Geschichte der scholastischen Literatur und der Theologie der Schlüsselgewalt,* Beiträge zur Geschichte der Philosophie und Theologie des Mittelalters: Texte und Untersuchungen 38/4 (Münster, Germany: Aschendorff, 1960), 78, and Mews, "In Search of a Name," 172–73 (with translation).

10. See Yukio Iwakuma, "'Vocales,' or Early Nominalists," *Traditio* 47 (1992): 37–111, and Jean Jolivet, "Trois variations médiévales sur l'universel et l'individu: Roscelin, Abélard, Gilbert de la Porrée," *Revue de métaphysique et de morale* 1 (1992): 111–55.

11. In what follows, the first view is that of scholarship up through Mews, introduction, *Petri Abaelardi opera theologica* 3, CCCM 13 (1987): 42–46. The second is that of Marenbon, *Philosophy of Peter Abelard,* 57.

as an attack on his onetime teacher, at which Roscelin struck back by writing Abelard a caustic letter. In response Abelard wrote Letter Fourteen to Bishop Gilbert of Paris. Another perspective would be that Roscelin got wind of the oral teaching that was the precursor to the drafting of the *Theologia "Summi boni"* and that he thereupon took Abelard to task for having succumbed to the heresy of Sabellianism by suggesting that the divine substance is singular. Rebuking Abelard for this supposed suggestion would have allowed Roscelin to reaffirm his own definition of the three persons of the Trinity as being three distinct things. To continue with this hypothetical scenario, in retaliation Abelard sent his letter (no longer extant) to the canons of Tours.[12] Roscelin obviously knew of the letter and in fact we are alerted to its existence by a mention of it in his own letter. The clash came to a crescendo, first with Roscelin sending his harsh missive to Abelard and then with Abelard incorporating into the second and third books of the *Theologia "Summi boni"* criticisms that did not name Roscelin but that were directed against him. The final act in the drama, at least as can be discerned in surviving documents, would have been Abelard's appeal to Bishop Gilbert (Letter Fourteen).

What are the certainties? In 1120 or thereabouts Roscelin read a treatise by Abelard called *De fide sancte Trinitatis* or heard about Trinitarian teachings by Abelard, in which his former student took issue with positions that he—Abelard—judged to be tritheistic. Although the extant text of the *Theologia "Summi boni"* makes no overt mention of Roscelin, Abelard's references to "pseudodialecticians" and a "dissimulating sophist" are clearly aimed at his teacher of yore.[13] In addition, Abelard sent a letter (now lost) to the canons of St. Martin of Tours to attack Roscelin. Roscelin reacted by issuing a bitter letter in which he assailed his erstwhile student on a variety of grounds, among them that the treatise contained heresies.[14] No other texts surely by Roscelin have come down to us apart from this vicious po-

---

12. Roscelin in his letter to Abelard refers to himself as a canon of Besançon; see ed. Reiners, *Der Nominalismus*, p. 65, lines 27–28.

13. Marenbon, *The Philosophy of Peter Abelard*, 57.

14. On the dating, often fixed between 1118 and 1121, see Smits, *Letters IX–XIV,* 197–99.

lemic against Abelard.[15] Letter Fourteen would appear to have been written after Roscelin's letter to the canons of St. Martin, which was itself a response to Abelard's earlier (lost) letter to the same canons, and after the *Theologia "Summi boni."* Possibly the back-and-forth amounted to nothing because Roscelin died or fell seriously ill. In any case, no more is heard of him, and no records survive of the public debate with Roscelin that Letter Fourteen requests Gilbert to organize.

Abelard's *Theologia "Summi boni"* enraged not only the heretic Roscelin but also some of the orthodox. Most importantly, Alberic of Rheims and Lotulf of Novara, who had studied under Anselm of Laon and who had nurtured a much greater respect for the older man than Abelard evinced in the *Historia calamitatum,* helped to orchestrate the Council of Soissons, where Abelard's book was condemned and burned and its author compelled to recite the Athanasian Creed.

Letter Fourteen makes mention of another Anselm (not to be confused with Anselm of Laon), namely, St. Anselm of Canterbury (1033–1109), also known after his birthplace as Anselm of Aosta. Years later Abelard would name St. Anselm in a possibly mocking context in the *Theologia Christiana,*[16] but here he is complimentary, partly because he appreciates being able to invoke an authority who had written disapprovingly of Roscelin; in a letter known as *De incarnatione Verbi* (On the Incarnation of the Word, written in successive drafts around 1093–1095) St. Anselm had accused Roscelin, without

15. With breathtaking crudity, the letter asserts that castration has reduced Abelard to nothingness, since he passes the test as neither cleric, layman, nor monk. Roscelin finds no way to categorize Abelard except as "Petrus imperfectus." In addition, a treatise "On Universals According to Master R." may offer a student's account of Roscelin's teaching; see John Marenbon, *Early Medieval Philosophy (480–1150): An Introduction* (London: Routledge & Kegan Paul, 1983), 134–35. As well, a commentary on Porphyry has been ascribed to Roscelin; see Iwakuma, "'Vocales,'" 58–60.

16. The passage is *Theologia Christiana,* Book 4, ed. Eligius Marie Buytaert, *Petri Abaelardi opera theologica 2,* CCCM 12 (1969): 304, lines 1206–33. On this episode, see Michael T. Clanchy, "Abelard's Mockery of St. Anselm," *Journal of Ecclesiastical History* 41 (1990): 1–23, and David E. Luscombe, "St. Anselm and Abelard," *Anselm Studies* 1 (1983): 207–29.

identifying him by name, of tritheism and had refuted Roscelin's distinction between God the Father and God the Son.[17]

Abelard's letter also refers to Robert of Arbrissel (about 1045–1117), so called after a village in Brittany, who was the founder of the Fontevrault order, an advocate of asceticism and also of syneisaktism (unconsummated spiritual marriage), a former master who had studied in Paris, and a celebrated preacher.[18] Like Abelard, Robert incurred criticism for his ministrations to women and for his refusal to conform to the stability of an existing order. Robert's order was a "double order" of monks and nuns who lived in separate convents under the rule of one abbess, and thus it put into practice an idea for which Abelard was the only twelfth-century writer to enunciate a theory in writing.[19] In view of these many parallels between their lives, it is understandable that in Letter Fourteen Abelard would have characterized Robert laudatorily as "that outstanding herald of Christ." Abelard needs to speak highly of both Anselm and Robert so as to buffer them from Roscelin's supposed vituperation of them—which, by the bye, Roscelin denies in his sole letter. Simultaneously, and even more to Abelard's advantage, praising the two men for their sanctity has the effect of putting him in good company. If

17. *Epistola de incarnatione Verbi*, in *S. Anselmi opera omnia*, ed. Franciscus Salesius Schmitt, 5 vols. (Edinburgh, Scotland: Thomas Nelson & Sons, 1940–1961), 2 (1946): 1–35. On the relationship between Anselm and Roscelin, see Constant J. Mews, "St. Anselm and Roscelin: Some New Texts and Their Implications: I. The *De incarnatione verbi* and the *Disputatio inter Christianum et Gentilem*," *Archives d'histoire doctrinale et littéraire du moyen âge* 58 (1991): 55–97; repr. in Mews, *Reason and Belief in the Age of Roscelin and Abelard*, Variorium Collected Studies CS730 (Aldershot, Hampshire, U.K.: Ashgate, 2002), and Mews, "St. Anselm and Roscelin: Some New Texts and Their Implications: II. An Essay on the Trinity and Intellectual Debate 1080–1120," *Archives d'histoire doctrinale et littéraire du moyen âge* 65 (1998): 39–90; repr. in Mews, *Reason and Belief*.

18. On Robert, see Berenice M. Kerr, *Religious Life for Women, c. 1100–c. 1350: Fontevraud in England* (Oxford, U.K.: Oxford University Press, 1999), 15–63. For an excellent dossier of texts in translation with commentary, see Bruce L. Venarde, *Robert of Arbrissel: A Medieval Religious Life* (Washington, D.C.: The Catholic University of America Press, 2003).

19. For an analysis of the concept as developed in the letters, see Georg Jenal, "Caput autem mulieris vir (I Kor. 11.3): Praxis und Begründung des Doppelklosters im Briefkorpus Abelard-Heloise," *Archiv für Kulturgeschichte* 76 (1994): 285–304.

being maligned by Roscelin means that Abelard is shown thereby to resemble Anselm of Laon and Robert of Arbrissel, then the slander is richly rewarded.

Among many points of interest, Letter Fourteen is fascinating for showing that Peter Abelard reacted to Roscelin's charges of heresy exactly as he would do to Bernard of Clairvaux's accusations a full score years later before the Council of Sens: he appeals to a bishop to coordinate a debate of the issues between the two disputants before judges whom he asks the addressee to select, so that they can decide who is right. With a few minor mutatis mutandis, this scenario is what Abelard sought unsuccessfully to orchestrate later at Sens.[20]

Letter Fourteen is extant in one manuscript that is of use in constituting the text, namely, Paris, Bibliothèque nationale de France, MS lat. 2923 (third or fourth quarter of the thirteenth century). This is the only letter in this volume that is extant in a medieval manuscript with the main set of letters exchanged by Abelard and Heloise (Letters One through Eight, without the Rule); the same manuscript also contains the *Soliloquium* and the *Confessio fidei "Universis."* The editio princeps of 1616 followed another manuscript, which has not been identified and which has not survived. The edition followed is that of Smits.

LETTER FOURTEEN

To G[ilbert], by the grace of God bishop of the see of Paris, and at the same time to the venerable clergy of the same Church P[eter] [sends] an eternal offering of due reverence.

It has been reported to us by certain students of ours as they arrived that the proud and ever conceited old foe of the Catholic faith, whose detestable heresy to confess and even to preach three gods has been condemned at the Council of Soissons by Catholic fathers and in addition has been punished by exile, spewed forth many slanders and threats against me after he saw a certain work

20. Zerbi, *"Philosophi" e "Logici,"* 49.

of mine *On Faith in the Holy Trinity,* which I had written especially against the aforementioned heresy by which he has earned infamy.[21] What is more, it has been announced to me by a student
of mine, to whom he spoke thereafter, that he was waiting for you
(who were then absent), to show you that I had implanted certain
heresies in that work, and to stir up against me you too, like all the
others on whom he relies.

But if it is so, that he continues even now in this, I beseech you,
champions of God and defenders of the holy faith,[22] that you call
together him and me at an agreed place and at a fitting time, and
that what he mutters against me when I am absent may be heard
before Catholic men of discernment whom you furnish (taking
your own counsel), and that either he be subjected to due punishment for imputing such a great accusation or I for such great te-
merity in writing. In the meantime, however, I render thanks to
God that if I endure the highest enemy of God and subverter of
the faith who is contrary in his faith, I too am compelled to sally forth on behalf of the faith in which we stand firm, and that I
seem already to be in the ranks of good men, owing to the hostility of this one who (it is plain) is ever hostile to good men alone;
his life as well as his teaching are apparent to everyone.

He dared to concoct an obstinate letter against that outstanding herald of Christ,[23] Robert of Arbrissel, and flared up so much

---

21. Peter Abelard's words to convey Roscelin's pride ("elatus ille et semper infla-
tus") differ from the term ("superbia") used by Anselm in his *De fide Trinitatis et incarnatione verbi* (first recension in 1092, second in 1094) and by Abelard in his *Theologia
"Summi boni"* (also known as *Tractatus de unitate et Trinitate divina*); see Picavet, *Roscelin,* 119
and 125. Still, the underlying preconception that heretics are driven by pride rather
than ignorance is the same. On this pride, see Clanchy, *Abelard,* 301–4.

The phrase *hostis antiquus* (old foe) had been used since late antiquity to designate
the devil and diabolic agents. See Augustine, *Sermo* 389, ed. Cyrille Lambot, *Revue Bénédictine* 58 (1948): 43–52, at 48: "ille hostis antiquus, id est diabolus."

22. *Athleta Domini (Dei, Christi)* and *defensor fidei* are also phrases conventional from
late antiquity on.

23. *Praeco Christi* (herald of Christ) is another conventional phrase of long standing
in Christian Latin; for instance, it is pronounced by a bishop when ordaining a deacon.

in affronts against that magnificent doctor of the Church, Archbishop Anselm of Canterbury, that for his basely shameless obstinacy toward the authority of the English king he was expelled from England and barely escaped with his life.[24] In fact he wishes to have a partner in his infamy and, so that he may take solace for his own infamy by the defamation of good people, he (who cannot stand to be good) does not hate anyone but a good man. Owing to the immoderateness of his insolence he was ejected with the highest dishonor from both realms in which he dwelt, which is to say, from that of the English as well as from that of the French; and, so they tell, he was beaten on various occasions by canons in the church of St. Martin [of Tours], of which he was called a canon (to its shame!); and yet he clung to his usual conduct. To indicate by name who this scoundrel is, I have considered superfluous; for the unique disrepute of his betrayal of the faith and of his life makes him uniquely notorious. Since he (being a pseudo-Christian, just as he is a pseudodialectician) asserts in his *Dialectic* that nothing but an utterance alone has parts, so too he shamelessly perverts the Sacred Scriptures so that in that passage [Luke 24.42] where the Lord is said to have eaten part of a roasted fish, he is compelled to understand part of this utterance (which is "roast fish"), not part of the thing.[25] What is the wonder, therefore, if he who was accustomed to "set his mouth against heaven" [Psalm 72.9] should rage on earth, and if he who persecutes the Lord should detract from the members of the Lord, and if he who cannot spare himself should spare no one else?[26] Farewell.

24. On instances in the lives of Roscelin and other heretics when they were physically abused or even killed by mobs, see Clanchy, *Abelard*, 289–92.

25. Abelard refers to pseudodialecticians in the *Theologica Christiana*, *Theologia "Scholarium,"* and *Theologia "Summi boni."* The word was his own coinage. In contrast, pseudo-Christian is attested much earlier in the Latin of Christian authors, particularly in the writings of Augustine.

26. The quotation of Psalm 72.9 is also found in *Theologia Christiana* 3.25, ed. Buytaert, CCCM 12 (1969): 205, line 308. The members of the Lord would be the constituents of the Christian Church.

BIBLIOGRAPHY

Selected Works of Peter Abelard

Apologia contra Bernardum. Edited by Eligius M. Buytaert. *Petri Abaelardi opera theologica* 1. CCCM 11 (1969): 359–68.

Carmen ad Astralabium. Edited by José M. A. Rubingh-Bosscher. *Peter Abelard—Carmen ad Astralabium.* Groningen, The Netherlands: n.p., 1987.

Carmen figuratum. Edited by Ulrich Ernst. "Ein unbeachtetes *Carmen figuratum* des Petrus Abaelardus." *Mittellateinisches Jahrbuch* 21 (1986): 125–46.

Collationes. Edited and translated by John Marenbon and Giovanni Orlandi. Oxford Medieval Texts. Oxford, U.K.: Clarendon Press, 2001.

———. *Ethical Writings: His Ethics or "Know Yourself" and His Dialogue between a Philosopher, a Jew, and a Christian.* Translated by Paul V. Spade. Indianapolis, Ind.: Hackett, 1995. Pp. 59–148.

Commentaria in epistolam Pauli ad Romanos. Edited by Eligius M. Buytaert. *Petri Abaelardi opera theologica* 1. CCCM 11 (1969): 41–340.

———. "Exposition of the Epistle to the Romans" (excerpt). Translated by Eugene Rathbone Fairweather. *A Scholastic Miscellany.* Library of Christian Classics 10. Philadelphia: Westminster Press, 1956. Pp. 276–87.

———. "Commentary on St Paul's Epistle to the Romans: Prologue and Beginning of Commentary" (excerpt). Translated by Minnis and Scott. *Medieval Literary Theory and Criticism.* Pp. 100–105.

———. *Expositio in epistolam ad Romanos = Römerbriefkommentar.* Translated by Rolf Peppermüller. Fontes Christiani 26. Freiburg im Breisgau, Germany: Herder, 2000.

Confessio fidei ad Heloisam. Edited by Charles S. F. Burnett. "'*Confessio fidei ad Heloisam*'— Abelard's Last Letter to Heloise? A Discussion and Critical Edition of the Latin and Medieval French Versions." *Mittellateinisches Jahrbuch* 21 (1986): 147–55, at 152–55.

———. Translated by Betty Radice. In *The Letters of Abelard and Heloise.* Pp. 211–12.

Confessio fidei "Universis." Edited by Charles S. F. Burnett. "Peter Abelard, *Confessio fidei* '*Universis*': A Critical Edition of Abelard's Reply to Accusations of Heresy." *Mediaeval Studies* 48 (1986): 111–38, at 132–38.

Dialectica. Edited by Lambertus Marie De Rijk. *Petrus Abaelardus, Dialectica, First Complete Edition of the Parisian Manuscript.* Wijsgerige Teksten en Studies 1. 2d ed. Assen, The Netherlands: Van Gorcum, 1970.

Ethica. See *Scito te ipsum.*

Expositio fidei in symbolum Athanasii. In *PL* 178: 629B–32C.

Expositio in Hexameron. Edited by Mary F. Romig. *Petri Abaelardi opera theologica* 5. CCCM 15 (2004): 1–III.

Expositio "Multorum legimus orationes." Edited by Charles S. F. Burnett. "'Expositio Orationis Dominicae'—*Multorum legimus orationes*—Abelard's Exposition of the Lord's Prayer." *Revue bénédictine* 95 (1985): 60–72.

Expositio symboli quod dicitur apostolorum. In *PL* 178: 617D–630A.

Historia calamitatum. Edited by Jacques Monfrin. *Abélard, Historia calamitatum.* 3rd ed. Paris: J. Vrin, 1967.

Hymnarius Paraclitensis. Edited by Joseph Szövérffy. *Hymnarius Paraclitensis: An Annotated Edition with Introduction.* 2 vols. Medieval Classics: Texts and Studies 2–3. Albany, N.Y.: Classical Folia Editions, 1975.

—————. *Hymn Collections from the Paraclete.* Edited by Chrysogonus Waddell. 2 vols. Cistercian Liturgy Series 8–9. Trappist, Ky.: Gethsemani Abbey, 1987–1989.

—————. *The Hymns of Abelard in English Verse.* Translated by Sister Jane Patricia. Lanham, Md.: University Press of America, 1986.

Letters One through Nine, Prefaces to the Three Books of *The Paraclete Hymnal,* Dedication Letter to *The Commentary on the Six Days of Creation,* Letter Sixteen: Prologue to *The Sermons,* Confession of Faith to Heloise (= Letter Seventeen). Edited and translated by Ileana Pagani. *Abelardo ed Eloisa: Epistolario.* Turin, Italy: Unione Tipografico—Editrice Torinese, 2004.

Letters One through Fourteen, Prefaces to the Three Books of *The Paraclete Hymnal,* Dedication Letter to *The Commentary on the Six Days of Creation,* Letter Sixteen: Prologue to *The Sermons,* Confession of Faith to Heloise (= Letter Seventeen). Translated by Carmelo Ottaviano. *Pietro Abelardo: Epistolario completo.* Palermo, Italy: Industrie Riunite Editoriali Siciliane, 1934.

Letters One through Six and Eight (entire). Letter Seven (summarized). *The Letters of Abelard and Heloise.* Translated by Betty Radice, revised by Michael T. Clanchy. London: Penguin Books, 2003.

Letter One. See *Historia calamitatum.*

Letters Two through Five. Edited by Joseph Thomas Muckle. "The Personal Letters between Abelard and Heloise, Introduction, Authenticity and Text." *Mediaeval Studies* 15 (1953): 47–94.

Letters Six and Seven. Edited by Joseph Thomas Muckle. "The Letter of Heloise on Religious Life and Abelard's First Reply." *Mediaeval Studies* 17 (1955): 240–81.

Letter Seven (entire). In *The Letters of Abelard and Heloise.* Translated by C. K. Scott Moncrieff. London: Guy Chapman, 1925. Pp. 105–42.

—————. In *Guidance for Women in Twelfth-Century Convents.* Translated by Vera Morton. Cambridge, U.K.: D. S. Brewer, 2003. Pp. 50–95.

Letter Eight. Edited by T. P. McLaughlin. "Abelard's Rule for Religious Women." *Mediaeval Studies* 18 (1956): 241–92.

Letters Nine through Fourteen. Edited by Edmé Renno Smits. *Letters IX–XIV: An*

Edition with an Introduction. Groningen, The Netherlands: Bouma's Boekhuis BV, 1983.

Letter Nine. In *Guidance for Women in Twelfth-Century Convents.* Translated by Vera Morton. Cambridge, U.K.: D. S. Brewer, 2003. Pp. 121–38.

Letter Ten. In *"Dacci oggi il nostro pane." Sermo 14 e Lettera 10.* Translated by Edoardo Arborio Mella. Testi dei padri della chiesa 49. Magnano, Italy: Edizioni Qiqajon, Monastero di Bose, 2001. Pp. 25–35.

Letter Thirteen. In *Abélard, ou la philosophie dans le langage. Présentation, choix de textes, bibliographie.* Translated by Jean Jolivet. Vestigia 14. Fribourg, Switzerland: Éditions universitaires, 1994. Pp. 150–56.

Letter Fifteen. Edited by Jean Leclercq. "Études sur Saint Bernard et le texte de ses écrits." *Analecta sacri ordinis Cisterciensis* 9 (1953): 1–247, at 104–5.

———. Edited by Raymond Klibansky. "Peter Abailard and Bernard of Clairvaux: A Letter by Abailard." *Mediaeval and Renaissance Studies* 5 (1961): 1–27, at 6–7.

Logica "Ingredientibus." Edited by Bernard Geyer. *Peter Abaelards philosophische Schriften.* Beiträge zur Geschichte der Philosophie des Mittelalters 21/1–4. Münster, Germany: Aschendorff, 1919–1933. Pp. 1–503.

———. *Glossae super Porphyrium* (Glosses on Porphyry's *Isagoge* = Edited by Geyer, pp. 1–109). Translated by Paul Vincent Spade. *Five Texts on the Mediaeval Problem of Universals: Porphyry, Boethius, Abelard, Duns Scotus, Ockham.* Indianapolis, Ind.: Hackett, 1994. Pp. 26–56.

Planctus. Edited by Giuseppe Vecchi. *Pietro Abelardo, I "Planctus": Introduzione, testo critico, trascrizioni musicali.* Istituto di filologia romanza della Università di Roma: Collezione di testi e manuali 35. Modena, Italy: Società tipografica modenese, 1951.

———. *Pietro Abelardo: Planctus.* Edited and translated by Massimo Sannelli. Littera 3. Trento, Italy: La Finestra, 2002.

Problemata Heloissae cum Petri Abaelardi solutionibus. In *Petri Abaelardi opera.* Edited by Victor Cousin, with Charles Jourdain and Eugène Despois. 2 vols. Paris: A. Durand, 1849. Vol. 1. Pp. 237–94.

———. In *PL* 178: 677–730.

———. *The Education of Heloise: Methods, Content, and Purpose of Learning in the Twelfth-Century* [*sic*]. Translated by Elizabeth Mary McNamer. Mediaeval Studies 8. Lewiston, N.Y.: Edwin Mellen Press, 1991. Pp. 111–83.

Scito te ipsum. Edited by Rainer M. Ilgner. *Petri Abaelardi opera theologica* 4. CCCM 190 (2001).

———. *Ethics: An Edition with Introduction, English Translation and Notes.* Edited and translated by David E. Luscombe. Oxford Medieval Texts. Oxford, U.K.: Clarendon Press, 1971.

———. *Ethical Writings: His Ethics or "Know Yourself" and His Dialogue between a Philosopher, a Jew, and a Christian.* Translated by Paul V. Spade. Indianapolis, Ind.: Hackett, 1995. Pp. 1–58.

Sermones 1–34. In *PL* 178: 379A–610D.

Sermon 35. "*Adtendite a falsis prophetis* (Ms. Colmar 128, ff. 152v/153v). Un texte de

Pierre Abélard contre les Cisterciens retrouvé?" Edited by L. J. Engels. In *Corona gratiarum. Miscellanea patristica, historica et liturgica Eligio Dekkers O.S.B. XII lustra complenti oblata*. 2 vols. Bruges, Belgium: Sint Pietersabdij / The Hague: Martinus Nijhoff, 1975. 2: 195–228 (1–34).

———. Translated by Chrysogonus Waddell. "Adtendite a falsis prophetis," pp. 371–98.

Sic et non. Edited by Blanche Boyer and Richard McKeon. Chicago: University of Chicago Press, 1977.

———. "Prologue to the *Yes and No*." Translated by Minnis and Scott. *Medieval Literary Theory and Criticism*. Pp. 87–100.

Soliloquium. "Peter Abelard *Soliloquium*: A Critical Edition." Edited and translated by Charles S. F. Burnett. *Studi Medievali*, 3rd series, 25 (1984): 857–94, at 885–94.

Theologia Christiana. Edited by Eligius M. Buytaert. *Petri Abaelardi opera theologica* 2. CCCM 12 (1969): 69–372.

———. Excerpts and paraphrase. Translated by James Ramsay McCallum. *Abelard's Christian Theology*. Oxford, U.K.: Blackwell, 1948. Pp. 45–97.

Theologia "Scholarium." Edited by Constant J. Mews. *Petri Abaelardi opera theologica* 3. CCCM 13 (1987): 203–549.

Theologia "Summi boni." Edited by Constant J. Mews. *Petri Abaelardi opera theologica* 3. CCCM 13 (1987): 39–201.

Works of Other Ancient and Medieval Authors

Ambrose. *De incarnationis dominicae sacramento*. Edited by Otto Faller. CSEL 79 (1964): 225–81.

———. *Expositio euangelii secundum Lucam*. Edited by Marcus Adriaen. CCSL 14 (1957): 1–400.

———. English: *Commentary of Saint Ambrose on the Gospel According to Saint Luke*. Translated by Íde M. Ní Riain. Dublin: Halcyon Press in association with Elo Publications, 2001.

———. *Hexameron, De paradiso, De Cain, De Noe, De Abraham, De Isaac, De bono mortis*. Edited by Karl Schenkl. CSEL 32/1 (1896): 3–261.

Anselm of Canterbury. *Epistola de incarnatione Verbi*. In *S. Anselmi opera omnia*. Edited by Franciscus Salesius Schmitt. 5 vols. Rome: n.p. / Edinburgh: Thomas Nelson & Sons, 1940–1961. 2 (1946): 1–35.

Arator. *De actibus apostolorum*. Edited by Arthur Patch McKinlay. CSEL 72 (1951).

———. English: *Arator's On the Acts of the Apostles*. Translated by Richard J. Schrader, Joseph L. Roberts III, and John F. Makowski. Classics in Religious Studies 6. Atlanta, Ga.: Scholars Press, 1987.

Augustine. *Confessions*. Edited by James J. O'Donnell. 3 vols. Oxford, U.K.: Clarendon Press, 1992.

———. *De baptismo contra Donatistas libri vii*. Edited by Michael Petschenig. CSEL 51 (1908): 43–375.

———. *De catechizandis rudibus.* Edited by J. B. Bauer. CCSL 46 (1969).

———. *De diversis quaestionibus LXXXIII.* In *PL* 40: 11–100.

———. *De doctrina Christiana.* Edited by Josef Martin. CCSL 32 (1962).

———. *De Genesi ad litteram liber imperfectus.* Edited by Joseph Zycha. CSEL 28/1 (1894): 457–503.

———. *De Genesi ad litteram libri XII.* Edited by Joseph Zycha. CSEL 28/1 (1894): 1–435.

———. *De Genesi contra Manichaeos. PL* 34: 173–220.

———. *Enarrationes in Psalmos.* Edited by Eligius Dekkers and Johannes Fraipont. CCSL 38–40 (1956).

———. *Retractationes.* Edited by Almut Mutzenbecher. CCSL 57 (1974).

———. *Sermones.* In *PL* 38–39: 332–1638.

———. *Sermo* 355. In *Sancti Aurelii Augustini Sermones selecti duodeviginti.* Edited by Cyrille Lambot. Stromata Patristica et Mediaevalia 1. Utrecht, The Netherlands: Spectrum, 1950. Pp. 123–31.

———. *Sermo* 389. Edited by Cyrille Lambot. *Revue Bénédictine* 58 (1948): 43–52.

———. *Sermo eiusdem de oboedientia* [Mainz 5]. In *Augustin d'Hippone: Vingt-six sermons au peuple d'Afrique retrouvés à Mayence.* Edited by François Dolbeau. Collection des études augustiniennes Série Antiquité 147. Paris: Institut d'Études Augustiniennes, 1996. Pp. 328–44. Reprint of *Revue des Études Augustiniennes* 38 (1992): 50–79, at 63–79.

———. *The Works of Saint Augustine. A Translation for the 21st Century: Sermons III/11. Newly Discovered Sermons.* Translated by Edmund Hill and John E. Rotelle. Brooklyn, N.Y.: New City Press 1997.

Augustine, Pseudo-. *Sermo* 222 "De sanctis apostolis" (= Hrabanus Maurus, *Homilia* 35). In *PL* 39: 2156–58.

———. *Tractatus de oratione et eleemosyna.* In *PL* 40: 1225–28.

Basil the Great. *Homélies sur l'Hexaéméron.* Edited and translated by Stanislas Giet. 2d ed. Sources chrétiennes 26 bis. Paris: Éditions du Cerf, 1968.

Bede. *Ecclesiastical History of the English People.* Edited and translated by Bertram Colgrave and R. A. B. Mynors. Oxford, U.K.: Clarendon Press, 1969.

———. *In Lucae euangelium expositio.* Edited by David Hurst. CCSL 120 (1960): 1–425.

———. *In Marci euangelium expositio.* Edited by David Hurst. CCSL 120 (1960): 427–648.

———. *Libri quatuor in principium Genesis usque ad nativitatem Isaac et eiectionem Ismahelis adnotationum.* Edited by C. W. Jones. Opera exegetica 1. CCSL 118A (1967).

———. *Retractatio in Acta apostolorum.* Edited by M. L. W. Laistner and David Hurst. CCSL 121 (1983).

———. *Super Acta apostolorum expositio.* Edited by M. L. W. Laistner. CCSL 121 (1983): 1–99.

———. English: *Commentary on the Acts of the Apostles.* Translated by Lawrence T. Martin. Cistercian Studies 117. Kalamazoo, Mich.: Cistercian Publications, 1989.

Bede (or Pseudo-Bede). *De titulis Psalmorum* (also known as *De Psalmorum libro exegesis*). In *PL* 93: 477–1098.

Benedict of Nursia. *Benedicti regula.* Edited by Rudolf Hanslik. CSEL 75 (1960).

Berengar of Poitiers. *Apologia.* Edited by Rodney M. Thomson. "The Satirical Works of Berengar of Poitiers: An Edition with Introduction." *Mediaeval Studies* 42 (1980): 89–138, at 111–38.

—————. Reprinted (with original pagination) in *England and the 12th-Century Renaissance.* By Rodney M. Thomson. Variorum Collected Studies Series 620. Aldershot, Hampshire, U.K.: Variorum, 1998. Essay 13: 89–138.

Bernard of Clairvaux. *Ad clericos de conversione.* In *Sancti Bernardi opera.* 4: 59–116.

—————. "On Conversion" In *Bernard of Clairvaux: Selected Works.* Translated by G. R. Evans. New York: Paulist Press, 1987. Pp. 65–97.

—————. "On Conversion: A Sermon to Clerics." In *Bernard of Clairvaux, Sermons on Conversion: On Conversion, A Sermon to Clerics and Lenten Sermons on the Psalm "He Who Dwells."* Translated by Marie-Bernard Saïd. Cistercian Fathers 25. Kalamazoo, Mich.: Cistercian Publications, 1981. Pp. 31–79.

—————. *Apologia ad Guillelmum S. Theodorici abbatem.* In *Sancti Bernardi opera.* 3: 81–108.

—————. Edited and translated by Conrad Rudoph. *The "Things of Greater Importance."* Pp. 232–87.

—————. *Apologia to Abbot William: Cistercians and Cluniacs.* Translated by Michael Casey. Cistercian Fathers 1A. Kalamazoo, Mich.: Cistercian Publications, 1970.

—————. *Epistola de baptismo (Epistula 77).* In *Sancti Bernardi opera.* 7: 184–200.

—————. Letters. In *Sancti Bernardi opera.* 7–8 (1974–1977).

—————. Letters. *Opere di San Bernardo.* 6/1–2. 2 vols. Edited by Ferruccio Gastaldelli. Translated by Ettore Paratore. Milan, Italy: Scriptorium Claravallense, 1986–1987.

—————. *The Letters of St Bernard of Clairvaux.* Translated by Bruno Scott James. Cistercian Fathers Series 62. Kalamazoo, Mich.: Cistercian Publications, 1998.

—————. *Le lettere contro Pietro Abelardo.* Edited and translated by Albino Babolin. Collana di "Testi e saggi" 3. Padua, Italy: Liviana editrice, 1969.

—————. *Sancti Bernardi opera.* Edited by Jean Leclercq, C. H. Talbot, and H. M. Rochais. 8 vols. Rome: Editiones Cistercienses, 1957–1977.

Biblia sacra iuxta Vulgatam uersionem. Edited by Robert Weber and Roger Gryson. 4th ed. Stuttgart, Germany: Deutsche Bibelgesellschaft, 1994.

Boethius, trans. Aristotle, *Categoriae vel praedicamenta.* Edited by Laurentius Minio-Paluello, Corpus philosophorum Medii Aevi: Aristoteles Latinus 1/1. Bruges, Belgium: Desclée de Brouwer, 1961.

—————. *In categorias Aristotelis libri IV.* In *PL* 64:159–294.

Capitula haeresum Petri Abaelardi. Edited by Eligius M. Buytaert. *Petri Abaelardi opera theologica* 2. CCCM 12 (1969): 473–80.

Cassian, John. *Conlationes XXIIII.* Edited by Michael Petschenig. CSEL 13 (1886).

Cassiodorus. *Expositio psalmorum.* Edited by Marc Adriaen. CCSL 97–98. Turnhout, Belgium: Brepols, 1958.

Chronicon Mauriniacense. Edited by Léon Mirot. *La chronique de Morigny (1095–1152).* Paris: Alphonse Picard et fils, 1909.

Cyprian. *Epistulae.* Edited by G. F. Diercks. CCSL 3A–D (1996–1999).

Epistolae duorum amantium. Edited by Ewald Könsgen. *Epistolae duorum amantium. Briefe Abaelards und Heloises?* Mittellateinische Studien und Texte 8. Leiden, The Netherlands: E. J. Brill, 1974.

———. Edited and translated by Chiavaroli and Mews. In Mews, *Lost Love Letters.* Pp. 190–289.

Eusebius of Caesarea. *Historia ecclesiastica.* Translated by Rufinus. *Die Kirchengeschichte.* Greek text edited by Eduard Schwartz, Latin translation of Rufinus edited by Theodor Mommsen. Eusebius Werke 2/1–3. Die griechischen christlichen Schriftsteller der ersten drei Jahrhunderte 9/1–3. Leipzig, Germany: Hinrichs, 1903–1909.

Fulk (Fulco) of Deuil. Letter to Abelard. In *PL* 178: 371–76.

———. Translated by W. L. North. Available online at *http://www.fordham.edu/halsall/source/fulk-abelard.html.* Accessed 1 July 2006.

———. Translated in Ferroul, *Héloïse et Abélard.* Appendix 2. Pp. 197–205.

Gerald of Wales. *Itinerarium Kambriae.* In *Giraldi Cambrensis opera.* Edited by James F. Dimock. 8 vols. London: Longman, 1861–1891. 6 (1868): 3–152.

———. *"The Journey through Wales" and "The Description of Wales."* Translated by Lewis Thorpe. London: Penguin Books, 1978. Pp. 63–209.

Gregory the Great. *Homiliae in Hiezechihelem prophetam.* Edited by Marcus Adriaen. CCSL 142 (1971).

———. English: *The Homilies of St. Gregory the Great on the Book of the Prophet Ezekiel.* Translated by Theodosia Gray. Edited by Juliana Cownie. Etna, Calif.: Center for Traditionalist Orthodox Studies, 1990.

———. *Registrum epistolarum.* Edited by Paul Ewald and Ludwig Hartmann. Monumenta Germaniae Historica: Epistolae 1–2. 2 vols. Berlin: Weidmann, 1887–1899.

Gregory VII. *Epistola 69 extra registrum.* In *PL* 148: 713CD.

Haimo of Auxerre. *Homilia 28.* In *PL* 118: 190C–203B.

———. *In omnes Psalmos pia, brevis ac dilucida explanatio.* In *PL* 1116: 193–696.

Heiric of Auxerre. *Homiliae per circulum anni.* Edited by Riccardo Quadri. CCCM 116–116A–116B (1992–1994).

Hilduin of St. Denis. *Vita s. Dionysii, sive Areopagitica.* In *PL* 106: 9–50.

Hugh of St. Victor. *Didascalicon de studio legendi.* Edited by Charles Henry Buttimer. Catholic University of America Studies in Medieval and Renaissance Latin 10. Washington, D.C.: The Catholic University of America Press, 1939.

———. English: *The Didascalicon: A Medieval Guide to the Arts.* Translated by Jerome Taylor. Records of Civilization 64. New York: Columbia University Press, 1961.

Irenaeus of Lyon. *Adversus haereses.* Edited and translated by Norbert Brox. Fontes Christiani 8/1–5. 5 vols. Freiburg, Switzerland: Herder, 1993–2001.

Isidore of Seville. *De ecclesiasticis officiis.* Edited by Charles M. Lawson. CCSL 113. Turnhout, Belgium: Brepols, 1989.

———. *Etymologiarum sive originum libri.* Edited by W. M. Lindsay. Oxford, U.K.: Clarendon Press, 1911.

Ivo of Chartres. *Decretum.* In *PL* 161: 48–1022.

————. *Panormia*. In *PL* 161: 1041–1344.

Jerome. *Commentarii in Danielem.* Edited by François Glorie. CCSL 75A (1964).

————. *Commentarii in Ezechielem.* Edited by François Glorie. CCSL 75 (1964): 1–743.

————. *Commentarii in iv epistulas Paulinas.* In *PL* 26: 307–618 (331–656).

————. *Contra Rufinum* (known also as *Apologia aduersus libros Rufini*). Edited by Pierre Lardet. CCSL 79 (1982): 1–72.

————. *Contra Vigilantium.* In *PL* 23: 339–52.

————. *De uiris inlustribus.* Edited by Aldo Ceresa-Gastaldo. Biblioteca patristica 12. Florence, Italy: Nardini Editore, Centro internazionale del libro, 1988.

————. English: *On Illustrious Men.* Translated by Thomas P. Halton. Fathers of the Church 100. Washington, D.C.: The Catholic University of America Press, 1999.

————. *Epistula praefatoria in Chronicis Eusebii.* Edited by Rudolf Helm. *Eusebius Werke* 7/ 1–2. Die griechischen christlichen Schriftsteller der ersten drei Jahrhunderte 47. Leipzig, Germany: J. C. Hinrichs'sche Buchhandlung, 1913–1926. 1: 1–7.

————. *Epistulae.* Edited by Isidor Hilberg. *Sancti Eusebii Hieronymi Epistulae.* 3 vols. CSEL 54–56 (1910–1918).

————. *The Letters of St. Jerome.* Translated by Charles Christopher Mierow. Vol. 1. Ancient Christian Writers: The Works of the Fathers in Translation 33. New York: Newman Press, 1963.

————. *Epistula ad Praesidium.* Edited by Germain Morin. *Bulletin d'ancienne littérature et d'archéologie chrétiennes* 3 (1913): 51–60.

————. *Homilia in Ioannem Euangelistam.* Edited by Germain Morin. CCSL 78 (1958): 517–23.

————. *The Homilies of Saint Jerome.* Translated by Marie Liguori Ewald. 2 vols. Fathers of the Church 48 and 57. Washington, D.C.: The Catholic University of America Press, 1964–1966.

————. *Liber interpretationis hebraicorum nominum.* Edited by Paul de Lagarde. CCSL 72 (1959). Pp. 57–161.

Justinian. *Corpus juris civilis.* Edited by Paul Krueger, Theodor Mommsen, Rudolf Schöll, and Wilhelm Kroll. 3 vols. Berlin: Weidmann, 1963–1965.

Origen. *In Canticum canticorum.* In *Patrologiae cursus completus: Series Graeca.* Edited by Jacques-Paul Migne. 161 vols. Paris: J.-P. Migne, 1857–1866. 13: 62–84.

Otfrid of Weißenburg. *Glossae in Mattheaum.* Edited by Cesare Grifoni. CCCM 200 (2003).

Otto of Freising. *Gesta Frederici seu rectius Cronica.* Edited by Franz-Josef Schmale. 2d ed. Ausgewählte Quellen zur deutschen Geschichte des Mittelalters: Freiherr vom Stein-Gedächtnisausgabe 17. Darmstadt, Germany: Wissenschaftliche Buchgesellschaft, 1974.

Pelagius. *Ad Celantiam* (= Pseudo-Jerome, Letter 148.1–2). Edited by Isidor Hilberg. CSEL 56 (1918, 2d ed. 1996): 329–56.

Peter the Venerable. *The Letters.* Edited by Giles Constable. 2 vols. Harvard Historical Studies 78. Cambridge, Mass.: Harvard University Press, 1967.

Philo of Alexandria. "On the Contemplative Life." Edited and translated by F. H.

Colson. In *Philo.* Edited and translated by F. H. Colson and G. H. Whitaker. 12 vols. Cambridge, Mass.: Harvard University Press, 1929–1962. 9 (1941): 103–69.

———. *On the Creation of the Cosmos According to Moses.* Translated by David T. Runia. Philo of Alexandria Commentary Series 1. Leiden, The Netherlands: E. J. Brill, 2001.

Quodvultdeus. *Adversus quinque haereses.* Edited by René Braun. CCSL 60 (1976).

Roscelin of Compiègne. Letter to Peter Abelard. Edited by Reiners. *Der Nominalismus in der Frühscholastik.* Appendix. Pp. 62–80.

———. Translated (excerpts) in Ferroul. *Héloïse et Abélard.* Appendix 2. Pp. 191–96.

———. Translated by Werner Robl, available online at *http://www.abaelard.de/abaelard/Main.htm* (accessed 1 July 2006).

Rufinus. See Eusebius of Caesarea.

Sulpicius Severus. Letter 3. Edited by Jacques Fontaine. *Vita S. Martini episcopi.* 3 vols. Sources Chrétiennes 133–135. Paris: Editions du Cerf, 1967–1969. 1: 316–44.

Tertullian. *De pudicitia.* Introduced, with commentary and index, by Claudio Micaelli. Edited and translated by Charles Munier. Sources chrétiennes 394–395. Paris: Editions du Cerf, 1993.

Thierry of Chartres. *De sex dierum operibus.* In *Commentaries on Boethius by Thierry of Chartres.* Edited by Nikolaus M. Häring. Pontifical Institute of Mediaeval Studies Studies and Texts 20. Toronto: Pontifical Institute of Mediaeval Studies, 1971. Pp. 555–75.

Thomas of Morigny. *Disputatio contra Petrum Abaelardum* (also known as the *Disputatio catholicorum patrum*). Edited by Nikolaus M. Häring. "Thomas von Morigny, *Disputatio catholicorum patrum adversus dogmata Petri Abaelardi.*" *Studi Medievali,* 3rd series, 22 (1981): 299–376.

Walahfrid Strabo. *Liber Psalmorum.* In *PL* 113: 483–1098.

Walter of Mortagne, *Epistola Gualteri de Mauritania episcopi ad Petrum Abaelardum.* In *Sententiae Florianenses.* Edited by Heinrich Ostlender. Florilegium Patristicum tam veteris quam medii aevi auctores complectens 19. Bonn, Germany: Peter Hanstein, 1929. Pp. 34–40.

William Godel(l) of St. Martial in Limoges. *Chronicon.* Edited by Léopold Delisle. *Ex Chronico Willelmi Godelli, Monachi S. Martialis Lemovicensis.* In *Recueil des Historiens des Gaules et de la France* 13. Paris: Victor Palmé, 1869. Pp. 671–77.

Modern Scholarship

Abélard en son temps. Actes du colloque international organisé à l'occasion du 9e centenaire de la naissance de Pierre Abélard (14–19 mai 1979). Edited by Jean Jolivet. Paris: Les Belles Lettres, 1981.

Anna, Gabriella d'. "Abelardo e Cicerone." *Studi medievali,* 3rd series, 10 (1969): 333–419.

Asni, Raffaella. "Abélard et Héloïse sur l'écran et la scène de 1900 à nos jours." In *Pierre Abélard. Colloque international de Nantes.* Pp. 185–203.

Astell, Ann W. *The Song of Songs in the Middle Ages.* Ithaca, N.Y.: Cornell University Press, 1990.

Barrow, Julia, Charles S. F. Burnett, and David E. Luscombe. "A Checklist of the Manuscripts Containing the Writings of Peter Abelard and Heloise and Other Works Closely Associated with Abelard and His School." *Revue d'histoire des textes* 14–15 (1984–1985): 183–302.

Baswell, Christopher. "Heloise." In *The Cambridge Companion to Medieval Women's Writing.* Edited by Carolyn Dinshaw and David Wallace. Cambridge Companions to Literature. Cambridge, U.K.: Cambridge University Press, 2003. Pp. 161–71.

Bautier, Robert-Henri. "Les origines et les premiers développements de l'abbaye Saint-Victor de Paris." In *L'abbaye parisienne de Saint-Victor au Moyen Age.* Edited by Jean Longère. Pp. 23–52.

———. "Paris au temps d'Abélard." In *Abélard en son temps.* Pp. 21–77.

Beer, Jeanette, ed. *Translation Theory and Practice in the Middle Ages.* Studies in Medieval Culture 38. Kalamazoo, Mich.: Medieval Institute Publications, Western Michigan University, 1997.

Benson, Robert L., and Giles Constable, eds. *Renaissance and Renewal in the Twelfth Century.* Cambridge, Mass.: Harvard University Press, 1982.

Benton, John. "A Reconsideration of the Authenticity of the Correspondence of Abelard and Heloise." In *Petrus Abaelardus.* Pp. 41–52.

Berndt, Rainer. "La pratique exégétique d'André de Saint-Victor. Tradition victorine et influence rabbinique." In *L'abbaye parisienne de Saint-Victor au Moyen Age.* Edited by Jean Longère. Pp. 271–90.

Bertola, Ermenegildo. "I precedenti storici del metodo del *Sic et non* di Abelardo." *Rivista di filosofia neo-scolastica* 53 (1961): 495–522.

Blamires, Alcuin. "*Caput a femina, membra a viris:* Gender Polemic in Abelard's Letter 'On the Authority and Dignity of the Nun's Profession.'" In *The Tongue of the Fathers.* Pp. 55–79.

———. "No Outlet for Incontinence: Heloise and the Question of Consolation." In *Listening to Heloise.* Pp. 287–301.

Borst, Arno. "Abälard und Bernhard." *Historische Zeitschrift* 186 (1958): 497–526.

Brooke, Christopher. *The Twelfth Century Renaissance.* London: Thames & Hudson, 1969.

Brown, Dennis. *Vir Trilinguis: A Study in the Biblical Exegesis of Saint Jerome.* Kampen, The Netherlands: Kok Pharos, 1992.

Burge, James. *Heloise and Abelard: A Twelfth-Century Love Story.* London: Profile Books, 2003.

Burrow, John A. *The Ages of Man: A Study in Medieval Writing and Thought.* Oxford, U.K.: Clarendon Press, 1988.

Buytaert, Eligius M. "Abelard's *Expositio in Hexaemeron.*" *Antonianum* 43 (1968): 163–94.

———, ed. *Peter Abelard. Proceedings of the International Conference, Louvain, May 10–12, 1971.* Mediaevalia Lovaniensia Series 1, Studia 2. Louvain, Belgium: University Press, 1974.

Bynum, Caroline Walker. *Docere verbo et exemplo: An Aspect of Twelfth-Century Spirituality.*

Harvard Theological Studies 31. Missoula, Mont.: Scholars Press, 1979.

————. *Jesus as Mother: Studies in the Spirituality of the High Middle Ages.* Publications of the Center for Medieval and Renaissance Studies, UCLA, 16. Berkeley and Los Angeles: University of California Press, 1982.

The Cambridge Companion to Abelard. Edited by Jeffrey E. Brower and Kevin Guilfoy. Cambridge, U.K.: Cambridge University Press, 2004.

Châtillon, Jean. "Abélard et les écoles." In *Abélard en son temps.* Pp. 133–60.

————. "Guillaume de Saint-Thierry, le monachisme et les écoles: À propos de Rupert de Deutz, d'Abélard et de Guillaume de Conches." In *Saint-Thierry: Une abbaye du VIe au XXe siècle: Actes du Colloque international d'histoire monastique, Reims-Saint-Thierry, 11 au 14 octobre 1976.* Edited by Michel Bur. Saint-Thierry: Association des Amis de l'Abbaye de Saint-Thierry, 1979. Pp. 375–94.

————. *Le mouvement canonial au moyen âge: Réforme de l'église, spiritualité et culture.* Edited by Patrice Sicard. Bibliotheca Victorina 3. Paris: Brepols, 1992.

Cipollone, Maria. "In margine ai *Problemata Heloissae.*" *Aevum* 64 (1990): 227–44.

Clanchy, Michael T. *Abelard: A Medieval Life.* Oxford, U.K.: Blackwell, 1997.

————. "Abelard's Mockery of St Anselm." *Journal of Ecclesiastical History* 41 (1990): 1–23.

Constable, Giles. *Three Studies in Medieval Religious and Social Thought: The Interpretation of Mary and Martha; The Ideal of the Imitation of Christ; The Orders of Society.* Cambridge, U.K.: Cambridge University Press, 1995.

Cook, Brenda M. "Abelard and Heloise." *Genealogists' Magazine* 26 (1999): 205–11.

————. "The Shadow on the Sun: The Name of Abelard's Son." In *The Poetic and Musical Legacy of Heloise and Abelard.* Pp. 152–55.

Curtius, Ernst Robert. *European Literature and the Latin Middle Ages.* Translated by Willard R. Trask. Bollingen Series 36. Princeton, N.J.: Princeton University Press, 1990.

Déchanet, Jean-Marie. "L'amitié d'Abélard et de Guillaume de Saint-Thierry." *Revue d'histoire ecclésiastique* 35 (1939): 761–74.

De Santis, Paola. "Abelardo interprete del Cantico dei Cantici per il Paracleto?" In *Pascua mediaevalia: Studies voor Prof. Dr. J. M. de Smet.* Edited by Robrecht Lievens, Erik van Mingroot, and Werner Verbeke. Leuven, Belgium: Universitaire Pers Leuven, 1983. Pp. 284–94.

————. *I sermoni di Abelardo per le monache del Paracleto.* Mediaevalia Lovaniensia 1/31. Leuven, Belgium: Universitaire Pers Leuven, 2002.

————. "Osservazioni sulla lettera dedicatoria del sermonario di Abelardo." *Aevum* 55 (1981): 262–71.

Dickinson, John C. *The Origins of the Austin Canons and Their Introduction into England.* London: S.P.C.K., 1950.

Dinzelbacher, Peter. *Bernhard von Clairvaux. Leben und Werk des berühmten Zisterziensers.* Darmstadt, Germany: Wissenschaftliche Buchgesellschaft, 1998.

Doyle, Matthew A. *Bernard of Clairvaux and the Schools: The Formation of an Intellectual Milieu in the First Half of the Twelfth Century.* Studi 11. Spoleto, Italy: Fondazione Centro italiano di studi sull'alto Medioevo, 2005.

Dronke, Peter. "Heloise's *Problemata* and Letters: Some Questions of Form and Content." In *Petrus Abaelardus (1079–1142). Person, Werk und Wirkung.* Pp. 53–73. Reprinted in Dronke. *Intellectuals and Poets.* Pp. 295–322.

———. *Intellectuals and Poets in Medieval Europe.* Storia e letteratura: Raccolta di studi e testi 183. Rome: Edizioni de Storia e Letteratura, 1992.

———. *Women Writers of the Middle Ages: A Critical Study of Texts from Perpetua (d. 203) to Marguerite Porete (d. 1310).* Cambridge, U.K.: Cambridge University Press, 1984.

Dronke, Peter, and Giovanni Orlandi. "New Works by Abelard and Heloise?" *Filologia mediolatina* 12 (2005): 123–77 (123–46 on *versus et ludi*, 146–77 on *epistolae*).

Duby, Georges. *The Three Orders: Feudal Society Imagined.* Translated by Arthur Goldhammer. Chicago: University of Chicago Press, 1982.

East, William G. "Abelard's Anagram." *Notes and Queries* 240 (1995): 269.

Engels, L. J. "Abélard écrivain." In *Peter Abelard: Proceedings.* Pp. 12–37.

Evans, G. R. *Language and Logic of the Bible: The Earlier Middle Ages.* Cambridge, U.K.: Cambridge University Press, 1984.

Ferrante, Joan M. *To the Glory of Her Sex: Women's Roles in the Composition of Medieval Texts.* Bloomington: Indiana University Press, 1997.

Ferroul, Yves. *Héloïse et Abélard: Lettres et vies.* Paris: GF-Flammarion, 1996.

Ferruolo, Stephen C. *The Origins of the University: The Schools of Paris and Their Critics, 1100–1215.* Stanford, Calif.: Stanford University Press, 1985.

Festa, Gianni. "San Bernardo di Chiaravalle tra *ipsa philosophia Christi* e *philosophorum ventosa loquacitas*." *Divus Thomas: Jahrbuch für Philosophie und spekulative Theologie* 96 (1993): 207–38.

Folz, Robert. "Otton de Freising, témoin de quelques controverses intellectuelles de son temps." *Bulletin de la Société historique et archéologique de Langres* 13 (1958): 70–89.

Fournier, Paul. "Les collections canoniques attribuées à Yves de Chartres." *Bibliothèque de l'École des Chartes* 58 (1897): 624–76.

Frank, Donald K. "Abelard as Imitator of Christ." *Viator* 1 (1970): 107–13.

Frugoni, Arsenio. *Arnaldo da Brescia nelle fonti del secolo XII.* Istituto storico italiano per il Medio Evo: Studi storici 8–9. Rome: Nella sede dell'Istituto, 1954.

Georgianna, Linda. "Any Corner of Heaven: Heloise's Critique of Monasticism." *Mediaeval Studies* 49 (1987): 221–53.

———. Reprinted in revised form as "'In Any Corner of Heaven': Heloise's Critique of Monastic Life." In *Listening to Heloise.* Pp. 187–216.

Godman, Peter. *The Silent Masters: Latin Literature and Its Censors in the High Middle Ages.* Princeton, N.J.: Princeton University Press, 2000.

Gouron, André. "'Non dixit: Ego sum consuetudo.'" *Zeitschrift der Savigny-Stiftung für Rechtsgeschichte. Kanonistische Abteilung* 105 (1988): 133–40.

Grant, Lindy. *Abbot Suger of St-Denis: Church and State in Early Twelfth-Century France.* London: Longman, 1998.

Grauwen, Wilfried Marcel. "Gaufried, bisschop van Chartres (1116–1149), vriend van Norbert en van de 'Wanderprediger.'" *Analecta Praemonstratensia* 58 (1982): 161–209.

———. "Het getuigenis van Abaelard over Norbert van Gennep." *Analecta Praemonstratensia* 63 (1987): 5–25.

————. "Nogmaals over Abelard, Bernard en Norbert." *Analecta Praemonstratensia* 65 (1989): 162–65.

————. *Norbert, Erzbischof von Magdeburg (1126–1134).* Translated by Ludger Horstkötter. 2d ed. Duisburg, Germany: Selbstverlag der Prämonstratenser-Abtei St. Johann, 1986.

Greenaway, George William. *Arnold of Brescia.* Cambridge, U.K.: Cambridge University Press, 1931.

Gregory, Tullio. "Abélard et Platon." In *Peter Abelard: Proceedings.* Pp. 38–64.

————. Reprinted in Gregory. *Mundana sapientia: Forme di conoscenza nella cultura medievale.* Storia e letteratura 181. Rome: Edizioni di storia e letteratura, 1992. Pp. 175–99.

————. *Anima mundi. La filosofia di Guglielmo di Conches e la scuola di Chartres.* Pubblicazioni dell'Istituto di filosofia dell'Università di Roma 3. Rome: G. C. Sansoni, 1955.

Griffiths, Fiona J. "Brides and *Dominae*: Abelard's *Cura Monialium* at the Augustinian Monastery of Marbach." *Viator: Medieval and Renaissance Studies* 34 (2003): 57–83.

————. "'Men's Duty to Provide for Women's Needs': Abelard, Heloise, and Their Negotiation of the *cura monialium.*" *Journal of Medieval History* 30 (2004): 1–24.

Grodecki, Louis. "Abélard et Suger." In *Pierre Abélard—Pierre le Vénérable.* Pp. 279–86.

Haskins, Charles Homer. *The Renaissance of the Twelfth Century.* Cambridge, Mass.: Harvard University Press, 1927.

Hödl, Ludwig. *Die Geschichte der scholastischen Literatur und der Theologie der Schlüsselgewalt.* Beiträge zur Geschichte der Philosophie und Theologie des Mittelalters. Texte und Untersuchungen 38/4. Münster, Germany: Aschendorff, 1960.

Illich, Ivan. *In the Vineyard of the Text: A Commentary to Hugh's Didascalicon.* Chicago: University of Chicago Press, 1993.

Iwakuma, Yukio. "Pierre Abélard et Guillaume de Champeaux dans les premières années du XIIe siècle: Une étude préliminaire." In *Langage, sciences, philosophie au XIIe siècle: Actes de la table ronde internationale organisée les 25 et 26 mars 1998 par le Centre d'histoire des sciences et des philosophies arabes et médiévales (UPRESA 7062, CNRS/Paris VII/EPHE) et le Programme international de coopération scientifique (France-Japon) "Transmission des sciences et des techniques dans une perspective interculturelle."* Edited by Joël Biard. Paris: J. Vrin, 1999. Pp. 93–123.

————. "'Vocales,' or Early Nominalists." *Traditio* 47 (1992): 37–111.

Jaeger, C. Stephen. "Peter Abelard's Silence at the Council of Sens (1140)." *Res publica litterarum* 3 (1980): 31–54.

Jeauneau, Édouard. "Denys l'Aréopagite, promoteur du néoplatonisme en Occident." In *Néoplatonisme et philosophie médiévale: Actes du Colloque international de Corfou, 6–8 octobre 1995 organisé par la Société Internationale pour l'Etude de la Philosophie Médiévale.* Edited by Linos G. Benakis. Société Internationale pour l'Etude de la Philosophie Médiévale: Rencontres de Philosophie Médiévale 6. Turnhout, Belgium: Brepols, 1997. Pp. 1–23.

Jenal, Georg. "Caput autem mulieris vir (I Kor. 11.3): Praxis und Begründung des Doppelklosters im Briefkorpus Abelard-Heloise." *Archiv für Kulturgeschichte* 76 (1994): 285–304.

Jolivet, Jean. *Arts du langage et théologie chez Abélard.* 2d ed. Etudes de philosophie médiévale 57. Paris: J. Vrin, 1982.

————. "Données sur Guillaume de Champeaux, dialecticien et théologien." In *L'abbaye parisienne de Saint-Victor au Moyen Age.* Edited by Jean Longère. Pp. 235–51.

————. *La théologie d'Abélard.* Paris: Editions du Cerf, 1997.

————. "Trois variations médiévales sur l'universel et l'individu: Roscelin, Abélard, Gilbert de la Porrée." *Revue de métaphysique et de morale* 1 (1992): 111–55.

Kearney, Eileen F. "Heloise: Inquiry and the *Sacra pagina.*" In *Ambiguous Realities: Women in the Middle Ages and Renaissance.* Edited by Carole Levin and Jeanie Watson. Detroit, Mich.: Wayne State University Press, 1987. Pp. 66–81.

————. "Peter Abelard as Biblical Commentator: A Study of the *Expositio in Hexaemeron.*" In *Petrus Abaelardus.* Pp. 199–210.

————. "*Scientia* and *Sapientia:* Reading Sacred Scriptures at the Paraclete." In *From Cloister to Classroom: Monastic and Scholastic Approaches to Truth.* Edited by E. Rozanne Elder. Spirituality of Western Christendom 3. Cistercian Studies Series 90. Kalamazoo, Mich.: Cistercian Publications, 1986. Pp. 111–29.

Kerr, Berenice M. *Religious Life for Women, c. 1100–c. 1350: Fontevraud in England.* Oxford, U.K.: Oxford University Press, 1999.

King, Peter. "Metaphysics." In *Cambridge Companion to Abelard.* Pp. 65–125.

L'abbaye parisienne de Saint-Victor au Moyen Age: Communications présentées au XIIIe Colloque d'Humanisme médiéval de Paris (1986–1988). Edited by Jean Longère. Bibliotheca Victorina 1. Turnhout, Belgium: Brepols, 1991.

Lanham, Carol Dana. *Salutatio Formulas in Latin Letters to 1200: Syntax, Style, and Theory.* Münchener Beiträge zur Mediävistik und Renaissance-Forschung 22. Munich, Germany: Arbeo-Gesellschaft, 1975.

Leclercq, Jean. "'Ad ipsam sophiam Christum': Le témoignage monastique d'Abélard." *Revue d'ascétique et de mystique* 46 (1970): 161–81.

————. German: "'Ad ipsam sophiam Christum.' Das monastische Zeugnis Abaelards." In *Sapienter ordinare. Festgabe für Erich Kleineidam.* Edited by Fritz Hoffmann, Leo Scheffczyk and Konrad Feiereis. Erfurter theologische Studien 24. Leipzig, Germany: Sankt-Benno-Verlag, 1969. Pp. 179–98.

————. *Etudes sur le vocabulaire monastique du moyen âge.* Studia Anselmiana 48. Rome: "Orbis Catholicus," Herder, 1961.

————. "Les lettres de Guillaume de Saint-Thierry à saint Bernard." *Revue bénédictine* 79 (1968): 375–91.

Lejeune, François. "Pierre Abélard et Jean de Salisbury." In *Pierre Abélard. Colloque international de Nantes.* Pp. 63–75.

Lemoine, Michel. "Abélard et les Juifs." *Revue des études juives* 153 (1994): 253–67.

Le Vot, Gerard. "Que savons-nous sur la musique des *Planctus* d'Abelard?" In *Abelard. Lamentations. Histoire de mes malheurs. Correspondance avec Heloise.* Translated by Paul Zumthor. Babel 52. Avignon, France: Actes Sud, 1992. Pp. 107–22.

Listening to Heloise: The Voice of a Twelfth-Century Woman. Edited by Bonnie Wheeler. New York: St. Martin's Press, 2000.

Little, Edward. "Relations between St. Bernard and Abelard before 1139." In *Saint Ber-*

nard of Clairvaux: Studies Commemorating the Eighth Centenary of his Canonization. Edited by M. Basil Pennington. Cistercian Studies Series 28. Kalamazoo, Mich.: Cistercian Publications, 1977. Pp. 155–68.

Lubac, Henri de. Exégèse médiévale: Les quatre sens de l'Ecriture. 4 vols. Paris: Aubier, 1959–1964.

———. English: Medieval Exegesis: The Four Senses of Scripture. Vol. 1. Translated by Mark Sebanc. Vol. 2. Translated by E. M. Macierowski. Grand Rapids, Mich.: W. B. Eerdmans, 1998–2000.

Luscombe, David E. "Abélard et le monachisme." In Pierre Abélard—Pierre le Vénérable. Pp. 271–76.

———. "Denis the pseudo-Areopagite in the Middle Ages from Hilduin to Lorenzo Valla." In Fälschungen im Mittelalter. Internationaler Kongreß der Monumenta Germaniae Historica, München, 16.–19. September 1986. Edited by Wolfram Setz. Schriften der Monumenta Germaniae Historica 33/1–5. 5 vols. Hannover, Germany: Hahn, 1988. 1: 133–52.

———. "From Paris to Paraclete: The Correspondence of Abelard and Heloise." Proceedings of the British Academy 74 (1988): 247–83.

———. "Monasticism in the Lives and Writings of Heloise and Abelard." In Monastic Studies: The Continuity of Tradition. Edited by Judith Loades. Bangor, Gwynedd, Wales: Headstart History, 1990. Pp. 1–11.

———. "Pierre Abélard et l'abbaye du Paraclet." In Pierre Abélard. Colloque international de Nantes. Pp. 215–29.

———. "St Anselm and Abelard." Anselm Studies 1 (1983): 207–29.

———. The School of Peter Abelard: The Influence of Abelard's Thought in the Early Scholastic Period. Cambridge Studies in Medieval Life and Thought: New Series 14. Cambridge, U.K.: Cambridge University Press, 1969.

———. "The School of Peter Abelard Revisited." Vivarium 30 (1992): 127–38.

———. "'Scientia' and 'disciplina' in the Correspondence of Peter Abelard and Heloise." In "Scientia" und "Disciplina": Wissenstheorie und Wissenschaftspraxis im 12. und 13. Jahrhundert. Edited by Rainer Berndt. Berlin: Akademie Verlag, 2002. Pp. 79–89.

Marenbon, John. "Authenticity Revisited." In Listening to Heloise. Pp. 19–33.

———. Early Medieval Philosophy (480–1150): An Introduction. London: Routledge & Kegan Paul, 1983.

———. "Life, Milieu, and Intellectual Contexts." In Cambridge Companion to Abelard. Pp. 13–44.

———. The Philosophy of Peter Abelard. Cambridge, U.K.: Cambridge University Press, 1997.

———. "The Platonisms of Peter Abelard." In Néoplatonisme et philosophie médiévale: Actes du Colloque international de Corfou 6–8 octobre 1995, organisé par la Société Internationale pour l'Étude de la Philosophie Médiévale. Edited by Linos G. Benakis. Rencontres de philosophie médiévale 6. Turnhout, Belgium: Brepols, 1997. Pp. 109–29.

Matter, E. Ann. The Voice of My Beloved: The Song of Songs in Western Medieval Christianity. Philadelphia: University of Pennsylvania Press, 1990.

McLaughlin, Mary Martin. "Heloise the Abbess: The Expansion of the Paraclete." In *Listening to Heloise.* Pp. 1–17.

———. "Peter Abelard and the Dignity of Women: Twelfth-Century Feminism in Theory and Practice." In *Pierre Abélard—Pierre le Vénérable.* Pp. 287–333.

The Medieval Translator 1– (1989–).

Meier, Heinrich Christian. *Macht und Wahnwitz der Begriffe. Der Ketzer Roscellinus.* Aalen, Germany: Ebertin, 1974.

Mews, Constant J. *Abelard and Heloise.* Oxford, U.K.: Oxford University Press, 2005.

———. *Abelard and His Legacy.* Variorium Collected Studies CS704. Aldershot, Hampshire, U.K.: Ashgate, 2001.

———. "The Council of Sens (1141): Bernard, Abelard and the Fear of Social Upheaval." *Speculum* 77 (2002): 342–82.

———. "Heloise, the Paraclete Liturgy and Mary Magdalen." In *Poetic and Musical Legacy of Heloise and Abelard.* Pp. 100–112.

———. "Hugh Metel, Heloise, and Peter Abelard: The Letters of an Augustinian Canon and the Challenge of Innovation in Twelfth-Century Lorraine." *Viator* 32 (2001): 59–91.

———. "In Search of a Name and Its Significance: A Twelfth-Century Anecdote about Thierry and Peter Abaelard." *Traditio* 44 (1988): 171–200. Reprinted in Mews, *Reason and Belief.*

———. "The Lists of Heresies Imputed to Peter Abelard." *Revue bénédictine* 94 (1985): 73–100. Reprinted in Mews, *Abelard and His Legacy.*

———. "Liturgy and Identity at the Paraclete: Heloise, Abelard and the Evolution of Cistercian Reform." In *Poetic and Musical Legacy of Heloise and Abelard.* Pp. 19–33.

———. "Nominalism and Theology before Abaelard: New Light on Roscelin of Compiègne." *Vivarium* 30 (1992): 4–33. Reprinted in Mews, *Reason and Belief.*

———. "On Dating the Works of Peter Abelard." *Archives d'histoire doctrinale et littéraire du moyen âge* 52 (1985): 73–134. Reprinted in *Abelard and His Legacy.*

———. "Peter Abelard." In *Authors of the Middle Ages: Historical and Religious Writers of the Latin West,* vol. 2/5. Edited by Patrick Geary. Aldershot, Hampshire, U.K.: Variorum, 1995.

———. "Peter Abelard on Dialectic, Rhetoric, and the Principles of Argument." In *Rhetoric and Renewal.* Pp. 37–53.

———. *Reason and Belief in the Age of Roscelin and Abelard.* Variorium Collected Studies CS730. Aldershot, Hampshire, U.K.: Ashgate, 2002.

———. "St Anselm and Roscelin: Some New Texts and Their Implications: I. The *De incarnatione verbi* and the *Disputatio inter Christianum et Gentilem.*" *Archives d'histoire doctrinale et littéraire du moyen âge* 58 (1991): 55–97. Reprinted in Mews, *Reason and Belief.*

———. "St Anselm and Roscelin: Some New Texts and Their Implications: II. An Essay on the Trinity and Intellectual Debate 1080–1120." *Archives d'histoire doctrinale et littéraire du moyen âge* 65 (1998): 39–90. Reprinted in Mews, *Reason and Belief.*

———. "The *Sententie* of Peter Abelard." *Recherches de théologie ancienne et médiévale* 53 (1986): 159–84. Reprinted in *Abelard and His Legacy.*

————. "The Trinitarian Doctrine of Roscelin of Compiègne and Its Influence: Twelfth-Century Nominalism and Theology Reconsidered." In *Langages et philosophie. Hommage à Jean Jolivet*. Edited by Alain de Libera, Abedelali Elamrani-Jamal, and Alain Galonnier. Etudes de philosophie médiévale 74. Paris: J. Vrin, 1997. Pp. 347–64. Reprinted in Mews, *Reason and Belief*.

————. "Un lecteur de Jérôme au XIIe siècle: Pierre Abélard." In *Jérôme entre l'Occident et l'Orient: XVIe centenaire du départ de saint Jérôme de Rome et de son installation à Bethléem, Actes du Colloque de Chantilly (septembre 1986)*. Edited by Yves-Marie Duval. Paris: Etudes Augustiniennes, 1988. Pp. 429–44. Reprinted in *Abelard and His Legacy*.

Mews, Constant J., with Neville Chiavaroli. *The Lost Love Letters of Heloise and Abelard: Perceptions of Dialogue in Twelfth-Century France*. New York: St. Martin's Press, 1999.

Meyer, Heinz, and Rudolf Suntrup. *Lexikon der mittelalterlichen Zahlenbedeutungen*. Münstersche Mittelalter-Schriften 56. Munich, Germany: W. Fink, 1987.

Minnis, Alastair J., and A. Brian Scott. *Medieval Literary Theory and Criticism, c. 1100– c. 1375: The Commentary-Tradition*. Oxford, U.K.: Clarendon Press, 1988.

Moonan, Lawrence. "Abelard's Use of the *Timaeus*." *Archives d'histoire doctrinale et littéraire du moyen âge* 56 (1989): 7–90.

Moos, Peter von. *Abaelard und Heloise. Gesammelte Studien zum Mittelalter* 1. Edited by Gert Melville. Geschichte: Forschung und Wissenschaft 14. Münster, Germany: Lit Verlag, 2005.

————. "Literary Aesthetics in the Latin Middle Ages: The Rhetorical Theology of Peter Abelard." In *Rhetoric and Renewal*. Pp. 81–97.

Murray, A. Victor. *Abelard and St Bernard: A Study in Twelfth Century "Modernism."* New York: Barnes & Noble, 1967.

Norberg, Dag. *An Introduction to the Study of Medieval Latin Versification*. Translated by Grant C. Roti and Jacqueline Skubly. Edited by Jan M. Ziolkowski. Washington, D.C.: The Catholic University of America Press, 2004.

Pagani, Ileana. "Il problema dell'attribuzione dell'Epistolario di Abelardo ed Eloisa. Status quaestionis." *Filologia Mediolatina* 6–7 (1999–2000): 79–88.

Penco, Gregorio. "S. Giovanni Battista nel ricordo del monachesimo medievale." *Studi monastica* 3 (1961): 7–32.

Pennington, M. Basil. "The Correspondence of William of St. Thierry." *Studia monastica: Commentarium ad rem monasticam investigandam* 18 (1976): 353–65.

Peter Abelard: Proceedings of the International Conference, Louvain May 10–12, 1971. Edited by Eligius M. Buytaert. Mediaevalia Lovaniensia Series 1/Studia 2. Leuven, Belgium: Leuven University Press, 1974.

Petrus Abaelardus (1079–1142). Person, Werk und Wirkung. Edited by Rudolf Thomas. Trierer Theologische Studien 38. Trier, Germany: Paulinus-Verlag, 1980.

Piazzoni, Ambrogio M. *Guglielmo di Saint-Thierry: Il declino dell'ideale monastico nel secolo XII*. Studi storici 181–83. Rome: Istituto storico italiano per il Medio Evo, 1988.

Picavet, François. *Roscelin, philosophe et théologien d'après la légende et d'après l'histoire. Sa place dans l'histoire générale et comparée des philosophies médiévales*. Paris: Félix Alcan, 1911.

Pierre Abélard. Colloque international de Nantes. Edited by Jean Jolivet and Henri Habrias. Rennes, France: Presses Universitaires de Rennes, 2003.

Pierre Abélard—Pierre le Vénérable. Les courants philosophiques, littéraires et artistiques en Occident au milieu du XIIe siècle—Abbaye de Cluny, 2 au 9 juillet 1972. Edited by René Louis, Jean Jolivet, and Jean Châtillon. Actes et mémoires des colloques internationaux du Centre National de la Recherche Scientifique 546. Paris: Éditions du Centre National de la Recherche Scientifique, 1975.

The Poetic and Musical Legacy of Heloise and Abelard: An Anthology of Essays by Various Authors. Edited by Marc Stewart and David Wulstan. Wissenschaftliche Abhandlungen/ Musicological Studies 78. Ottawa, Canada: Institute of Mediaeval Music, 2003.

Powell, Morgan. "Listening to Heloise at the Paraclete: Of Scholarly Diversion and a Woman's 'Conversion.'" In *Listening to Heloise.* Pp. 255–86.

Radding, Charles M., and William W. Clark Jr. "Abélard et le bâtisseur de Saint-Denis. Études parallèles d'histoire des disciplines." *Annales ESC: Économies, sociétés* 43 (1988): 1263–90.

———. *Medieval Architecture, Medieval Learning: Builders and Masters in the Age of Romanesque and Gothic.* New Haven, Conn.: Yale University Press, 1992.

Rebenich, Stefan. "Jerome: The 'vir trilinguis' and the 'hebraica veritas.'" *Vigiliae Christianae* 47 (1993): 50–77.

Reiners, Josef. *Der Nominalismus in der Frühscholastik. Ein Beitrag zur Geschichte der Universalienfrage im Mittelalter.* Beiträge zur Geschichte der Philosophie des Mittelalters: Texte und Untersuchungen 8/5. Münster, Germany: Druck und Verlag der Aschendorffschen Buchhandlung, 1910.

Rhetoric and Renewal in the Latin West 1100–1540: Essays in Honour of John O. Ward. Edited by Constant J. Mews, Cary J. Nederman, and Rodney M. Thomson. Disputatio 2. Turnhout, Belgium: Brepols, 2003.

Richter, Michael. "*Urbanitas—rusticitas*: Linguistic Aspects of a Medieval Dichotomy." *Studies in Church History* 16 (1979): 149–57.

Ritter, Adolf Martin. "Die Absicht des Corpus Areopagiticum." In *Christian Faith and Greek Philosophy in Late Antiquity: Essays in Tribute to George Christopher Stead, Ely Professor of Divinity, University of Cambridge (1971–1980) in Celebration of His Eightieth Birthday, 9th April 1993.* Edited by Lionel R. Wickham, Caroline P. Bammel and Erica C. D. Hunter. Supplements to Vigiliae Christianae 19. Leiden, The Netherlands: E. J. Brill, 1993. Pp. 171–89.

Rizek-Pfister, Cornelia. "Die hermeneutischen Prinzipien in Abaelards *Sic et non.*" *Freiburger Zeitschrift für Philosophie und Theologie* 47 (2000): 484–501.

Robl, Werner. *Heloïsas Herkunft: Hersindis Mater.* Munich, Germany: Olzog, 2001.

Rochais, Henri. "Ipsa philosophia Christus." *Mediaeval Studies* 13 (1951): 244–47.

Rudolph, Conrad. *The "Things of Greater Importance": Bernard of Clairvaux's Apologia and the Medieval Attitude toward Art.* Philadelphia: University of Pennsylvania Press, 1990.

Sapir Abulafia, Anna. *Christians and Jews in Dispute: Disputational Literature and the Rise of Anti-Judaism in the West (c. 1000–1150).* Variorum Collected Studies Series CS621. Aldershot, Hampshire, U.K.: Ashgate, 1998.

Saxer, Victor. *Saint Vincent, diacre et martyr: Culte et légendes avant l'An Mil.* Subsidia hagiographica 83. Brusells: Société des Bollandistes, 2002.

Schmitz-Esser, Romedio. "Arnold of Brescia in Exile: April 1139 to December 1143." In *Exile in the Middle Ages: Selected Proceedings from the International Medieval Congress, University of Leeds, 8–11 July 2002.* Edited by Laura Napran and Elisabeth van Houts. International Medieval Research 13. Turnhout, Belgium: Brepols, 2004. Pp. 213–31.

Silvestre, Hubert. "A propos d'une édition récente de l'*Hymnarius Paraclitensis* d'Abélard." *Scriptorium* 23 (1978): 91–100.

————. "Aratus pour Arator: Un singulier lapsus d'Abélard." *Studi medievali,* 3rd series, 27 (1986): 221–24.

————. "Pourquoi Roscelin n'est-il mentionné dans l'"Historia calamitatum'?" *Revue de théologie ancienne et médiévale* 48 (1981): 218–24.

Smalley, Beryl. "Ecclesiastical Attitudes to Novelty, c. 1100–1250." *Studies in Church History* 12 (1975): 113–31.

————. "*Prima clavis sapientiae:* Augustine and Abelard." In *Fritz Saxl 1890–1948: A Volume of Memorial Essays from His Friends in England.* Edited by D. J. Gordon. London: Thomas Nelson and Sons, 1957. Pp. 93–100.

————. *The Study of the Bible in the Middle Ages.* 3rd ed. Oxford, U.K.: Blackwell, 1983.

Smith, Anne Collins. "The Problemata of Heloise." In *Women Writing Latin, Vol. 2: Medieval Women Writing Latin.* Edited by Laurie J. Churchill, Phyllis R. Brown, and Jane E. Jeffrey. Women Writers of the World. New York: Routledge, 2002. Pp. 173–96.

Southern, Richard W. *Scholastic Humanism and the Unification of Europe.* 2 vols. Oxford, U.K.: Blackwell, 1995.

Stäblein, Bruno, ed. *Hymnen (I): Die mittelalterlichen Hymnenmelodien des Abendlandes,* Monumenta monodica Medii Aevi 1. Kassel, Germany: Bärenreiter-Verlag, 1956.

Szövérffy, Joseph. "'False' Use of 'Unfitting' Hymns: Some Ideas Shared by Peter the Venerable, Peter Abelard and Heloise." *Revue bénédictine* 88 (1979): 187–99. Reprinted in Joseph Szövérffy, *Psallat Chorus Caelestis, Religious Lyrics of the Middle Ages, Hymnological Studies and Collected Essays.* Medieval Classics: Texts and Studies (Berliner Reihe) 15. Berlin: Classical Folia Editions, 1983. Pp. 537–49.

————. *Hymns of the Holy Cross: An Annotated Edition with Introduction.* Medieval Classics 7. Brookline, Mass.: Classical Folia Editions, 1976.

Taylor, Andrew. "A Second Ajax: Peter Abelard and the Violence of Dialectic." In *The Tongue of the Fathers.* Pp. 14–34.

Teeuwen, Mariken. *The Vocabulary of Intellectual Life in the Middle Ages.* CIVICIMA Etudes sur le vocabulaire intellectuel du moyen âge 10. Turnhout, Belgium: Brepols, 2003.

Tomasic, Thomas Michael. "William of Saint-Thierry against Peter Abelard: A Dispute on the Meaning of Being a Person." *Analecta Cisterciensia* 28 (1972): 3–76.

The Tongue of the Fathers: Gender and Ideology in Twelfth-Century Latin. Edited by David Townsend and Andrew Taylor. Philadelphia: University of Pennsylvania Press, 1998.

Tristram, Hildegard L. C. *Sex aetates mundi: Die Weltzeitalter bei den Angelsachsen und den Iren: Untersuchungen und Texte.* Anglistische Forschungen 165. Heidelberg, Germany: C. Winter, 1985.

Turner, Denys. *Eros and Allegory: Medieval Exegesis of the Song of Songs.* Cistercian Studies Series 156. Kalamazoo, Mich.: Cistercian Publications, 1995.

Van den Eynde, Damien. "Chronologie des écrits d'Abélard à Héloïse." *Antonianum* 37 (1962): 337–49.

———. "Détails biographiques sur Pierre Abélard." *Antonianum* 38 (1963): 217–23.

———. "Le recueil des sermons de Pierre Abélard." *Antonianum* 37 (1962): 17–54.

Venarde, Bruce L. *Robert of Arbrissel: A Medieval Religious Life.* Washington, D.C.: The Catholic University of America Press, 2003.

Verbaal, Wim. "Sens: Une victoire d'écrivain. Les deux visages du procès d'Abélard." In *Pierre Abélard. Colloque international de Nantes.* Pp. 77–89.

Vergani, Fiorella. "'Sententiam vocum seu nominum non caute theologiae admiscuit': Ottone di Frisinga di fronte ad Abelardo." *Aevum* 63 (1989): 193–224.

Verger, Jacques. "Saint Bernard vu par Abélard et quelques autres maîtres des écoles urbaines." In *Histoire de Clairvaux. Actes du Colloque de Bar-sur-Aube/Clairvaux 22 et 23 Juin 1990.* Bar-sur-Aube, France: Némont SA, 1991. Pp. 161–75.

Vicaire, Marie-Humbert. *L'imitation des apôtres. Moines, chanoines, mendiants IVe–XIIIe siècles.* Tradition et spiritualité 2. Paris: Editions du Cerf, 1963.

Waddell, Chrysogonus. "*Adtendite a falsis prophetis*: Abaelard's Earliest Known Anti-Cistercian Diatribe." *Cistercian Studies Quarterly: An International Review of the Monastic and Contemplative Spiritual Tradition* 39 (2004): 371–98.

———. "Cistercian Influence on the Abbey of the Paraclete? Plotting Data from the Paraclete Book of Burials, Customary, and Necrology." In *Perspectives for an Architecture of Solitude: Essays on Cistercians, Art and Architecture in Honour of Peter Fergusson.* Edited by Terry N. Kinder. Medieval Church Studies 11. Studia et Documenta 13. Turnhout, Belgium: Brepols, 2004. Pp. 329–40.

———. "*Epithalamica*: An Easter Sequence by Peter Abelard." *Musical Quarterly* 72 (1986): 239–71.

———. "Heloise and the Abbey of the Paraclete." In *The Making of Christian Communities in Late Antiquity and the Middle Ages.* Edited by Mark Williams. London: Anthem Press, 2005. Pp. 103–16.

———. *Hymn Collections from the Paraclete.* 2 vols. Cistercian Liturgy Series 8–9. Trappist, Ky.: Gethsemani Abbey, 1987–1989.

———. *The Paraclete Statutes Institutiones nostrae: Troyes, Bibliothèque municipale, Ms. 802, ff. 89r–90v. Introduction, Edition, Commentary.* Cistercian Liturgy Series 20. Trappist, Ky.: Gethsemani Abbey, 1987.

———. "Peter Abelard as Creator of Liturgical Texts." In *Petrus Abaelardus.* Pp. 267–86.

———. "Peter Abelard's *Letter 10* and Cistercian Liturgical Reform." In *Studies in Medieval Cistercian History 2.* Edited by John R. Sommerfeldt. Kalamazoo, Mich.: Cistercian Publications, 1976. Pp. 75–86.

———. "St. Bernard and the Cistercian Office at the Abbey of the Paraclete." In *The Chimaera of His Age: Studies on Bernard of Clairvaux.* Edited by E. Rozanne Elder and John R. Sommerfeldt. Studies in Medieval Cistercian History 5. Cistercian Studies Series 63. Kalamazoo, Mich.: Cistercian Publications, 1980. Pp. 76–121.

Waldman, Thomas G. "Abbot Suger and the Nuns of Argenteuil." *Traditio* 41 (1985): 239–72.

Weinrich, Lorenz. "Peter Abaelard as Musician I." *Musical Quarterly* 55 (1969): 295–312.

—————. "Peter Abaelard as Musician II." *Musical Quarterly* 55 (1969): 464–86.

Weyns, Norbertus Iosephus. "A propos des Instructions pour les clercs (De Institutione clericorum) de Philippe de Harveng." *Analecta Praemonstratensia* 53 (1977): 71–79.

Williams, John R. "The Cathedral School of Rheims in the Time of Master Alberic, 1118–1136." *Traditio* 20 (1964): 93–114.

Wulstan, David. "*Novi modulaminis melos:* The Music of Heloise and Abelard." *Plainsong and Medieval Music* 11 (2002): 1–23.

Zerbi, Pietro. "Guillaume de Saint-Thierry et son différend avec Abélard." In *Saint-Thierry, une abbaye du VIe au XXe siècle, Actes du colloque international d'histoire monastique, Reims-Saint-Thierry, 1977*. Saint-Thierry, France: Association des Amis de l'Abbaye de Saint-Thierry, 1977. Pp. 395–412.

—————. Reprinted in *Ecclesia in hoc mundo posita: Studi di storia e di storiografia medioevale raccolti in occasione del 700 genetliaco dell'autore*. Edited by Maria Pia Alberzoni. Bibliotheca erudita: Studi e documenti di storia e filologia 6. Milan, Italy: Vita e pensiero, 1993. Pp. 549–76.

—————. "'Panem nostrum supersubstantialem.' Abelardo polemista ed esegeta nell'*Ep. X.*" In *Raccolta di studi in memoria di Sergio Mochi Onory*. 2 vols. Milan, Italy: Editrice Vita e Pensiero, 1972. 2: 624–38.

—————. "*Philosophi*" *e* "*Logici*": *Un ventennio di incontri e scontri: Soissons, Sens, Cluny (1121–1141)*. Istituto storico italiano per il medio evo: Nuovi studi storici 59. Rome: Nella sede dell'Istituto, Palazzo Borromini, 2002.

—————. "San Bernardo di Chiaravalle e il concilio di Sens." In *Studi su s. Bernardo di Chiaravalle nell'ottavo centenario della canonizzazione: Convegno internazionale, Certosa di Firenze: 6–9 novembre 1974*. Bibliotheca Cisterciensis 6. Rome: Editiones Cistercienses, 1975. Pp. 49–73.

Ziolkowski, Jan M. "Heloise, Abelard, and the *Epistolae duorum amantium:* Lost and Not Yet Found." *Journal of Medieval Latin* 14 (2004): 171–202.

GENERAL INDEX

Boldface page numbers indicate translations in this volume

Aaron (brother of Moses), 164

Abelard, letters of, xxxvii–xxxviii; One,
xlin52, 40n9; Three, xxxix, xlin52, 4,
6, 34, 38, 40n9, 59, 65; Five, xlin52, 4,
34, 38, 65; Seven, xxxviiin49, xli, 16n41,
19n46, 28n78, 34, 38, 65, 71n16, 152,
165n51; Eight, xxxviiin49, xxxix, xli, 5–6,
34, 38, 58n20, 65, 66, 71n16, 91n37, 156,
161n37, 161n38, 162n42, 165n51; Nine, xxx,
xli, xlii, 3–10, **10–33**, 38, 54, 65, 72n18, 81,
105n15, 156, 171n66; Ten, xxx, xliii–xliv,
xlv, 22n58, 35, 36, 77, 78–80, 82, 84,
85–98, 109n23, 135, 172n68; Eleven,
xxvii, xlv, xlvi, 13n29, 29n80, 55, 133, 135,
137–38, **138–46**; Twelve, xxviii, xlv, 85n26,
97n57, 147, 152–54, 156–57, **158–74**,
171n66; Thirteen, xvi, xlv, 31n87, 176–78,
179–87; Fourteen, xvii, xxvi, xlv, xlvi,
103n8, 104, 188, 192–94, **194–96**; Fifteen,
xxxiii, xliv, 99, 103–8, **108–10**, 189; Sixteen, 38, **70–72**. *See also* correspondence
of Abelard and Heloise

Abelard, Peter: abbot of St. Gildas, xxviii, xxxi; affair with Heloise, xiv–xvi,
xxiii–xxiv; biblical commentaries, xxx,
xxxvi; biography, xv; birth and parentage, xvi; castration of, xxiv, xlii, 46n27,
150, 155–56, 156, 189, 192n15; charges of
heresy, xv, xxxii–xxxiv, xliv, 104, 105n14,
106, 116–18, 120, 125, 133, 188, 192; chronology of works, 6, 10, 38, 52, 65–66, 76,
77, 79, 105, 112n4, 114, 133, 178, 188–89,
190–92; on Cistercian liturgy, 36, 78,
83–84, 92–96, 135; commentaries on
liturgical texts, xxxvi, 10; commentary
on Song of Songs, 4; confinement at
St. Médard, xxvi; convalescence, xx;
death and burial, xxxiv; education,
xvi–xxi, xxi, 55, 189; on education of
nuns, xlii, 5–10, 25–26, 28, 33; on female
monasticism, xv, xxx, xxxiii, xlii, 3–10,
33, 34–36, 50, 54, 59, 66, 152, 153; on free
will, 117 126–27; Lord's Prayer, xxxi, 36,
78, 81–82, 85–90; marriage to Heloise,
xxiii–xxiv; on Milanese rite, 83; on monasticism, xlv, 152–57, 158–64, 166–67,
169, 171, 172–73; names and epithets,
xiv, xvii, 149, 192n15; patrons of, xx; as
pedagogue, xix–xxii, 149; poetry of,
xxxvi–xxxvii; as saint, 105–6; sister of,
xxiii; as songwriter, xiv, 37, 49n32; son
of, xxiii; on translation, 23–24, 25, 30–31,
81. *See also* Abelard, letters of; Abelard,
sermons of; *and individual works by title*

Abelard, sermons of, xxxvi, xlii, 3, 6–7,
26n72, 54, 59, 64–72, 76, 81n16, 118n22;
prologue to, xxx, xlii, 5, 35, 38, **70–72**;
Sermon 8, 11n24, 165n53; Sermon 14,

Abelard, sermons of *(cont.)*
  10, 81n16; Sermon 16, 11n24; Sermon 18,
  6; Sermon 23, 165n51; Sermon 24, 157;
  Sermon 26, 11n24; Sermon 27, 66n8;
  Sermon 29, 4n2, 11n24, 52, 54n5, 54n6;
  Sermon 30, 66n8; Sermon 31, xxxviiin49,
  54n5; Sermon 33, 65n7, 66n8, 118n22,
  149n4, 149n7, 152, 153n20, 155–57, 161n38,
  162n42, 165n53, 169n62, 177n4; Sermon
  35, 76, 156, 169n62
Acts of the Apostles, xxvii
Adam (abbot of St. Denis), xxvii, xlv, 133,
  135, 138
Ad Celantiam (Pelagius), 26n74
Ad clericos de conversione (Bernard of Clair-
  vaux), 102
Adrian IV (pope), 101
"Adtendite a falsis prophetis" (Abelard,
  Sermon 35), 76, 169n62
Adversus haereses (Irenaeus of Lyon), 86n29
Adversus quinque haereses (Quodvultdeus),
  184n20
Aeneid (Virgil), 15n39
Against Five Heresies (Augustine of Hippo).
  See Adversus quinque haereses
Alberic of Rheims, xxii, xxvi, 192
Alexander the Great, 12–13, 16n42
Alexandria, 25
alleluia, performance of, 69–70
All Saints, Feast of, 159, 160n35
Amboise, François d', 70, 157
Ambrose, 42, 44n20, 55, 89, 93n42, 144
Ambrosian rite. *See* Milanese rite
Andrew of St. Victor, 25n70
Andria (Terence), 119
Annunciation, Feast of the, 66, 72n19
Anselm of Canterbury, 192, 196
Anselm of Laon, xxi–xxii, xxvi, 53, 91n36,
  192–94
Anthony the Hermit, 162
Apollinarianism, 25n65

Apollinarius the Younger, 25
Apollo, 19
Apologeticum. See Apologia contra Bernardum
Apologia against Bernard of Berengar (Abelard),
  xlix
Apologia contra Bernardum (Abelard), xliv, xlvi,
  97n57, 111–15, 116–29
Apologia for Abbot William (Bernard of Clair-
  vaux), 76–77
Apostles' Creed, xxxvi, 94
Aquila, 19
Arator, 137, 145–46, 145n26
Aratus. *See* Arator
Aratus Latinus, 145n26
Aratus of Soli, 137, 145n26
Areopagite. *See* Dionysius the Areopagite
Argenteuil, convent of, xxiv, xxix–xxx,
  xxxii, 5, 189
Arianism, 96n53
Aristotle, xvii, xxi, xxii, 12, 16n42, 57, 59, 181
Arnold of Brescia, 100–101, 104
ars nova, 181n12
ars vetus, 181n12
Ascension, 66
Asella, 9
Assumption of the Virgin Mary, 66
Astralabe, xxiii, xxxvi
Athanasian Creed, xxvi, xxxvi, 10, 94–95,
  116n16, 192
Athanasius of Alexandria, 15, 105
Athens, 136, 139
Athleta Domini, 195n22
auctoritas, xxii, xxv, 41n12
Augustine (bishop of Canterbury), 91
Augustine (bishop of Hippo), 58, 59, 62,
  63, 90–91, 106, 117n21, 118, 128, 143, 145,
  151, 171, 177, 178, 180–81, 183, 184, 187,
  195n21; *Sermo* 1, 117n21; *Sermo* 355, 118n22.
  See also works by title
Augustinian Canons, 148
Aurelian (Roman emperor), 136

Ausonius, 184n21
authenticity of liturgical texts, 35

baptism, 165, 166n56
Barak, 18–19
Baraninas of Tiberias, 25
Basil the Great, 55
Bede, the Venerable, 11n24, 55, 133, 135,
    137–38, 140, 142–46, 167n57
Benedictine order, 35–36, 147. *See also* Rule
    of Benedict
Benedict of Nursia, 93n43
Berengar of Poitiers, 111, 114–15
Bernard of Clairvaux, xix, xxviii, xxx–xxx-
    iv, xxxix–xl, xliii–xliv, xlv, xlviii, 35–36,
    54, 63n33, 75–85, 97n56, 97n57, 99–106,
    108, 109n24, 109n25, 116n16, 125, 149–51,
    155–56, 177n4; letter 332 to Guy (Guido)
    of Città di Castello, 18n45
Besançon, 191n12
Bethany, 165n53
Bethlehem, 25, 32n88, 170n63
Bible. *See* Douay-Rheims Bible; King James
    Bible; scripture; *Vetus Latina;* Vulgate; *and
    Index of Scriptural References*
Black Canons, 148
Blaesilla, Saint, 22
Blois, xviii
Boethius, xxi, xxii, 57, 62n31, 71n17, 116,
    181n12
Bonne-Espérance, 154
Book against Jovinian (Jerome), xxiv
Book of Sentences, 112, 118
breviary, 37
Buytaert, Eligius M., 114n12, 115, 116n16
Bynum, Caroline Walker, 151n14

Caiaphas, Joseph, 164
Calcidius, 57
canonical hours. *See* divine office
canons, 147–48. *See also* Regular Canons

capitula of William of St. Thierry, 112
Carmen ad Astralabium (Abelard), xxxvi,
    71n17, 107
Carmen figuratum (Abelard), xxxvi
Carolingian Renaissance, xiii
Cassian, John, 90n35
Cassiodorus, 48n29
Categories (Aristotle), 57, 62
Cato, 142n18
Celantia, 26
Celestial Hierarchy (Pseudo-Dionysius the
    Areopagite), 134
Celestine II (pope), 18n45, 105n13
Châlons-sur-Saône, xxxiv
Charlemagne, 41n13
Chartres, xxxii
Chartrian Neoplatonists, 57
Christian Hebraism, 24n63
Chronicle of Morigny, 79
Chrysostom, John, 163
Cicero, 97, 118, 145n26
Cistercian liturgy, 35–36, 78, 82–83, 93–96
Clarembald of Arras, 55
Clement I (pope), 136, 146
Cluny, xxxiv, 149
Collationes (Abelard), xxxvi, 16n43, 24n63,
    107, 180n10, 181n11, 183n16, 187n28
Commentaria in epistolam Pauli ad Romanos
    (Abelard), 30n83
Commentary on the Six Days of Creation (Abe-
    lard), xxx, xxxvi, xlii, 3, 4–5, 35, 40n9,
    49n34, 52–53, 56–59, **60–63**, 64n3, 71n16
Confessio fidei ad Heloisam (Abelard), xlvi,
    40n9, 105, 114–15
Confessio fidei "Universis" (Abelard), xlvi, 10,
    115, 118n22, 119n23, 194
Confessions (Augustine of Hippo), 56, 128,
    175
Conlationes (Cassian), 90n35
Cono (bishop of Palestrina), xxvi
Corbeil, xix, xx

Corpus Areopagiticum, 134

Corpus iuris civilis, 90n36

Corpus Paraclitense, xxx, xli–xlii, 3–7, 66

correspondence of Abelard and Heloise,
xxxv, 3, 65, 156, 194; authenticity of,
xv–xvi, xxxi, xxxvii–xxxviii, xl; dedicatory letters, 34–35, 37, 40–41; distinction between personal and public, xliii;
letters of direction, xxx, xxxvii, xxxviii,
xlii–xliii, xlviii; manuscript transmission, xlviii; nonepistolary considered as,
34–35; personal letters, xxx, xxxvi, xxxvii, xxxix, xl, xlii–xliii, xlviii, 59. *See also
Lost Love Letters of Heloise and Abelard*

Cyprian of Carthage, 14

Dacian, 106, 109n26

Damaris, 136, 141

Damasus I (pope), 31n86

David, 142n19

De actibus apostolorum (Arator), 145n26

Deborah, 18–19

De catechizandis rudibus (Augustine of
Hippo), 58n18

Decius (Roman emperor), 136

Decretum (Ivo of Chartres), 84, 91n36,
91n37, 171n171

De dignitate clericorum (Philip of
Harveng[t]), 154

De diversis quaestionibus LXXXIII (Augustine
of Hippo), 58n19, 184

De doctrina Christiana (Augustine of Hippo),
187

defensor fidei, 195n22

De fide sancte Trinitatis (Abelard), 189, 191, 195

De fide Trinitatis et incarnatione verbi (Anselm
of Canterbury), 195n21

De Genesi ad litteram liber imperfectus (Augustine of Hippo), 56n13

De Genesi ad litteram libri XII (Augustine of
Hippo), 56n13

De Genesi contra Manichaeos (Augustine of
Hippo), 56n13

De incarnatione Verbi (Anselm of Canterbury), 192–93

De incarnationis dominicae sacramento (Ambrose), 89

*De institutione clericorum. See De dignitate cleri-
corum*

De inventione (Cicero), 118

Denis, St., xxvii, 134, 135–42, 144, 146

De principiis (Origen), 21n53, 32n88

De sanctis apostolis (Pseudo-Augustine), 72n18

De Santis, Paola, 70

De sex dierum operibus (Thierry of Chartres), 55

De syllogismo categorico libri duo (Boethius),
71n17, 116n15

De unitate et Trinitate divina (Abelard), 189

dialectic, xvi–xvii, xxi, xxxix, xlv, 116n15,
122n29, 175–78, 179, 180–81, 183–85

Dialectic (Roscelin of Compiègne), 196

Dialectica (Abelard), xxii, xxxvi, 176, 182n13

*Dialogue between a Christian, a Philosopher, and a
Jew* (Abelard), xxxvi, 107

Didascalion (Hugh of St. Victor), 175n1

Didymus the Blind, 25

Diocletian (Roman emperor), 106

Dionysius. *See* Denis

Dionysius of Corinth, 136–42, 144, 146

Dionysius the Areopagite, xxvii, 133–34,
135–41, 144, 146

*Disputatio catholicorum patrum. See Disputatio
contra Petrum Abaelardum* (Thomas of
Morigny)

Disputatio contra Petrum Abaelardum (Thomas
of Morigny), 113–14, 126

Distichs of Cato, 142, 179n8

Divine Names, The (Pseudo-Dionysius the
Areopagite), 134

divine office, 35, 37, 39, 43, 50, 51, 92, 93n42,
94–96

Domitian (Roman emperor), 136
Douay-Rheims Bible, li, 143n22, 165n54, 187n27
Du Chesne, André, 70, 157

Ecclesiastic History. See Historia ecclesiastica
Eight Beatitudes, 86
Eleutherius (companion of St. Denis), 138
Elijah (prophet), 143, 156, 162, 164–65, 174
Elisha (prophet), 162, 164n50, 165, 174
Elizabeth (cousin of Mary), 164n49
Enarrationes in Psalmos (Augustine of Hippo), 117n21, 143n23
Ephesus, 19n47
Epigrams (Martial), 119
Epiphanius of Salamis, 20n50
Epistles (Horace), 16n43
Epistola ad beati Martini Turonensis ecclesiam (Abelard), xlvii
Epistolae duorum amantium. See correspondence of Abelard and Heloise
Epistulae morales (Seneca the Younger), 170
Epithalamica, 69n15
Étampes, 79
Ethica seu Liber "Scito te ipsum" (Abelard), xxxvi
ethics, xxi, xxxvi
Eugenius III (pope), 108, 149n6
Eusebius of Caesarea, 29n81, 136
Eustochium, 9, 15, 17, 22n59, 23, 170n63
Exhortatio ad fratres et commonachos (Abelard), xlvii, 157
Explication of the Lord's Prayer (Abelard), 81n16
expositio, 71n17
Expositio euangelii secundum Lucam (Ambrose), 144
Expositio in Hexaemeron (Abelard), xxx, xxxvi, xlii, 3, 4–5, 35, 40n9, 49n34, 52–53, 56–59, 60–63, 64n3, 71n16
Expositio Orationis Dominicae (Abelard), 81n16

Fabiola, 24n64, 169
Farsitus, 155
female saints, 42
Fidentinus, 119
Fontevrault order, 193
Frederick Barbarossa (Holy Roman emperor), 101
French Revolution, xxxiv
Fulbert (canon of chapter of Notre Dame), xxii–xxiii, 155
Fulk (prior of Deuil), xlviii, 84

Gallican Church, 41
Galo (bishop of Paris), 188n3
Geoffrey of Lèves, xxxii, 107
Gerald of Wales, 107
Gesta Dionysii. See Historia Dionysii
Gesta Frederici imperatoris (Otto of Freising), 111, 112n4
Gilbert (bishop of Paris), 188, 194
"Gloria", 95
Glossae in Mattaeum (Otfrid of Weißenburg), 119n26
Glossa ordinaria, xxi
Goswin (prior of St. Médard), xxvi
Gothic architecture, xxix
Greek literature, 13, 17
Gregory, Tullio, 116n17
Gregory the Great, 11, 44n20, 44n21, 91–92, 118, 143
Gregory VII (pope), 91
Guy (Guido) of Città di Castello, 18n45, 105n13

Haimo of Auxerre, 119n26
Hannah (mother of Samuel), 15
Hannibal, 170
Haskins, Charles Homer, xiiin1
Hebrew language, 7–8, 10, 13, 23–24, 25n70, 26, 28–32, 40, 48, 89, 143
Heiric of Auxerre, 120n26

Heliodorus, 160n36, 161, 173

Heloise, 55, 56, 78, 85, 152, 169n62; affair with Abelard, xiv–xvi, xxiii–xxiv; as deaconess or abbess, xxxviii; as instigator of Abelard's works for the Paraclete, xxx, xxxviii–xxxix, xlvi, 3–5, 34–35, 39, 40, 46, 52–53, 59, 64, 66, 70, 161n38; as leader of the Paraclete, xxxvi, xxxviii, 3, 7; linguistic abilities, 7–8, 28; marriage to Abelard, xxiii–xxiv; as mother of Astralabe, xxiii; as "sister" to Abelard, 40, 59, 67, 70, 72; as student of Abelard, xxiii; taking the veil, xxiv. *See also Corpus Paraclitense*; correspondence of Abelard and Heloise; Heloise, letters of; Paraclete

Heloise, letters of: Two, xlin52, 4; Four, xxxviii, xlin52, 46n24, 169n62; Six, xlin52, 153, 156; request for hymnal, 35, 41–46

Henry Sanglier (archbishop of Sens), xlix, 103

Herman (abbot of Tournai), 155

hexaemeron: commentaries before Abelard, 55

Hexaemeron (Ambrose), 55

Hilarion, 162

Hilary of Poitiers, Saint, 15, 42

Hildebert of Lavardin, xlvii

Hildegard of Bingen, xxxix

Hilduin (abbot of St. Denis), 133, 135, 141n16

Historia calamitatum (Abelard), xv, xvi, xxvii, xxx, xxxi, xxxvi, xxxvii, xxxix, xl, xlv, xlvi, 3, 27n75, 38, 53, 60n25, 64, 65, 79, 83, 105, 107, 118n22, 133, 135, 150, 154, 155–56, 177n4, 185n25, 189–90, 192

Historia Dionysii (Hilduin), 133, 135

Historia ecclesiastica (Eusebius of Caesarea), 29n81, 47–48, 136, 137, 139, 141–42, 146

Holy Spirit, 143, 178, 185–86. *See also* Trinitarian theology

Holy Week, 83, 94n47, 95

Homilia ad monachos (Pseudo-Jerome), 170n63

Homiliae in Hiezechilhelem prophetam (Gregory the Great), 118, 143

Homiliae per circulum anni (Heiric of Auxerre), 120n26

Homilia (Haimo of Auxerre), 119n26

Homilies on the Hexaemeron (Basil the Great), 55

homoousion, 96n53

Honorius II (pope), xxx

Horace, 16n43, 107

hostis antiquus, 195n21

Hrabanus Maurus, 72n18

Hugh Metel, xlix

Hugh of Amiens, 113–14

Hugh of Fosses, 155n24

Hugh of St. Victor, xix–xx, 77, 175n1

Hugo Farsitus, 155n24

humility topos, 48n30, 50n38, 59n23

Hymnarius Paraclitensis (Abelard), xxx, xxxvi, xli–xlii, 3, 4, 36–40, 52, 59, 65, 67–68, 71n16, 72n19

hymns, xxx, xxxvi, 34–39, 70; authorship of, 41–42; Cistercian, 83, 93, 95; composition of, 47–48, 50; of the cross, 51; Heloise on need for new, 38, 41–46; incongruities of texts and contexts, 43–45; melodies of, 42; musical notation for, 37; prosody of, 49n32

hymns, incipits cited: "Aeterna caeli gloria" (Prudentius), 44, 45n21; "Aeterne rerum conditor," 83, 93, 94n43; "Ales diei nuntius" (Prudentius), 44, 45n21; "A solis ortus cardine" (Sedulius), 43n17; "Aurora iam spargit polum" (Prudentius), 44, 44n21; "Aurora lucis rutilat," 44, 45n21; "Beata nobis gaudia," 185; "Christe, redemptor omnium," 159; "Consors paterni luminis" (Ambrose), 43, 44n20; "Deus qui corpora"

(Abelard), 49n33; "Ecce, iam noctis" (Gregory the Great), 44, 44n21; "Iesu, salvator saeculi," 160; "Iste confessor Domini," 46, 46n25; "Martine, par apostolis" (Odo of Cluny), 46, 46n25; "Nocte surgentes vigilemus" (Gregory the Great), 43, 44n20; "Nox atra rerum contegit" (Ambrose), 43, 44n20; "Nox et tenebrae" (Prudentius), 44, 44n21; "O quanta qualia" (Abelard), 37, 49n31; "Rerum creator optime" (Ambrose), 43, 44n20, 46, 46n24; "Salvete flores martyrum" (Prudentius), 43n17; "Summae Deus clementiae," 44, 44n20, 46, 46n24; "Te decet laus," 93n42; "Te Deum laudamus," 93n42; "Tu Trinitatis unus" (Gregory the Great), 43, 44n20

hymnus angelicus, 95n50

In Canticum canticorum (Origen), 60–61
Incarnation, 66
Innocent II (pope), xxxiv, xlix, 79, 82, 101, 103n6, 104, 105n13, 112, 115n14
Innocents, Feast of, 42
Innocents, Feast of Holy, 67
Irenaeus of Lyon, 30n81, 86n29
Isidore of Seville, 7
Ivo of Asbach, 156
Ivo of Chartres, xxv, xlvii, 91n36, 171n171

Jabin, 19n46
James the Apostle (the Less), 144, 160
James (the Greater), 144
Jeremiah, 162
Jerome, xxiv, xxviii, 7–11, 13, 16–18, 26, 30n81, 31–32, 54, 59, 72n18, 143, 147, 153, 156, 163n45, 177; Apologia adversus libros Rufini, 32n88, 86n30; Commentarii in Danielem, 27n76; Commentarii in Ezechielem, 61; Commentarii in iv epistulas Paulinas, 22; Contra Rufinum, 32n88, 86n30; Contra

Vigilantium, 169; De uiris inlustribus, 137, 140, 145–46; Epistula praefatoria in Chronicis Eusebii, 145n26; Homilia in Ioannem Euangelitam, 163n46; Liber interpretationis Hebraicorum nominum, 143–44n23; "Praefatio in Evangelio," 96; "Praefatio in libro Psalmorum," 40n10, 48n29; "Prologus in libro Iob," 48n29; "Prologus in Pentateucho," 86
Jerome, letters of: Epistula ad Praesidium, 173–74; 14 (to Heliodorus), 160, 161, 169; 39 (to Paula), 22–23; 53 (to Paulinus of Nola), 184; 58 (to Paulinus of Nola), 161–62; 60 (to Heliodorus), 173; 65 (to Principia), 18–19; 70 (to Magnus), 182; 84 (to Pammachius and Oceanus), 24–25; 107 (to Laeta), 12–13, 14–16; 108 (to Eustochium), 23; 117 (to Oceanus), 169–70; 125 (to Rusticus), 11, 164–65; 127 (to Principia), 19–21
Jerusalem, 17, 25, 29n79, 151
Jesus Christ, 7, 15, 25n65, 25n68, 28n78, 58, 81, 88n32, 95n48, 97–98, 144n24, 164n47, 165, 168, 186
Jewish Antiquities (Josephus), 163n45
Jewish War (Josephus), 163n45
Jews and Judaism, 24, 24n63, 25, 60, 178, 186
John of Salisbury, xlvii
John the Baptist, 88, 152, 153, 162–64
John the Evangelist, 144
Josephus, Flavius, 163
Julian the Hospitaller, 162
Justinian I (emperor), 90

King James Bible, li, 143n22
Klibansky, Raymond, 108

Laeta (daughter-in-law of Paula), 9, 11, 13n29, 15n38, 17n44, 139n11
Lament of Dinah (Abelard), 53, 68
Laon, xxi, xxii, xxvi, 154

Lateran Church, 96

Laurence of Liège, 155

Lazarus (sister of Mary and Martha), 165n53

Leah (sister of Rachel), 168

lectio, 71n17

Leonides, 12n27, 13

Le Pallet, xvi, xvii, xxiii

letter collections, medieval, xlvii

Letter on Baptism (Bernard of Clairvaux), 77

Letters of Abelard and Heloise (Radice), xli, xlii–xliii, xlviii

liberal arts, 175–76

Liber sententiarum, 112, 118

Libri quatuor in principium Genesis (Bede), 55

litanies, 94, 159

liturgical reform, Cistercian, 35–36

Loches, xviii, 189

logic, xvi–xvii, xxi, xxii, xxxvi, xlv, l, 57, 122n29, 175–76

Logica "Ingredientibus" (Abelard), xxxvi, 62n31

logica nova, 181n12

logica vetus, 181n12

logos, xlv, 177, 178, 184–85

Lord's Prayer, xxxi, xxxvi, xliii, 36, 78, 81–82, 85–90, 94, 135

Lost Love Letters of Heloise and Abelard, xxxviii

Lotulf of Novara, xxii, xxvi, 192

Louis the Pious (emperor), 135

Louis VI the Fat (king of France), xx, xxviii

Lucilius, Gaius, 170

Lucius Verus (Roman emperor), 140–41

Luke, 86–90

Lyon, Church of, 97

Macarius the Elder, 162

Magnus (Roman orator), 182

manuscript transmission and witnesses: Apologia contra Bernardum, 113; Expositio in Hexameron, 60; *Hymnarius*

Paraclitensis, 36–37, 50n37; letters, xlviii, 6, 10, 80, 84, 107–8, 137–38, 194; *planctus*, 68; *Sermones*, 65, 70

Marcella, 7, 32

Marcella (Saint), 19–21

Marcus Aurelius (Roman emperor), 140–41

Marenbon, John, 114n12

Mark, 47, 86n28

Martha (sister of Mary and Lazarus), 165, 167–68, 172

Martial, 119

Martin of Tours, 166

Martyrology (Bede), 146

Mary Magdalen, 42n17

Mary (sister of Martha and Lazarus), 165, 172

Masson, Jean-Papire, 70

Matthew, 29n81, 85–90

Matthew of Albano, xxx

Maximian (Roman emperor), 106

medieval society, 152

Melun, xix, xx

memorizing, 13–14

Merchant of Venice (Shakespeare), 119n26

metaphysics, xxi

Milanese rite, 83, 93n42, 94n43, 96–97

monachus, 147

monasticism, 147–53

Monophysites, 190

Montier-la-Celle, 45n21

Mont Ste. Geneviève, xx, xxvi, xxxi, 101

Moos, Peter von, 178n6

Morigny, 79

Moses, 50n36, 164n47

Mystical Theology (Pseudo-Dionysius the Areopagite), 134

Nantes, xvi

Nathan (prophet), 142

Neoplatonism, xxii, 57, 134, 136. *See also* Platonism

Nepotian (nephew of Heliodorus), 173

Nero (Roman emperor), 146

Nicene Creed, 96n53

Nicodemus, 25

Nogent-sur-Seine, 189

nominalism, xviii, 190

Norbert of Xanten, xxviii, xxxii, xlv, 148, 154–55, 157

Notre Dame, school of, xviii–xx, xxii, 76

number symbolism, 67, 81, 87–88

Oceanus, Saint, 24, 169

Odes (Horace), 107

officium, 153

On Baptism (Augustine of Hippo), 90–91

On Christian Doctrine (Augustine of Hippo), 180–81

On Eighty-Three Different Questions. See De diversis quaestionibus LXXXIII

On Faith in the Holy Trinity (Abelard), 189, 191, 195

On First Principles (Origen), 21

On Mercy (Augustine of Hippo). *See Tractatus de oratione et eleemosyna*

On Order (Augustine of Hippo), 180

On the Creation of the Cosmos According to Moses (Philo), 55

ordinary gloss. *See Glossa ordinaria*

Organon (Aristotle), 181n12

Origen, 21n53, 23, 30n81, 32n88, 59, 60

Otfrid of Weißenburg, 119n26

Ottonian Renaissance, xiii

Otto of Freising, 111, 112n4, 189

Ovid, 106–7

Pammachius, Saint, 24, 32

Panormia (Ivo of Chartres), xxv, 91n36

Papias, 29n81

Paraclete, xxvn26, xxxiv, xxxvi, xli, xlii, 3, 18n45, 37, 38, 53, 65, 150, 156; education of nuns, xlii, 5–10, 25–26, 28, 33; found-

ing, xxviii, 5; liturgy and rule, xxx–xxxi, xxxiii, xlii, xliii, 4, 35–36, 39, 45n21, 48–51, 59, 66, 78, 80, 83; papal recognition, 79–80, 81, 85n25; visit of Bernard of Clairvaux, 78–79. *See also Corpus Paraclitense*

Paraclete codex, 64–65

Paraclete Hymnal, xxx, xxxvi, xli–xlii, 3, 4, 36–40, 52, 59, 65, 67–68, 71n16, 72n19

Paris, xvii, xxii–xxiii, xlv, 104, 107, 110, 113, 188, 189, 193, 194

Paris, University of, xx

Passion of Christ, 116n18

Patrologia Latina, xl–xli

pattern poetry, xxxvi

Paul, 8, 47–48, 81, 86–87, 96, 126, 134, 136, 138, 139, 141, 143, 145–46, 165, 173, 186

Paula, 9, 15, 17, 22, 23, 170n63

Paula (the younger), 9, 11–16

Paulinus of Antioch, 20n50

Paulinus of Nola, 161, 162n42, 184

Paul the Hermit, 162

Pelagius, 26n73

Pentecost, 66, 178, 185–86

Père Lachaise, cemetery of, xxxiv

Periarchon (Origen), 21n53, 32n88

Peripateticus Palatinus, xvii

Peristephanon (Prudentius), 106

Peter, 142, 144, 145–46, 172

Peter of Blois, xlvii

Peter the Venerable, xxxiv, 8, 75, 115

Phaedrus, 179n8

Phaenomena (Aratus of Soli), 145n26

Philip I (king of France), xx, 107

Philip (king of Macedonia), 12

Philip of Harveng(t), 154

Philo of Alexandria, 47, 55

philosophia, 177n4

planctus, xxxvi, 3

Planctus (Abelard), xxxvi, 3, 53, 68

Platonism, xviii, 21n53. *See also* Neoplatonism

Porphyry, xxii, 181n12

Possidius, 171n67

Posterior Analytics (Aristotle), 181n12

praeco Christi, 195n23, 196n24

Praesidius (deacon), 173

Premonstratensian Order, xxviii, 148

Prémontré, 148, 154

Principia, 18–19

Prior Analytics (Aristotle), 181n12

Priscilla, 19

Problemata Heloissae cum Petri Abaelardi soluti-onibus, xxxviii–xxxix, xlvi–xlvii, 3, 5–6, 9, 10, 22n57, 35, 38, 57, 65, 161n38, 169n62

prosa. See sequence

prosopography, xlvi

Provins, xxvii

Prudentius, 42, 43n17, 44–45n21, 106

psalmody, 23, 41n14

psalter, 4, 41

Pseudo-Augustine, 72n18, 183n16

Pseudo-Chrysostom, 153

Pseudo-Cicero, 97n57, 171

Pseudo-Dionysius the Areopagite, 134–37

Pseudo-Jerome, 26n74, 170n63

Purgatorio (Dante), 46n24

Pythagoras, 22

quadrivium, 57

quaestio, 57

Quincey, Abelard's hermitage at, xxvii, 5, 149

Quodvultdeus, 184n20

Rachel (sister of Leah), 153, 168

Radice, Betty, xli

Raoul le Vert, xxvi

reading aloud, 13

realism, xviii

Redemption, 116n18, 126

Regular Canons, 148, 150–56, 150–57, 158–59, 171–72

religio, 153

Remedia amoris (Ovid), 106–7

Retractatio in Acta Apostolorum (Bede), 145

Retractationes (Augustine of Hippo), 59, 63, 143n20

Rheims, cathedral school of, xxii

Rhetoric to Herennius (Pseudo-Cicero), 97n57, 171

Robert of Arbrissel, 193–94, 195

Rogation Days, 66

romance of Abelard and Heloise, xxiii–xxiv, xxxv, xxxix, 53–54; modern artistic representations of, xvi

Rome, 15, 17, 19, 21, 22n59, 26n73, 170n63, 170n65, 182

Roscelin of Compiègne, xviii, xx–xxi, xxvi, xlvi, xlix, 103n8, 155, 188–94

Rufinus of Aquileia, 20n51, 21n53, 32n88, 136, 139n12

Rule of Benedict, 39, 93, 93n42, 149

Rusticus, 138

Rusticus of Narbonne, 11, 164

Sabellianism, 191

St. Ayoul, xxvii, 45n21, 149

St. Denis, xxiv, xxvii, xxviii–xxx, xlv, 5, 45n21, 133, 135, 148, 150, 189

St. Germain des Prés, synod on monastic reform at, xxix

St. Gildas, xxviii, xxxi, 54n5, 65, 79, 149, 152

St. Hilary, 101

St. John the Baptist, Feast of, 67

St. Léon, xlix

St. Marcel, xxxiv, 149

St. Martial, 8

St. Martin-des-Champs, 113

St. Martin of Tours, xlvii, 191–92, 196

St. Médard, xxvi, 149

St. Peter's, 96

St. Stephen, Feast of, 67

St. Victor, xix–xx, 10, 25n70, 76

Ste. Marie de Footel, xxx
salvation of man. *See* Redemption
Samson (archbishop of Rheims), xlix
Samuel (prophet), 142
Scholasticism, 75, 150
scientia, 31n87, 180n9
scriptural languages, 7–8, 13, 22–23, 25–26, 28–33, 81
scripture: Acts of the Apostles, 14, 145, 164n47; Chronicles, 14; Deuteronomy, 182n14; Ecclesiastes, 14; Epistle to the Galatians, 21–22; Epistle to the Romans, 30n83; Esther, 14; Ezekiel, 53, 55; Ezra, 14; Genesis, 60–63, 153; Gospels, 14, 17, 164n47; Heptateuch, 14; Kings, 14, 162n41; Job, 14; Luke, 81; Matthew, 29, 81; Prophets, 14; Song of Songs, 14, 52–55, 60–61, 153. *See also Index of Scriptural References*
Second Crusade, 108
Secular Canons, 148
Sedulius, 43n17
Seneca the Younger, 170
Sens, Council of, xxxii–xxxiv, xliv, xlix, 75–77, 76–79, 82, 84, 99, 103, 104, 105n14, 110, 111–12, 114–15, 194
Septuagesima, 94
sequences, 67–70
sermo, 6
Sermones (Abelard). *See* Abelard, sermons of
Sermon on the Mount, 81, 86, 88
Shakespeare, William, 119n26
Sheba, queen of, 27
Sic et non (Abelard), xxiv–xxv, xxxv, xxxix, xlvi, 13n29, 15n37, 16n42, 22n57, 41n14, 57, 62n31, 63n32, 78, 84, 97n57, 105n13, 129n34, 133, 135, 137, 139n11, 181n11, 183n16, 187n28
Soliloquium, xxxvi, xlvii, 177n4, 184n17, 194
Silo, 16n41
Silvestre, Hubert, 190n8

Siricius (pope), 20n51
six ages: of human life, 58; of the world, 57–58
Smits, Edmé, 157, 165n54, 171n67, 178, 184n18
socius, 108n21
Soissons, Councils of: in 1092, xviii, 189–90, 194; in 1121, xxvi, xxxii, xxxiv, 27n75, 77, 104, 106, 107, 133, 192
Solomon, 27–28, 142n19, 182
sophia, xlv, 177, 178, 185
sophism, 182, 184n18, 187
Sophistical Refutations, 181
Stephen, 173; relics of, 103
Stephen of Garlande, xx, xxviii, 76
Stultilogia, 102–3, 109
Suger (abbot of St. Denis), xxvii, xxix, xxxii, 5, 135
Sulpicius Severus, 166n56
Super Acta Apostolorum expositio (Bede), 133, 137
Susanna, 27
syneisaktism, 193
Szövérffy, Joseph, 40

Tenebrae, 95
Terence, 119n24
theologia, xxxv
Theologia (Abelard), xlix, 99, 102–3, 105n13, 107, 109, 176
Theologia Christiana (Abelard), xxvi, xxxv, 118n22, 129n34, 157, 176n3, 181n11, 182n13, 182n15, 184n20, 187n28, 192, 196n25, 196n26
Theologia "Scholarium" (Abelard), xxvi, xxxv, 22n57, 97n57, 113, 121n28, 124, 129n34, 180n10, 181n11, 182n13, 182n15, 183n16, 184n20, 187n28, 196n25
Theologia "Summi boni" (Abelard), xxv–xxvi, xxxv, 97n57, 128n34, 176n3, 181n11, 182n13, 187n28, 188, 190–92, 195n21, 196n25

theology, xxi, xxv

Thibaud, Count, xxvii, xxxii, 135

Thierry of Chartres, 27n75, 55, 57

Thomas Becket, xxxix, xlviii

Thomas of Morigny, xlix, 111, 113–14, 126

Tiberius (Roman emperor)

Timaeus (Plato), 57

T-O maps, 29n79

Topics (Aristotle), 181n12

Tours, xviii, 189, 191

Toxotius, 9

Tractatus de oratione et eleemosyna (Pseudo-
    Augustine), 183n16

Tractatus de unitate ac trinitate divina (Abelard),
    xxv–xxvi, xxxv, 195n21

Trinitarian theology, xviii, xxv–xxvi, xxxiii,
    29, 95n49, 109, 116–17, 120–28, 190–91

tritheism, 190, 193, 194

trivium, 57

Troyes, 189

Twelfth-Century Renaissance, xiii

universals, xix

Valerius (bishop), 109n26

Vetus Latina, 31n86, 41n13

Vincent, Saint, 106, 108

Virgil, 15n39

Vita Augustini (Possidius), 171n67

vocalism. *See* nominalism

Vulgate, li, 31n86, 81, 143n22, 187n27

Waddell, Chrysogonus, 4n3, 36n3, 39, 65n6

Walter of Mortagne, xlix, 109n25

White Canons, 148

William Godel(I), 8

William of Champeaux, xviii–xxi, 76–77,
    155

William of St. Thierry, xxxii, xlix, 77,
    99–100, 109n25, 112, 116n16

Wimund (bishop of Aversa), 91

Zachary (father of John the Baptist),
    164n49

INDEX OF SCRIPTURAL REFERENCES

Genesis
1.1–2.25, 52
29–30, 168
34, 68
35.18, 68
37.7–9, 68
42.36, 68
43.14, 68

Exodus
17.8–16, 50n36
15, 22n55

Leviticus
26.10, 31

Deuteronomy
17.6, 29
27.9, 23

Judges
11.29–40, 68
13–16, 68

2 Kings
1.17–27, 68
2.11, 163n43
3.26–39, 68
7, 142n19

3 Kings
10.1–13, 27
19.4, 143

4 Kings
4.38–39, 164n50

1 Chronicles
17.1–15, 142n19

2 Chronicles
9.1–12, 27

Psalms
1, 19
1.2, 32
5.18–19, 47
7.1, 143
35.7, 68
44, 18
62.7, 43
72.9, 196
72.18, 169
89.10, 141
90.11, 119
118, 19
118.55, 43
118.62, 43
118.164, 43

Proverbs
1.1–6, 182
10.7, 50

Ecclesiastes
1.7, 32

Song of Songs
5.2, 166, 171n66
5.2–7, 167n57
5.3, 166–67
5.6, 168

Isaiah
11.2–3, 87n31

Ezekiel
1, 60–61
40–48, 60–61

Daniel
12.4, 31
13.2, 27
13.3, 27

Ecclesiasticus
37.23, 181
44.1, 50

Matthew
3.7, 174
4.4, 172
4.6, 119
5.1, 86
6.9–13, 87
11.12–14, 163n43
12.42, 28, 33
15.14, 179
17.1, 144
17.12–13, 163n43
18.15–17, 101
18.16, 29, 142
19.21, 161
24.24, 186
26.30, 49

Mark
9.12–13, 163n43

Luke
1.36, 164n49
3.21, 165
6.12, 86
6.17, 86
7.24–26, 163n43
10.38–42, 165n53, 168
10.42, 172
11.1, 88

Luke *(cont.)*
11.1–4, 87
11.9, 183
21.15, 185
24.39, 123n31
24.42, 196

John
1.1, 177, 184
1.6, 163
1.12–13, 123
1.17, 88n32
4.24, 123n30
4:36, 46n27
12.1–8, 165n53
14.6, 91, 186n27
16.30, 125n33
21.15–16, 172
21.17, 172

Acts of the
Apostles
17.28, 145n26
17.34, 134, 136,
    139, 140, 141
21.8, 173n71

Romans
1.7, 138
8.23, 87
11.5-6, 126
11.36, 123
12.5, 167n58
14.5, 90, 98

1 Corinthians
1.22, 186
1.24, 185n24
4.7, 126
8.6, 123
12.10, 97n58
12.27, 167n58

12.28, 97n58
14.10, 97n58

2 Corinthians
11.28–29, 165
12.11, 63

Galatians
1.19, 144
2.11, 143

Ephesians
4.25, 167n58
5.18–19, 48
5.30, 167n58

Colossians
3.16, 47

1 Timothy
1.7, 179
2, 20

2.7, 47
6.20, 96

2 Timothy
4, 20

Hebrews
4.13, 121

1 Peter
1.1, 30
3.15, 183

James
1.1, 30
1.19, 23
5.16, 160

Apocalypse
1.11, 30

Letters of Peter Abelard, Beyond the Personal was designed and typeset in Monotype Centaur by Kachergis Book Design of Pittsboro, North Carolina. It was printed on 60-pound House Natural Smooth and bound by Sheridan Books of Ann Arbor, Michigan.